To Pat

Happy to Hear
about your way
the camino. How far
us Both. Enjoy my way
Keep following your path.

thanks

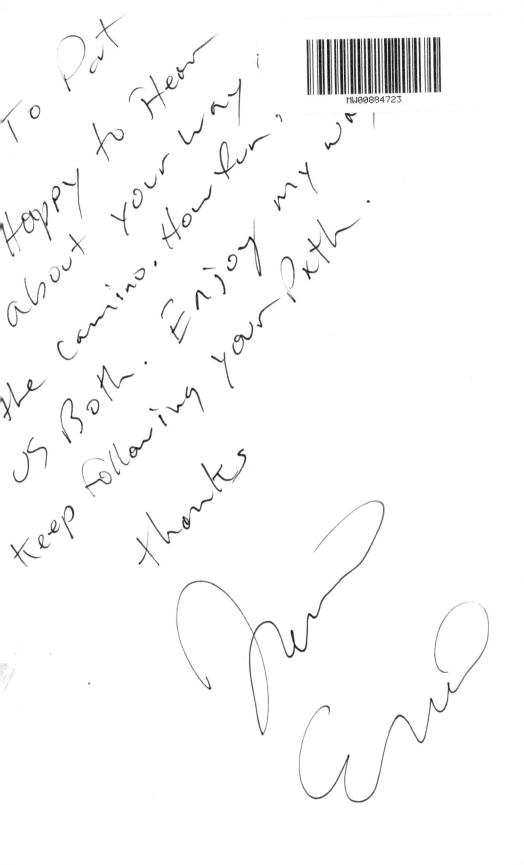

a private journal
on facebook
posted by...

drew eric

adventure
path
road
trek
follow my...   journey
of self discovery...

overcoming fear, anxiety, loneliness, divorce, pain,
while discovering europe, peace, friends, love, me...

Table of contents

Table of contents

Without you, this book wouldn't be written…

Way back, during some holiday with my family, I shared my crazy idea about backpacking Europe. With excitement and words of encouragement, my crazy idea was planted deep into the soil of a small cracked ceramic pot, sitting in a corner of my tiny bachelor apartment in America. With water and careful planning, my crazy idea grew. The plan it became outgrew that small ceramic pot and had to be replanted in the ground to grow into an adventure.

I would like to thank all my family, Daron, Ana and Vivian who were the first to water my little crazy plan. Damon, Lisa, Tarissa, Will and Avery for sending me off with love and support on my adventure.

To my ex-husband, who instilled a love of travel and adventure in me, and spent so many years sharing my life. I am forever grateful for your joining me as I grew into the man I am today. With our union and life together, you greatly contributed to my betterment with your love and support. You were my best friend for 20 years and I will always be grateful for that. You taught me so much for so many years, and when our learning was complete, we separated with kindness and ease. Thank you. This book is dedicated to you for so many reasons.

To all the kind souls I met while on my journey of self-discovery, I thank you. Prior to leaving America I had troubled relationships. I read once in a blog that I would meet new travel buddies and make lifelong friends. I couldn't imagine this for myself until the journey unfolded for me. Now I have all of my travel road buddies to thank for your love, gifts and kindness. There are too many to name here but know in your hearts that you are named in mine. Thank you, thank you and thank you for the deep meaningful contributions you made in my life.

To Jeanne Looper Smith, my editor and friend, your love and support before, during and after my adventure has been endless. With each new chapter you encouraged me. With each new paragraph you said just what I needed to hear. With each new sentence you told me I was on the right track. This perfect book is because of your guidance. Don't forget I can edit the published book so if you see any follow up corrections email me :)

To Janet Weissman, my spiritual teacher and friend, thank you. My spiritual foundation is based on your teachings. You were there for me when my marriage came to its completion. You were there for me while I built a new life for myself and you were there to send me off into the world with a granite path to walk upon, my new found spirituality. I thank you and the teachings of "A Course in Miracles" for everything you contributed. Clearly, you shaped my story, chapter by chapter, and helped me develop a new way of seeing the world.

To Ralph Barber, my best friend, thank you. Before, during and especially after, you have been there for me. All those days of endless writing, you supported me—even when you asked me how long it takes to write a book, saying it seemed like forever. Your love and support during the months after my journey contributed to my happiness—which greatly impacted my ability to write and complete this book. Don't worry; I have two more books planned so you can keep on keeping on. Thanks for sharing my life.

To all my new friends and all my old friends, each and every one of you has taught me so much. Even in your absence, I learn and grow. Because of you, I am the person you see today. Even if we share little now, please know how much our once connected lives meant to me and my personal development on this journey.

So many kind souls covered my sleeping head with a roof and a warm home, before, during and after my year-long homelessness. I couldn't have accomplished so much without the kindness of others. I received so much love in so many ways whether it was financial, a roof, food, quality time or friendship, it was all equally appreciated. I thank you all.

To my little inside "Drewbie," thank you for letting me befriend you in Europe. Thank you for showing up and taking me on the adventure of a lifetime. You were always there for me, guiding me on where to go, what to do, what to say and to whom. You, my friend, are with me always. I might have been solo but I was never alone, I always had you by my side, my shadow.

Prologue

My story first began some time before my actual adventure. I decided to create a blog as a marketing tool for my new coaching business. I believed at the time that a blog would communicate who I am and what I believe in for all my future clients. With a blog, I could share with followers how to live their best life.

But I have never written before and had no idea how. With fear as my friend, I jumped in anyway. With each new blog, my writing hand got stronger. After my marriage of 20 years ended, I decided to take a journey of self-discovery to Europe and find myself. I chose to blog about my fears and challenges while preparing to take the journey of a lifetime. With just over six months of preparation, I wrote several telling stories about my own anxieties. I felt vulnerable, scared but I chose to move past the anxiety and trek on.

Once on my adventure, as I continued to blog, I discovered I had a knack for suspense which translated well through my storytelling. I found my writing pace and loved it. Then the difficulties and true hardships began and I had to choose again. Do I really want to put my "crazy" on the page and publish it for all to see on Facebook?

Prior to leaving home, my blog was edited and polished before publishing. However, on my journey I chose not to be encumbered by the time it takes to polish a short story. So I chose to write, read it through once and post the ugly, unedited story on Facebook. These stories are filled with mistakes, misspellings and incorrect words in places that make you think, "Oh, he meant to write "clothes" instead of "cloths" here."

This is when Facebook became a character and a friend on my journey. I gained so many followers and supporters I felt Facebook, contributed to my growth. A dialog began through Facebook with people from my past, present and followers I had yet to meet. I felt their presence and love with me throughout my journey. Thus began my journal through Facebook.

In this private journal on Facebook (pun intended) I have included comments, words of encouragement, conversations and dialogs I have had with everyone from my school days to my ex-husband. I observed healing from both sides of the pond. I was told by followers my journey is their journey, my adventures are their adventures. We were all sad when our journey reached its end.

This is how my private journal on Facebook came to life. This is how my book wrote itself. I manifested an amazing adventure. I journaled about it on Facebook and now I'm sharing my deepest, innermost thoughts and emotions with all of you, my new followers, so you too can take this journey with me. My adventure is now your adventure.

follow my… adventure

Posted on May 25, 2016 by Drew Eric

Chapter 1 Can I do this?

Departure day, I packed and unpacked several times prior to leaving for the airport. I still had not weighed my pack for walking the El Camino de Santiago. Morning of my flight I am still in preparation mode to travel abroad.

I have two adventures planned. The long adventure is backpacking Europe, lasting four to twelve months depending on my money, Visa and enjoyment. The shorter adventure is walking the El Camino de Santiago (a 500-mile pilgrimage through northern Spain).

Now that the day is here I am reflecting on the last month, shutting down my old life, packing away my belongings, all in an effort to begin my adventure. I have been reviewing my Facebook posts and reading peoples comments and words of encouragement. I feel so inspired by all the love and well-wishing on Facebook.

It is amazing how many inspirational quotes are coming up in my Facebook feed that are directly related to what is happening in my life. I keep sharing them out for others to be inspired. These words are no coincidence when they arise in my feed at the exact moment I need them to appear.

This will be an adventure of #LifeLessons.

Facebook, April 15—Drew is feeling overwhelmed—
"More is less. For me, having more means having to insure it, protect it, polish it, worry about it, try to double it, brag about it, price it, maybe sell it for a profit, and on and on."—Dr. Wayne Dyer

— This is so timely when I literally am carrying all of my belongings on my back and I have officially moved out of my apartment and have stored the remainder of my belongings—what I didn't donate or sell—until I return someday, if I return someday. My adventure is open-ended so who knows. I have no ties left to come back to, necessarily. I am free to wander the world if I so choose. Wow, I never would have imagined this for myself. This IS my adventure. Sadly, I have released my pups to my ex-husband for his care while I am away. I will miss them terribly. The hardest part about leaving the country is leaving my pups behind.

9

—James—

You are on a spiritual journey. Forget about "stuff". Store the memories in a photo and when you see it, you will feel the experience again.

Facebook, May 16—Drew is feeling grateful—

I spent my first night Couch Surfing at a friends home. This is the first of many homes until I depart for my adventure. I wanted to practice sleeping around, pun intended. Giving up my bed, pillows and comfortable apartment will help me move into my adventure sooner. Why wait for when I fly away, I want to feel the road beneath my feet now. Bring it baby.

Facebook, May 11—Drew is feeling nostalgic—

Teaching my last yoga class before I fly away. It's getting real in here.

Facebook, May 14—Drew is feeling stressed—

"Today I refuse to stress myself out by things I cannot control or change."—unknown

—Drew—

I have been working all day on reservations with hostels, signing up for Couch Surfing and looking for a host. I'm getting pretty nervous now that it's getting closer, I don't feel prepared. But I wonder if I will ever feel prepared. I have never traveled like this alone. Only a couple trips here in the U.S. since my divorce. My inexperience is daunting. I leave in four days. eeeekkkkkk! I'm worried about where I will be staying over the next four months, so much anxiety.

Facebook, May 16—Drew is feeling determined—

"You want to know the difference between a master and a beginner? The master has failed more times then the beginner has ever tried."—unknown

—Drew—

I am willing to fail if that's what I need to master this.

Facebook, May 17—Drew is feeling excited—

Wow, I can't believe this day has come. I can't believe its here. One day left before I leave Florida. I am getting pretty nervous. I am flying to my brothers for my niece's wedding then leaving America from Boise on the 24th.

Facebook, May 22—Drew is feeling optimistic—

"Walk yourself out of your bad mood. Studies have shown that every 10-Minute walk immediately boosts brain chemistry to increase happiness."—unknown

—Drew—

Wow, I will feel amazing in June when I start walking 500 miles.

Facebook, May 23—Drew is feeling exhausted—

"Everything comes to you in the right moment. Be patient."—unknown.

—Drew—

I really need this today. Getting anxious for my flight to Barcelona tomorrow at 2:17 p.m. and still finding a Couch to Surf on or a Hostel. It's getting real up in here. I arrive in Barcelona at 8:30 a.m. Wednesday morning, getting nervous now, I mean excited, both really, I'm conflicted.

Facebook, May 24—Drew is feeling lucky—

"There are times in our lives when we just need to get away from everything, take the adventure, just go."—Drew Eric

For backpacking Europe the two packs are heavy—50 pounds or more. Fortunately, I will only be carrying all my belongings when I change locations every three-four days moving between hostels. I don't know what countries I will be visiting during the long adventure and I am scared/thrilled about it.

I'm not sure what I'll take for the El Camino pilgrimage, so I unpacked everything and packed only the belongings for the walk. My pack weighed up to 19 lbs, which is too much. I chose to take out items I could get again if I needed them. One of the items not to make the cut was a second walking sun protection shirt. I can just wash the same walking shirt every day by hand as I only have one pair of walking pants anyway.

Before I left I had to spray everything with bedbug repellent for obvious reasons and leave them outside to dry.

With the second walking shirt gone and a couple other items, this brought the weight down to about 16 lbs. I was happier. The recommendation is 10-12% of your weight in your pack at the most. All walkers have said they eliminated items after the first few days, so I decided to eliminate mine prior to leaving. I wonder if I am still taking too much stuff overall.

With this done, I repacked all the items that made the cut and head to the airport with my much-loved niece as the driver. It's special being chauffeured by this high school senior who is so important to me.

I've allowed plenty of time to get through TSA and boarding.

Facebook, May 24—Drew checked in @ Boisepolis International Airport—
Catching my plane now, next stop Atlanta, then Barcelona baby.
 —Carrie-Ann—
So incredibly proud of you my friend...enjoy every minute. Excited to see and read all of the fascinating opportunities you are about to experience. Wishing you much love and safe travels.

Unfortunately, I discovered a glitch in the plans when I arrived at the ticket counter. Europe has a three month Visa to all visitors who stay over a six month period. Meaning I can come and go in/out of Europe as long as I am only in the European Union Visa (Schengen Visa Treaty) area for three months. I booked a four-month return flight (which is changeable for an additional $150, affordable enough if I so choose to stay longer).

The problem arises when the ticket agent asks for my Visa number. She is as confused as I am. Nobody really understood what needed to happen next. I have no Visa number since it isn't required and I wasn't told when booking I should even have a return flight. I just guessed it would probably be a good idea to get one and show I'm not moving indefinitely to Spain.

She got on the phone and starting piecing together questions and answers. I gave her my limited information about the EU and Schengen Treaty Visa. I told her I thought that leaving the EU for a month would be perfectly fine as long as my passport is only stamped in the EU for three months. I am not entirely sure how informed she is on international flights and such. I believe her knowledge might be limited.

Quickly it became apparent, in order to fill the blank in the computer with the ticket agent, I need another plane ticket leaving the EU. Presumably this would also alleviate any problems in Spain when I arrive.

My original ticket was purchased with frequent flier miles donated by a generous friend who was inspired by my blog writing and travel plans. Since it's summer in Europe all other flights would cost more points. This is not viable since I can't get more points.

The ticket agent was on the phone with central command determining less costly options until central command and she decided I just needed to buy another ticket on my own.

As information, I am just divorced from my husband of 20 years who loved to travel and relished making all the travel arrangements. And I let him. So my habit of just showing up, packed and ready did not serve me well in this situation.

Facebook, May 24—Drew is feeling restless—
"It is hardest in the beginning, do not give up. The best is yet to come."—Drew Eric
—Julie—
Drew, thank you for being a bright light in such a dark world. Safe travels. XO.

I have no idea what to do. Time is running out and I am thinking CAN I DO THIS? Will it work, do I have enough information to pull this off and get into Spain? Where do I fly out of and when?

The agent thinks I need to leave out of Spain but that doesn't make any sense to me. My gut says I can leave from anywhere and land outside the EU Visa area.

In checking flights she came back with $500+ ticket fees. That is not in my budget. I'm looking at options. How far is my niece? Should I just miss the flight and work harder at figuring all this stuff out? OMG, what the hell, I have no idea if I can pull this off in just a few minutes!

Facebook, May 24—Melvin—
I will hold you in prayers every day!

I need prayers now, after the initial panic, I pick a cheap airline website. I believe Ireland is out of the EU and choose them as a destination. I CAN DO THIS! I want to go to Ireland anyway. Ok, what is close to Ireland and would be a short, possibly cheap flight? Amsterdam—which I will visit anyway. Ok when? I'll be walking until early July so anytime mid-July will work. I pick July 12th off the cuff with a return flight to Amsterdam two weeks later. BOOM! $225 round trip. See, I CAN do this!

Got my information, check! Credit card, check! Ticket agent asks me for my date leaving, check! She says hurry up! I fill in the final blanks, hit the button and done. Confirmed ticket purchased. What is the confirmation number? Where is it in the confirmation, where is it? THERE!

13

She puts it in, takes my luggage, gives me the ticket and says RUN! Luckily I am TSA pre-checked. I make it through security and arrive at the gate just in time for boarding. Again, hoping this will satisfy Spain with all their requirements since nobody really knows.

Here I am, sitting on the plane now flying to Barcelona. Cross your fingers they accept my last minute flight arrangements as I exit the plane. I can do this.

#LifeLesson —1 When life turns crisis, be still, breathe, confidence can overcome and make it so.

Facebook, May 24—Drew is feeling ecstatic—
In Atlanta waiting for my flight to Barcelona. Got a seat, ticket and all looks good. Got some food, sleeping pillow and my computer for writing. Here goes, no turning back now. On the plane baby, Barcelona next stop. My adventure begins.
—Jeanne—
So excited for everything that will be a piece of this journey! Love from me goes with you.
—Josi—
Take a moment and think back at what you've already accomplished... pause & be present there. Now take the next step without looking too far ahead. Remember, when we think too far ahead we miss the now.
—Kitty—
Safe travels Drew! I cannot wait to hear and see the pics and posts as you go. I am so happy for you.
—Rosa—
My dear Drew Today is the beginning of the rest of your life. Wishing you all the fun, good times and memories you can have. May your path be always green and the rain brings a new start each day. Take lots of pictures and keep us all well updated. The Camino will bring exactly what you need, Buen Camino Peregrino

follow my… adventure

Posted on December 7, 2015 by Drew Eric

Chapter 2 Can I take a Journey-of-Self-Discovery?

This new blog post is based on a potential adventure to Europe I am considering for the end of May 2016. Between now and May I will be writing about my fears, challenges and lessons learned until the day I am potentially leaving for my adventure. At which time I would continue with the blog while on my adventure discussing new fears, challenges and lessons learned.

"One new decision can alter your adventure in a totally new direction."—Drew Eric

My intention for this blog is to become a book on overcoming fears, facing challenges and learning through self-discovery and having some fun in a foreign land. I do hope you will join me on my adventure.

Can I leave my life here in Fort Lauderdale and spend a year traveling Europe? Leave my family, three dogs, car, possessions, friends, community, everything that I identify with, for a life on the other side of the pond? Can I face all my fears and overcome all my obstacles for the unknown? Can I do this?These are my questions today.

"Goals need to be giant, to where you must learn and grow into the person who can achieve such heights."—Drew Eric

It's Sunday after Thanksgiving, November 2015. Only 16 days ago Paris was attacked and the world changed for the second time since 9/11.

Yesterday my ex-husband went on a ten-day cruise with his new partner. We ended our relationship early January, just five months short of our 20th anniversary. We met when I was 27 years young. I spent eight years as an adult prior to meeting my husband and 20 years as an adult coupling. So I have very little experience traveling as a single man. Can I travel Europe without a travel partner?

When I was in 10th grade my home life was less then what I wanted for comfort and support. This was the last year I lived with my father and stepmother prior to moving to Fort Lauderdale to live with my mother and stepfather. It was then the dream of traveling Europe was first introduced to me.

I met a friend in one of my classes the last half of the school year and she invited me on a European vacation with her family. For the next several months, until the school year concluded, we talked about the adventure and it gave me hope, something to dream about. Of course shortly before the school year finished she pulled away. It was then I realized the gift she gave me that very difficult year. Hope!

The dream never left me. Whether it was a book or a movie that involved other lands that dream would reignite in me. The first movie was "Summer Lovers" starring Daryl Hanna based in Mykonos. My second Mykonos movie was "Shirley Valentine". An amazing movie with Shirley, leaving her husband and grown daughter and son, for a two-week vacation in Mykonos, Greece, where she falls in love with herself and the far-off land then decides to stay and create a new life. This deeply moved me and still does to this day. Especially now as I find myself "starting over".

"Under the Tuscan Sun" was such a book so rich with description that you could envision the land in your mind's eye. My takeaway from this reading was the incredible detail of the culture and the way of life. So many details of the food, home and furnishings with interesting local characters. It was like being there.

Elizabeth Gilbert's "Eat Pray Love", I can't even imagine how many lives were impacted by this story. How many people left marriages or took an adventure of their own to discover themselves and/or both. "Attraversiamo" is the "word" Elizabeth loved the most in Italian, meaning "Let's Crossover". For her it was taking a risk and crossing over to another land for a calling to her soul that needed answering.

Can I "spend the summer" in Mykonos and choose me as my "Valentine"? Can this moment be my "Moment in the Tuscan sun"? Can I "Crossover" to another land and challenge my fears, identities and all I hold dear?

Can I be emotionally ready in a short amount of time to take such a big adventure? The Sunday prior to Thanksgiving—on a road trip with my brother and his family—I shared my interest in traveling Europe in about a year possibly. Their excitement and words of encouragement were overwhelming. They were very clear "don't wait a year, DO IT SOONER". They screamed. Which I replied "But I'm not ready, I have so much to prepare and do prior to leaving including being emotionally ready for the adventure" anxiety and fear immediately flushed my face.

I got very present to my fears over the next couple days and thought "maybe they are right, maybe I should crossover sooner than later". My lease is up in April and my niece is getting married in May. Maybe, just maybe the end of May could work. SCARE!

This is where I am today. I am single, debt free, in a rented apartment working as a residential appraiser which stopped being rewarding after the real estate crash in 2006. I have possessions, not as much as I had before the divorce, but still more than makes me feel comfortable. I have some money in the bank from the sale of our home. I do own a Fiat convertible that I "Attraversiamo" with all the time. I have three Maltese pups named Kiko, Kobi and Kai, Hawaiian names were chosen after two visits to the Hawaiian Island and our first non-legal wedding on the shores of Kauai. They would be a huge loss if I left them behind.

I have many "Identities" that would be my challenge to overcome. I will list some now. I make good money. I am 47 years old and I have possessions/belongings. I live in a nice, upgraded condo and I have a nice car. I am a charitable, reliable, giving member of my community. I have a very large network of friends and colleagues in my community and even more acquaintances from living in Fort Lauderdale for more than 25 years. All of my identities wouldn't travel with me.

Facebook, December 5—Drew—
"You are never too old to set another goal, or to dream a new dream."—C. S. Lewis

Can I take an adventure to Europe and leave all my identities? All the parts of me that make up my life here in Fort Lauderdale. All the identities I have grown to believe are ME in an effort to grow and find new identities and new ways of being ME. This, is terrifying.

I have however already started my journey to happiness through self-discovery and exploring spirituality. This eventually led me to realize the marriage was at its end. The day after my separation I went back to my spiritual discussion group "A Course

17

in Miracles, ACIM" and have been attending every Tuesday this year. It has helped me immensely move past my separation with love, kindness and compassion for myself and my husband. We will be divorcing presumably at the end of this year.

Through "A Course in Miracles, ACIM" I learned forgiveness, practicing non-judgment and seeing the light in my soon to be ex-husband. By practicing these principles, I was able to let go of past hurts, angers and find love in myself again.

This new spiritual path along with living alone for the first time in 20 years left me with questions of who am I and who do I want to be in my future. What do I like to do and who do I like to spend my time with? Friendships have been a lifelong learning opportunity for me. As I have witnessed since the separation, I spent too much time focusing on my troubled marriage, and not enough time nurturing deeper relations with friends. Not an uncommon theme for divorcées.

When I was a child I attended six elementary schools prior to fifth grade. Kindergarten and first grade two different schools. I started second grade at a third school when I asked my mom, "if you don't find me a dad, then I want to live with mine". Which means I switched schools mid-semester to live with my father and step-mother. They were married when I was four years old and she brought me a stepbrother nine months older than I.

As a seven-year-old learning about life, I wasn't able to comprehend the diverse way of living with my new parents. By the end of that semester I chose too not to return for the new school year and I was back with mom and two brothers. Third grade came the fifth school of course. Halfway through fourth grade my father requested full custody of his three boys and we moved to Seminole, FL where I landed at my sixth elementary school. Clearly my education wasn't consistent and I was held back for a second year in fourth grade.

Childhood is where we learn about friendships and how to maintain long-term relationships. Mine were happening so fast I did not develop helpful skills that were beneficial. What I did learn was when you trade your brownie for friendship, they laugh at you, while eating your brownie.

Can I overcome my fear of being alone and spend a year in Europe traveling alone? Friendships mean the world to me. I am still learning helpful skills to this day like, how to be a good friend. I have learned past many unhelpful personality traits and I feel I am currently fine-tuning who I want to be for others.

Most of my childhood I didn't have consistent friends and found myself alone a good percentage of the time. This is my biggest FEAR! Not having friends and being alone. People that know me see me as a highly social person when I am out and about however I really feel uneasy going out alone attending parties or events without a companion to share the experience. Sometimes I feel out of place like I don't belong.

I have worked from home since 2003 and rarely leave the comfort of home to work outside in a coffee shop or restaurant. I am sitting in Starbucks writing this in an effort to challenge my comforts. When work slows, It takes all of my energy to be productive. Usually I just extend my work from a couple hours to as long as it takes till I get busy again. As opposed to finishing early and doing something fun.

Facebook, December 7—Stefan—
Yes you can...I felt like you when I traveled all alone around the world for months. Would I be alone? What would I encounter in a foreign country without knowledge of the language? It all worked out, I met wonderful people.
—Fernando—
Don't be afraid, my friend, I was 42 when I was forced to leave my country and come here with my 6-year-old son. Little money, no English, no friends or family here.

Can I overcome my fears, comforts and social anxiety to travel Europe? Traveling to unfamiliar places gets me anxious causing me to reach for my anxiety fixes that are common for most, food, alcohol, sleep, phone apps, sex and television. I stress/comfort eat when I get anxious especially sugar. I get tired and down when I anticipate doing something outside my comfort zone and struggle with motivating myself. I have been known to escape with my favorite T.V. shows and programs. Exercise seems to slow to a crawl when I am feeling the need to escape. Unfamiliar social situations can be calmed with a glass of wine or two. If I was to take the adventure, I want to be present to my "fixes" and not succumb to them but to remain present in my life.

Can I be spiritually ready in such a short amount of time to take such a big adventure? So this is my plan: Between now and the

19

end of May I want to create the new ME. I'm not going to focus on whether I am taking this adventure or not. I am going to put my attention on all my fears, challenges and identities along with anything else that doesn't serve me. I plan on figuring out who I want my future self to be and work on becoming that person now. Letting go of old habits and creating new ways of being. This way I am focusing on today, and not my tomorrow adventure. At the end of five-ish months I will be a new person with new ways of being and prepared for my new life. I hope I can do this.

Facebook, December 7—Vinny—
There is no better time than the present. I think this will be an amazing experience for you. I spent almost 2 months in SE Asia and it was the experience of a lifetime. Go. Enjoy. Grow. Embrace. Learn. Love. Live.
—Tom—
Hey, Drew...What will I do for a yoga teacher when I come back from my adventure to West Africa? Another question to ponder! It's very interesting to read your blog...at the onset...because it will change very much as your adventure progresses. When I turned 21, I went into the Peace Corps...for two years! A boy from Ohio being sent into a tropical rain forest in the Ivory Coast...I had no idea of what I was getting into...didn't even know where the place was and couldn't find it on a map! And soon after getting there, wondering what I had done to myself and why! I ended up staying for four years! The point is: to know yourself, you must see all you describe in your blog from a very different and foreign perspective...THAT will answer those questions. I doubt you will answer them BEFORE you go...Isn't that the purpose of going in the first place? To discover???

follow my… adventure

Posted on May 26, 2016 by Drew Eric

Chapter 3 Can I survive my first few days in Europe?

Barcelona Day 1; Wow, what an adventure! Arriving this morning and all went well through Customs. Found the bus into the city where my Couch Surfing host picked me up and escorted me back to his place. He's got a great apartment in Gothic Barcelona, with my own private room, so far, loving Couch Surfing.

couchsurfing.com is a website designed to bring travelers and host together in an exchange of experiences, conversations and sharing of one's space. No money is involved since the only collateral is your dynamic personalities. In return you get a roof over your head and a place to sleep. Sleeping arrangements vary from a private room with a bed, to a couch, shared bed or even a yoga matt on the floor, all depending on what the host has available. Similarly to Uber, you are rated as the host and the guest equally. The intention is to share your adventure with others while traveling.

I spent the day exploring all around my area but not venturing too far from home base. I decided to head in the direction of the water, exploring the port area. Lots of tourists—and lots of vendors trying to sell them Barcelona bags, sunglasses and selfie sticks along with touristy knickknacks.

I am really bad with memory retention—a symptom of dyslexia—but I have a really good sense of direction. I have not been able to remember any street names yet but I have done well with navigation.

The food is really enjoyable so far. I had a classic cheese, bread, fruit and yogurt breakfast offered by my host. Then my host and I went for lunch later in the day—an inexpensive three-course meal, only 12 euros.

My host told me about a meet-up group at the local gay bar that meets every Wednesday night. I got directions and after exploring the port area a bit more, it was off to check out the meet-up.

I met some really nice people and had a couple of drinks. I enjoyed myself immensely, I am happy I went. It was a pleasure to meet some locals. It was a good first-day activity. The drinks were poured well and I was a little tipsy.

Time to head back to my host flat. I pulled up google maps, then my phone went black. No battery left. (Cue danger music.) My keen sense of direction worked well in an area I had explored. However, I wasn't as familiar with this side of town. I had the address on my phone but I don't have any street names memorized yet.

Since it was getting late I took a taxi. The only detail I can remember about the area where I live is the Picasso Museum isn't too far from his place. So, I chose that as my drop off point.

Just before grabbing the cab, I stopped and got a chicken sandwich—from Burger King of all places. I hadn't eaten since the late lunch at 4 p.m. I finished the sandwich and arrived near the museum. I paid the cabbie, grabbed my garbage and jumped out.

Panicking now about my keys to get in the flat. Hoping I didn't leave them in the cab as it drives away. I find the keys then check my belongings. Where's my phone? SHIT!

I'm wearing a running belt or a money waistband for my wallet and keys—a European traveling precaution. I didn't realize I'd left my phone since I was focused on looking for my keys. Nothing I can do about it now other than calling the cab folks tomorrow. Crossing fingers.

Facebook, May 25—Laurie—
OMG!! You are so Adorable!! I'm so excited for you. This is A Book, I just want to turn the page. And you should too. NEXT!!
—Janet—
If not a book – definitely a movie script. Can't wait for the next scene. Big Hug.

On I walk in the direction that seems correct. It is not. Ok, so much for my great sense of direction. I am completely turned around and have no idea where I am. I'm certainly not seeing anything familiar. An hour later I try another cab driver who only spoke Spanish and didn't seem interested in my dilemma. So, it's out of the cab and walking again.

Facebook, May 25—Denny—

I got lost in Barcelona myself and learned more about maps, addresses and remember those feelings of anxiety when I didn't know where I was. All part of the adventure.

I stopped in a bar to ask for directions. I got a helpful response and the number for the taxi company's lost and found department. This I'll have to handle tomorrow—with the help of my host.

One last cab ride. This time I remembered the two roundabouts near the water. The driver was Jamaican and spoke English. We drove away from where he picked me up toward the circles and past the water. Now I have my bearings and I tell him to go back the way we came. Finally, a boulevard and a church and plaza whiz by and finally I'm on the small street where my Couch Surfing host lives. I'm home—two hours later.

During the walk I was freaking out. I couldn't believe that I'm in an unfamiliar country, with no phone, no directions and very few identifiers. All kinds of things are crossing my mind. Will I be sleeping on the street? Be robbed of my backpack and my camera? Will I ever find my Couch Surfing flat? Crazy thoughts!

I kept asking my intuition to guide me. I did my best to ignore the frightening thoughts that kept intruding—pushing them out of my head and asking for guidance.

In "A Course in Miracles, ACIM" we have several phrases we repeat in any difficult situation."I turn this over to holy spirit to solve." "Universe guide me now." "God, show me who I should see, speak to and where I should go." I was using them all at this point, telling myself I am ok and it will all work out.

#LifeLesson —2 When you are in dire need of assistance, turn it over to your inner guidance and listen intently for the answer and direction. You always know best.

Facebook, May 25—Sherry—

Praying for you Drew! Sending Love! So glad you are safe!

—Eric—

Thank you for sharing. I'm so excited for you and know you are ready for this journey. I think two important lessons for all of us. 1. The answer is always within. 2. Don't drink in new surroundings.

Lol. More pics. More writing

The panic subsided when I was back at the flat, safe and sound. I believed my phone would turn up because these kinds of things always work out for me. I'm more centered now and I am sure the cabbie will turn my phone into the lost and found.

Facebook, May 25—Mark—
Isn't this type of adventure the exact reason you decided to go on your walk-about? #becarefulwhatyouaskfor
—Will—
This is the journey... Conquering your fear on a minute by minute basis... So jelly... God bless...

I was concerned about disrupting my host coming in so late on my first day staying with him, so I was extra quiet. Realizing how much adrenaline I had running through my body, I took two Xanax and tried to settle down for bed. After a bit more time I knew I needed to top those off with one more, which finally put me out.

I slept five-½ hours the night before, then caught the redeye to Barcelona. I slept three hours on the plane, then spent the entire day awake site seeing. Now it's 2:30 a.m. and I'm finally, comfortably down for a full nights sleep

Facebook, May 25—Rick—
Drew, I can relate to your misfortunes. In 2008, I was in Berlin, Germany. A few of us took a cab back to the German army barracks. As I got upstairs to my room, I realized I left my wallet in the cab which fell off my knee. Long story short, I had to drive 8 1/2 hours to Spangdalemn Air Force Base in Germany to get a new military ID card. Otherwise, it would've been impossible to leave the country and return back home. I lost about $100 in that ordeal but believe it or not, a few months later, my wallet and drivers license was returned back to me in the mail. Everything else was gone. Moral of the story, be patient and ensure you have all your belongings before moving about. Thanks for your story and keep posting. Safe travels.
#LifeLesson —3 Relying on old ways of coping with stress that is destructive, brings no peace, i.e. comfort eating and drinking. Create new pathways relying on inner strength and concentration of breathe. "I choose peace over this." Peace will envelop you in its arms, holding you tight.

Barcelona Day 2; I roll over, pulled open my computer and read the time. Sleeping until 3:45 p.m. shocked even me. I can't remember the last time I slept until midday. Obviously jet lag has taken its toll and the three Xanax. My host was equally surprised and was even concerned if I was in the room at all.

Facebook, May 26—Drew—
"Everyday we wake up, breathe in the new day, smile and begin again."—Drew Eric

I share my story about getting lost and losing my phone. He was a bit surprised and did help me call the taxi company to put in a lost and found claim.

This kind of thing always seems to works out for me. So, I focused on not letting it overwhelm me throughout the day. I turned on "Lost my iPhone" but the battery was dead and it didn't register.

Facebook, May 26—Drew—
Have faith and hope knowing everything will be ok and everything happens for a reason that will be clear, someday.

The rest of the day I continued to put the phone out of my mind. I can text and use Facebook on my computer however choose not to for the day.

My host—a kind man from England who works as a translator—made a delicious late lunch which we ate together. He shared how he "made a special effort" preparing the meal. I was greatly appreciative.

I venture out for some more exploration, this time really paying attention to where I am and where I am going.

Facebook, May 26—Nicole—
Drew thank you so much for sharing your adventure and thoughts with us. I am so excited for you. We are brief acquaintances many years ago, with friends in common. I am living vicariously through you. I wish I were doing it! You are brave and will have amazing things come from this journey! I am sure of it. I wait anxiously for your next entry!!! Safe travels!

My host and I discuss the various ways for me to travel to Pamplona–train or car share for a fee—which sounded interesting. I tried to book a ticket but it didn't go through so I put it off for later.

My host said I could stay until Sunday if I wanted and I left that option open since I hadn't booked a ticket to Pamplona and I am waiting for my phone to turn up.Really, everything is on hold at this point. No sense in making plans until the phone situation is resolved. It's too early for total panic.

My host made another great dinner which we shared while chatting. He is a sweet man.

I work with my host and google maps coordinating directions and old-school items such as paper, pen, printer and a paper map. This time I have the address of the flat written down.

Facebook, May 26—Mark—
How all very exciting, Your attitude is perfect, And that is everything! Looking forward to hearing more about your amazing adventure. Enjoy each precious moment and know that the universe has put you exactly where you are as part of your journey. Even your disappearing phone. Some of my best adventures traveling and in life came because I was lost.

It's now early evening and I decide to grab a drink at one of the gay bars—possibly meet some nice locals again. No reason to stay in and worry about my plans or phone. I'm a little nervous about getting lost again and told my host I would probably take a taxi instead of walking.

Facebook, May 26—Mike—
One day you will laugh about the phone being a chapter in your adventure. Stay positive and patient and roll with it.

I am looking at the street signs on the corners and they don't make sense. They have arrows and names but they do not appear to be street names. Finally I realize the street names are on the corners of buildings, unlike in America where they are posted on the corners of roads. I am on the right street, going in the right direction. Hmmm, that's good to know.

Facebook, May 26—Josi—

We are never "really lost" just "redirected".

I find the bar and meet a nice Italian man visiting from Paris—two visitors talking in a local hangout. It was a pleasure. I was able to relax and live in the moment.

Facebook, May 26—Kitty—
I am impressed how you are handling losing your phone. I would be a mess. Funny though, how couple decades ago you wouldn't have had a phone to lose and now, this is such a necessary piece of our lives. What's happened to you makes me reflect on how dependent I've become on mine, for good or ill. Best wishes, hope things work out!

As it's getting late, I decide to head home so not to disturb my host with my late arrival. After a short taxi ride, I am home safely. I set an alarm on my hiking watch and fall asleep with a plan to wake up the next day at a respectable 8:30 a.m. to the good news that my phone is located and all is well. I can do this, even without a phone.

Facebook, May 26—Drew—
"Everything always works out for my best interest, Universal law."—Drew Eric
—Marco—
If you stay positive and in the present, your adventure will turn out better than anything you could have planned. #stayintheflow the universe will carry you

follow my… adventure

Posted on February 5, 2016 by Drew Eric

Chapter 4 Can I overcome so many fears and travel Europe?

"Success arrives when our mind repels fear-thinking while focusing on our heart's desires."—Drew Eric

30 Fears, 30 Solutions; I'm planning to backpack Europe starting at the end of May. It's an adventure I hope will last for a year or more. I haven't pinned down where I'll start my adventure; it could be Germany to visit a friend or it could be Paris with a couple of friends starting their own adventures–so many unknowns.

While considering my adventure, fear has percolated to the top. I don't know how long I will be gone. I don't know all the places I will go. I don't know all the people I will meet. However, I'm committed to challenging these fearful conversations. I want to step up to these fears, look them squarely in the face and relegate them to walking behind me in my shadow.

Elizabeth Gilbert, author of "Big Magic" said, "Fear goes everywhere with you." She accepted fear as her companion, however she told fear to "Shut up, don't speak, you're welcome to come on this trip, but you are not allowed to drive."

I understand the importance of fear; it keeps us alert. But it also keeps us small. Fear keeps us aware of pitfalls and potential dangers, but it doesn't have to rule our world. I am choosing to overcome many fears, today, now, in Fort Lauderdale.

In the books, "Wild" by Cheryl Strayed and "Eat Pray Love" by Elizabeth Gilbert, both women used their adventure to challenge and change their life. This is a fantastic concept that I want to embrace as I travel to a new continent.

But I'm not waiting to leave before I begin focusing on my personal growth and creating the person, I've always dreamed of being. By working on my inner "stuff" I'm creating a more powerful life now.

It's mid-January 2016 and I've had plenty of time to face my fear head on and plan an amazing adventure. For the last couple months, I have increasingly gotten more comfortable with the adventure and here's my list of things to work on:

30 Fears to Overcome:
1. Is this adventure a good idea
2. Meeting new people
3. Social anxieties
4. Being in uncomfortable situations
5. Being around angry people
6. Not liking the people I meet
7. Not having my friends with me
8. Traveling and being alone
9. Not being in control
10. Not speaking the language
11. Not liking the food
12. Not having a place to stay
13. Not being able to sleep
14. Sleeping in unfamiliar spaces
15. Sleeping with strange people
16. Not having my bed
17. Not having my five pillows
18. Not having a permanent home
19. Not having my belongings
20. Not having a home when I return
21. Not having my pets
22. Not having television
23. Not earning a living
24. Not making money on the adventure
25. Not putting money into retirement
26. Not having a job when I get home
27. Not having a car when I return
28. Living off the kindness of others
29. Not completing projects
30. Traveling like a 20-something when I am 48 years old

I feel like I've lived a "safe" life. I was in a relationship for almost 20 years. Several times during the long relationship came moments of questioning–questioning whether continuing was the best decision for both of us, I played it safe and stayed, instead of taking action and separating.

During our long relationship we lived in the same home for 17 years, another example of "safe". Being risk averse had a tremendous effect on my wellbeing and personal growth. I was stunted, distracted and too busy focusing on a broken marriage. As a result, I didn't work on my own growth.

30 Solutions for today:
1. Donate, sell and trash most of my belongings. Shrinking my stuff to what is needed when I return–releasing old belongings in an effort to feel free of my past identity.
2. Complete unfinished projects— i.e. a quilt made from my mother's clothing almost 20 years after her passing.
3. Finish my continuing education for a Real Estate Appraisal license and a Real Estate license.
4. Become the person I think I am or let go of the dreams—Become a runner—Have a daily yoga practice of my own. (I am a yoga instructor without my own practice)
5. Have a morning and evening spiritual practice including meditation, "A Course in Miracles" daily lessons and taking care of my body Run a half marathon–I love a healthy challenge.
6. Run a half marathon–I love a healthy challenge.
7. Create art. (I went to one of the top art schools in the country, Ringling College.)—Learn photography-a lifelong desire—Work with pastels.
8. Sell my car–this one is big. It makes me feel vulnerable and afraid to lose.
9. Couch Surf the final 45 days in America with friends and family.
10. Put my current clients and my appraisal business on hold.
11. Complete my coaching certification with University of Miami and get my Professional Certified Coaching (PCC) with the International Coaching Federation (ICF).
12. Create self-help videos on my YouTube channel promoting my coaching business.
13. Complete my taxes–always a chore.
14. Finish a book, "A New Year, A New You." (Working title.)
15. Recreate my website.
16. Build a following on social media.
17. Write blogs about my fears, challenges, anxieties and learnings, for my new book, "Can I Do This?" about preparing for and traveling through Europe.
18. Let go of my television addiction.
19. Lose weight to be lighter on my adventure.
20. Research backpacking Europe and walking El Camino de Santiago, a pilgrimage through northern Spain.

21. Create a weekly road-bike practice, so I can bike ride while traveling.
22. Explore my city.
23. Get up at 6 a.m. on work days.
24. Devour audiobooks for learning.
25. Drink less.
26. Learn to sleep anywhere and without earplugs.
27. Read more books.
28. Reduce bills.
29. Control emotional fixes i.e. stress eating, drinking, sex, comfort T.V.
30. Learn to be alone.

Facebook, February 3—Drew—
"Hope, Faith and Desire are the three things stronger than fear."—Drew Eric

This is an important adventure for me to take. I believe I will be changed forever. I have dreamed of such a challenge all my life. Now is the time to create that reality by taking action, not, to play it safe.

I can do this, I will overcome fears.

Facebook, February 4—Drew—
"The only person you are destined to become is the person you decide to be."—Ralph Waldo Emerson
Facebook, February 5—Ray—
Drew, I myself did something similar that you are about to embark on. Two years ago, when I retired with the fire department, I sold everything or gave away everything I owned, including my house here, bought an RV and traveled the entire United States for almost a year by Myself. In doing so I found out more about me than I had ever done before. I was very inspired by the children's book written by Dr. Suess "Oh the places you'll go" so much so I have that written on the back of my RV. Get out there and don't worry, just let it happen, let it play out, its opener there in the wide open air. Enjoy my friend!
—Ralph—
Good Drew - when I was fired I was filled with a lot of fear and was really pissed. I was challenged to write a letter to Dear Fear for 30 days. First few letters were filled with hate i.e. f--- y-- fear.

But as I continued to write each day I began to change and see fear as a friend that was always there with me. Fear was the thing that made me challenge myself and overcome my insecurities. So take fear with you and walk hand in hand.

follow my… adventure

Posted on May 28, 2016 by Drew Eric

Chapter 5 Can I pull up my big boy pants and take care of myself?

Barcelona Day 3; I wake up before the alarm and pop out of bed. My host is at the gym and I make coffee and grab some bread and cheese with a little jam, which is breakfast in Europe. I look online for notification on my phone with no word. Now what?

I decide a yoga class in a studio just down the street would settle my nerves. The class was in Spanish with some Sanskrit but I was able to follow along. Nice to forget about my troubles.

Facebook, May 27—Sally—
You're not going to come across anything you don't know how to handle. You just need to take time to think it through. You can buy a cheap disposable phone or even rent one in Europe and use that if it makes you feel better. I love you!

I remember that on the day I lost my phone I'd stopped at Burger King. Maybe I left it there. Following my intuition, I decided to head that way after yoga and find out. But first I check in with my host

I arrive home and talk with my host about calling the taxi company. He seems a bit put out. I am noticing his energy has shifted. I don't want to make him feel burdened by my problems. He calls and the taxi company has no further details. No phone.

I shower, get ready for exploring and finding my phone at Burger King at the least. Out the door this time taking my computer just in case I need to get online.

No phone at Burger King even though they often advertise that you can "have it your way"! Apparently, that just applies to their burgers…

Facebook, June 27—Drew—
"I give up, will not be writing by my hand in my story."—Drew Eric

Holy shit. My phone is gone. The reality of the situation hits me full force. Do I buy a phone in Europe? Do I buy a phone at home and have it shipped? Holy fuck, now what? I'm Couch Surfing until

Sunday. I have no place to ship a phone and my host is a bit put off so I can't live with him till my phone comes in.

I head back to the flat and scooted into my room to figure things out. As if on cue, my host comes in and asks about my plans for leaving. When I say "Sunday, to see if the phone turns up like you mentioned" and ask if that is okay, he answers with a resounding "no" followed by a "just kidding" and a hit on the arm. From what I know about people and reading our conversation, I got the hint.

I hear my intuition speaking loud and clear. Pull your Big-Boy-Pants up and handle this. Make it happen! Get it done! FIGURE THIS SHIT OUT NOW!!! "Figure this out" is fast becoming my new mantra.

Facebook, May 27—Jacob—
Life is a journey, literally for you now. Breathe and keep using your mantras! I think you are on your way, also literal, Camino style!!! Writing is therapeutic and you have a great ability, keep it up!! You got this!!!

I reached T-Mobile through the internet on my computer and was able to text an agent. I choose to purchase a new phone and have it mailed overnight to my friend's home in Florida. I text my friend through my computer, the phone will be arriving and can he ship it to me SOMEWHERE in Europe. I will let him know where—when I know where!

Facebook, May 27—Drew—
#ActOfKindness —1 My friends, who let me stay in their spare bedroom for two weeks prior to leaving America and who are receiving all my mail and holding it for me and depositing any checks that come in after I leave and who are writing any necessary checks that need writing while I am gone, agreed to mail me a new phone to someplace in Europe when it arrives at their home. They are so kind to do so much for me. I love them for that.
Facebook, May 27—Mark—
It seems the loss of the phone is a test. The one thing that you were completely reliant on was taken from you. Maybe the Universe is simply showing you that you do not need it after all? Safe travels. -m
—Sherry—

34

Drew- I am sooo proud of you at how you are handling all this stretching beyond your comfort zone!!! Remember, God is with you. You are never alone and you and God together can do anything!!! Know that I am keeping you in prayer and sending love!!

Next, I found the hostel in France where I can reserve a bed starting Sunday through Wednesday. Done, I got my address and let me friend know.

I am feeling a huge sense of accomplishment right about now, the Big-Boy-Pants are up.

Facebook, May 27—Suzanne—
My prayers for you last night were for wisdom and understanding and that you would grow in your confidence during this adventure. So glad to read this update. Sometimes the path isn't the one we planned, but you'll end up where you need to be. Keep moving forward—one day and one step at a time!

I need to get out of Barcelona. Another Camino walker told me about flying into Madrid and taking a train to Pamplona and then a bus to Saint Jean Pied de Port to start the Camino. This indicated to me as the best means to get to Saint Jean since it is a smaller town, probably without an abundance of transportation options. I decided to follow what had already worked.

I went online for a train ticket to Pamplona and picked the first booking company that came up. I put all the info in and hit purchase. Done! Holy fuck! I just purchased my first train ticket in my life.

Sidebar-I am tearing up writing this. So proud of myself! This is such an adventure—me, diving into the deep end of the pool!
Facebook, May 27—Greg—
One of the most revealing aspects of traveling (as opposed to touring) is what you learn about yourself. Seeing the world is great and those memories will be with you forever. But the truly lasting effect will be on your self-perceptions and self-knowledge. You are doing great!

I let my increasingly reluctant host know that I'm leaving on Saturday.

Now, for a place to stay in Pamplona. Couch Surfing has nothing. I email all the hostels and everything is booked for Saturday night.

I jump over to Airbnb to rent a cheap room. I go through the sign-up process and, after some frantic moments and the support of a friend who texted me my confirmation number, I'm signed up.

I need to pick a host on Airbnb and I decide to choose a cheap option and a woman host, I am not entirely ready to be hosted by a straight man. I send the request and pay with my card. Of course, there's the time lag waiting for my host to confirm while Jeopardy music plays in my head.

Facebook, May 27—Chris—
What an adventure! It is in between the planned and the unplanned that we find the dropped pieces of who we once thought we could be....BRAVO!

Here's the recap: I've ordered my replacement phone, had it shipped to my friend in the States who is sending it to France where I'm staying until it shows up. I have a train ticket out of Barcelona to Pamplona on Saturday where I have put in a request to stay the night with a lovely Airbnb woman host.

Facebook, May 26—Drew—
"Something will grow from all you are going through, and it will be you."—unknown
Facebook, May 27—Michelle—
U make me want to jump on this plane and hold ur hand through this. Ur so strong. I am so humbled by what ur going through. I am here for u and can mail stuff to u. U can use my address. Whatever I can do to help u I will. Yoga in Spanish☺.
#OneDayAtAtime#YouGotThis love u Drew. Keep us posted.

This took me all day! I had no idea it would take so long. I thought it would be a little bit easier finding places to stay but it was a day of learning. Gratefully, I am my own Prince-In-Shining-Armor, I am my own Prince who swooped in and saved me. I saved the day. ME!

Nothing left to do but wait for the Airbnb host to reply to my request. My Barcelona host and I head out to dinner. He's in great spirits and we have a lovely meal. I want to take a couple of night photographs of some Gaudi buildings and he decides to join me. Off we go into the night walking and talking.

We arrived home after 11:00 pm and said our goodnights. I caught up with some friends through text on my computer, feeling the comfort of connecting with home before I took my Xanax and welcomed sleep. I totally nailed it today, I can do this. Until tomorrow…

Day 4 Barcelona/Pamplona; I wake up at a respectable 8:45 a.m. I give the phone one more try but still, nothing. I grab a shower, make a coffee and start the packing process. My host I assumed was at the gym however he later rolled out of bed which was quite a surprise since he has been such an early riser the last three days. He inquires if I received confirmation yet for a room stay from the woman in Pamplona and I mention "no".

After some more packing I check again, still nothing. Now it's 15 minutes before I leave for the train. I decide to choose another host from Airbnb. I choose a guy, register and the site tells me I have two bookings do I really want two separate bookings. I cancel the guy. Hmmm, what now?

The guy sends me a message to tell me I can have the room. Wow, that worked out. I cancel the woman's reservation and book him again. I inquire about the address and he says he will pick me up at the train station. I tell him the time of arrival and sign off to run out the door and catch my train. It looks like things are working out better.

My host escorts me to the station and helps me through the process. I get the impression from him that I might be in over my head with the traveling thing. He is right. However what he doesn't know is "I CAN DO THIS!"

I looked back one last time and feel a twinge of safety walking back to his home. I am alone again. I turn, down the escalator to go. I smile sand say to myself. This is awesome. This is so cool. I can am going to rock this. I am the man, I can do this! Off I go to my train.

I CAN DO THIS!

Facebook, May 27—Drew—
"My blessings far exceed my problems at the end of this day. I am grateful!"—Drew Eric

37

#LifeLesson —4 We are stronger then we think. When life presents difficulties, strength is always available to us.
   —Drew—

   #ActOfKindness —2 First Couch Surfing host, offered a private bedroom, food, drink and quality time. Such a beautiful experience to share someone's home, life and see first hand how different it is to live in another country. Thanks Barcelona for all you gave me. Thanks my friend for all your kindness. I am forever grateful for your generosity in welcoming me on my first day of my new adventure.
   —Anne—

You don't need a Prince my friend!! YOU are your own Prince! You are learning every day, with every challenge. Not only can you do this... You ARE doing it. Carry on!!
   —Elizabeth—

You are on the adventure of a lifetime!
   —Ann—

It's amazing what can be accomplished with a clear mind and no distractions... Only you can be distracted by you at this point. Congratulations for pulling those pants up and getting it done... When you arrive back in Florida I would love to meet and talk with you about your journey and all that you have learned from it. Remember... You're a big boy now.... ❤ Sending you peace and love and enlightening...
   —Kenny—

Drew. Stepping out of our comfort zone is always not the easiest thing to do. There are good people who will cross your path and help you along your way. Look at the police stations for truth. You have this and what a story you will have. Sometimes it is uncomfortable but with a positive non judgemental attitude you will ROCK!

Posted on December 23, 2016 by Drew Eric

Chapter 6 Can I Overcome My Social Anxieties?

Facebook, December 20—Drew—
"Peace: Remaining calm within, while you are surrounded by noise, conversation, distractions and work."—Drew Eric

Last night I attended a colleague's, Christmas party. Many of the guests in attendance were new to me. As I made my way through the room, I found my anxiety rising as I wasn't finding the safety of a familiar face. When this happens I usually get the sense of wanting to leave, head home and enjoy some of my favorite comfort T.V. I have relied on television as a friend for so long, he will be missed while I backpack Europe.

When I first thought about backpacking Europe it terrified me. How will I live without all my comforts; My bed, five pillows positioned all around me, three pups also positioned all around me, Fiat Convertible, nice upgraded apartment, belongings, job, friends and safety/security of home? If I am going on this adventure, I have to start overcoming my fears and face a life living outside my comfort zone. Without my favorite T.V. shows to escape.

"How can a book describe the physiological factors a person must prepare for, the despair, the alienation, the anxiety and especially the pain both physical and mental which slices to the very heart of the hiker's volition, which are the real things that must be planned for. No words can transmit those factors". Charles Long, published in "The Pacific Crest Trail Volume 1: California.

Cheryl Strayed described reading this quote in her book "Wild" after hiking three miles on her first day. I am hearing this quote more than five months prior to my backpacking Europe. I fear to feel alienated and anxious as described by Charles at some point on my adventure, especially since I feel it now in life.

Traveling in lands where I do not speak the language could cause a feeling of alienation. I will be meeting new people each and every day creating some anxiety within. However, I want to challenge my fears and anxieties. If I work hard today, I can create new patterns of wellbeing and minimize future anxieties. I want to have the adventure be heartfelt with an abundance of learning and personal growth. I want to allow others to truly see me and not hide my inner self as to protect. On the upside, I don't plan on actually hiking 1000 miles so hopefully, I don't have to experience the physical pain Cheryl endured hiking the Pacific Crest Trail.

Today, I am acknowledging the social anxiety in my life and plan on surrendering it. Last night, facing my first challenge, I worked through anxiety, not letting it win. Typically, I would reach for alcohol as a social lubricant. Not tonight, I enjoyed one glass of wine then switched to bottled water. Moments before the bottled water, the "go home" anxiety started to surface, which through positive reinforcement of safety, subsided swiftly.

Facebook, December 22—Drew—
"There's nowhere you can be that isn't where you're meant to be."—John Lennon

Usually, I enjoy attending events with a group of friends. Having a friend in tow gives me someone to partner and share the experience while alleviating some of my social anxiety. Someone to always come back to when a lull in the event happens. For the past 20 years I had a husband by my side, but no longer.

Last night I felt no different. I quickly engaged with a friend and his partner for conversation and choose them as my social partners for the evening. Eventually, they slipped away for another conversation leaving me ALONE, my biggest fear.

I used to do an extensive amount of business networking. I knew this expression well "work the room" and in my mind, meant "say hello to as many friends and colleagues as possible." In my opinion, this ties back to my childhood pattern of never sticking in one place long enough to have close relations. A pattern that felt very familiar and comfortable. When I became present to this pattern, I was able to discern the destructive nature it had on my relations. I then chose to surrender this pattern of behavior.

Now, I have grown accustomed to a new pattern, patient and calm, while engaging in long conversations. I find this tremendously rewarding. I truly enjoy getting to know someone for more than a few passing seconds. I allow them the chance to see me and get to know the real me on a deeper level. Two friends this year have given me feedback, they felt I am more myself and relaxed. My life has become richer and happier. However, this doesn't eliminate my feeling of anxiety and fear when I am standing by myself.

Moving through the party, I found another friend for conversation. Through sharing, my confidence was building and anxiety dissipate. However, I noticed we were too close within reach of the buffet area, always a means of comfort for anxiety. I picked and poked at the nibbles. In an effort to save calories I deconstructed food as a pastime. Saving calories isn't reason enough to pick at food while at a party feeling anxious.

My old patterns of comfort while being social, are as follows:
- Attend with a friend
- Find a social partner to stick with if I attend alone
- Drink for comfort
- Eat for comfort
- Go home and escape with television.

In order for me to enjoy my adventure in Europe, I have to choose growth and alter my experiences in social settings.

Someone recently told me when referring to backpacking Europe, "I assume it must change you as a person. You will probably not see people the same again. You would probably see them more similar than different. See different cultures of people more as the same then separate". He said it more to himself while thinking really, then saying it to me. He shared with a dreamy look in his eyes as if he wanted to imagine feeling the experience for himself. Hearing his words, I stirred with excitement over the possibility of my European adventure, allowing the adventure to forever alter how I see others in the world. I heard him and imagined the depth of personal growth I will have.

When I arrived at the party I realized I do see people as different, separate from me. I didn't feel I was sharing the experience of the party, I felt outside the party. It took some time before I did relax and ease into a comfortable space. Through my studies in "A Course in Miracles," I have learned we are all joined, one and the same. We are not separated by religions or nationalities, gay or straight, we all carry the same blood in our veins and are brothers on this earth.

With just days away from Christmas, 2015, Donald Trump has been trending on social media by declaring our separateness from other religions and nationalities. He is stating "we need to build a wall to keep THEM out. We need to ban THEM from entering our country. THEY are and WILL do us harm." Donald Trump is saying this in an effort to win the Republican parties vote to represent Republicans in the presidential election of 2016.

I, on the other hand, am taking a different view. I see Donald Trump as the same as me. Doing the best he can in his life with the personal growth he has accomplished. "Namaste" is a respectful greeting of hello and goodbye in the Indian language of Hinduism, Buddhism, and Jainism. "Namaste" means "I see the light in you as the same light in me". Donald Trump, WE are the same you and I. We are both brothers in this world. I see the light in you as the same light in me. Namaste and peace be with you, Donald. I hope someday you'll join us.

Imagine:
Imagine no possessions
I wonder if you can
No need for greed or hunger
A brotherhood of man
Imagine all the people sharing all the world, you

You may say I'm a dreamer
But I'm not the only one
I hope someday you'll join us
And the world will be as one—John Lennon

Notice the lyrics that reflect oneness. "And the world will be as one." and "A brotherhood of man." This is how we need to see the world. This is how I and John Lennon want to see the world. This is the intention I am setting for my European adventure. I want to be at ease, without anxiety, fear, feeling of separation and aloneness. I want to be comfortable enough in my own skin, not to rely on my past comforts when anxiety arises. I want to be my best self for others to see and get to know. I can do this! I can release separateness and see the world as one.

The party took a collective fun turn when someone pulled up Ellen DeGeneres's hilarious game "Heads Up" on their phone and we gave it a few rounds. Even I took the vulnerable step of giving it a try, guessing what the partygoers were all screaming at me, at the same instance. I allowed them all to see me, my flaws and lack of pop culture knowledge. It was funny. What was once a regular party with people mingling around all having their own joyful experience, turned into a group of participants in a game, "a brotherhood of man." We all joined in for the common experience "and the world will live as one."

P.S. I felt pretty good with my learning last evening. My party going experience lasted more than three hours. I observed my uncomfortableness, disease and pushed past it. I noticed my need to leave, eat for comfort and overcome my feelings. I started the party feeling alone and separate and ended the party feeling the collectiveness and oneness. I can do this! I can travel Europe with social ease and comfort. I hope someday you will join me and we will be as one.

Facebook, December 23—Laz—
Beautiful insights, well written. As an introvert I relate very well to parties where all are strangers and the panic that brings. Was great to understand how you process that and work your way through it.
—Denise—
Just know you're not alone on this!!!

43

Posted on May 29, 2016 by Drew Eric

Chapter 7 Can I relax and have fun in Pamplona?

Pamplona Day 4; I watched several YouTube blogs about backpacking and the Camino. One big take away is to blog on travel days. Nothing to do but sit on the train, look out the window at the scenery and write.

I have spent the last four days writing about my experience. This is proving to be a bigger adventure then I could have imagined—anxiety, lost phone, learning to navigate travel arrangements. Talk about throwing myself into the deep end of the pool, I am treading water now!

But it doesn't stop there—the adventure is just beginning.

Facebook, May 28—Elizabeth—
I am jealous of you in Europe, makes me want to be there! Loved living in the UK for 3 years and traveling all over. Such great memories you are making! Have more fun, I will live vicariously!

Next up, I'm meeting my Airbnb host in Pamplona.

My female Airbnb host didn't message back and I had to scramble quickly before I left Barcelona and secure another Airbnb host.

He meets me at the train. He's attractive, thin, 35ish and a typical skateboarder type guy. We walk the short distance to his flat, talking, happily speaking English along the way. I'm anxiety ridden for many reasons. First, I'm a gay man—straight men make me nervous. I never know how they are going to feel about "The Gay". So, I mention nothing about it.

#LifeLesson —5 Vulnerability is showing up in the face of uncomfortableness and moving into it for your own betterment.
Facebook, May 28—Chris—
What a great day/night! I did a lot of traveling around Europe by myself also, as a gay man, and I have very similar anxieties, but with the exception of one or two negative experiences what I found is that the people of Europe care so much less about sexual orientation than people in America do, and they value the quality

of your character far more than who you like to sleep with at night! Hope you have a wonderful new day!

I'm also anxious about learning a new city and getting lost in one. I am trying to be hyper sensitive to my surroundings. I have an excellent sense of direction, but I need landmarks to imprint into my consciousness.

I have just completed my first Couch Surfing experience, now I am meeting my first Airbnb host. Couch Surfing has a component of sharing time with the host since you're not paying for the room/couch. In Barcelona, we mostly shared meals. However, the last day we spent the evening walking the city after I took my host out to dinner as a thank you. He turned out to be a kind man and a great host. With Airbnb you're renting a room, so I don't really know if the host will be a guide or leave me on my own entirely.

His place is clean and spacious, two bed, two bath—really quant flat. He made some furniture out of pallets which he is very proud to share with me. I like the home with its skater-type decorations around the space—its "Skater Chic". I have a private room and bath. Once I'm settled in, he offers cool reading material along with maps of the town and the essential WIFI details. It's like a real hotel but I'm sharing the space with the owner.

After reviewing the maps I get the lay of the land a little but I'm still pretty anxious. I need to buy a bus ticket to Saint Jean Pied de Port, France. He offers me a beer and I politely decline so he offers coffee to which I say, "Si." He has the beer.

He mentions a Couch Surfing Meet-up and inquires if I would like to join him. I reply with an affirmative "guay" which means "cool." OK, I'm totally kidding I don't know Spanish at all so I really said "cool". Moving on. Now I'm anxious about meeting a bunch of straight people. I have no idea how this will play out. Anxious! Anxious! Anxious!

For all of my straight friends reading this, please know these are real feelings some gay people have when we are in any new situation, not knowing how religious, crazy or bigoted people can be. This is something I am clearly working on while on this adventure. I have chosen this adventure purposely to put myself in "uncomfortable" situations so I can stretch and grow as a person.

45

We sit on the couch talking as he finishes his beer with a Snoop Dog video playing on T.V. "I like rap" he says. I tell him about my experiences in Barcelona—getting lost and losing my phone. He finds it amusing. I tell him I need to buy a bus ticket to Saint Jean Pied de Port, France and he shows me on the map where the station is. At this point I still don't know if we are hanging together or he is ditching me for his friends. I am trying my best to study the map, directions and expect the unexpected.

I decide to bring my computer and camera in my backpack so in case anything goes wrong I can get online. The camera is for sightseeing shots since I don't have my camera phone. It's about 5 p.m. in the afternoon as he grabs a beer for the road and offers me one as we head out the door. I decline the beer since I am focused on not getting lost and buying a bus ticket. I learned that lesson in Barcelona, no need to repeat it.

Off we go. My host is talking the whole time, telling me all about Pamplona, the running of the bulls, churches and cool places to see. I mention the bus station again and we head that way, I think. I can't be sure since his focus is a bit all over the place, it could be the beers. The whole time we are walking and talking I am taking as many mental notes as possible—noticing landmarks to help me find my way, in case we get separated. He pops in a store and buys a beer before we reach the bus stop.

He takes over with the bus ticket agent, I hand over my card and it's done. I now have a ticket to Saint Jean where I will start the Camino—after I receive my phone. So far, people have been really helpful and kind on this adventure. Maybe they recognize my lack of travel experience and feel compelled to assist. And it does help when you have someone speaking the language.

It starts raining and I have nothing but my lightweight backpack and a long sleeve shirt and t-shirt underneath. He puts on his skater hoodie. I get the first clue on how to be a Pamplona resident as he tells me, "You know how you can tell a Pamplona resident? They have a sweater hanging over one shoulder." I look around and he was right.

We duck into a church to wait for the rain to stop and continue chatting comfortably. My anxiety is lessening now that my ticket is purchased and I am ready for a beer and something to eat, however, not in that order.

We eat a slice of pizza while the rain is finishing. He says, "It rains, then stops, then rains again all the time. We're always prepared for a little rain in Pamplona". He's pretty adorable. We are getting along nicely.

The streets are blocked off for a festival in old town. No particular occasion, just a manufactured reason to have a party in the street, he tells me. And that is exactly what everyone is doing in old town Pamplona. Partying! Wow. People are everywhere in this old city. He gives me the impression that this is the real Pamplona.

We are staying in the entrance of a cool bar. This place is AWESOME. They are playing a mix of '50s, '70s, '80s and early '90s music from America and Spain, the soundtrack from *Grease*, punk, alternative, Diana Ross and lots of Spanish stuff I don't recognize.

He introduces me to people and I stand there kinda not knowing really what to say or do. But I like this place. He tells me it's a hipster, cool hangout. Which means this 48 year old white, gay, American is hanging out with a bunch of hipster Spaniards! I love it. This is how I want my adventure to be. This is what I imagined for myself. I AM IN LOVE WITH PAMPLONA!

Facebook, May 28—Laz—
Awesome indeed... Congrats on one step at a time. I spent a few weeks in Pamplona years ago and you had a better time

My brother married a Cuban woman when I was in my early 20's so I have been around Spanish speaking people most of my adult life. I have no problem not understanding a word they are saying. Doesn't bother me in the least. So I am completely comfortable with this part of the experience.

A couple of the girls chat me up and I begin to find my rhythm as an American in Spain. Hola, Americano, Ingles? Drew, Andres. Drew. "Repeat, repeat, repeat." Yes, this is working well since most all of them speak English. So this is really a treat for me.

A girl from France shows me her Pamplona specialty drink —red wine, coke and a lime. She lets me try it, surprisingly it's really good. Try it, you'll see. It's called a "Calimocho."

Sidebar- By the way I am on the bus to Saint Jean writing and the scenery is incredible. We just about hit a car coming

47

around a sharp bend on the winding road—mountains, homes, old cities with high brick-walls. Incredible!

The bar clears a bit and we're off to the next bar as a group. I'm wishing I didn't have this backpack, computer and camera.

I decide to hold off on a second beer. I really want to be sober for the unexpected situations in my future and minimize the chance of getting lost again. But that doesn't stop him from ordering along with his friends and all the other partiers in town.

The new place is a dance bar and it's playing a mix of American and Spanish music again. The people look really different here in Pamplona than in Barcelona—very casual, messy casual, hipster casual. Whatever their fashion is, it's pretty cool.

It's getting late and I get a good natured scolding by a female partier, in Spanish, about having a full backpack in a crowded bar. I decide to take a risk and head back to the flat to drop off the backpack and try to find my host again among the partiers. I have little faith I will see him again if I leave him. But it's worth the risk.

He is really concerned about my getting lost. I reassure him that I will find his building and I will meet him back at the fountain in one hour. He agrees to meet me in an hour and off I go into the unknown.

Sidebar- As I'm writing this, my bus ride just ended in St Jean Pied De Port. I, along with the other 11 Camino walkers, am dropped off in the middle of town. We are all looking around like lost puppies, confused and unsure where to go and for what. Anxiety is rising again.

My Pamplona host brought me one way. I see all the markers around me. I see the map. I am GOOD, I got this, I can do it. Walking, walking, walking I go. I am making good time. He said it takes 20 minutes at a good pace. I'm right on target. There it is, that's his building—the one with seventh floors.

SHIT, I don't know what floor or unit he is in. I don't have a phone or his number. I'm screwed. I totally didn't see this coming as I was so sure I'd remember the markers along the way. I was never thinking about the apartment or the floor.

I try the door, it's the right building. I look, was it the seventh floor or the fifth? I try five. The elevator door opens and there are people in the hall. I ask about my host's apartment, no, not here. I go up a floor. Knock, no answer. Yes, I stick the key in the lock and try it like a thief at the door. It does not work. I go up one more floor. SHIT, SHIT, SHIT. I'm such an idiot. Why didn't I write down the unit and floor?

I reach the next floor. I see a door. I try the door with the key... It turns. It's his apartment. In I go, drop off the backpack and head out the door to find/never find him again. Dust is starting to settle in and even if I rush, I won't make it in time to meet him.

I went one way with him, came back another way on my own, then a third way back, but I found the fountain. Its 10:15 p.m. which means I'm late. The square is full of people so I just people watch and grab that wine/coke/Calimocho drink, delicious.

Facebook, May 28—Julie—
I freaking love your posts! I feel like I'm there. I'm so incredibly proud of you Drewby. XO

Low and behold there he is—drink in hand. I can't believe it. He found me. We walk as a happy partying group back to the first bar and dance for a while to the crazy American/Spanish music. I LOVE PAMPLONA! This is the adventure I always wanted— filled with people, dancing and new friends. Totally awesome!

It's very difficult to figure out who is gay or just being Spaniards because there is so much touching and hugging. They are total space invaders and linger past the point of acceptable touch. I mean, the men hang on each other for five minutes or so. It takes some getting used to. In America I could get my ass kicked for this type of behavior in a party atmosphere.

Facebook, May 28—Sherry—
Ok Drew! You are naturally one of the most outgoing friendly people I know whether you are around straight or gay you are a hugger and a people lover!!! If the past 25 years or so have changed that sense of being then this adventure will remind you who you are and restore your confidence in life!!! You are a "Go getter and lover of life! Enjoy every moment!!
—Drew—

49

It's a secret I don't tell people about my anxieties. On the surface I look all fun and outgoing. Inside I get scared sometimes. But who doesn't.

—Sherry—
Yes Drew, you know how to "Do it and conquer the fear" though- you've done it your whole life! You've got this – "God has not given you a spirit of fear, but of power, love and a sound mind!

My host leans in and says. "Can I ask you a question?" Oh, here we go. I didn't want to go there, but ok, sure, ask. "Do you like girls or boys?" "BOYS" I yell over the music. Ah, yes, it's cool. If you would prefer a boy's bar we can go later. I said, "Ok, whatever, I'm good, this is fun," and he buys us a drink.

We danced and danced. Some of his friends left. I never was sure if he knew them at all or if they were new friends. So many unanswered questions?

He taught me a new Spanish expression, "Chi Cha" I asked it's meaning and he said, "Nothing, nothing, chi cha, chi cha, chi cha, nothing, nothing, nothing." Not really sure what it means but I LOVE IT.

Facebook, May 28—Lynn—
Your life will never be the same! Enjoy!

He takes me to Nicolett's, clearly a gay bar from the rainbow flag and looks of the place. We go in and he buys us yet another round of beers. I am not sure where this is going but these are my people, so I'm in.

My host introduces me as the American from Miami. No kidding, my straight host, in a gay bar, seems more comfortable than me.

Facebook, May 28—Mark—
This restores a little faith in humanity. How refreshing to read about open minded, kind, free spirited people just enjoying life. There is far too little of that over here. Thanks for sharing. Safe travels. -m

He introduced me to an American from New York that I immediately liked. I gave him a travel card I had made for my journey of self discovery and he invited me to stay over and Couch Surf if I make it back to Barcelona.

Facebook, May 28—Ann—
I am so glad you are finding such wonderfully warm, friendly people on your travels. Loving reading about your adventures!!!

It's 2 a.m., and I'm just following my host, hoping he remains vertical and find our way home.

Did I say how much I LOVED PAMPLONA? The evening was terrific. Who cares how late it is. I can sleep in and still make my bus tomorrow at 2:30 p.m. to France.

Keep an eye out for my next update. This is the craziest thing I have done in my life. I LOVE IT! I CAN DO THIS!!!

P.S. This adventure is bringing up a roller coaster of emotions. I'm tearing up, right now, sitting in a cafe in France, drinking wine and listening to French disco music in the background. My life is clearly crazy awesome!

#LifeLesson —6 Sometimes you just have to throw caution to the wind, be present to where and what you are doing and have a little fun without worry or anxiety.

#LifeLesson —7 Always believe in the kindness of others first. Making fear around people not liking you is an assumption not worth carrying.

#LifeLesson —8 The first time doing anything can be uncomfortable, with the second time it's a little less, the third time barely noticeable and so on until the uncomfortableness of the first time is a distant memory.

Facebook, May 28—Drew—
#ActOfKindness —3 Thank you my first Airbnb host for your hospitality, welcome beer, assistance with my ticket purchase, tour of your beautiful city and night on the town. I will always cherish my time spent in Pamplona. Such beautiful sights, such beautiful people you introduced me to and an amazing night out on the town. I LOVE you Pamplona, I am grateful for your kindness, Airbnb hosting and a tour guide, who could ask for more. Great night, wish I stayed longer.
—Ayal—

On a journey of self discovery you'll find out all the things you thought you couldn't do are actually doable. Once you become self reliant, you'll NEVER doubt yourself. Your journey sounds amazing. Very happy for you. Keep yourself open and let the experience take you wherever. You will end up in places that you did not know exist. You'll find out how much there is to you.

—Michelle—

Wow! Sounds like such a great time. You can do all of this! Your journey of self discovery is so KOOL!

—RJ—

Bold & dynamic. I feel as I'm along the journey

—Robert—

Drew – thanx for sharing your experiences! I feel that I am walking with you during your internal journey!

—Juan—

Hey Drew, maybe after this adventure you could relate more to my life. I read your long description and I enjoyed it. Glad you are stepping out of your comfort zone to expand yourself …

—Daphne—

So proud of you constantly going outside of your comfort zone over and over, and being authentic in your sharing. Be brave, be strong, and enjoy every moment.

follow my… adventure

Posted on May 30, 2016 by Drew Eric

Chapter 8 Can I make it to France?

Day 5 Pamplona/St Jean Pied de Port; I wake up later in the day then early, 10 a.m., but still with plenty of time to catch my bus to St Jean Pied de Port at 2:30 p.m. I start packing up and texting with my friend in Florida checking to see if he shipped out the phone yesterday/Saturday. I am expecting the phone to have arrived Saturday in Florida since I paid for additional overnight shipping. My friend has the address of where I am staying in France so all should be well. It's good to confirm anyway.

My friend says, "It never came." OMG

I immediately get on text with Tmobile my provider. I raise the roof on them. The agent explains what the previous agent should have said was "Next business day not next day." OMG. you have got to be kidding. "I was expecting the phone to arrive on Monday or Tuesday and now I'm finding out it hasn't even shipped to the residence in Florida where it will be, then again, shipped to me in France." I typed.

I politely inform them, "I have made reservations for lodging, purchased transport tickets accordingly and instructed the lodging to expect my package. While I am in Spain today getting ready to move to France to pick up my phone when it arrives."

"DO YOU UNDERSTAND WHAT KIND OF ARRANGEMENTS I AM MAKING HERE IN ORDER TO BE IN ONE PLACE TO RE-CEIVE MY PHONE IN SHIPMENT." I typed/text in all CAPS. This went on for an hour back and forth I told them of my arrangements and plans according to what I was told. OVERNIGHT, which to them really means, its "Friday and you will get it Monday." OMG, you are kidding me.

They offered me a rebate of my $24.95 for additional shipping fee. I said "Absolutely not!!! I have made travel plans according to your instructions. My adventure would have been completely dif-ferent. I would have made other travel plans if I had known. Now I must stay in the same city/hotel for several additional days. ARE YOU UNDERSTANDING THE INCONVENIENCE THIS IS CAUS-ING ME. I AM IN EUROPE ON VACATION." I type again in all text.

Slowly the rebate goes up. I put the pressure on a little harder. We settled in the end. I received a $300 rebate to my account. I feel much better. Even if the phone cost more then the rebate.

Facebook, June 2—Drew—
"Life is an adventure, don't let money or possessions or situations limit your adventure."—Drew Eric

That took a long time out of my morning. Now I have to really speed up the packing and getting out of here. My host is not up yet. I grab my cheese and bread, make some coffee and shower. Time is really running out now. My host is not up yet and it's 1 p.m.

Yesterday I went to the bus station so I generally know where it is. Looking at the map I plan my route. I figure I can grab a taxi if time runs out. I leave him a note of thanks and one final check for my stuff and out the door. It's 1:15 p.m. I CAN DO THIS! I will find the bus station and I will make the bus to St Jean, out I go.

In a completely new direction from where I have gone before. It's hot. My two packs weigh 50 lbs and it is HOT walk/running. I am sweating. I CAN DO THIS! I am such a lucky person I am sure a taxi will see my hand out any minute and pick me up.

Where am I? Not sure, not sure, not sure! I ask someone on the street for directions. They point and say something in Spanish. On I go. I CAN DO THIS! I will make it in time.

I ask someone else, they again point in the direction. On I go never once putting my hand down for a taxi. OMG. I have 15 minutes. My legs are hurting I'm walking so fast. I read the street signs, I am on the right street. GO, GO, GO, I CAN DO THIS!

I come around the corner of the building and BAM, there is the station. It's a beautiful sight. However, it's 2:30 p.m. I choose to run, sweaty, with 50 lbs on my back. Maybe, just maybe they don't leave on time, like Delta or other airlines. Down the escalator I go. The booth where I bought my ticket is closed. I look for the busses... none are boarding. It's 2:34 p.m. I didn't do it. The bus left without me. I can't do this. What the hell do I do now?

Facebook, June 2—Drew—
"A hundred moments can break me into tears, while a million moments can make me smile and laugh."—Drew Eric

I start laughing. Another learning lesson. How many of these difficult lessons are there in store for me? I mean really! LOL.

Ok, the automated ticket booth is there. Yesterday my host helped me buy the ticket. Now I have to put on my "big-boy-pants" and buy it again. I guess that's my lesson here. Take care of myself. Ugh, where is my Prince-In-Shining-Armor? Ok, the machine is in Spanish, of no surprise to anyone reading this. I put in St Jean Pied de Port, I put in my information, I assume that is my passport number, I assume that means pay now, I assume that means debit pin number. Hit conclude and printing receipt. I just purchased my first bus ticket. I CAN DO THIS!

Now I have three hours to kill till my bus leaves. Hmmm, what to do, what to do? I am completely sweaty. There is a park right outside the station. I think a little yoga in the middle of Pamplona is in order here. Just the right thing for me to do and relieve all this built up stress. Just a quick switch of clothing in the men's room at the bus station and up I go, out into the park.

It's spectacular out here. I assemble a clothesline with my pack and stick and hang my wet clothes to dry. I have a quick apple for energy and on the mat I go. I feel amazing. Just what I needed.

Facebook, June 2—Peter—
UNLIKE travel in the U.S. buses & trains in Europe leave on time. Give yourself a little extra time so you don't have the added anxiety. Buen Viaje!
Daphne—
I love that the lesson is to remember you always have yoga to find the calm in the storm. Remember that every day and your journey will be easier. Sending love from the other side!

I even hear my good friend Laurie in my ear saying, "You are so crazy, I love it!" Maybe my lesson is to remember yoga? They are all lessons, they are all good. One thing I know for sure is I am always in the right place at the right time doing the right thing with the right people. So I was meant to miss the bus and meant to do some yoga before I leave the city I love.

I finish yoga before the rain—because every hour you can expect a quick sprinkle in Pamplona. I grab a sandwich for the road. Quick change in the bathroom and I am back to normal again.

I stop at the ticket office that is now open again and inquire about the bus I lost earlier. She offers me a refund for the first bus

I missed since I purchased another ticket already. I am forever grateful. Everything usually does work out for me. I can do this.

I use the bus station WIFI to find the hostel where I am staying. I put the address in google map and leave it open so when I arrive I have a map to find my way since I have no printer or phone. All set. On the bus I go. I pulled up my big-boy-pants and said. I CAN DO THIS! Nothing will stop me now... Famous last words.

Saint Jean Pied de Port Day 5; The bus is moving swiftly through Spain and its beautiful countryside. While the landscape flies by, I am writing about my adventures—it's a travel timesaver. There are about 12 of us on the bus, a mixed bag of men and women. All of us, I noticed, have backpacks and walking sticks under the bus—which means we are all walkers heading to Saint Jean Pied de Port to start the Camino. I assume they will all be starting their adventure tomorrow even though I will be waiting several days for my phone to arrive from America.

Since making my backpack selection, I am mesmerized by them and seeing my fellow traveler's backpacks gives me a thrill. I analyzed my pack for all its uses and hidden compartments and now I look at everyone's packs to get a new use or tip for my own.

"BOOM," I hear a sound coming from outside the bus. Hmmm, that didn't sound good. It doesn't feel like a blown tire but after traveling a short distance we pull over.

Facebook, May 29—Rick—
Your stories are so suspenseful. KEEP WRITING!

Several of us disembark; the driver has the back engine hood up which is never a good sign. We all clearly see a thick hose has separated from the thingy-ma-jig and the driver has no tools. MacGyver we are not.

Come to find out, this is a bus with only Camino Pilgrims. None of us carry tools on the walk so all these men are looking at this easy fix and no one is able to fix it. It's amusing. You can see the challenges of wanting to fix it themselves, but not being able to do that.

Rather than just staring at the broken bus we start chatting and get to know each other. As a group, someone is from almost all continents, Brazil, South Korea, Germany, Mexico, America, Russia. All we need is Australia and Africa.

Hearing these people share their stories was exciting. We hear the "I am walking the Camino because..." and the "What I left behind was..." stories.

We got on the bus as strangers and now we are pilgrims sharing the same adventure.

A repairman shows up with the necessary tools. Hooray! It added a little more time onto our short adventure but the camaraderie we shared was worth it.

Once back on the road, the rolling hills and mountains are spectacular. It's hard to believe I'm seeing all this first hand versus watching it in a movie or seeing it on someone's Facebook page. My eyes are seeing this in real time.

In what seemed like a second, we pull into Saint Jean Pied de Port. Anxiety hits me again along with that feeling of "Don't get lost".

We file off the bus in what seems like the outskirts of town—no bus station or signs directing us anywhere. Next to us is a big medieval stone gate with the name of the city. All of us are standing there like lost puppies. No one really knows where to go or what to do next. As anxiety creeps up, I remember I'm prepared. I open my computer to pull up the Google map I downloaded before I left the bus station. It's there complete with directions—I'm not lost.

We, as a Camino pack, seem to migrate over to the first hostel we see and a couple of men ask about rates. The pack seems disinterested and leaves. I, on the other hand, am prepared, I HAVE A RESERVATION! I got one before I left Barcelona as I needed an address where my phone could be shipped. Anticipating needs and being prepared are signs of big growth for me. I show the hostel clerk the map and he points through the stone arch. I stumble away scared and alone, leaving my Camino pack, looking for my destination.

Still carrying my open computer, I wander for some time before finding my hostel. I must look unusual walking around town with an open laptop. I see the host and he asks for my Compestella passport, I'm confused. He explains I need to go to the registrar office for the El Camino de Santiago. Once I register they will give me a passport for the pilgrimage.

He offers me the 17 euro room with 10 beds or the semiprivate room with two beds and a curtain with a shared bathroom. I choose the semiprivate room since the last thing I want to do is share my anxiety with a room full of people.

He shows me to my room and instructs me to leave my stuff with the assurance that it's all safe.

It's a bit premature for me to trust this new way of life. I leave my big pack and carry my smaller pack with the computer and camera, He directs me to the Compestella office to register for the pilgrimage and to get my passport.

The office is up an ancient medieval road, over a bridge and up a steep incline. People have been walking this path since 1000 BC. The city looks cool and certainly different than anything I've ever seen.

I find the office, check in and a woman there gives me a packet with a passport booklet, directions, a shell to hang off my back-pack and notes. I am barely hearing what she is saying as she's speaking so fast and my anxiety is too high to take it all in. I literal-ly just got off the bus 15 minutes ago and now I'm registered for the pilgrimage. I thank her and step outside.

Once outside it hits me. I have been waiting for this moment for months. I just registered for the El Camino de Santiago and like in the movie "The Way" I am going to walk the Camino. I AM IN FRANCE ABOUT TO WALK THE Camino, I scream in my head.

I burst into tears—I don't mean slight tears coming down from the corner of my eyes I mean the big, ugly tears, chin moving and all. I am overwhelmed with emotion. I have been emotional since I moved out of my apartment choosing to be homeless so I could travel Europe without ties, now, its real. I'm in another country about to walk 500 miles, me, not Martin Sheen in the movie "The Way," but me.

By the time I get back to my hostel I have control of myself.

(I did take a selfie to capture the ugly tears with my big camera) I have decided to give you all the good, the bad and the ugly tears.

Facebook, May 29—Alisha—
I'm loving your adventures, big ugly tears and all!

It's early evening and I'm not sure what to do next. I'm scared, vulnerable and emotional. I think its time to eat and maybe drink wine—sounds like a good time for French comfort food and drink.

I've always dreamed of sitting in a French cafe with my Mac computer typing away while the city around me buzzes and hums.

It's the dream of being a regular resident sitting in a cafe sipping coffee or wine, eating a baguette—a slow and enjoyable moment.

So as not to get lost, I carefully walk away from my hostel. I walk back the way I came and see the medieval gate I walked through when I arrived. There, across the street is a restaurant where I can grab a bite and perhaps get WIFI. I feel its safe and not too far from my hostel.

I sit at a table next to a couple of 20-somethings. I pick something French with a cream sauce and a glass of wine to settle my nerves. I sit and listen to the street sounds, drinking in, literally and figuratively, the French aromas while feeling the energy of this ancient town. I hear the people speaking French all around me. In the background is French disco music accompanied by lots of loud voices coming from inside the bar. I'm observing, calmly breathing.

My creamy meal comes along with the wine. Food and alcohol are two things that I often reach for to soothe my anxiety. I've found both.

Once my meal is finished, and my second glass of wine comes, I take out my computer. The waitress helps me log into the WIFI and, viola, I'm online again. After chatting with friends through Facebook I get back to finishing the story I was writing on the bus. My dream has materialized; I'm sitting in a French café—writing— while the world spins around me.

Facebook, May 29—Shannon—
I am loving your adventures and your honesty. I completely under-stand the joy of sitting in a French café and absorbing all the sights, sounds, tastes and textures of it and feeling like you were meant to do this. (Maybe it's the artist in us? I love you, Drew! I can't wait for your next installment!

Now I'm curious about the happenings inside the bar with lots of 20-something patrons, loud and having fun. They are all so touchy, touchy and I wonder if I have come into a gay bar by accident.

Some of the boys start talking me up. One even comes over and offers to buy me a drink. He is a boy. Barely legal to drink probably and he's a bit tipsy. European men are so comfortable with themselves and friendly. I ask what he is drinking because it has a red color to it. He says beer and he gives me a sip. All I can say is it kind of tastes like a raspberry flavored beer. He offers to buy me one and I accept.

Facebook, May 29—Drew—
#ActOfKindness —4 Thank you to the kind young man who bought me a welcome beer after arriving in Saint Jean. So warm and welcoming. I hope I am offered many more on this adventure of mine and I hope they are equally as warm and welcoming.

We talk for a second as he gets distracted with someone who comes in. Two other patrons chat me up and then the question. "Hey, what do you like, girls or boys?"

Oh God, I'm just going to be honest and say boys. He replies, "Oh, ok, that guy in the yellow, he likes boys too."

These people are so nice. We talk for a while longer. I finish the beer and I'm feeling less scared. The way men interact here seems much more fluid than in America. There are fewer taboos in how they interact with each other. I'm remembering this seemed true with the men in Pamplona also.

I head back to the hostel close to midnight. I start setting up my bed and personal belongings. I unpack the "sheet set" that is on the bed, at least that's what it's called. All I see is a thin bed liner and a matching pillow liner. It looks so flimsy and transparent but I put it on, organize my things and crawl into my sleeping bag liner that protects me from the mattress. I did spray all my belongings with bed bug repellent prior to leaving home, so I should be protected. We shall see.

I am so keyed up and excited to be here that I have to take three Xanax to finally fall asleep. I CAN DO THIS! Until tomorrow…

Facebook, May 29—Julie—
You are killing me with the 3 Xanax again. You are not a horse! You are fine, doing fantastic sweetie. I love you.
—Janet—
Remember to breathe and you will need less Xanax

follow my… adventure

Posted on February 25, 2016 by Drew Eric

Chapter 9 Can I run a half marathon?

I love a physical challenge. But, I didn't sign up right away for the Valentine's Day marathon. I created a running schedule leaving open the possibility of not actually completing the half-marathon.

All kinds of questions came up for me. How do I train? What if I get hurt and can't teach yoga? Can I actually run 13.1 miles when I have never run farther than 3.5 miles?

On a deeper level I knew I wanted to challenge myself to see what I'm made of. When it gets hard, will I quit or will I keep running? I had a concern I wasn't a finisher. Here's my pattern: lots of great ideas—mediocre completion.

I went to art school and completed their three-year curriculum but never finished the non-art courses necessary to get a bachelor's degree. I didn't have a strong support system encouraging me to complete my academics. It was easier to just let it go.

That's when I started the training routine. Short distances at first with increasing miles slowly. My training time was short, only two months at most. From not running at all to a half-marathon in just under two months, was I was crazy?

I learned running wasn't so bad. Wouldn't say I liked it but I didn't absolutely hate it. When I start anything new it begins with anxiety which must be overcome in order for me to learn and finish.

Here's the info I picked up along the way—not all shoes are for everyone. My left ankle started to hurt and a friend told me to get a new pair of shoes fitted for me at a running store. With only two weeks before the half-marathon I was concerned about running in new shoes. But despite my concern I got a new pair made just for me. Apparently I prone in (never heard of that) and my shoes didn't counter my proning, causing my ankle to get sore.

I started running to the beach in an effort to see the ocean and love my city just a little more. The halfway stop and short break at the beach allowed the aches and pains to subside and I filed that tidbit of information for later.

Two weeks before the half-marathon I ran my longest run—eight miles. Everything hurt. I was concerned about how ready I was at this point. The week prior I ran three short runs. I did learn that when I took an extended break—the week off waiting for my new shoes—the next run hurt considerably more. So I ran a 5k on Saturday, the day before my half-marathon.

Just before the half-marathon, I shifted my intention to complete the run. My strategy is to be flexible. Maybe I will run the whole thing, maybe I will walk/run, and maybe I will run half and walk half. Finishing became the focus.

"If you are willing to try, only then can you really see how far you can go."—Drew Eric

Race day… Surprisingly I was calmer than expected. I met up with two friends and got in line with the other 4000+ participants. My friend asked if I looked over the race route. Laughing a bit I realized how much of a novice I was.

Apparently when you're a seasoned runner you train longer, build up your distance, become familiar with the route, get your shoes special fit and break them in long before the run. A little late for me but good information to have.

Bang, the race starts. Not so bad, 1-mile, 2-mile, 3-mile markers go by—all is well. We enter the park and now I'm seeing the runners in the lead passing me on the right. That's cool.

I reach the 5-mile marker and consider using the restroom soon. But I'm running with my friend at a nice pace and if I stop to use the facilities, we'll separate. However, if I occasionally slow down and, at some point I'll lose him anyway.

I see the bathroom and inform my friend of my plans. The pit stop was a welcome break from running. My legs feel much better now, so back to the run.

It was then I chose to run alone. Doing anything alone is not in my comfort zone. The reason I chose this run for my first half-marathon is that it was my friends first too and we could share the experience of running our first race together.

I leave the park running up A1A. Still running past the folks ahead of me and feeling good. I pass the 8-mile marker and realize this is it. I am officially past my longest run with five more miles to go. My legs hurt a bit but my ankle feels good. I see the turn up ahead that brings me back down A1A towards the finish line and feel excited.

I make the turn. This is now unknown territory as I've never run this far. Now my legs are starting to hurt. I am running past other runners and I immediately start a dialog of negative thoughts:
- I'm not good enough
- My training wasn't long enough
- My friend is a better runner than I am

I easily recognize when my EGO is working hard at convincing me to believe a lie. Immediately I realize what's happening and counter the ego with positive statements of truth.

I've also learned when I am not feeling well, i.e., running in pain, my EGO mind steps up to try to take control by criticizing, comparing and attacking myself and others.

This lasted through the 9-mile and into the 10-mile marker. These are the mantras I used to combat my Ego mind:
- I am running a half marathon
- I trained long and hard
- I am a good runner
- I am good enough

After the 9-mile marker the muscles in my feet, legs and thighs are in pain. I remembered in my practice runs that when I stopped at the bathroom, a break helps relax the muscles. Then when I start running again they feel better.

"The pain I am feeling now will eventually disappear, I can count on this!"—Drew Eric

So I tried walking a short distance. Still in pain, I started running again, "WOW, that didn't help AT ALL." This never happened before. The pain always subsided after a short pause. Why didn't it work now? Never having run longer than eight miles this was new information.

I tried walking again to see if it would make me feel better. "NOPE, not better," I thought.

I'm faced with the reality that I would be in pain for the remainder of the half-marathon. So, I dug deep and chose to run in pain. The ego was quieted as I made the choice. Big life lesson happening for me and I was keenly aware of it while running.

#LifeLesson —9 When life gets painful you can quit or you can push past the pain and finish what you started.

Running is an emotional experience for me. On New Year's Day during a 5K I cried somewhere in the middle of the run. I learned you can't cry and run at the same time. Crying requires you to hold your breath which is bad for running. Who knew?

But I was able during the 5K run to realize that it was New Year's Day and I wasn't hung over and tired. I was healthy, alert and running! I'd completed my first year alone as a single man and I felt transformed.

Now running my half-marathon, I felt that familiar emotion rising up again. When you cry in yoga while in a posture, it's referred to as a release. Releasing anything deep inside that doesn't serve you. So, I'm not afraid of the experience.

The finish line is within a mile at this point. I'm seeing people walking around wearing their finish medals. The medals are big and look pretty cool.

I can see the finish line now. I'm full on crying, in pain, flooded with emotions. I am running alone. I'm thinking "I am finishing a half-marathon, ME"

The ugly cry overcomes me–chin is moving and all. I see the finish. The clock says 2:26 minutes. I want to finish under 2:30 minutes so I pick up the pace, crying all the way in.

I cross the finish line at 2:27 minutes, weeping.

Not quite sure what to do next. I have just spent the last 2 hours and 27 minutes running. Can I really stop running now? Is that it? Just stop running? So I finished? So I stop running and walk now? It's all hard to comprehend through my exhausted mind.

So I did, I stopped running.

I pulled myself together, got my huge medal, saw my friends and joined them.

While reflecting back on my run later in the day, I honestly couldn't remember 2:27 minutes of running. It didn't seem that long. I remember only snippets of the run. It seemed more like 30 minutes worth of running. I was very present the entire time so not remembering the entire run felt weird.

Since yoga is very important to me and I'm concerned about my body's wellbeing, I don't know if I will run a half-marathon again.

After the big event—to give my ankle a rest—I didn't run for a week. I missed it. I felt like running was a friend that I missed having around.

I made friends with running that day and we shared a once in a lifetime experience together.

At the end of May I will start my pilgrimage. I can now officially say I understand a physical challenge. I will be in pain, I will be emotional, I will want to stop. I will have to choose to finish.

Now I know I have what it takes to finish.

I am someone who finishes. I can do this because I totally did it, I ran a half-marathon, ME.

#LifeLesson —10 No pain, no fear, no emotion can stop you from finishing when you set your mind to do just that… Finish!

Facebook, February 14—Drew—
Finished 2:27 hours. Whoohoo. Runner 198 in my age group out of 274 runners age 47 runners 2393 leaving me in the top 34% of runners 10K finish at 1:08:06 Start of race to finish 2:27:40 My time 02:22:07 pace overall 10:51
Facebook, February 25—Angel—
Compelling writing, excellent reflections, emotionally releasing end. You had me at "I can see the finish line now. I'm full on crying."

follow my... adventure

Posted on June 3, 2016 by Drew Eric

Chapter 10 Can I chill in France?

Mid-week of my stay in Saint Jean, I decided to go for a walk. I have explored the city (it is as big as a stamp, my fear of getting lost was unfounded) and I'm getting antsy to start walking the Camino, especially since that's why I came to Saint Jean. However, I have to stay in town to wait for the new phone. I decide to hike up the mountain because, well, the mountain is there.

I did several practice walks in Fort Lauderdale and averaged about five hours of time with each walk. So I decide to hike up the mountain 2.5 hours and back down again, no biggie. Saint Jean is 180 meters above sea level. Orisson is the first hostel up the mountain and is almost 800 meters above sea level. I have no plans on getting all the way to Orisson since my goal is a total of five hours and I am sure 620 meters will take longer than that.

I'm pretty anxious with all my pent-up energy around leaving America and living in a foreign land. Perhaps this hike will settle some nerves.

The sky is perfectly clear, I can see for miles. There are rolling mountains, random farmhouses, goats and horses. I am hiking up the mountain, this is something I have dreamed about for months and it's actually happening. The landscape looks like something from a Pyrenees picture book. This area is on the border between France and Spain, where, in 1813, Napoleon's Battle of the Pyrenees took place. His troops were on their way to Pamplona to relieve French garrisons

There are two patches on my backpack to signify where I am from and what I'm interested in—an American flag and a blue and yellow patch that says, "A Course in Miracles." The work of "A Course in Miracles" is part of my daily practice and, at home I enjoy a weekly discussion group.

I am hiking along at a nice pace, up and up I go, taking pictures left and right. I see a woman that I assume to be an American. As I pass her I call out "Buen Camino" which is "Good Way" in Spanish and the expression we say to each other on the path. She replies with the same greeting.

Then I hear her say, "A Course in Miracles!"

This is exactly what I wanted to happen! I wanted people to recognize the patch and start a conversation. And someone did! That is totally cool. I'm walking backward now, facing her. I threw up both hands and repeated: "Yes, a Course in Miracles". The next thing she said stopped me dead in my tracks, I LOST IT! I don't mean I lost my cool, I mean I went into the straight up, shoulder moving, ugly cry in seconds. Once more, here come the tears.

She patted my shoulders and repeated her statement. I am trying to get the words out through my tears as she continues to pat my shoulders. She has said the very thing I wanted my adventure to be about. The same quote often discussed in my study group and the one handed to me on a card and used as wallpaper on my phone—the phone I lost in Barcelona. She and the card and my phone are all saying,

"Trust, would settle every problem, now!" —*A Course In Miracles ACIM*

#LifeLesson —11 Always believe in your inner guidance system. Trust it will always lead you on the correct path and all problems will have solutions.

Facebook, June 1—Janet—
ACIM is translated into 27 languages, This is just the first of many connections you will have

Clearly my emotions are running just like this hike, up and down the mountain. Several more days here in Saint Jean are probably just what I need most to lower my stress and draw my emotions in.

Facebook, June 1—Chris—
We know the universe is finely tuned for these connections, and yet they still surprise us all the same! I love where these tears are carrying you and the joy you will spread with them! (Imagine her story about this encounter!)
—Drew—
I have to share this. It's 7 p.m. here in France. I like to sit in the center of town and write. I am here around this same time every day. Its when the bus drops off all the Camino pilgrims. I keep seeing these confused puppies wandering the street looking just like I was, scared and alone. I have informed over 20 pilgrims over

a couple days where to go and what to do. I have been like the Camino ambassador here in Saint Jean Pied de Port. I love it.

—Mike—Helping others is a cure for a lot of things. 😊

—Sherry— No surprise that you chose to be an ambassador of encouragement and support! 😊😄

Facebook, June 2—Drew—
I realize now I have been in the dark night of the soul this past week. Denial, fear, everything. Today I am realizing the blessing for ME to be in one place for so long waiting for my phone. Today I am calmer. I slept well. Got up early with the other pilgrims. Today I am being more one with myself. Today I am at peace.

—Suzanne— Drew, I am so happy to see that you finished this post with, "today I am at peace." That has been my prayer for you the past two days!

—Drew—
I have a pilgrim friend staying at my hostel, great guy. He is inspiring me with his budget. I have decided to keep my budget between 30 and 50 Euros a day. We are looking at trash now and seeing how we can use it on our pilgrimage. My sister-in-law gave me a bag of trail mix. It has a ziplock top. When its empty it will make a great storage bag for cheese and bread, the breakfast of choice here. Plastic storage bags make a great container for sandwiches also. This is really fun getting creative on this path.

Now it's time, I am finally leaving the place I have called home for the past six days. I have gone to the post office to mail my belongings to my new friend Kelly in the Netherlands. All the items I am not taking on the pilgrimage. Maybe I brought too much stuff on this adventure. The package weighed 35 pounds, C'est la vie.

Facebook, June 3—Sally—
Kelly will take care of you! Reach out to her if you need help. Love you!

—Kelly—
Drew it's easy, just relax and enjoy!! You are in my favorite country in the world (& I have seen a few). The Spanish will take care of you and then we will follow up with the perfect time in A'dam!

Figuring out how to get from Santiago to Amsterdam in time to make my flight to Ireland is a huge, daunting task I want to avoid. I have little experience or confidence in regard to making travel arrangements. Now, I am faced with the stressful business of learning how to navigate the travel industry.

Where is my Prince now? How do I make all my arrangements? I haven't even started walking the Camino and look at me, I'm a nervous wreck already worrying about things that will take place after the Camino.

#LifeLesson —12 Focus on today, here, now. Allow the future to remain with the past, on a different day than today.
Facebook, June 3—Drew—
"I welcome the people I will love, the places I will go and the memories I will make on this path that is my life."—Drew Eric
—Drew—
Today my path begins. I welcome the new. And so it is
—Robert—
Making me nervous for you!
—Shannon—
Public transportation in Europe is so much easier and more prevalent than in the U.S. You will be fine, my friend! You've got this!
—Ann—
You don't need a Prince my friend!! YOU are your own Prince! You are learning every day, with every challenge. Not only can you do this… You ARE doing it. Carry on!!

After mailing my package at the post office, I had separation anxiety. What If I need something today that's gone? I am even second guessing my destination. For $12 more I could have had the package shipped to Santiago, giving me four additional days with my stuff.

#LifeLesson —13 Be present to your belongings, how much you have versus how much you need. Are you carrying too many burdens?
Facebook, June 3—Keyla—
The secret of health for both mind and body is not to mourn for the past, worry about the future, or anticipate troubles, but to live in the present moment wisely and earnestly. – Teachings of Buddha

Along with all the stress of becoming homeless, Couch Surfing with friends, packing up my belongings, sending my dogs to live with my ex-husband and his new family, leaving the country, losing my phone, making travel arrangements, etc., I decided to switch from Windows to a Mac book Air. Nothing like adding that into the mix and then trying to get up to speed on how to use the damn thing. I keep having to refer to Google and YouTube for instructions. Bring on the challenges! I am clearly crazy. My constant question reappears, "Can I do this?" My answer today is, "Yes I CAN."

Facebook, June 3—Kevin—
If you wanna run with the pack, ya gotta piss like the big dogs!! You got this and I'm so happy for you and proud of you. Godspeed.
—Karen—
You are the bravest man! Thank you for keeping all of us up to speed on your adventures
—Ray—
I say don't breathe, just hold your breath as long as you can and just pass out, that way when you wake up you will have forgotten what was making you anxious.
Drew, the first week out on my one year journey traveling the U.S. I contemplated turning around and I asked myself "What am I doing?"
Then I realized — "'MY DREAM!"
Go grab yours! You've got this!
—Drew—
Looks like I start walking tomorrow. YAY! My replacement phone has arrived. YAY! You will now get updates in real time and pictures. My anxiety is rising again. Nervous, nervous, nervous!
—Rosa—
Buen Camino Peregrino
—Sherry—
Happy Trails!!! Hee Hee 😘
—Drew—
"Trust yourself. Are the words I remind myself every day. I have survived this long I will survive what is to come."—Drew Eric

follow my… adventure

Posted on February 12, 2016 by Drew Eric

Chapter 11 Can I walk 500 miles/800 kilometers?

Top 6 reasons I am walking 500 miles:
1. Journey-of-Self-Discovery
2. Overcoming Fears
3. My Love of Physical Challenges
4. To Meet Like-Minded Pilgrims
5. For My Mom
6. The Path to Enlightenment

It was a Sunday in November when I wrote my first blog about traveling to Europe. Making a decision about backpacking across Europe is monumental in my life. I didn't know then if I should go on a **1.Journey-of-Self-Discovery.** The journey would force me to let go of identities and learn through **2.Overcoming Fears.**

It was thrilling to think about such an adventure even if I questioned whether the idea was yet another half-brained scheme to distract me from my life.

I have a never-ending supply of creative ideas flowing through my mind. Some I follow up on, other great ideas seem a bit bonkers, yet are a fun way to entertain me during periods of boredom.

My Bonkers Idea:

Once when boredom struck, I spent 18 months re-stuccoing my home to make it an Art-Deco masterpiece. Looking back, it was too much time spent on something that didn't improve my quality of life or add to my growth. I don't even own the Art-Deco masterpiece anymore. Here's a bonkers idea that could have been left undone.

So when I mentioned my idea to family and friends, I was shocked with the enthusiasm and encouragement I received. I was expecting them to say, "That's a sweet idea, but maybe you should concentrate on your coaching career and such." Not the case. My family said "Do it and don't wait. Do it soon!" I was thinking, in a year, maybe next fall, that would give me time to prepare mentally, emotionally and physically. They again encouraged sooner.

"You get one shot at this, choose shooting for what will make you happy."—Drew Eric

As time has passed, I've been blogging and talking about the adventure more consistently and with more conviction than before. Even with the growing conviction, I've questioned whether the idea is crazy, should I undertake such an adventure or is this the greatest idea since when I decided to get married in Hawaii? Hmmm, maybe not the best example since I am now separated.

As I'm getting closer to my departure time of mid-May the concerns have transformed into "Oh, HELL yes, I am taking this adventure!"

My Wonderful Idea:

One fantastic Friday night while bowling with a group of friends, someone said, "Hey when you're on your adventure, you should do El Camino de Santiago."

"WAIT A FREAKING MINUTE," I thought. I know that name, what is it? And from the back of my mind, I remember a book I read written by Shirley MacLaine. It was about a really long walk she did through some country that I can't remember now. I hope it was based in Europe since that is where I'm traveling. Oh, I hope so. I AM TOTALLY DOING THAT! YES, YES, YES!!!

3.My Love of Physical Challenges:

The reason this resonated with me so deeply is, I LOVE a physical challenge. For the last eight years, I have ridden The Smart Ride (165-mile bike ride from Miami to Key West for HIV/Aids charities in Florida).

This past year I chose to train with a close friend who is a really strong rider. It took everything I had to keep up with him and his Band-of-Brothers. After multiple rides it dawned on me, I am stronger, better, faster--kinda like the Bionic Man. The rush and adrenaline were intoxicating. I finally understood the benefits of riding fast and hard.

While training for The Smart Ride 2015, I considered the idea of riding the Aids Lifecycle (ALC) ride when I turn 50 years old (two years from now.) ALC is a 545-mile ride through the mountains of California from San Francisco to Los Angeles raising awareness and funds for HIV/Aids. Several friends have completed the ride and maybe the challenge would be a great way to kick off my 50s.

Another bonkers idea surfaced over the winter holidays. Why don't I run a half marathon, 13.1 miles on February 14th? After the holidays, I set a schedule of running three days a week with increased miles each day. I have only recently become a 5k (3.1 miles) runner over the past couple years. My longest run ever was probably 4.5 miles. So running a half marathon was way outside my comfort zone. But hey, what the hell, I do love a physical challenge. So, let's do it.

Testing my physical endurance doesn't stop there. I've been a student of yoga since 2006, the same year I quit smoking. After seven years of being a student of yoga, I decided to try my hand at teacher training. My level of knowledge about the practice and postures were strong and deep enough that I felt I was perhaps ready to teach.

It changed my life, depended my practice and, within that, supported a deeper spirituality that brought forth a new passion for sharing with others. I highly recommend teacher training even if you have no interest in being a teacher. It changes everything you feel about yoga. I now teach three days a week as a hobby and love it.

"A comfort zone is really a fortress with high stone walls preventing you from seeing the adventure just outside your comfort zone."—Drew Eric

Back to My Wonderful Idea:
As fate would have it, a few moments after the mention of El Camino de Santiago, another friend started a conversation with, "I read your blog about your adventure, you should consider walking El Camino while in Europe." My world was rocked. Two separate, unrelated friends mentioned the same pilgrimage and suggested I should do it. Here's confirmation of the same thought I had more than a decade prior when I read Shirley MacLaine's The Camino.

WOW, there are no coincidences. When life directs you, there is no shortage of signs. Kismet!

"The first step towards getting somewhere is to decide that you are not going to stay where you are."—J.P. Morgan

El Camino De Santiago:

El Camino de Santiago (The Way to Santiago) is a pilgrimage from Southern France across the northern portion of Spain to the city of Santiago near the Atlantic coast. This is an ancient trail that pilgrims have traveled for centuries. Some pilgrims have spiritual experiences on the trek. Others have simply challenged their strength and endurance by walking 500 miles/800 kilometers over 30 days.

Pilgrims are identified on the walk by carrying a staff and hanging a scallop shell off their gear. Pilgrims walk an average of 16 miles a day (26 kilometers) from city to city. There are Albergues in each city for the hundreds of pilgrims walking the path. Albergues are large roomed hostels with many bunk beds or mattresses on the floors for sleeping. Albergues can have up to a hundred pilgrims staying the night–conditions can be noisy.

Starting in France at Saint Jean Pied de Port, you receive a passport/booklet for your journey. In each city passed through, your booklet is stamped marking your visit along The Way. At the end of the pilgrimage to Santiago, you receive a certificate of completion. Every day is a ceremony at The Cathedral of Santiago de Compostela for the pilgrims finishing their journey. Once you complete the pilgrimage you receive your Compostela(certificate of completion).

Restaurants serve pilgrim meals for $10/$12 Euros, which are 3-course meals including a drink–wine most likely since it's Spain's second beverage of choice. Each city has fountains of water for the pilgrims. One city has two spigots–one for water and the other for wine. No joke.

Pilgrims mention the camaraderie you feel and the friends you make along The Way. Your fellow pilgrims help, encourage and wish you well with Buen Camino (good path). If you are choosing the spiritual path, it is recommended to maintain some aloneness throughout the way. Some days you see the same people over and over again. Some days you meet new travelers that you may never see again. They say you will be tempted to stay with your new friends. However, the path is your journey alone and, as such, should be walked, at times, alone.

"Everyday is a new day to change your life. If not today, then when?"—Drew Eric

Back to My Wonderful Idea:

One of the biggest fears I have about backpacking Europe for a year is the unknown. Although I don't have an exact blueprint of the countries I'll see or the places I'll stay, I have the beginning of a plan.

I will spend the first month of my year traveling, walking El Camino de Santiago. While walking the Camino, there are several things I'm sure about. I'll be traveling through centuries-old cities. I'll be challenging my body physically by walking such a long path. It will be amazing and I will love it.

Pilgrims from all over the world will be walking the path with me. I know I will make friends. My intention is to allow destiny, the path and the people I meet to impact my life and I plan to share my travel plans—Journey-of-Self-Discovery—with all my new friends. I'll let my pilgrims know that I am a free agent looking for new cities to explore and taking suggestions for spectacular places to visit. I will tell them about my quest **4.To Meet Like-Minded Pilgrims** to invite me into their homes and share in my journey with kindness and support. I will allow mother-destiny to guide me along The Way.

Walking with **5.My Mom.** Once my mother was given a walking staff from a client who carved it out of her Christmas tree. It has leather strings and feathers with an owl's head carved at the top. Even though my mother passed many years ago, I wonder if she has worked her magic and encouraged this destiny.

I feel her all around me these days. She was a student of metaphysics and leader in her own spiritual circles. Oh, how I wish we could be sharing this time in my life together. I learned so much from her. She taught me to always be curious and always challenge myself for personal growth.

I will start my Journey-of-Self-Discovery with her staff. I will bring my mother along The Way, tied to this walking staff. I know she will be with me physically and in spirit-together, we'll be tied to the staff.

Thanks, mom, for the gifts. The gift of the staff, the gift which is my life and the loving encouragement to find my way on my Journey-of-Self-Discovery. I will finish the path you started and encouraged me so many years ago. It's **6.The Path to Enlightenment.** I can do this with your help mom.

#LifeLesson —14 Sometimes a bonkers idea is the brightest idea.

(For more information about El Camino de Santiago, watch the movie "The Way" starring Martin Sheen and Emilio Estevez. Available on Netflix.)

Note: This was my first post on Facebook about El Camino de Santiago. I was a little off on the details, too funny.

Facebook, January 16, 2016—Drew—
I can't believe I forgot about "El Camino de Santiago trail". A walking pilgrimage from France to the Atlantic Ocean through Spain, 622 miles, 1000 kilometers over four months. It is called a spiritual pilgrimage. Also made famous by Shirley McLain and her book "The Camino: A Journey of The Spirit" which I read a decade ago. This sounds perfect for my spiritual journey. OMG, I think I want to do it in the month of June. 51/2 months from today. I must be crazy. Can I walk the El Camino de Santiago trail?

Facebook, February 12—Berta—
Oh my goodness Drew!!! How can you do this to me??? Ugh, got the itch now. Officially in my bucket for 2017! Dude! God planted the seed, grow, grow, grow! You deserve it and will TOTALLY rock this! You are amazing! Hope you didn't put your journals in storage - you will need plenty of those! Now get out there and change the world young man :-) Big hug my friend!

—Josi—
YES YOU CAN! It's not the destination, it's the journey.

—Annaleah—
Sounds glorious! Especially the Spanish wine part. Will be living vicariously through you, although you are a bit tougher than I. ;-) #glamping

—Cheryl—
I've seen that trail... It's incredible. Words fail to adequately describe.

—Karen—
Hi Drew... I wish you a great path, especially over the Pyrenees... One of the most visually awesome places on the planet! Buen Camino! Look forward to hearing your shares.

—Elizabeth—
I miss your Mom lots, she would be so proud of you! She was so proud of all of you!

—Lisa—

I miss her a lot. She was always so joyful and full of life. Happy you are taking her along. Love this sweet homage!

—Heather—

I miss her too! She was like a second mom to me when I was young.

—Bart—

3 summers ago in June, Sarah and I were in Spain. We passed, the pilgrims several times. They looked very peaceful. Maybe just tired.

—Adam—

OMG, I am so excited for you Drew!!! You are so brave for leaving everything behind, so strong for letting go and so empowering for taking this big step. Good luck to you my friend, many blessings and great things your way😘😘

—Tarissa—

To live will be an awfully big adventure.—Peter Pan XOXO Your niece 😘

follow my… path

Posted on June 11, 2016 by Drew Eric

Chapter 12 Can I navigate this path?

Facebook, June 4—Drew—
"You don't have to see the whole staircase, just take the first step."—Martin Luther King

El Camino de Santiago Day 1; My path on the Camino started like any path would start. Yeah, right! Humor aside, this was unlike any beginning of any path I've undertaken.

I started, walking almost straight up the mountain to a mere 4520' above sea level with a 17% up to 19% incline, pretty hard stuff.

The Camino is a popular pilgrimage that begins on the border of Spain at the base of the Pyrenees Mountains in Saint Jean Pied de Port, France. Pilgrims today are walking for an array of reasons—spiritual, physical, personal and religious to name a few.

As legend has it, the remains of Saint James (Apostle of Jesus) were brought to Spain by boat and then carried through northern Spain until reaching Santiago where they are alleged to have been buried. This route has become The Way to Santiago.

In 1984, Don Elias, a parish priest, had the vision to rescue, clean and mark the trail we call "The French Way" that begins in the city Roncesvalles. As the story goes, he had been researching the pilgrimage and was so inspired he set out to mark the path painting blue arrows for the onslaught of new pilgrims that will be following the path. Not too many days into his marking, he ran out of blue paint.

With his drive to proceed, he asked some local men working on the streets if he could have some paint to complete his project. This is when the arrows changed from blue to yellow since the only paint available was yellow street paint.

He marked the path all The Way to Santiago. Today there are stone markers, blue and yellow arrows along with wall signs and street signs marking The Way.

In 2015, 263,000 pilgrims shared in the Camino experience. I knew I would meet people and make friends but overall I imagined walking in solitude. I planned on listening to audiobooks, meditating, writing and enjoying the scenery for hours in peace with nature. This isn't quite how it unfolded; it never is how you expect it will be.

#LifeLesson —15 You can plan all you want but when reality arrives, no planning prepares you for unexpected realities.
Facebook, June 4—Shannon—
There I was, sitting in my NJ backyard with my coffee, when all of a sudden I was transported to Spain and this crazy-wonderful adventure you are on! Thank you for sharing your journey!

From what I heard about the Camino, you start as an individual and end with deep, meaningful relationships beyond what you ever imagined. When I first heard about the friends you make, I thought it would be nice but I couldn't imagine the reality of it.

My path begins through the gates of Saint Jean and up the mountain I go. I am alone, highly emotional, scared, insecure and anxious. I have been waiting five months for this day. Over the first few hours I meet some really sweet people and strike up conversations. It would seem most of us are feeling the same thing, as today is the first day for us all.

Facebook, June 4—Drew is feeling amazing—
"I feel most alive, right here, now, this point in my life. This place in time is right where I need to be."—Drew Eric

Nobody really knows how this works or what to do. Do you want to be alone? Do they want to be alone? Do you chat? Do you walk by? Do you keep a walking pace with a stranger? It's really weird. You can see the gears turning for everyone attempting to understand this path.

I eventually meet a couple of Italians—I suspect that one of them is gay. As a gay man, I am always looking out for other gays to feel safe and secure. I never know who I am meeting and what their belief systems are or how they feel about gay men—how they will feel about me. I have anxiety around how to act when I am with straight men. I don't really know how to be myself, I am overly concerned about them feeling uncomfortable or offending them.

In an attempt to fit in with my new Italian friends I start speaking English/Italian, meaning speaking English with an Italian accent.

Or at least I think I am speaking English/Italian well, but probably not. It's going pretty well and they seem nice. The two of them met on the flight over from Italy and started the path together.

Through conversation I find out one of the men is gay and has a partner at home. I'm pleased to meet someone on the path with whom I can feel safe. So I keep pace with these new friends, that pace is pretty fast, I struggled.

The path to Roncesvalles is about seven hours so we have a lot of time to talk and get to know each other. When I say a lot of time, that is all we have. We walk and talk, walk, talk, walk, talk. If you do walk with someone I learned that first day, its pretty much nonstop walking/talking.

I'm not really sure when I met "The Boy," possibly sometime around lunch. He and his cousin, who encouraged him to do the pilgrimage, are originally from a southern state in America.

Facebook, June 4—Drew—
"People walk across your path for many reasons; a lesson, a blessing, a relationship, a friendship. There are no accidental meetings."—Drew Eric

I thought he was pretty cute and that was about it since he was so young. Somehow we all ended up walking together, Italians included, sharing our personal details of work, and schooling and most importantly, "Why did you decide to walk 500 miles through northern Spain?"—the first question asked in every conversation.

Late in the day at the top of the mountain, we came to a fork in the road. I had been told that the path directly ahead of us was a treacherous downward climb while the path to the right was an easy decline although possibly a few minutes longer. The Italians choose the first path while the cousins and I choose the later. I see now there is no coincidence on the metaphor of the fork in the road and who chooses what path. This chance choice changed my life into another trajectory.

This was our first real chance to get to know each other more deeply. In our more private time together, I decided that the boy is pretty cool. He has a sensitive nature and a gentle manner. As I describe my coaching and tell him I am a yoga instructor, he is really intrigued. It would seem he is at a crossroads in his life as I am. He's just graduating from college with a Bachelors degree in Finance. He has multiple interests and is truly unsure of what his

80

next direction is—so many choices. I offer my coaching services while we are on the Camino. He tells me about his deep interest in yoga as a possibility as it seems we have that in common.

We reach Roncesvalles and call it a day. I expect to see him several more times over the next few weeks since we are walking in the same direction—The Way to Santiago. I am still unsure of how this all works and how much time I will be spending with anyone on the Camino.

Facebook, June 4—Erick—
You, my son, are writing from your soul. Powerful! Just like these experiences. Allow it to flow. Life is gifting you with exactly what you need. I'm so happy for you. You are becoming such an explorer!

Dinner and social time finish up as people are scurrying around getting their responsibilities done prior to heading to bed early so we can all get up and do it again, for the next 30 days. There's laundry, packing our backpacks for the next day along with general bedtime activities. I head into the men's shower area where the boy is brushing his teeth.

"Um, you wanna walk out together tomorrow?" He strikes up a conversation with downcast eyes and a sweet nervous look on his face. I'm intrigued but yet confused. I am a 48-year-old man. Why would two young kids want to walk down a mountain with some old guy when there are plenty of other people their ages around to meet and hang with? (I find out later he was keeping an eye out looking for me. He and his cousin both agreed they enjoyed my company and wouldn't mind walking with me. This confuses me.)

Facebook, June 4—Josi—
Friendships come in all colors.

You see, I have many friendship issues combined with worthiness issues. Just coming out of a divorce, my support system and friendships seemed to fall apart leaving me insecure and confused. This is why I chose to come to Europe and walk the Camino, to explore my new life and grow past these worthiness issues. I also have attachment and letting go issues which I plan on overcoming while on this adventure.

I reply to the boy, "Sure, of course. I'm planning on walking out with the Italians but I am sure you are more than welcome to come with us". I put little faith into this. He is low on my radar due to our age gap. I'm thinking the Italians are around my age and we probably have more in common.

I asked him to wake me up in the morning since I don't have an alarm. I also ask the Italians to do the same so I am sure I will be included and we will all get out in time for another day of walking.

That's pretty much how it all began, low-key, low expectations, easy peasy. Well, let me tell you, this has been anything but easy. This has been a rollercoaster of fun mixed with equal amounts of discomfort in a mountain setting. I never expected the depth I would go and the growth I would experience on the Camino. It's as if the Camino itself has an electrical current plugged into my body. I'm telling you it's a freaky experience.

In the beginning, the boy and I were just two people getting to know each other. We were sharing our life stories and experiences and learning about each other's similarities and differences. There were more similarities than differences.

Facebook, June 4—Drew is feeling ready—
"Leaving your comfort zone is where you can grow without limitations. Accepting awkwardness and moving ahead towards a new self is the result."—Drew Eric
Facebook, June 4—Janet—
I am so thrilled for your self-discovery- now we all know why you are there. Missing & Loving You – Heart to heart hug

It was all fun and games in the beginning but then there were some subtle shifts. There was a vulnerability and more sharing of authentic emotions. It occurred little by little but gradually increased.

It lasted eight days. During those eight days we fought, talked, got real, cried, exposed our true selves and challenged each other in ways neither of us expected, wanted or imagined.

#LifeLesson —16 Judging limits the openness that is required for others to cross our paths and walk into our lives contributing abundant rewards beyond our wildest dreams.
Facebook, June 4—Ray—
"The little things? The little moments? – They aren't little"

follow my... path

Posted on June 12, 2016 by Drew Eric

Chapter 13 Can I open my heart and feel again?

When God delivers someone to your life, you don't ask questions. You receive them with a happy blessing. This boy is everything I would ever want in a guy, kind, sensitive, interested in talking nonstop about my interest in spirituality, life lessons and personal growth. He has a powerful energy coupled with what seems to be some real psychic abilities and possibly mental telepathy. I guess no one is perfect because "he seems" almost perfect and is just what I have been asking for—except for the fact that he could be a little older and... into guys!

Facebook, June 4—Sherry—
Drew you are awesome!!! Love your sharing, and know God is up to something!!!

However, this isn't a love story, this is a story of how two very different people came together and got real, vulnerable and really uncomfortable, all in an effort to grow personally and spiritually. It's so hard to believe it for myself and It actually happened to me. I imagine it as a book and a movie—it was that powerful.

Facebook, June 4—Bart—
Good friends can be straight.
—Drew—Yes they can my good friend

Let me get back to the boy. I'm going to call him a young man now because he is more of a young man than a boy. I'd like to tell you more about him.
From what I observed, he appears to have no boundaries and is very open. It appears to be one of his many requirements on how friends should act and be with each other. He is the kinda guy that has a yogurt, eats half then hands you the rest along with his spoon and would be personally offended if you didn't finish his yogurt "using his spoon" thinking all the while "what could possibly be wrong with my used spoon?"

He has such an amazing spirit and incredible energy. There's extremely powerful energy exuding from him at all times. Sometimes it seems a little out of control. I never know how the energy will show up, whether in warmth, kindness, flirting, excitement, even a little sexual which is confusing and complicated for sure.

Facebook, June 5—Drew—
"If you give your life as a wholehearted response to love, then love will wholeheartedly respond to you." —Marianne Williamson

We are both Pisces and I mention this because Pisces are very intuitive and emotional. Both of us are similar when it comes to emotions and intuitive nature. We can get into each other's heads. I have rarely met anyone with whom I could do this. I never expected to meet someone so intuitive here on the Camino.

Here's an example: We were out walking the path, something happens that causes me to go within and reflect, I was very raw and emotional. I quieted for a few seconds and I pulled my energy back, in order to contemplate something. I decide, "I am not going to open up to him about this, it is just too raw and I am just going to take a break from opening up." Not 10 seconds later he says, "Hey, what's up, you ok?" You have got to be kidding me. Get out of my head!

"How did you know just then something was wrong?" I asked him. "How did you know?" He replied, "Well your breathing changed and I sensed a shift in your energy." I was astounded. He is so sensitive and in tune with me, he can feel my energy and hear my breathing and tell I was contemplating something heavy and a concern for me. He's good—like a freaking physic or empath. All this while walking in nature and knowing each other only a few days.

Sometimes I feel like I can almost hear him talking to me, in my head, without using his words.

At one point he said, the very words I have been saying for years about spirituality, life and learning lessons. "This is all I ever really want to talk about," He said. That totally freaked me out.

Facebook, June 5—Laurie—
These Stories Blow My F*cking Mind! I'm amazed every time I read a post. This is so beautifully written. And the connection is

84

Awesome. It's like turning a page of a book that I NEVER want to stop reading. Thinking of you My friend. Xo

I have already told you he has no boundaries. It's one of his many requirements. He requires physical touch. In his presence you just feel him wanting a big bear hug, to be so close to you like he almost wants to be one with you, non sexually, just to be that close. It's like physically sharing your energy. In addition to touch, he has no food boundaries; you must share all his food, from his fingers, into your mouth—even sharing from the same bite.

He loves to push buttons and brings up the most obviously uncomfortable conversations. It gives him an electric charge, it's his passion. When he wants something, he is relentless. Never giving up, never backing down, and never walking away.

He is full of energy, firing energy out in all directions with all intentions, with little to no self-control. It can be very confusing whether it's intimate, loving or sexual. He is a mixture of charming, just himself and a flirt, his words. It's a bit of a messy mix.

He appears to be very emotional—typical Pieces—vulnerable, scared to cry and feel, but is desperate for it at the same time. I don't know this for sure but I bet he would love nothing more than to live in a world where men cried, shared, touched and talked endlessly with each other about spirituality, life lessons and personal growth.

The first three days were going well. I was meeting people, making connections, doing a little coaching with the fellow pilgrims, all in good fun. The young man was very friendly and doing the same with all the people we were meeting. He was also staying close to me and bidding for my attention

When we reach Pamplona things started getting a little more intense—making me more uncomfortable. I have never been around young straight men before so I have no reference to how the millennial generation works and how I should act. I have since learned.

Facebook, June 7—Kenny—
Drew, we all are human and chemistry happens. Develop these friendships without thinking of his orientation.

While running around Pamplona, doing some errands and shopping with several pilgrims, the young man started making gay jokes, laughing all the while and saying, "Why am I doing this, I just can't stop." This was getting closer to an inappropriate conversation. Eventually, as it does go sometimes, he started asking questions about "being gay". At this point, alarms are going off in my head. All I could hear was "Danger Will Robinson, danger" a line from a very old television show, "Lost In Space." (Unfortunately, it's a reference that would be "lost" on him.) I didn't answer his questions and eventually got away from the topic.

I didn't sleep well that night fretting about where this was headed. I didn't want to be "The old gay guy that turned that young man while walking the Camino." This was not the reason I came on the Camino. I did not know what to do. Of course, this might not be where he was headed but it sure felt like it was going in that direction.

The next day I made a plan. Just ignore him and his attempts to "get my attention". So that afternoon when he was asking me to help him with his handstand, I said no. He sulked and walked towards the river looking confused about my reluctance to help him. He was still in my line of vision and I could see his pain and the confusion from my behavior.

It was then I realized I was at another fork in the path. This time it was about who I wanted to be on this path. Do I want to be the guy who pulls away without explanation and hurting someone's feelings or do I want to be the guy that challenges himself even in difficult situations? Clearly I chose the challenging path.

#LifeLesson —17 At any given time in our life we need to pause and check-in on who we want to be in the world and determine, are we being true to that person.

What this meant was my next task was figuring out what to say, how to proceed and deciding what I want from this young man. I didn't know what I wanted or what to say. I realized I didn't have to know. All I needed to do was be honest with him. Then let him figure it out on his own.

#LifeLesson —18 We do not always have to have the proper words to express ourselves. Sometimes honesty is the easiest and best expression.

Before we started walking again I joined him by the river and asked if we could speak. He was a bit mopey but agreed.

I proceeded to explain the best I could, "I don't know what is happening here, and I just want you to know I am very uncomfortable. You're attractive, young, kind and we get along really well. Your questions last night made alarms go off in my head and I wanted to let you know why I was pulling back and treating you the way I just did. I didn't want you to question our friendship and wonder if you did something wrong because you didn't. I don't have an answer here, I just want you to know I am feeling uncomfortable around you, that's all. This type of friendship is new to me and I am in unchartered-territory. You're a young, impressionable guy. I feel uncomfortable and I just wanted you to hear it from me. If you saw me pulling away, this is why."

There, I said it; I was honest and shared my innermost feeling of discomfort not knowing what he will do with the information. Well, lo and behold; he takes this information as an invitation to be even more present with me. This did not elicit a shy response from him. I all but told him how I liked him and my feelings towards him and he chooses to stay—just as close and perhaps even closer than before.

Surrender, that's what I kept hearing and what there was for me to do. Ok, clearly this guy isn't going away even after I told him how uncomfortable our connections were making me feel. What the hell, I give up then. I surrender. This horse has left the stall and I can't seem to do anything to get him back in the stall. I give up. I will go wherever this takes me and let it unfold just the way the Universe wants it to unfold. So that's what I did.

#LifeLesson —19 Surender is allowing the goodness in the world to reward your life in unknown, infinite ways.
Facebook, June 8—Adam—
It's been very rewarding for me as a gay man to strike up a friendship with straight men. Those that are cool and not threatened by the idea of homosexuality have been great teachers, students and friends. I've shared this connection with a few men over my lifetime. Their acceptance and platonic love, sometimes called a "man-crush" or "bromance," has had a healing effect for me and them. I had fear of "men" into my 30s. Becoming "close" with these straight guys has been very empowering. This only happens

if I allow them in fearlessly. Thank you for such a beautiful story!
Sigue El Camino!

—Drew—I usually feel the same. I tried to blow the kid off but
he saw something in me and pursued a bond.

Deeper and deeper our bond formed. Our connection grew and our like for each other grew also. People were coming and going all around us while we were walking the Camino but the three of us stayed together, the cousins and me. I couldn't imagine what other people and even his cousin was thinking. How did it look to her? Again, I surrender.

Our best day was in Estella, Spain where we "Estayed" an extra day. It was a bizarre beginning that ended taking on a whole new meaning with an unexpected direction.

He pulled out these ridiculous brightly colored yoga pants and I laughed. He dared me to wear them and I offered up an outfit for him to wear in reprisal. After we put on each other's clothes we became the other person for the day. Totally random, totally ridiculous, totally crazy and really, really fun. Something girlfriends might do, something I had never done at home in America.

We left the hostel and ventured out into the city for provisions and errands. I was wearing his super weird, bright yoga pants and his hiking hat; he was in my purple tights, sleeveless shirt and sports visor. We looked like some bizarre gay couple with bad fashion sense. Hilarious!

What ended up happening was pretty awesome. He realized how people were looking at him/us and realized what if feels like to be judged as gay. He said, "Dude, they keep checking out my crouch." I'm thinking, now he knows how it feels to be objectified—similar to how women feel every day. I got a kick out of the experience. It made me laugh.

When we were in Pamplona I was attracted to his look and couldn't put my finger on why. I didn't want to be a 20 something. I have now realized I admire his carefree attitude and how it translates into his appearance. I wanted that for myself, to be carefree.

So we went off to shave my head. Before I came to Europe I wanted to shave my head but chickened out at the last minute. Here on the Camino I really felt the need for something new. His head is shaved. I see him as comfortable in his own skin with his own relaxed, almost hippie style—he's wearing a big round hat for shade. I want to be more like him.

I thought about getting a bigger hat before I came and thought against it thinking it would be too weird, not gay stylish. But now that I'm here it doesn't seem that out of place. I choose the visor instead which is great when it's hot.

I mention this because I'm present to how much of my life I worry about how I look. I don't want to look too gay, not gay enough, too weird or not weird enough or not be seen as gay stylish. Clearly I over-think everything.

Once we found the hair salon, I got in the chair and cried the entire time while she was buzzing my head. It was such a release to be the person I am now on the Camino, a real shedding moment. Letting go of who I was before the Camino to the person I am here, now, on the Camino.

It was liberating being in someone else's clothes. I have a picture of us with me in the pants, wearing the hat and him in the tights, sleeveless shirt and visor. The snapshot caught me looking happy, healthy and joyful.

We talked quite a bit that day, deeply personal stuff. Ran around town then picked up groceries for meals. It was a very easy and intimate day between two men. Something a gay man only gets to do with his close gay friends in a safe space. Here we are in Spain, in ridiculous clothes and have only known each other for a few days. Yet, we quickly fell into a deep comfortable intimacy.

Facebook, June 7—Drew—
"To love ourselves and support each other in the process of becoming real is perhaps the greatest single act of daring greatly."—Brene Brown

This whole thing has been a whirlwind of emotions and personal growth. It's very overpowering at times and yet enjoyable. Neither of us appeared to know how to explain it or rationalize it. So we didn't.

We decided we would call ourselves brothers. That made us laugh and it felt comfortable. I have a friend in America that said his two sons hold hands all the time while walking in public. They have always been intimate with each other when together. Calling ourselves brothers made sense to me.

I was very impacted with the affection between men in Pamplona. I have never seen men be so intimate with one another. I thought they were gay they were touching each other so much and were so close. In America they would be considered space invaders, encroaching on one's personal space, but here it's chicha, chicha (nothing, nothing, Pamplona slang I was told). Here I am, a week later having a similar experience in Pamplona while walking the Camino with a young man.

I explained how energy works and how NOT to fire off all your energy in all directions. I'm really good at sensing energy and I pick up feelings and emotions easily, always have. His energy is all over the place and very confusing. He needs to decide what energy he wants to send out and from where, mind, heart or below the waist.

That afternoon when we were doing yoga in the park I could sense a real control in his energy he didn't have before. He later explained, he feels my description about energy is the most impactful thing he has learned from me. He never knew about energy and looking back at his past, he sees how his unfocused energy has impacted his life and his friendships.

That was an amazing day. Great learning, sharing, exploring our bond and shedding inhibitions all while exploring Estella, Spain. However, the next day went to shit.

His cousin got ill and we got a late start to the day. All three of us were irritable. When I'm with family and someone is not well, I turn into a super supporter. I did this for years with my mother-in-law, who had bad knees. I would silently reach out and help her downstairs or a curb. She would silently accept my help without us ever discussing anything. However today on the Camino it wasn't working so well, nor was it appreciated, it seemed.

That's how I learned about my requirements. I require my family and extended family to accept my help. It's how I share love. I learned this from the book *"The 5 Languages of Love – Acts of Service."*

That afternoon, after we reached the next town the cousins went off to nap while I took a walk-about to get my head on straight. It was then that clarity came.

Facebook, June 10—Drew—
"There is no need to look for love, simply give it away and love will find you."—Drew Eric

90

Reflecting on how I express love, I realized it was the catalyst inspiring my "moment on the mountain." I kept trying to defend my behavior, having a mental argument with the young man.

While I was on the mountain I realized I don't need to defend my behavior, It's just me and that's ok. It's my way of expressing love and it doesn't need to be defended. I don't need to change me to suit someone else. This is the second time in a week I told myself that I will not apologize for being me! It was powerful.

#LifeLesson: —20 Being our authentic self requires no apologies. None!

I found "myself" that day on the mountain realizing that I am great just being me. It's the people around me that aren't ok with me. If they and others can't see the love I have to offer, and the way I express it, then someone else will. I don't need to change who I am to make someone else comfortable. I am great just the way I am. It was a powerful moment.

I climbed that mountain in flip-flops on a small rock/root path. It was a really high mountain with the ruins of an old monastery at the top. Halfway up the mountain my energy changed, I thought more clearly and could not only see the whole countryside, I could also see the answer for my current situation. It was intense, emotional, draining, crazy and incredible, but its time to walk on. I need to find my path alone. If I can climb this mountain in flip-flops I can walk this Camino alone, again.

#LifeLesson —21 It is not necessary to climb a mountain to prove you can do anything. You just need to believe and repeat to yourself, "I can do anything!"
Facebook, June 10—Courtney—
What a great story. I loved the video of you on the mountain. It brought tears to my eyes. "I can do this!"

follow my... path

Chapter 14 Can I be my authentic self?

I've heard that you need to resist the urge to walk with your new friends at all times. You need to leave yourself some personal time. You need to walk it alone at times. I have not been doing this since the first day and it is time. I need to go within, in solitude.

While getting to know him and his requirements, I learned a great deal about myself. I learned I can celebrate what I love about myself-my own requirements. I offer you this, the reader, acknowledge what you love about you—that's your authentic self.

I am going to get vulnerable and real. I am going to tell you my requirements, my authentic self. The reason I am telling you this upfront is that I want anyone who is not interested in learning more about my authentic self to stop reading and move on, un-friend me on Facebook, let's not hang out.

I am realizing today I have my own requirements and I love that about myself.

For so many years I have tried to squelch my needs—to live for other people's requirements and not my own, let my needs go in order to live inauthentically for others. I realize now how detrimental that is to my well being. I am not going to be a good fit for everyone, I am happy about that now. If you are able to meet my requirements, then let's hang out. If you aren't, DO NOT ASK ME TO LET MINE GO. We are not a fit. I have needs; you will meet them or move on.

Facebook, June 9—Drew—
"First, foremost, #1, start with, loving yourself!"—Drew Eric

Here are my requirements/needs:
- No food boundaries, I'm the kind of person who wants to take the first bite of food off your plate. 😊 I will resist, but this is true.
- I am passionate about friends. They mean the world to me. If you call me your friend you will meet my needs, period. If you choose to not meet my needs but want to be my friend, we are not friends.

92

- You will meet my needs, if I am hungry, feed me. If I am doing too much, help me. Be a partner in my life, not an observer or critic.
- I will take care of everyone around me. I will be nurturing, attentive and helpful. If you are the kind of person that is so independent that you won't accept help, we are not a fit. I will no longer allow people to tell me to change this about myself. I am a natural nurturer, it is my passion, and it is my "Love Language" Non-negotiable!
- I am a take-control leader. I will naturally fall into the leadership/ project manager role. This clearly rubs some people the wrong way. I will not apologize for this, it is who I am.
- I enjoy being challenged and pushed to grow. I require people to stand up to me and put me in my place if needed. If you let my large personality steamroll over you without a response, we are not a fit. I can feel your lack of response, I know something is not being said, I require you to speak up and challenge me. If this is not you, and you want to run from speaking your truth, then move on. It's either challenge me, speak your truth or don't talk to me.
- Family is everything to me. I do not take the family feeling lightly. If you say we are family you need to mean it, good, bad, ugly, nasty, warts and all. When the shit hits the fan and we are family, stand up with me and be a family, MAN UP. Find what needs to be done and do it.
- Quality time is required. You must spend quality time with me doing any and everything. Let's hold hands and watch a movie. Let's do yoga together then skip down the street holding hands. Let's share clothes. Let's run errands. Let's just be together.
- I am not perfect! I will make mistakes! I will be a jerk at times; I will get excited and talk over you! I will sometimes not listen. I require you to tell me I am doing any or all of these things so I can adjust my behavior and be a better person for you, but I will not tolerate people getting mad at me for not being perfect. I am loud and high energy and I make mistakes. Tell me to calm down and we will do fine. Get mad at me and hold a grudge, we are not a fit.
- I require a flow of positive energy. If you are withholding in any way, we are not a fit. I can't hang out with you. It doesn't work for me. I need a constant flow of loving energy. If you are negative, bitchy or mean-spirited, please walk on the other side of

the street. Not a fit! I require love and will not accept anything less than loving energy. You can certainly get mad at me but after you process you need to come back with love in your heart.

- Positivity is a must, no complaining, loving conversations work best for me. If you are the type of person to just simply complain, go away.
- I love conversation about personal growth, life lessons and spirituality. If this makes you uncomfortable, please block me out of your life. My foundation is betterment for me and others, Non-negotiable.
- I am dyslexic; I can't spell and make tons of incorrect word choices. If you are counting the mistakes in any of my writings, why the hell are you reading it? Go read DICKens.

THIS IS SO LIBERATING... I feel so much better getting this off my chest. I will no longer try to fit others needs or feel bad for being who I am. This is who I am, take me or please leave me. I can certainly dial some things down to fit the needs at the moment and will. But do not ask me to stop any of my requirements because you are uncomfortable. You need to walk away, we are done here.

I am weird and needy and crazy. I love that about me. If you do too, please call me. Let's share food and talk endlessly about ourselves. Let's spend quality time together.

Facebook, June 9—Drew—
"You are emerging from the cocoon of your former self. There are no limits to the extent of the transformation that's possible for you."—Marianne Williamson

I have spent so many hours hanging out with people that don't meet my requirements. If you are reading this and seeing yourself not meeting any of my requirements and you call yourself my friend, please take this as a warning. I am not interested in you anymore. No apologies, no regrets.

Facebook, June 10—Drew—
"First, you must heal, the rest will fall into place."—Drew Eric

I met a young man who was weird, friendly, liked me for me and met many, many of my needs. He taught me I can attract the right people to my life. He helped me realize I can be me and people will still like me. He is a young straight guy who should technically not respond to my requirements. However, he stepped up to the plate, learned and met my needs and still wanted to hang out with me.

That shocked the shit out of me. It made me believe in myself and made me believe there are people in the world who will like me. There are people in the world with similar requirements and similar needs; I just need to find them!

This story is about my falling in love with myself and falling in love with a straight young man who taught me to love myself. I am forever changed. I have him to thank. I have the Camino to thank. I have all the people who are not interested in me and my needs to thank. This is for all of you.

Take me as I am and I will love you too. This is my moment on the mountain. This is my "Manifesto". This is me, raw and authentic.

I'm feeling this urge to say, "If this isn't you then Go Fuck yourself." but that would just be rude so I won't. Wink 😊 *(Channeling my dear friend Laurie who loves the word fuck—she is fucking awesome)*

P.S. Immediately after writing this I felt an enormous shit.
(I meant to type shift in the original story, you can see why I am leaving it now; it fits with my last requirement). Something happened when I was writing this story. When I started writing about my requirements, my fingers started flying, pounding even, on the keyboard. It was as if each time I hit a key, I unearthed another pain, another source of anger. Then, like magic, the pain and anger were released into the Spanish air, never to darken my soul again. In that afternoon, I released my husband, I released friends, and I released my soul from the life-debilitating pain of my past.

I realize I was harboring anger with all the "you need to change" people in life. I had real anger for the people who wanted me to "be different, be less me".

Good news is I don't need to be angry anymore. I can let them all go. They are not for me. I love myself too much to allow naysayers in my life. Are you with me? I can do this, I can let go and be free from my past hurts.

#LifeLesson —22 All one needs to do is stand still, be authentic and you will attract loving people who are interested in your authenticity.

#LifeLesson —23 Never allow others to influence you into letting your needs go. Needs are not negotiable.

Facebook, June 10—Sarah—

I love your "weird, needy, crazy" self...glad to see you are learning to love that person too. And, as a side note...I remember sitting in a GLBX meeting with you when we first met, and you leaning over and sharing my breakfast. It was ok with me then, and it's ok with me now! LoL

—Mark—

I read Huge growth! Good for you 😊 Just like the velveteen rabbit you ARE discovering what it feels to be real.

—Tamara—

Gotta be you... Everyone else is already taken. Sarah- that's a great line "glad you are learning to love that person too." This may just be my new mantra!

—Anne—

If you learn nothing else from your journey then it's been a success. You should love yourself, especially if you're weird!!!

—Kimberly—

We've only met once and I'm loving getting to know you better through these posts! When you come back to Fort Lauderdale I'd love for you to come eat off my plate!

—Kitty—

It's funny, though we have been friends for many, many years, I realize as I read your posts how little I really have known you, though I suppose you might state that, until recently, you didn't know yourself this well either. 😉 It's been really interesting and cool to learn more about the person you are in the process of finding yourself. Thank you for sharing Drew!

—Annaleah—

Wow. How evolved for you to have not only identified but articulated what you need, Yay for you, my friend. P.S. Read your P.S. I snickered a bit. You probably felt a 'shift'?

—Laurie—

I fuckin Love this! I got chills reading this and laughed out loud when I read my name. You inspire me in so many ways. And I'm exactly the same as you in so many ways. Especially about the

96

food, that's me! Your journey is a blessing to so many. You are helping us, or at least me, learn more about myself through your experience and beautiful words. I can't put the book down. I want more! With happy tears flowing. I'm honored to be your friend. And I Fuckin Love you!! Xoxo

Posted on June 18, 2016 by Drew Eric

Chapter 15 Can I walk away?

While on the Camino I met a young man who was weird, friendly, liked me for me and met many, many of my needs. He taught me I can attract the right people in my life. He helped me realize I can be me and people will still like me. He made me believe in myself. OMG I love myself. I am weird, needy and even crazy sometimes. That's what I love about me.

Here's what the young man taught me:

- Live life for me, through my clothes and personal style. I am allowed to be weird if I want to be. *#LifeLesson —24 If you're weird be weird. Allow your authenticity to shine through.*
- I spend way too much time concerned about straight people and what they might/might not think. I need to be more honest in public and not worry about my safety or making others uncomfortable. I've made it a bigger deal than it is. *#LifeLesson — 25 Worrying about what others might think or do if they knew the true you, shrinks your authenticity.*
- I can meet people who will be attracted to what I have to offer— even with all my weirdness. *#LifeLesson —26 Authenticity comes at a high price, people might actually like you.*
- I have requirements and I don't have to change for someone else. I have needs that will be met. There are people that will like my requirements. I met him, I will meet others. *#LifeLesson —27 There are people in the world that will like your needy, crazy, loving self.*
- I don't need to apologize for being me, I just don't. *#LifeLesson —28 When you are authentic, people won't expect you to apologize. They either like your authenticity or they won't, no apology necessary.*
- I can see young men as friends and find common ground with them. This was my first time forming a bond with a young man. *#LifeLesson —29 Forming friendships are easy when you are willing to show your true self and allow others to see your shared commonalities.*

That night I shared with him my thoughts on walking ahead without them. He was pretty upset with himself as he reflected back on how he reacted to my nurturing ways. He told me he was having an argument in his head, wanting me to dial down my attention to his cousin. He didn't want to have our last walk together end with him and his anger towards me.

This was the most emotional moment we shared together. I was still elated from my hike up the mountain and he was crying uncontrollably for quite a long time. I continued to console him as he poured his heart out about us, himself, his life at home, everything. He even commented that he expected me to be crying when this day came, not him. I was honored to have shared this intimate moment with him.

Facebook, June 10—Drew at Albergue Villamayor de Monjardin—
I just had one of the most profound conversation in my life. I will never forget this moment. Life can get better for me!

As I shared before, it always felt like we were in each other's head. I have shared a similar experience two other times in my life when I was in college. Both men were straight and we had an incredible connection. Both of those experiences ended with my cutting them off, they were way too intense, way too powerful, way too emotional.

I'm reminded of them today. That's a bit unsettling because I am wondering if this friendship will suffer the same fate. I am friends with one of the guys on Facebook, not sure if he is reading this, if so, please know I remember our time together fondly.

On the Camino you might encounter the same people all the time or only come across them once. You never know. It's really up in the air whether we will cross paths again. Since the past seven days have been such a whirlwind of emotions, both of us need a break. At least I do.

Facebook, June 10—Drew—
"Get still and listen to your intuition. No one knows your path better than your inner guidance. It will always direct you well."—Drew Eric

I promised him then we would walk in the morning and have fun. Conflict won't dominate our last day walking together and it didn't. We had great fun that next day.

Apparently his cousin and I needed to finish on a better note also. We didn't split up that afternoon like I expected but walked and stayed over in another hostel together. His cousin and I were able to complete our family moments over dinner before bed. My favorite time with them both was eating. She gave us both a bite of her pasta, right off her fork. Apparently none of us have food boundaries. It was a nice evening.

The next morning I walked out of the hostel, alone again. He and I said our goodbyes not knowing what was in store for us, how to process what happened or even comprehend all the learning and intenseness.

I gave him my amethyst bracelet and a t-shirt. He gave me those pants I wore and his neck buff that I was attracted to since day one. It was a pretty gay moment saying goodbye. We hugged deeply, but no crying this time.

I explained to him that our connection is real, for sure, however we are living in a land with a false bottom. Meaning, our lives are put on hold while we are here, growing and learning. Once we return home, all this will be a distant memory but we will be forever changed. Our connection is real, but, our life here without stresses or outside worries, isn't. Who knows, we could be great friends someday, or maybe not.

I know the tendencies to attach myself to others runs deep. I also have separation anxiety that can complicate matters. But If I can climb that mountain in flip-flops, if I can fly across the world to a foreign land, if I can meet a straight boy and form a bond, I can do anything.

Facebook, June 10—Drew—
"I will continue to give love knowing it will find me in return."—
Drew Eric

I miss that young man. He was my friend, but not my boyfriend. I still love him. Who wouldn't?

This was a story about me falling in love with myself and creating a bond with a straight young man who taught me to love myself. I am forever changed. I have him to thank. I have the Camino to thank.

100

I can climb a mountain, I did that! I can walk 500 miles alone,

Facebook, June 10—Drew—
An amazing loving evening. I finally opened my heart to the Camino. It will not close again. It only took 11 days opening and closing down. Now it is fully open and it feels good. I can feel again. I can feel again, I can feel... Tears
—Drew—
#ActOfKindness —5 My heart has been opened and I am so blessed to have met the young man. Thank you for your kindness, generosity, friendship, warmth, food, support, gifts, conversation, quality time, connection, intimacy and love. You helped me on this path in ways that will be with me forever. I am sure I will continue to grow from knowing you for the unforeseeable future. I will look back on this time, here with you on the Camino and it will truly bring a skip in my heartbeat and a smile to my face and fill my body with warmth in remembering us, together. Thank you for so much, gratitude sounds such a small word for how I feel for you.
—John—
I love your spirit and how this journey has opened your mind and soul to yourself. I don't often read a post that is more than a paragraph long but you pulled me in and I read every word. I love being your friend. If you ever walk to Maine you have a place to stay in our home. Continuing to send you love and of course positive thoughts. John.
—Andy—
I am not quite sure I understand all of this!! are you looking for "real" connections or sexual ones? Why should his sexuality matter? He can still be a soul partner. Seems to me you still have a lot of soul searching to do and understand what "IT" is that you are actually "asking" for...Your life's journey seems to be just beginning...
—Drew—
Yes, it is very much just beginning.
—Courtney—
Love it!
—Drew—
I thought a lot about you today, writing this.
—Courtney—
That's awesome. We're connected.
—Drew—

I thought carefully about my message and what I wanted to convey to you. This experience has been pretty special.

—Courtney—

That means so much. Truly.

—Drew—

It's true, you made me step up my game by sharing.

—Courtney—

Gotta get out of that comfort zone.

—Drew—

Oh lord, don't give me no more lessons today! Couldn't be more uncomfortable every day. It's terribly wonderful.

—Courtney—

Right!!!!!! Love that terribly wonderful (title of your book! 😊)

Posted on January 25, 2016 by Drew Eric

Chapter 16 Can I find peace after a breakup?

"Reaching for the stars is impossible when you are to busy scrummaging in the soil for yesterday's regrets."—Drew Eric

My life is different than one year ago. One year ago today, January 5th, 2015, my husband and I choose to end our almost 20-year marriage. On this day, I became single, alone. I remember choosing to be alone with my three pups and my yoga mat. Choosing to take my almost nonexistent income to a place that could sustain me to live alone. Choosing a new life over the life I had, which was no longer serving either one of us.

Those first few months were stressful. I immediately focused on signing up for new appraisal management companies for work. I moved to the spare bedroom. My ex-husband took his first vacation without me. We had our third wedding anniversary three days before Valentine's Day. My birthday is six days after Valentine's Day. We divided up our belongings. We had a garage sale for all the items neither of us needed or wanted in our new lives. Found a place to live five days before move-out-day. Moved! Took the final exam for coaching at the University of Miami. Finished my last week of classes at UM. Spent our first holiday—Easter—apart. Sold our home at a slight loss. Then, came adjusting to living alone for the first time in 20 years.

"When life doesn't go as planned, don't close the book. A new chapter is a page turn away."—Drew Eric

Once the dust settled a bit and I was comfortably moved in my new 600sf apartment, I was able to breathe and get my bearings. For about a hot second. The energy I put towards growing my appraisal business brought in new clients, in turn creating my highest income month ever. I completed thirty—record-breaking—appraisals in one month. Working was a blessing since it helped keep my mind occupied and off the stresses of my new life. Working also brought confidence in my abilities to support myself in my new life alone.

It wasn't just working that got me through those difficult days, it was "A Course in Miracles, ACIM" I relied on most. I find it no co-incidence, that the day after my husband and I split was the first ACIM study group session of the new year. According to ACIM, there are no coincidences.

"You cannot but be in the right place at the right time."—A Course In Miracles

I learned the following four insights that saved my sanity while attending my weekly ACIM group meetings throughout 2015.
1. Do not place blame
2. Be Non-judgmental
3. Do not create a story
4. Come from a place of love

1. Do not place Blame
Right from the start I worked hard on resisting blame. When anyone leaves a relationship the easiest thing to do is place blame on others. It's nearly impossible, without an extensive amount of work, to take the blame or look at your own contribu-tion. I choose the latter; I choose to look for my contribution. I knew instinctively I played a big role in the demise of our relation-ship. Instead of focusing on all the things he did wrong, I looked at all the things I did and examined how they might have impacted him. I looked at how I treated him, how I communicated, I even examined how I loved myself, for any hidden insights.

It was loving myself where I found insights on my contribution. I didn't feel worthy of love and I didn't feel I deserved love. Not from my husband exactly, more in general. This was a huge discovery. By figuring out I had a lifetime of not feeling worthy of love, I was able to see how he fit into the puzzle that was my life. Not be-cause he didn't love me, he did, very much so. I was too busy looking for my specific love language and wasn't able to see the love "love language" he was offering.

In "The 5 Love Languages" written by Gary D. Chapman, he explains how we all give and receive love in primarily five ways:
1. Acts of Service
2. Physical Touch
3. Quality Time
4. Receiving Gifts

5.   Words of affirmation.

We can also be any combination of the five ways. I receive love through "2. Physical Touch" most of all, with "3. Quality Time" coming up second and "5. Words of Affirmation" coming in 3rd. "1. Acts of Service" is a love language I had to learn to recognize especially since I believe that was my husband's strongest love Language.

My husband provided me with a steady household income, which enabled us to own a beautiful home for 17 years. We had everything we wanted in life, new cars, trips all over the world, cruises, we even flew the Concord to Paris. We never left the house without each other, friends always. My Husband was also very free with "I Love You." I felt the love for what he provided. But I didn't feel wholehearted and loved because I subconsciously didn't feel I deserved love. So when It came to blaming him for not loving me, I was able to see the blame was on me. I needed to feel I deserve love and I am worthy of love before I can feel the love from anyone else.

#LifeLesson —30 By blaming others for our misfortunes we are taking the burden off ourselves, dispersing to the outside wheel. We are always the central cause, we are the axel that allows the wheel to spin.

2. Be Non-judgmental
Practicing non-judgment was new to me. I did want to judge my husband, judge me, judge how we could have worked harder and judged how we could have worked smarter. But with my new learning from ACIM judging others only keeps us separate, in a state of fear and comparison.

"Instead of judging, we need but be still and let all things be healed."—A Course In Miracles

If we want to feel whole and complete we need to live a life free of judgment because we are all the same. We are all doing our best at every moment. All of us are children of God. All of us are living, breathing, wonderful human beings. I realized I needed to see the light in him as the same light in me (the definition of Namaste). Only by seeing my ex-husband as a wonderful being of light, can I have peace in my own heart. We are the same him and I, both wonderful people with a beautiful shining light. Namaste.

#LifeLesson —31 Judgment, is immensely time consuming and unfulfilling. Letting go of judgment releases the burdens of right and wrong and allows the freedom of what is, oneness.

3. Do not create a Story

Creating a story is the ego-mind's job. We as humans are always filling in the blanks, making up a story so we feel complete and in control. However, we never have the entire story. We are always seeing any given situation from our vantage point which again, is always muddled with interpretation and filling in the missing pieces of the story. I learned in ACIM not to believe the stories I was creating. "He didn't love Me enough. He could have done more. He could have participated more." None of this is true. All of it is me trying to fill in the blanks and create a story so I can stand behind my story and feel right or better. None of it is real.

"When I am upset, it is always because I have replaced reality with illusions I made up."—A Course In Miracles

The reality is "He did the best he could, at the moment in time, no more, no less." So I learned not to create and believe my story as truth. Simply to let it go.

"Would you rather be right or happy?"—A Course In Miracles

#LifeLesson —32 Being right never leads to inner peace. Someone is blamed for being wrong. Being happy leads to inner peace.

4. Come from a place of Love.

Recently I had two friends share with me, how happy they are to see me grow and handle the breakup with such grace, love and kindness. I believed I was coming from love myself, and it was reassuring to hear my friends saw it too. Coming from a place of love brings me much peace. My ex-husband is in a new relationship and I am very pleased for his happiness. I see them together on trips, with friends, family and I send them love with a silent prayer or post/like on Facebook. Whether it's verbal or silent love has been extended with an open heart. I was with my husband for 20 years and still, to this day, I want nothing more for him than happiness. I can see my wishes are coming true. The only thing that is real is love, everything else is an illusion stemming from fear is a summary from ACIM. I do not need fear in my life. I am no longer in a relationship with fear. I am in love with LOVE.

"Nothing ever goes away until it has taught us what we need to know."—Pema Chodron

I did my work throughout 2015. Today I am reaping the rewards of my hard work. I feel at peace with myself, with my ex-husband, with friends and family. A couple other friends shared how they thought I was more authentic now, more myself. I feel calmer, relaxed, present and at peace. Apparently, peace within me is shining from the inside out.

"I enjoy this place I reside now, together."—Drew Eric

#LifeLesson —33 Coming from love reaps the rewards one longs for, peace and light shining from within, for all the world to see.

Facebook, January 26—William—
Drew, your words brought tears to my eyes. I too went through an 11-year breakup. After which I soon lost my mother. I fell deep into alcoholism. I feel God sent me my partner of almost 18 years, Mike, to fill the overwhelming void I was feeling. We married last September on our 17th anniversary. I now enjoy being married, taking yoga, personal training 3× a week, getting tattoos and realizing how lucky I am at the ripe old age of 59 to be where I am today. Your thoughts are such an inspiration to me, you are a very strong-willed person to do this on your own, and I feel VERY fortunate to now have you in my life! I wish you nothing but the absolute best in your future and hope we will always be friends. Sincerely, Bill
—Elizabeth—
Can you find peace? I think you have! May you continue to live and love who you are!
—Michelle—

Thank you so much for sharing the events that have brought you to a better YOU! Inspiration comes from adversity!

—Roberto—

Such an honest story. I admire your ability to be vulnerable. It seemed to have made you stronger. I think growth is a beautiful thing to share. Thank you for doing that!

—Marcia—

Drew, thank you so much for sharing this. I will be reading it several times as I think there is a ton of great helpful stuff in there. We all have struggles and need help dealing with them. Again thanks!!

Posted on June 23, 2016 by Drew Eric

Chapter 17 Can I overcome my worthiness issues?

It's the midway point in my pilgrimage. My journey has taken me over breathtaking mountains, hills and countryside. These are sights I have never seen growing up in the flatlands of Florida.

The solitude of this journey has flooded me with emotions and realizations. Sometimes it's overwhelming and I just want it to slow a bit. I wonder if others here on the electrically charged Camino feel the same way.

Facebook, June 18—Drew is feeling alone—
Just leaving Borgus. Alone again. Who shall I meet today? Who shall I see? Where will I sleep? How far will I walk? I have no idea. I am alone on this path. Until I am not. I love not knowing anything. I live in the flow of life. I am in love, with the Camino path.
Facebook, June 19—Drew—
I had a breakthrough/breakdown this morning. I was feeling a little lonely last night, a little excluded on occasion. I knew I was looking at something incorrectly. This morning I realized an old habit of mine. This sucks to say at my age. I was chasing after the popular kids. The ones I saw as cool and interesting, excluding others as possible friends. Old habits are hard to quit. I didn't even notice I was doing it. I am open to all people in my life.

After the separation with the young man. My "I am not worthy" got triggered because I felt alone, possibly rejected. Depression set in, sadness overcame me and I started to isolate.

When I was a child, I moved around to many elementary schools. This stunted the development of my social skills. I wasn't able to experience and learn from long-term friendships. I felt lonely and rejected in each new school, being so young and not understanding how life and friends really work.

When I landed in my father's home at the age of nine, halfway through fourth grade, it became evident I had a subpar education and was held back in an effort to strengthen my math and reading skills. Today I realize undiagnosed dyslexia probably contributed to my learning problems. Repeating fourth grade brought the same old feelings of loneliness and rejection. It wasn't for another few years until the same younger students—now seventh graders—started to be a little friendlier and I began to feel included.

It was then I developed the habit of designating the "cool kids." My thinking was, by hanging out with them, I'd be cool, worthy even, a better person, because on my own I'm not worthy—or so I thought.

Today, here on the Camino, I am finding people who like me and want to spend quality time with me. These are people I thought were cool, attractive and popular. This puzzled me. "Why do they want me around, I'm not worthy." I even felt that way with the young man from the first week on the Camino. "I'm 48 and gay, why does a 23-year-old straight boy want to hang out with me?"

During my school years, whenever people went out of their way with a kind gesture, I would always be so touched. In high school, a friend, Kim gave me her car to get my driver's license. We weren't even that close. Another friend, Julie offered to wash my clothes when my laundry piled up and I had nothing to wear. (I wasn't allowed to use the laundry machines due to family disputes.)

Facebook, June 11—Julie—
Love you then, love you now. You inspired me then, you inspire me now. Hugs and prayers. Stay safe my friend.

I chose people to hang out with, because with them, I would be a better person. People would like me because of that association. I chose people Like Wendy and Jennifer in my sophomore year because they were cool.

Facebook, June 11—Wendy—
Love and strength to you, Drew!!!! 😊 *You were important to me then and you are important to me now. Big hug from across the universe.*
—Drew—You like me calling you out. You were important to me in my school days. Thanks

In my junior year I changed high schools from the West Coast of Florida with my father, to the Southeast coast with my mother

110

and again I found myself in a place where I chose new people, the most pretty, popular and fun.

My high school had a Lip-sync contest and I saw this as an opportunity to choose the cool kids as my band members. I was Robert Palmer and I chose the beautiful and talented, Laurie and Tammy, Casandra and Christine as my guitar–holding backup girls in black miniskirts and bright red lips. Our cover song was "Addicted to Love." Just imagine how amazing that was. I had a mullet and the girls were all identically dressed and expressionless with red lips and slicked back hair—just like in the video.

Facebook, June 11—Cassandra—
I ♥ u Drew! Always have and always will. Stay strong on this journey and know you are worthy.
—Tammy—
Dear Drew, You may not be aware of this but Laurie and I went to 16 different schools before Plantation High School. We weren't popular (we had great hair and Thank you for the "PRETTY" compliment). Above all we were authentic and genuinely loved the company we kept. You inspired me then and still do to this day. We were seeking REAL Souls during the time we befriended you. Thanks for proving us all right after all these years. Perhaps you made US COOLER!!!??? I Love You! xoxo

In college, the habit continued, so I chose, Wendy, Jen, Michelle, Sally, Julie, Shannon and Kevin, I wanted to be liked by them; I was desperate to be loved.

I mention their names because we're Facebook friends and have remained close. They are following my post, sending me love and words of encouragement while I walk my path and find myself. After all these years the people that I thought I wasn't worthy of, are telling me how inspired they are by my adventure and my blogging. The people I thought would make me a better person are telling me how I am helping and inspiring them. I am overwhelmed with gratitude. I am worthy of all this love. I am worthy of receiving their love.

Facebook, June 11—Sally—
You are so inspiring, but more than that, you are brave. I doubt you realize the influence you're having on people's lives simply by being you. Keep going... I love you!!

—Shannon—

Oh Drew, I love this post and I love you. Thank you for sharing all your revelations about yourself, no matter how painful. You're making me analyze myself more. And for the record, I was amazed you wanted to be MY friend, and I was intimidated by you at first. You are, and have always been, fabulous, gregarious, loving and a great friend. I can't wait to read more about your journey!

—Julie—

Ok! I've been looking forward to your posts everyday...Today, I stopped to grab a bite before running to teach a class. I thought I would check in with Drew while I was eating to see if you were feeling better, if you were walking or resting etc. Such a powerful post. I teared up again, so I had to go to class with red eyes. (I'm going to have to be more careful about when I read your posts.) Just to be clear you were and are the cool one. Hard to believe you wanted to hang out with me! I'm a dork, (don't get me wrong I like being a dork.) You were always up for anything, a trip to the beach, hang out, go to eat, draw, see music, always with a smile. I'm happy you now can see yourself as others have always seen you. Much love to you!

—Jennifer—

I always thought you were worthy, glad you see it too.

Looking back on my 20-year relationship and marriage with my ex-husband, I realize the marriage was over many years before it actually ended. We were very close friends but our friendship didn't resemble a marriage. When those familiar feelings of loneliness, closely tied to feelings of rejection overcame me, I was all too familiar with them. I didn't realize that my life didn't have to be this way. I didn't have to stay in a finished marriage that was no longer working for either of us. It took several years of hard work convincing myself I am worthy and deserve to be happy in my life, whether I'm in this marriage or single. Then the day came when single was the answer for us both.

When a marriage dissolves, it's not uncommon for one's friendships to transform. I felt my support system, literally running through my fingers like beach sand. I couldn't help but feel unworthy and rejected. All the people I spent the last few years with were less communicative, leaving me feeling lonely and confused. I didn't understand why the people I cared for the most weren't

there, reaching out with conversation, quality time and loving support. I believe this is a common occurrence in a divorce, but still,
not an easy situation. I was working so hard to convince myself
that I was worthy, I am ok and yet I had to comfort myself through
this difficult time.

This morning, on the Camino, I found myself with the same
overwhelming but familiar feelings. Feelings I have been pulling
around my entire life, like a piece of an old car on a trailer being
pulled behind a donkey, for the last 48 years.

I chose a group of people I felt were cool, hip, and beautiful. I
found myself chasing them on the path, chasing their attention,
wanting to share in their conversation and music.

In the afternoon I started writing this blog not knowing where it
would take me. I was sitting on the grass near the "cool kids" writing when a young man turned in his chair and started a conversation.

He was attractive, very young and friendly. We asked the basic
questions everyone asks including, "Why are you walking the
Camino?" He got a phone call and I went back to my writing.
Eventually he moved inside while I remained in my sad state on
the grass.

I finally realized "I" was isolating myself by sitting on the grass
alone, on my computer. So I shook off that uncomfortable feeling
of sadness, closed my computer and walked into the dining area
where the same young man was talking with others. I joined them
and we spent the next several hours sharing and eating. It was a
truly enjoyable evening. I felt a real connection with all of them.

Facebook, June 10—Drew is feeling loved—
"Acquaintances talk when they have time while friends free their
time to talk."—Drew Eric

I was so focused on the people I selected as potential friends to
make me feel better about myself. I missed the people who wanted my company—the people who fit my needs and are interested
in me and what I bring to their life.

For several days, I followed the large group of cool kids, being
kind, showing my authentic-self and always giving them a kind
warm greeting sometimes with little reciprocation. Some were very
kind and inclusive, while some remained distant even ignoring my
kindness and warmth.

Now I have realized my mistake. I was reaching out to a group of individuals who weren't interested in what I had to offer. This is foolish of me and it's not why I came on the Camino. I came, in part, to connect with people who are interested in my company and what I have to offer, my authentic self.

I have learned one thing on the Camino, I don't have to do anything but be open and I will attract people who resonate with me. If I close down or feel desperate, I get nothing. If I love myself and remain open, my needs are met. I just have to see things differently.

Those individuals I met that afternoon and shared dinner and stories are still walking with me today. They are kind, receptive to my love and want me to join them on their path. They are worthy of my love. They are receiving my love.

If you're open and receptive to my love then you are deserving of my attention and time. If you are withholding of yourself in any way and not appreciative of me, then we are not a fit. Thanks but no thanks.

This is a huge realization. I cried for about an hour when I realized and grew from this experience. It was overwhelming.

When I am feeling sad, insecure, depressed or rejected, it triggers my lack of worthiness. I will do my best, in the future, to be present in my life and recognize when I am off course. There are no individuals in the world to make me better because I am better. I am perfect and whole just the way I am.

#LifeLesson —34 Worthiness is not tied to the people you are in close proximity with. Worthiness comes from within and attracts people who are worthy of you.
Facebook, June 11—Drew—
"Each and every day is a new opportunity to begin anew. Wake up, breathe in, smile, take that first step."—Drew Eric

On the Camino, we are all walking as a group, one big tribe heading in the same direction, towards Santiago. The cool kids are still all around except instead of longing for their attention, I am choosing to send them love, silently. Each day I feel better, confident and worthy.

The cool kids don't have to like me. I can choose to send them love. So each day I am smiling and feeling the love in my heart for them all. I'm not giving them a warm embrace, however I do offer a smile and warm loving energy. Because everyone deserves that from me, everyone deserves my loving energy. I will not withhold my love from anyone. I can do this, I can walk the Camino and know, I AM WORTHY and full of love for all human beings.

I AM WORTHY!

Facebook, June 10—Drew is feeling grateful—
"To be grateful to the lessons your past has taught you is how to release and heal. Thank you past."—Drew Eric

Update: Originally when I wrote this I was feeling rejected, lonely and scared. I said that my ex-husband had rejected me. The truth is I only felt rejected by him. I have since changed the wording around to better reflect that truth.

My statement that he rejected me spurred him to comment on Facebook. He asked me to consider what I write since so many of our friends and family are reading my story/Facebook post about my journey. When I saw his public comment, I private messaged him and everything changed that day. No longer was I on this journey alone.

Here is how it went in the private message, I hope you can see the friendship we share:

—Drew—
I understand, I will be more considerate of what I write. I am really oblivious to people reading it. On my end, it doesn't seem like very many people are reading it.

—Ex-Husband—
Many people read it–trust me.

—Drew—
Really? I had no idea.

—Ex-Husband—
If you get 30 comments–300 people probably read it, if not more.

—Drew—
I only see a few people comment on it. No Shit? I'm shocked. I guess that's my worthiness issue then.

—Ex-Husband—
Happily, I don't see 'everyone' all that often but when I do, I, too, am shocked at your audience.

—Drew—

I am standing on a sidewalk in Spain crying right now. I cry every day here. Thanks for telling me. I didn't know anyone was following me.
—Ex-Husband—

It is impactful, people are jealous, think you are crazy, think you are brave, think it's stupid, think it's awesome, don't understand, don't want to understand, wish they could do it, want insight about us (Was he always like this?) It's a plethora (love that word!)of emotions and thoughts–the point is, you are impacting many, which is part of your intent with posting. When you write, I want you to think about your closest friends reading it, your family and my family. Those are the people that matter now, mattered in your past and matter in your future.
—Drew—

Ok, that's helpful. I didn't know anyone reads it. I don't hear anything from anyone.
—Ex-Husband—

Well–trust me–it is not falling on deaf ears. I see your story as a book... Now a little disjointed through posts but when you finish, I can see you reviewing your 'journal' and creating something awesome. You got this!
—Drew—

That means a lot, I can't stop crying.
—Ex-Husband—

Please make them happy tears if they are not already.
—Drew—

I'm shaking, this is really overwhelming, thank you, thank you, thank you.
—Ex-Husband—

I can only imagine. You're welcome.
—Drew—

You don't know what this means to me. And of course it's you, you know my crazy well.
—Ex-Husband—

Of course I do know what this means to you in the context of who you were. I can only imagine what it means to the person you are, now.
—Drew—

Thanks, I'm better now. "Was he always like this?" that's my favorite...
—Ex-Husband—

I actually had 50 comments on this post along with 73 likes. This was a turning point when I realized people are following my path and I am impacting many lives with what I am doing. I thought I had this little journal thing on Facebook where I could write whatever I wanted and a few people would read it. I was wrong, immensely wrong.

It was this story that started a real response from people in all parts of my life. I saw healing from not just myself but from others whose lives I was touching. I decided Facebook would become a character in my story. I have been including Facebook comments throughout my story and now I am sharing the inspiration for that idea.

I am worthy of followers and all the kind loving words from friends and family. Thank you.

I AM WORTHY!

Facebook, June 11—Drew is feeling loved—
"Loving oneself alters the relationships in your life for the better."—Drew Eric
—Christine—
You are worthy Drew… Everyone in the world is worthy of love, kindness and acceptance. I think everyone feels the way you do Drew all throughout our lives. There's always good, bad, happy, stressful, unloving, scary, crazy, can I hang on another minute, I don't like myself, where do I fit in, how can I better myself, am I doing all I can to be my best. I think all of the millions of these questions that we ask ourselves are the mere things that help us to stop and to come back to center. To do a reality check on how we're living our lives.
I feel from the bottom of my heart that you always were and still are, one of the kindest people I know and you always have been. I also feel that you are so blessed to be on this path. You are not only finding yourself in some of the rawest, scared and vulnerable places in your soul but you're standing up, facing, addressing and making yourself a better person. You are truly finding you. The you that we see.
You may see things in me and your friends and you think one way about us but you don't know all the struggles we have and we hide.

I love you Drew and as you know life is a day by day, one foot in front of the other, make life happen, kind of a journey. We are not guaranteed anything, so do your part in the world to make things better and people will see that. Some will follow and some won't. But in the end you'll love yourself. If that's all you have then it was all worth the climb.

You sometimes really never know, even in a mere quick conversation, how you may have touched someone by something you said. You may have just changed their bad day into a good one. You may never know, but they will not forget it or you.

I am so proud of you, I would not have the courage to do what you're doing, you're popular with me and many others. God Bless you my dear friend and safe journey and happy healing along the way♥✖○

P.S. The skit we all did in high school is one of my favorite memories😎

—Peter—

Keep on growing! And remember, all those other people have their own journeys. Maybe someone who ignored you is on a journey where they decided before they started they would latch on to a small group (or maybe they planned to walk as a group of friends) and not expand to include others—maybe they want to see how deep a relationship they can make if they focus on just one or two others for the entire walk. Point is, you don't know their background or their journey, where they come from emotionally, how mature or prejudiced they are about different things and people. And they don't know of your want to connect, especially if they are just oblivious. You are learning that if you are focused on something that may not be real, or reciprocal, then you are missing a beautiful view, an interesting little flower aside the road, a fascinating conversation with a person you don't notice is there just a few feet away. Keep on growing, Drew!!!!

—Drew—

Yes you are correct on all levels. I completely agree. Thanks for adding to my long blog. It's perfect.

—Ralph—

Yes, your heart has been cracked open = I am not being a prick but I am so grateful for that. Stay with your vulnerability that is your gift, stay grounded in your vulnerability, it is not an imperfec-

118

tion, it is just a feeling. I breathe in, I calm my body, I breathe out, I smile.
  —Kevin—
Without vulnerability, joy becomes foreboding–Brene Brown
  —Tammy—
I always thought of you in high school as someone that was very self-possessed, self-assured, and confident. I was intimidated by you and your friends. I'm glad we got to know each other better as adults. We all find comfortable masks to wear through every stage of our lives, and it's a revelation when you realize you've been wearing one and can remove it without fear.
  —Ayal—
My dear, everybody deserves your love. You can love and share your love without expecting to be loved in return. The act of love and being a loving person is your reward. The deserving people will come and gravitate towards you because your love is unconditional and is offered free with no conditions. You will find as you move on your journey, that a lot of people will come and go, but the worthy ones will stay. There are not going to be many of them, but the few that will stay will make your life full and rich and loving. You are worthy.
  —Caresse—
Yes! You get to choose your reality. If you see yourself as an unworthy soul who complains all the time, then that is what is reflected. If you see yourself as Magic, Love and ONE with everything, then your reality shifts. Drew, you are LOVE. Once you realize what other people think of you is NONE OF YOUR BUSINESS, you will free yourself to be the BEST, authentic Drew you can be. Rock On Little One!
  —David—
Love this insight...but also be cautious that those same people you think are ignoring you or not worthy because they appear to be pushing you away are also the very same people that also may be suffering from not feeling worthy. The sweetest thing you wrote was, "I gave unconditionally and expected nothing in return." Shouldn't that be the way with most your interactions?
A: You'll never be disappointed because the expectation was never there in the first place.
B: if love is reciprocated, what a pleasant surprise.
  ♥ The second observation that was interesting is how often we isolate ourselves, then claim we are unloved. Truth be told, we

119

pushed everyone away. Be open to meeting new people along life's journey. Look into their eyes with the understanding that they too are dealing with life's issues and simply smile and say hello, how are you? Who knows where that step will take you. Keep the writing coming... living through your experiences and enjoying the journey.

 —Annaleah—

You are not alone with so many of the things you are discovering. Again, I applaud you for being so honest about your discoveries. Having always searched out the cool kids, and wanting to be accepted, for different reasons, I see my truths in yours as well. Hang in there. You are definitely worthy (oh, and you are cool too!)

 —Richard—

Drew – Your insightful comments remind me of my class trip to WDC in high school. I was popular in high school. However, when it came time to choosing hotel roommates, I was not picked by friends who I knew since first grade. My three roommates and I were just regular guys. Not popular enough to room with the 'crowd!' We had a fun time without any pretense! We became good friends after graduation–some on a regular basis–some on FB after many years. Drew–I, too, am gay and have seen you at a number of gatherings and always thought of you as cool yet aloof. I wondered what would it take to crack that exterior and get to know the real Drew. Now I see that we are all in the same boat. I, too, feel that at times however witty and jolly I appear–I am still questioning myself–what do they really think of me. Am I worthy of their friendship? Am I worthy of my persona? I realize I can only be me. It's okay to be me. I can't be anyone else. What you see is what you get! As I write this note–at 2:11 a.m.–I am content! Thank you for being so honest and upfront! I love you! Richard

 —Susan—

You are becoming comfortable in your own skin. This is one good trait that comes with age. Good to see you growing inside. You are a good person. Shine in the light of your positive energy.

 —Trinity—

Drew, I have to be honest, I never knew you very well in school. I was a dork and in my own cliche of misfits. I was never one of the popular kids. I always felt unwanted and unwelcome. I saw you as one of those special "popular people". You were always smiling and nice to people that I saw but we were in totally different circles. One thing that I have learned in my years is we are all in the same boat no matter who we are. We all have emotions and feelings of unworthiness. I think it is part of growing up and finding ourselves. I chased people and things I thought would make me happy. We have been through many trials and it is only through the grace of God that I have made it through. Now I find happiness in my family and the simple things in life. I love that you have embarked on this spiritual journey and allowed us to follow. Even though everyone takes a different path in life we are all in this together. We are brothers and sisters. May God bless you and keep you safe on your travels.

—Lisa—

Makes me teary. How could you possibly not realize how wonderful you are???!!! I'm so glad you are finding yourself. You always have my love. L

—Drew—

Thanks everyone, you are all healing me with each and every comment.

—Drew—

#ActOfKindness —6 Wow, is all I can say. Giving love is the kindness of all. Supporting something through kind words is true giving from the heart. I am moved beyond expectations from everyone's words of love and support here on my path. All the Facebook friends from home and around the world that are sending me well wishes I thank you, thank you, thank you. All of you are greatly contributing to my growth while on this path. I never expected my small little journal post to gain such a momentum as it has and I cherish it. I am healing in so many ways. I hope my stories are healing and giving back to you all. Thank you, sincerely and with love.—Drew Eric

Posted on June 14, 2016 by Drew Eric

Chapter 18 Can I overcome the fear of my own safety
as a gay man?

Facebook, June 12—Drew is feeling heartbroken—
It saddens me to hear about Orlando. You are in my prayers from
over here. Heart to heart hugs for Orlando.
   Facebook, June 14—Drew—
I have a long way to go. I send you love from Spain to all my
friends. Be safe. #orlando

So I finally had a breakdown/breakthrough (however you view it)—on the Camino—thousands of miles from Orlando, Florida.

I was walking with a man (make note that I am working on not distinguishing gay or straight when I refer to men) and we were talking about why we are walking the Camino. It's the first question you ask when you meet someone on this path.

As we walk he is talking about his life—his work, his divorce, everything, that's not unusual here. We start a story that may take hours or minutes to complete. Last week I summed up my life story with a fellow pilgrim in two hours—including everything from my childhood to today. There is beauty in the sharing that goes on and that connects us in a deeper place than just the path on The Way to Santiago.

This stranger was willing to be vulnerable and transparent, revealing intimate details about his life. How his girlfriend's son has taken residence in his heart. How he cannot have children due to a low sperm count—one of the reasons for the ending of his previous marriage. How he has returned to the Catholic Church and plans to marry this new woman in his life. This level of intimacy makes me panicky, unsure and unsafe.

Now it was my turn and this is what I wanted to say. "The reason I came to Europe, in general, is because I want to overcome my fears and anxieties along with putting myself in as many uncomfortable situations as possible in order to grow personally and spiritually, and believe me, the opportunities to do this are at every turn!"

122

Now mind you, this would be the third man I have shared with at this level of intimacy on the pilgrimage. The first was a young man with whom I had a bromance. Then another was a man I met earlier today who was curious about the bromance. I remained open to his questioning. It was difficult but I was choosing to be uncomfortable versus shutting down and talking about surface things. So I answered all his questions and he accepted me just the way I am. The Universe is bringing me people on the path who probe and prod me and I get to put my money where my mouth is in regard to facing my fears and anxieties.

Facebook, June 12—Drew—
"We can choose to step back into safety or we can choose to step forward into growth. I chose to step forward."—Drew Eric

So this new friend asks the requisite question, "Why, the Camino?" instead of saying my filtered comments, I immediately spat out "I recently divorced my husband of 20 years." Bam, right out in front, I put it right on the table then kept going. "I'm finding myself as a single person, learning and growing" blah blah blah. I, of course, explained how I want to put myself in as many uncomfortable situations as possible.

Then I said, "For example, this conversation is uncomfortable for me. I have no idea how straight men—or anyone for that matter—will feel about my being gay."

He seemed to brush off my comments but I kept talking, nervously.

"I live in a gay city and spend most of my time with gay friends, I'm rarely in a non-gay environment. So coming here on the Camino..."

I start to tear up as I continue, "I never know how safe I am." Crying now... "Look at what happened in Orlando."

He had no idea. I explained through tears about the tragedy in Orlando's Pulse Nightclub. He seemed to understand.

I explained, "We gay people are always concerned about this type of situation, concerned about our safety, how we look, dress and act in public."

I keep crying and talking, "I am now truly realizing the impact this has on my life and how I am outside the gay world. It's scary! I have no safety net. Usually, gays try to signal to each other, at least I do. We're always looking for that little recognition so we can feel safe and not alone."

Now I'm full-on crying, in front of a man I've just met, on a dirt path, in the middle of a wheat field. I'm trying to explain how being in a foreign country away from my safety of Wilton Manors is uncomfortable.

Facebook, June 12—Drew—
"Live in a world free of worry, because one day you will realize you worried too much and wish you had."—Drew Eric

At that moment I put it all together. It's understandable where the fear comes from, where the bigotry comes from, where the, "We are right and you are wrong" comes from. I am from a generation that had to grow up with fear and bigotry, we still are. Look at the reactions to the bathroom situation with transgendered humans beings, it's horrifying.

Here I am emotionally raw and naked. I'm telling this man how much pain is happening in America, in my community, in my neighborhood and on Facebook. A friend from South Florida visiting Ireland posted a picture of a burning candle with a tribute to the gay community in Orlando and I have been seeing them discuss Orlando all over Spanish television.

The world is sad today. I am sad today.

I will continue to grow from this experience. I will continue to talk to men—gay and straight—and tell them my story. Tell them about my life and my reality and I will grow each time I do it.

And perhaps they will too.

I love you Orlando, I love you Wilton Manors, I love you Gay Community. We will all grow together. Land or sea will not keep us apart. I am with you today. You are with me every day. We are not alone in this tragedy.

Love Always Wins ❤ ❤ ❤

#LifeLesson —35 All there is in the world is love and fear. I choose love over fear every day. Love always wins.
Facebook, June 14—Asmus—
Drew, I want to tell you I really enjoyed this post. As a straight man myself sometimes I forget how much of a privilege that can be at times.

Posted on December 14, 2015 by Drew Eric

Chapter 19 Can I be ME while traveling Europe?

"The greatest discovery in life is finding you, the second greatest discovery is being happy with you."—Drew Eric

While I am now preparing for my path to Europe next summer I have chosen to face any and all fears that arise in my life. By overcoming my fears, I will be more prepared to risk everything for the experience of my lifetime. So this is a short story about my fear of looking ridiculous.

Last week I ordered a kilt. I have always wanted one and have often thought how comfortable it would be to wear since jeans, pants and shorts get bunched up and restricting along with warm. So I would say I have always had skirt envy especially in hot summer months.

My kilt arrived this past week and I want to break it in. I had it on around the house and wanted to wear it to the grocery store and a coffee shop to do some writing. Looked in the mirror a dozen times and chickened out.

Today I went to Miami with my brother and his family to see the play "Kinky Boots" which is about a man who has a 100-year-old shoe factory and decides to make Kinky boots for drag queens to save the factory and all the jobs. I went to bed Saturday and woke up Sunday thinking about what to wear with the kilt and if I will wear it at all. I choose to put on a nice pair of pants and a button-down shirt with cufflinks. Boring!

Now, mind you when I saw "Priscilla Queen of the Desert" the musical, there were plenty of boas and fun accessories in the audience. So if I was going to wear a kilt out in public, a play with a drag queen in it would be the right time to do it. But still, I didn't put it on.

While looking in the closet mirror doors at my pants and button down, I saw my favorite jacket with a batik-style pattern. The one I bought at a thrift store when I was 15 years old and have been dragging out every holiday and special occasion since. Hmmm, If I pair the jacket with the kilt then the jacket would be the focus and

125

the kilt would be a cool and necessary accessory. I changed my outfit.

This time, I take a picture and send it to a friend asking if I look too ridiculous to venture out in public. He says I look great and with reluctance, I leave my apartment to join my brother and his family for breakfast prior to the show. I arrive only to find his wife's family present for breakfast since they are attending the play with us. Immediately I hear my ego voice saying, "Great, now you look like the gay brother in a skirt, oh right, you are the gay brother and you are wearing a skirt" This was the wrong outfit to wear. Ugh.

Funny things started to happen. A waiter and a guy on the street complimented my coat. I arrive at the theater and people are staring along with nodding and complimenting me including the ushers. One man asked to introduce me to his family because he liked my artistic style so much. Maybe I don't look too ridiculous for the public? Maybe!

A week ago I executed the "Glitter Beard". I had plans to attend three Christmas parties on that Saturday and thought If I choose to give the glitter beard a try then attending so many parties in one night would make a big sparkle, pun intended.

I went to the store, picked out the colors along with some Elmer's glue and walked to the register. While standing in line, I gave it one last thought in an effort not to waste money on something I might eventually choose not to do. I made the purchase and put my fears aside for the moment.

While getting ready that night I toiled over the decision again. I saw the pictures of other glitter beard's online and thought they made great images. I grew the beard recently and I really don't know if I will have a beard again next year. My last thought was "Do I really want to go out of the house looking this Ridiculous"? I did choose to look that ridiculous and it was a big hit. So much so this past weekend people were expecting me to wear it again.

I guess the glitter beard helped me practice looking ridiculous. When I recognized not wearing the kilt was fear-based I knew then I had to do it and soon since this is who I want to be in the world. Someone who overcomes fears and takes a risk.

I am scared about traveling Europe. Will people like me? Will I be vulnerable enough to walk up to strangers and allow them to see the real ME?

Austin, Texas has a wonderful slogan "Keep Austin Weird". Can I be ME, weird, silly and fun loving? Maybe I can.

Maybe I do look ridiculous in some people's eyes. But more importantly, maybe I like that. I like to find humor in myself and If I can bring humor into situations with what I am wearing then all the better. Laugh with me and or at me. A smile is a smile.

I can be ME and the world won't end.

#LifeLesson —36 Looking ridiculous is so much more fun than being the same as everyone else. Let you be you.
Facebook, December 14—Mike—
Be yourself. Everyone else is taken.
—Sheriann—
"Do more of what makes you sparkle."—unknown

follow my… path

Posted on June 20, 2016 by Drew Eric

Chapter 20 Can I be a man among men?

Facebook, June 18—Drew—
"What I most want I cannot have. What I most want to avoid I must face."—Drew Eric
—This Camino sucks sometimes. Good morning all!

The Camino is teaching me how to be a Man. I have been a gay man all my life and all my life I have been uncomfortable around men. Incoming on the Camino, I am learning how to be a Man. Not a gay man but a man.

You see, I am sensitive, emotional and loving. This is who I am. I never thought I could be myself. I was certain that only gay men are sensitive, emotional and loving. So I show up differently, depending on who I'm with—never dreaming I can be the same person with everyone.

I am meeting men every day who are teaching me how to be a man in this world— a world with the Orlando tragedy at Pulse Nightclub.

Facebook, June 18—Drew—
Every day I have to force myself to tell people I am gay. Every day I cry. Every day I tell men who I really am. Every day I am healing from the pain that is ORLANDO. I cannot hide Me on the Camino.

From the beginning of my Camino I have been coming closer to the point where I find myself today. I came on the Camino scared, alone and confused. What I didn't know is how confused I was about my sexuality. So the first thing I did when I started my Camino is attract confusion with a young man. Hardly a surprise, as confusion attracts confusion.

(As I write this, I have been crying and can't stop as I am overtaken with emotions in these realizations I had no idea were under the surface, now uncovered with rawness)

The confusion I feel has impacted how I relate to other men. I have men in my life that I love dearly—Bill, Bart and John—But with these men, I still held back some of me to suit what I thought was appropriate. Here on the Camino it's different, I want to be more authentic.

Men here are teaching me how to be intimate, caring, to embrace physical touch and to share conversation without discomfort.

I came on the Camino confused, attracting the first Camino relationship based in confusion. We crossed boundaries, had emotional intimacy and talked deeply about life and each other. The nature of the relationship soon became entwined with emotions both plutonic and loving, for either or both of us, I don't really know. Today I now know its ok to love another man, from the heart and this loving transcends sex.

This first Camino relationship taught me to open my heart and trust what happens. My normal tendency is the shutdown, run and/or close off. But every day I chose to work hard at opening my heart and accepting what the Camino offered.

Facebook, June 19—Drew—
Not every night is incredible. But I'm still in Spain so that makes up for it.

Another man walked into my Camino path just days after the Orlando attack. On the Camino we take turns sharing our "Why"— why are you walking the Camino? He told me that he recently came back to the Catholic Church and my anxiety rose. I was feeling unsafe in his presence.

When it was my turn to tell my "Why" I burst into tears right in the middle of the path. Being Brazilian, he hadn't heard about the Pulse Nightclub attack and I told him, through tears of sadness and fear, about how I, and many other gay men, feel unsafe, every day, in the world. It was my Orlando breakdown on the Camino.

I explained how scary it feels to be a gay man in a foreign country without the comfort of my gay community. No one here has my back. No one here is able to step up and defend me if I feel unsafe and vulnerable. Everyone I meet is straight and I, potentially, am alone as a gay man, to defend myself against bigots, religious

129

zealots and anyone else who is uncomfortable with my being a gay man.

He was so warm and kind as we walked the path. Since the day we met, he has continued to give me a big smile when I see him. The last time I saw him he came up behind me with a big, affectionate bear hug. "Who the hell is giving me a big bear hug on the Camino?" I thought

On and on I walked, eventually walking upon two more men. The first question that comes up is about the Orlando attack. I'm like, "Shit, I just can't hide here on the Camino".

So again I launch into my story, my divorce, then the Orlando breakdown, my big fat gay life in general. They were amazingly supportive.

As we shared, I noticed they had an ease with each other, comfortable, relaxed, intimate—it was beautiful to see. They just met and have been walking together only a few days.

Here on the Camino we are all raw, open and unfiltered. Everything is on the table and it's incredible. Regardless of sex, age, country of origin, language—there are no boundaries.

I observed these men over a couple days. They were so in touch with themselves, they were able to be physical with each other while maintaining their masculinity. As one was having shin pain, the other massaged his leg and did some healing work. I hadn't seen two men able to give and receive touch without it being weird or homosexual.

Facebook, June 19—Drew—
Some days I walk alone, some days I don't.

When I was in Pamplona I was amazed at the level of intimacy between men there. They would hold each other while talking, greet each other in an embrace and stay embraced beyond a period that's comfortable for American men. This was the beginning of my heart opening. This was the beginning of me being taught how to be an authentic man.

Facebook, June 19—Drew—
This is how I start my days now. Quiet, alone and in the dark. I have no idea how each day will unfold. I know I will walk my path.

Every day I wake up with these questions that have become like a mantra:
Who shall I meet?
Who shall I talk with?
Who shall I walk with?
Who shall I eat with?
Where will I go?
Where will I sleep?

My mantra keeps my heart open and grounded for all possibilities. This lets me freely walk with no expectations, letting God/Universe shed light on my path, guiding me where I need to be for maximum growth and betterment.

As my path continued, I walked upon another young man. Over a span of six hours together, we opened up and went deep. We laughed, shared and found so many commonalities including being fans of Eckhart Tolle.

Facebook, June 19—Drew—
I met the most amazing man today. We connected on such a deep level. This is crazy. This makes twice on the Camino I have connected so deeply. I am blown away. He is 23. I guess there are no men my age walking or maybe I am really a 23-year-old trapped in a 48-year-old body.

Once I mentioned chakras and energy, all of a sudden everything shifted. We moved from two people sharing a deeply philosophical conversation, then connected energetically, then intuitively into one another's thoughts. This reminded me of the young man I shared time with the first week on the Camino. However this time without the sexual confusing energy between us, our time together was magical.

I was present to the experience the entire time, amazed that this could happen so soon with another man. I began to wonder how many more men I would share with so deeply. I'm learning that I can attract like-minded people willing to go deep and get real with emotions and connections.

I have had this connection with four men now in my life—amazingly two show up this week. All four have been straight men. I was blown away. I couldn't put my finger on why but I knew something was shifting for me.

131

The following day the Universe brought me two more men who blew my mind. They just met three days prior and, wow, they were amazing. They are the inspiration for this final breakthrough.

We talked for perhaps two hours. I have seen them a few times around on the path but never joined them in conversation. One was from South Africa, the second from England.

When they first met me I was wearing the bright pants given to me by the first young man I met here on the Camino. I am wearing a bright aqua long sleeve hoodie for sun protection and my walking stick is decorated with multi-colored Tibetan prayer flags. I am a colorful sight. Feeling so comfortable in my own skin I am letting everything fly, including the flags.

When I saw them again I held up my walking stick and yelled a friendly hello. I knew instantly they were going to be my next "share" on the Camino.

When our pace synced, they kept saying that I am the most colorful person on the Camino. One of the walkers was looking for some words to express how he saw me and finally settled on "Peacocking," then apologized and asked if that's ok to say. I explained I am attempting to be my authentic self—letting my flags fly. This launched us into an unbelievable life-affirming conversation.

Talk about intuitive, their physic powers were off the chart and they were extremely in-touch men, firing on all emotional cylinders. They kept me on my toes, bombarding me with questions about my personal growth and my authentic self. The English man later explained he uses his intuition to ask questions rather than stating what he thinks—a great coaching technique.

He was helping me see what I might not be seeing, just like I do in my coaching conversations. I am always listening for the unsaid, subtle things that go unnoticed by my client. They were so in-tune and called me on all my garbage. They had a followup question to see if I was missing the point. They were drilling me hard. I loved it. These are guys I could hang with all the time.

Let me remind you that this connection is new and yet they have formed a relationship that is intimate, intelligent and deeply spiritual. The Universe provided me with a dream pair of men.

Interestingly, they were the first people I met on the Camino who said they are "celebrating life" not searching for answers. Everyone else, and I mean everyone I've encountered, is in a transition from one thing to another and came on this path to discover something about themselves, but not them. This must have a positive impact on their relationship and how they were able to form such a deep bond and ease.

They were familiar with "A Course In Miracles," and Eckhart Tolle's "A New Earth" along with Brene Brown's books, all my bibles of spirituality. They had their shit together, I loved it, I was in awe. After a couple of hours, I felt it was time to move forward and leave them for some of my own personal reflection time.

I was now processing all I learned from all the men on my path, assembling together the pieces of my pilgrimage. My pace was quickening, I felt my energy rising and realizing something was shifting in me and I was patiently waiting to see what would come forward.

Then it hit me, with tears flowing, I stopped dead on the path. All these men have been teaching me, showing me how to be a man in the world. Not a straight man or a gay man but a man that is emotional, in-touch and able to feel deeply. They modeled men not threatened by their own sensitivity but men willing to share themselves with other men.

All I see in America are sports guys, dudes, kids and men who are detached and unemotional. However here on the Camino, and in Europe, I am seeing an inspiring level of intimacy and connectedness. Maybe it has been in America and I just hadn't noticed.

They are teaching me that it's ok to be myself. They are showing me I am not alone and there are other men in this world who are sensitive, emotional like me who aren't gay or bisexual. They are masculine men in touch with their feminine side and completely comfortable with themselves, complete with their duality.

Best of all, they are showing me that when I put out loving energy into the world, I will attract other people like me. I don't have to worry or fear anything, anymore. I can be my authentic self and the people who are attracted to my energy, my colors, and my flags will find me.

Facebook, June 19—Drew—
"Teach only love, for that is what you are."— A Course In Miracles

I am learning for the first time how it feels to be a man-not a gay man or an old man or a young man—but an authentic man.

From this point forward I will work hard at not labeling people, no more sexual identity, religions, no more separations. We are all one. We are all just people learning to grow and be better individuals in a confusing and sometimes scary world.

I am choosing to be a man. I am manning up and letting my flags fly.

I can do this; I can be myself in a world of MEN.

#LifeLesson —36 Own your authenticity. If you are a sensitive, loving, kind, affectionate person then own it and show up for everyone just how you are. The rewards are great.
Facebook, June 14—Drew—
#ActOfKindness —7 To all the men that have crossed my path who have received me with kindness, respect and love. Your tutelage on how to be a man in this world has been deeply profound and an unexpected, rewarding privilege to receive. I knew not, how much I need you men on my path. I knew not, how deeply wounded I was. I thank you for your kindness and support and just being you. Especially my Brazilian friend who hugged me when I was balling, that day in Spain, in the middle of the wheat field, while walking the Camino. You, my friend, are a great man. You showed me how a man can extend love to another man, comfortably for all. I thank you all.
Facebook, June 19—Wendy—

134

Love all of this, Drew, but your second to last sentence hit home. "We are all just people learning to grow and be better individuals in a confusing sometimes scary world." So perfect. Thank you.
  —Drew—
Love You... It's so nice to hear one of my lines back. How cool...
  —Wendy—
This journey is for you but you are also touching many lives near and far.
  —Kimberly—
That has been my mantra this week in the aftermath of Orlando! Thank you for sharing your story Drew!
  —Kelly—
I can't even begin to tell you how moving your writings are! Every day I check to see what you've shared. It's like a wonderfully inspiring novel that I just can't wait for morning to read the next chapter. You are truly making us all think and reflect.
  —Ann—
I have walked with you since day one... And can't wait until your morning shadow peeks through my screen... Sending you finally the Man... Love and peace...
  —Drew—
That touched me, thanks...
  —Carlos—
Such an amazing read! I keep checking on you because thru you I am seeing the world, even thou I've been there, we have to live it to learn it! I just can't stop reading, your journey is so powerful and transformational! Thanks for sharing and don't stop... Keep going... I am traveling with you in every word you write! 😊
  —Rosa—
I am so happy for you Drew, The Camino gives us exactly what we need at exactly the right time. Keep enjoying your Camino and keep us posted. That was a beautiful read, much love and light your way my friend 🌁
  —David—
Beautiful! I've been struggling with the same issues all my life. Thank you for sharing your journey with us Drew! 🙏
  —Maria—

Wow MAN! This is such an amazing writing from the heart, your Heart which is full of love and wisdom. It's a pleasure to read this my friend! 👏 ✨ 💕

—Daphne—

Raw, unfiltered and beautiful. More men should be like you...Recognize the need for growth, for introspection, realize that they have much work to do... Choose a "Camino" to pave the way to a better understanding of their heart and soul. Thanks for sharing your journey. Sending love, light and blessings to stay safe for the rest of the Way!

—Richard—

Looking forward to bumping into you and giving you a MAN hug! Reading your thesis, "Yes! I Am A Man" made me aware of my questions, thoughts, fears, doubts and concerns. I experienced the same transition—albeit on a much smaller scale—was my participation in 'Direct Centering' in NYC in 1984. Gay, straight, bi, etc., we are all men in the universe! Keep writing, breathing, laughing, crying, touching, hugging, kissing and being who you are—a wise man for all times! Love, Richard

—David—

May I just offer that those that have been trained to be all knowing often are the ones unwilling to learn or listen beyond what they already think they know. It sounds like you have broken free of that mold, allowing yourself to break down those walls and be willing to learn even more (even when it might be painful or prove to yourself you never really knew). How liberating!

—Caresse—

What beautiful words Drew. 🖤 🖤 🖤 *Welcome to you're Awakening. When you return to Florida, stay in that energy and you will attract like-minded souls. I am one.*

—Erick—

Powerful and beautiful. Thank you for taking the time to share with us about this incredible journey. And thank you for opening up and sharing your emotions with us. It's as if you're shedding those things that no longer serve you. Better yet — expanding your awareness. Keep writing brother.

—Jeanne—

Raw, real and radically authentic. You are changing lives on the path to your own reality of truth and self-love.

—Ayal—

How wonderful for you. Learning to love another man is a lesson that we as a gay man are not taught. We confuse passion and physical attraction as love. Until you love another man without the sexual component, you don't know how to love a man, and loving yourself. I am so happy for you for discovering your self. You flaunt your peacock feathers as bright and as brilliant as you want them to be. You earned them. Sending you big hugs and love from the old hood.

—Drew—

I'm so touched, thanks Ayal.

—Ayal—

I am so proud of you. There are so many things I want to say and talk to you about, but this is not the place or the right format. When we meet, until then I am following your growth and share your journey from afar.

—Sarah—

Being a "man" means so many different things to different people. I'm so happy for you that you are learning what being a man truly means to you.

—Elizabeth—

When the student is ready, the teacher will appear. You are ready Drew to be the person you were created to be. Love hearing about your journey! Thanks so much for sharing!

—Allie—

You are such an inspiration! Thank you so much for sharing… You are courageous!

Posted on June 25, 2016 by Drew Eric

Chapter 21 Can I create a Camino Family?

Facebook, June 21—Drew—
By the way, I am halfway complete with the Camino as of today.
390 kilometers to go. 245 miles ish. I love walking. I love you all.

Meeting my Band-of-Brothers. The Camino is a funny place. Relationships start; they burn hot and can have a life-span of a few minutes or a few days. In this world of fast-paced connecting, we have what has affectionately been coined "The Camino Family" which constitutes a group of individuals walking together and staying together for whatever time they last.

I haven't seen very many of these families last much longer than eight days. My first Camino family lasted that long. My second and third Camino family lasted even less. Enter family four.

What I've learned on this journey has been based on attaching, separating and learning how to be ok with what is. We learned to honor our individual needs and to walk together in a way that best supports us all. It is an enlightening experience to pay close attention to energy and subtle body language.

I came up with this explanation and many fellow pilgrims agreed. The Camino is about 30 days in length. If you equate that to the length of the relationships you have here on the Camino then one day equals one year, ten days equals ten years. (A Camino flip on dog years!)

For shorter encounters, six hours might equal six days and one hour could be an entire day in the real world.

So, imagine 30 years of your life and the people who will impact you during that time. Imagine meeting them all in a day, a week or a month. This is a lifetime of learning, meeting and growing at warp speed.

So when I say my Band-of-Brothers is still walking together after so many days, that's quite an accomplishment.

I met one of my brothers the day I climbed the mountain. He was staying in my albergue. We didn't talk much at all. He is from Australia and currently lives in England. I will call him the Aussie. I learned that the Aussie is two months younger than I am, and it's

138

a kick to remind him of that. He is walking with a coworker, originally from Canada.

This past week I was feeling pretty sad and lonely. It was then that I met another brother from Sweden. He turned in his chair and started talking to me in his slight Swedish accent. On the attractive scale he is pretty damn adorable and is in his mid-20s. I will call him the Swede. I certainly didn't mind chatting with him even though my feeling of worthiness was at a low and I was feeling a little afraid of him.

I joined him at the table for conversation just before he received a phone call. I moved back to my writing on the lawn, still feeling sad. Eventually, I realized the only person isolating was me. It was time to take action.

I got up, put my computer away and looked in the dining area to see who was around. The Swede, Aussie and his coworker were in conversation at a table. A lovely woman joined us completing our new group of friends. We spent the next five hours talking, drinking and eating, all without getting up from the table. It was a special evening.

The Swede was sitting across from me and was very attentive throughout the evening, making long eye contact with me while we talked. I could clearly see we had a connection and would probably spend some time together in the next few days.

As it turned out we were all sharing a room and the Swede seemed quite interested in me as he kept up a conversation in between teeth brushing and getting ready for bed. Now my intuition was telling me he wanted to walk with me tomorrow.

Facebook, June 23–Drew—
Good morning world, hello from the other side. No shadow photo yet, soon…

Walking with someone is essentially going on a first date here on the Camino. If you walk for more than an hour that means the date has been going well. You really don't know what's going to happen. It could end in an hour, last many hours or continue for days.

I wake up every morning not knowing who I will walk with, meet, where I will stay or how fast I will walk. Everything is up in the air, which is exciting and scary at the same time.

139

Facebook, June 23—Drew—
Because of my confusion and chasing the popular kids, which I no longer am, I got a cold. Please send me healing energy. It's very mild so no worries.

On this morning I woke up with the realization I was chasing the popular kids—a recurring theme. It was very heavy on my heart and I could tell something was about to happen for me, including a shift in perception. I could feel my heart racing with the heaviness.

At 5:30 a.m. my alarm went off. I was getting ready but the Swede was still sleeping. I wanted to run out of the albergue, but I had this intuition he really wanted to walk with me. I was torn, I had something to process and he was still sleeping. So I reach over to his bunk and tapped his foot figuring if he wakes and starts the morning process then maybe we will walk, but I'm not counting on it.

My foot tapping worked, he rises and starts slowly buzzing about his stuff. His belongings appear to be everywhere as he begins packing them up. In other words, to me, he was a typical 20-something trying to get ready. I saw he wasn't moving fast enough and I chose to leave. I didn't see him before I left and felt bad because I just really knew he was reaching out for connection.

I took off, out the door, on my way in the dark of early morning. Still not knowing who I would walk with, who I would see or where I would sleep and still trying to figure out what the hell was going on in my head about the popular kids. I eventually had my realization and cried, leaving me raw and emotional.

I came across a beautiful bridge with pollen fluff on the ground that looked like summer snow. The light was just coming over the mountain. Across an amazing stone bridge was a tiny home with unusual metal furniture, artwork and benches. It was a beautiful setting to do some writing.

I also thought I would wait for the Swede to catch up. I was ready to spend some time walking with him after having an "aha moment" during my writing. Halfway into my writing he walked up and said, "I was looking for you this morning but I didn't find you." I replied and said, "Yeah, I know you were looking for me. That's why I am waiting here so we could walk together." He seemed surprised and pleased. It was several days later when he told me about some girl accidentally hitting his foot that morning. I told him it was me waking him up. He had no idea and was tickled it was me.

I closed my computer and we walked on. Now remember, most pilgrims go deep and vulnerable in a matter of seconds. This was no different, we immediately jumped in.

Perhaps an hour in, I said something that really hit home for him. So much so he needed to stop walking for a second. I saw he needed a minute so I told him I would walk ahead and see him in a bit. When this happens you never know if you will walk again or not. The Camino is that unpredictable.

When I found a place to pause again he walked up with the Aussie from the night before and the three of us walked the rest of the day, sharing and opening up about ourselves and our lives—my favorite conversations.

The Aussie was a bit angry, shut down and closed off. He barely smiled but was willing to walk with us. The Swede was full of stories about Sweden. He continually talked about Sweden, it was a hoot. Like white noise, I can still hear his accent in the background of my Camino, I loved the sound of his accent, I wanted to record it so I could play it later and find peace in the tones.

We spent that first day together and I could feel a real connection between us. Not really sure what would unfold but I was willing to stick this out and go for the ride. By now, I have grown quite accustomed to being in the company of men on the Camino so I wasn't having an issue with letting my flags fly and being myself.

Actually, I started to realize that I am attracting these men. They both seemed sensitive and emotional and somewhat giving. I could see the Aussie was struggling with opening up but I am the type of person who doesn't really let someone get too comfortable in their comfort zone. I push them right out of it with my coaching ways.

After another long day of walking we began a tradition of drinking beer for the electrolytes (after marathons they give out beer for that exact reason). During our first full day, I have pushed buttons, made them leave their comfort zone and forced a deep conversation about themselves, their lives and surprising me, they still stuck around for more.

That is an amazing feat. When I get going with my coaching/spirituality conversation, it can be overwhelming for some people. I could see I was pushing them and they both loved it. I even set

141

some ground rules for our discussions and they were happy to oblige.

- You can't use the word "but" as in "yes but".
- You can't use the word "sorry".
- You don't have to answer a question right away, you can defer for a later time.
- You must be open for possibilities, not closed to new ways of thinking.
- It's your Camino you do what you need on your Camino.
- "It's your Camino, NAMASTE" a way to keep a little humor in our conversations. (Sidebar: In the Whole foods parking lot, Namaste can have a slightly different meaning. That was my parking spot, NAMASTE. That was the last grocery cart NAMASTE. You're not going to put your cart back, NAMASTE! Are you getting the meaning? I believe there is a youtube or something).

I was astounded that they enjoyed the rules. When we talked and were all open, it was a beautiful experience as we were open all the time.

We established patterns like purchasing supplies after a long day walking to make sure we had a pre-dinner beer and wine for our long conversations.

After our second day of walking I saw a young man sitting alone on the front stoop of the albergue. He looked as if he wanted a hug. So I asked him to join us for pre-dinner wine and he accepted. That small invitation lasted far longer then we all expected.

"I want a hug" is from Germany so I will call him the German. His English sounds pretty good but you can tell he gets a bit lost if we speak too fast. I never expected him to stay long because of the language barrier and there are lots of Germans on the Camino for him to hang with.

The German is a little bear type kid whom you want to constantly squeeze or hug or both. He is so kind he exudes a loving presence out of every cell in his body.

I literally saw him pick up three snails off the road and move them to the grass on the opposite side. I doubted that he'd ever get to Santiago if he picked up every snail on the way. He even picked up a couple of worms and moved them. He told me once, "I don't want it too easy for the birds to get their food. It is impor-

142

tant for the birds to exercise while hunting." (His words, no kidding.)

Facebook, June 23—Drew—
I don't know what's happening but I like it.

So let's review who the characters are...

The Swede is super cute, great accent and a bit flirty to anyone around him. He is flirty, confident and himself all at the same time —a real charmer who likes to push your buttons and boundaries. You can see he is sensitive, emotional and open.

This would be the second person I encountered on the Camino with those traits and I had fallen in love with the first one. But this time I was more present to this type of behavior and knew not to get sucked into the trap of his allure.

The German was clearly sensitive, open and highly emotional with a loving manner you don't see in many men or people in general—just a bear of a boy.

The Aussie was a different story. I couldn't figure out why he was there and walking with us. I wasn't sure if he was interested in conversation, being emotionally open or just enjoying the energy and flirting tension that could be thrown about in our new boundary-less environment.

He was angry and pretty closed down when I met him. He was struggling with his Camino and traveling with a work colleague. Who wouldn't have a difficult time traveling with a work colleague? So I sat back and waited to see just what the Aussie wanted to get from our new Band-of-Brothers.

I am highly emotional, my sensitivity and intuition are off the charts. I just had my heart opened on the Camino so I was ready for anything the Camino was going to bring forth. I was so ready and prepared for these guys to walk onto my path at just the right time.

My belief system is, "Every conversation and experience has a benefit and a purpose." I believed we were forming a Camino family that would serve a purpose for each of us. I was excited to see where it would go and what the lessons would be.

Facebook, July 21—Drew—
"You need to associate with people that inspire you, people that challenge you to rise higher, people that make you better. Don't

143

waste your valuable time with people that are not adding to your growth. Your destiny is too important."—Joel Osteen

Clearly I can attract sexual tension as seen earlier on the Camino. I am also attracting emotional, sensitive, loving and kind individuals. This makes me really happy. All these men seemed to be comfortable with themselves, each other and me. I have never felt this level of comfort before with other men. In three days time (three years on the Camino) I felt at home. I felt a calmness wash over me, a peacefulness. I felt they had my back and I didn't have to be afraid any longer, especially in the wake of the Orlando tragedy.

Facebook, June 21—Drew—
I am loving myself so fiercely right now

On the second day we walked, I was just a little unsure about the Swede because he seemed a bit snappy during the day. This turned out to be a benefit since a great lesson unfolded for me. I pulled back a bit in an effort to give him space since I know I can be a bit overwhelming at times.

On the Camino you can have a relationship so intense that it feels like a Roman candle shooting high into the sky. Once a Roman candle burns out, it's done. I didn't want this new Band-of-Brothers to burn out so fast.

On that second day I decided not to shine so brightly in an effort to keep from igniting the Roman candle. It seemed to work because none of us tired from being together. So much so we would walk and talk all day then grab some beers and wine and drink and talk till bedtime. Our beds were even in close proximity to each other. Then we would wake up and repeat, day after day. It was like summer camp for all us boys; it was like a family, a Band-of-Brothers

#LifeLesson —37 Sometimes a little quiet time is saying so much more.

The Aussie, slowly but surely, started to soften. He started to smile. Ever so slowly he showed signs of opening up. I kept pushing him with questions and wouldn't let his answers be surface ones. I wanted to really hear the truth from him, he hated/loved it.

144

He had nowhere to hide and wasn't interested in walking away; he stood there, clearly outside his comfort zone and grew.

One special morning we were walking to the big cross. Here is where pilgrims leave their burdens. The idea is to bring a rock from home that represents our life burdens and leave it at the base of the cross. This is a particularly emotionally difficult part of the path. We were all emotional and had feelings of foreboding about the experience that morning. Eventually we split up and arrived at the cross, claiming our own space.

However, prior to our splitting up, I started to cry about my burdens, about losing my mom and my divorce this past year. On my mother's nightstand, when she transitioned, was a baby Jesus from a miniature nativity scene. I have held it all these years. When I was moving out of my apartment, someone told me to bring one thing with me from home. Then said, "I'd know what item to take when I saw it". When I packed and found the baby Jesus I knew it was the one item to take with me. I also had a rock from the garden at my first apartment as a single man. I was now choosing to leave both burdens at the cross.

The Swede saw me getting choked up and started to reassure me it would be all right. He told me to go ahead and feel. I am not sure all he said but it was working. I cried harder as we walked. It was like he was channeling my mother.

Then he surprised me by telling me to forgive my mother, to let it all go. I was in full blown tears; he was bringing up pain that I needed to get out. Eventually the crying slowed along with the talking. We eased back into our own worlds and continued getting closer to the cross.

When it was my turn to find the cross, I climbed the rocks on its base that were left by other pilgrims. I found the spot and placed my mother's baby Jesus and my divorce rock next to a lovely bracelet and a flat rock with the date on it written in chalk. I took a picture through my tears and felt the emotion of the experience.

In sharing our emotional rawness, I showed the Aussie the picture of my baby Jesus and the rock, he was flabbergasted. Without knowing it, I placed my burdens against his rock. We both have pictures of the same spot. We were stunned how divine intervention played its part on bringing our burdens to the exact spot —no coincidence there.

Facebook, June 23—Drew—

145

"Pictures, places, memories, moments, are all so priceless. I remember them with laughter in my heart and tears in my eyes."—Drew Eric

My Band-of-Brothers and I had such an ease with each other we never once questioned anyone's feelings, emotions or actions. It was like we had a psychic connection and we understood. We would walk separate, take a different pace then come back together with ease and love. When someone would slow a bit or walk ahead we all knew that they were taking the reflection time and the personal space they needed. We were all attached to the flow of the Camino and one another's flow, effortless, smooth, loving and beautiful.

Facebook, June 24—Drew—
"Meaningful conversations enrich your life far more than gold in your pockets."—Drew Eric

The German required the most space. He floated in and out all the time. He would be with us one minute, we would look back, and he is furrowing for critters along the path. He loved the animals of the Camino, truly loved them. That was his Camino.

He also talked with his hands incessantly. He held them close to his head and shook them about, however his hands didn't further any conversation, they just shook about. It was totally awesome to watch his boyish energy and loving charm. I could sit and look at him all day, just watching him talk, or sitting quietly. He often caught me looking at him and would instinctively know how much I cared for him—and I could feel his affection for me. He was the most loving individual I met on the Camino. I love him and he loves me.

Facebook, June 24—Drew—
#ActOfKindness —8 He picks up snails on the road and puts them in the grass. I saw this three times. He is always looking at flowers and searching for little critters. He requires you to share his food. We drank each other's wine, had endless conversations and he was always there for me if I ever needed or wanted anything. We most often would split groceries and carry each other's food. And always looks like he wants to hug you. This is how a man should

146

be, kind, warm and loving. He is German and I love him. Thank you my friend for being your loving self.
—Jay—
When you come back, (if you come back) remember these lessons learned…

The Swede has such charisma and you could feel his loving energy. Sometimes I felt it a little too much. He could use a little practice dialing some of that energy down a bit.

Luckily now, I was better prepared for intoxicating young men and I was able to resist this one's charms. I was able to accept him for who he is and I did love him, in a safe way, for him and me. He is the most charismatic loving person on the Camino.

Facebook, June 24—Drew—
#ActOfKindness —9 He is emotional, vulnerable and kind. He exudes love in every direction, always talking, always sharing, always looking for connecting. We laughed and shared, made jokes and got drunk several times, it was so much fun. He is so free with his love which is intoxicating. We shared wine, beer, food, money all my needs are met whenever we are together. I thank you for all the gifts and quality time you gave me. You are so kind and giving of yourself, so inclusive. I will always cherish your endless stories of home. He is from Sweden and I love him and he loves me.
—Ray—
With everyone you meet, they have a story of their own, then you become a part of their story forever. That's cool…

The Aussie is the most transformed individual I met. He went from a caterpillar to a beautiful schmetterling (the German word for butterfly). He now freely uses the word love and openly gives hugs. On those first few days he described his home life as nice, pleasant, and good. Now, he uses expressions like "fucking fantastic," "incredibly cool" and" totally awesome." The words he uses now have passion in them. The man has gotten way sexier, happier and has a bounce in his step when he walks. He appears so fucking happy to be alive and walking the Camino. I am sure there is no other place in the world he would rather be than here, with us, in Spain.

I once asked him a question and he answered with, "That was nice" I shot back with, "just nice? That's the best you can do?"

Several days later after an in-depth share I said, "That was a nice exchange, thanks." He looked me dead in the eye and shot back, "NICE?" Wow, the student becomes the teacher.

Facebook, June 24—Drew—
#ActOfKindness —10 My younger brother. He smiles and I see the boy he tries to hide. I have watched him be reborn from a caterpillar to the loving soul he shows off today, exuberant with a boyish energy. Today, he is the most passionate man I have met on the Camino. With our endless conversations we shared our souls. He grew to be a person I could lean on and always be frank with. One day he even loaned me money and he said, that is a huge deal for him. I thank you my brother from another mother. I will always cherish our friendship and all the gifts you gave me. He is from Australia and I love him and he loves me.
—Ray—
Just when the caterpillar thought the world was over, it became a butterfly…
#LifeLesson —38 Masculinity is defined as loving, caring, sharing and kindness.
–Mark—
Cannot wait to read your book… If you could only see your journey from this side. Emotional-Raw-Masculine-Real… Your shadow will always be with you.
—Drew—
Today is a good day. Last night over wine we discussed a plan we all agreed upon. The five of us would get up at 5:15 a.m. and walk early into Leon, Spain. Spend a long day in Leon at a nice albergue, then leave a little late the next day. Which means we will be spending the day together exploring Leon. It was a relaxed walk and short. The company was perfect. These are good men. We walk well together. We fit well together. Today is a good day with my Band-of-Brothers.
—Erik—
Wow! Awesome my friend. The frame in which you see and experience all others will never be the same. The power of traveling…

When we were together in Leon we had a blast. We were tired and wandered around the city trying to figure out what we wanted to see and do. Several ideas were thrown about with no real interest. We finally ended up near the Leon cathedral and I said, "Ok, it would appear all we really want to do is find a bar, sit, drink and talk more. So let's make a circle around the cathedral, completing our sightseeing, then we can sit in a bar somewhere for the rest of the night." That made everyone happy.

After the fourth day together I made a decision. With all I've learned up until now about men and how to be comfortable with them, I decided not to withhold anything about me, including my need for physical touch and expression. Yes, I was going to get physical with these men and they were going to like it. I wasn't going to hide my affection for them, I was going to touch them and kiss them in a way that is acceptable for them, mostly.

I decided I was going to wake them up with kisses and that's just what I did. I even told them what my plan was after our walk, over electrolytes—beers. We talked about everything. I talked about my blog, everything I'd learned thus far and falling in love with a boy on the Camino. I even shared what the men of the Camino, including them, are teaching me. I told them everything and they didn't walk away. I felt their love all the time.

The next day the Swede and German were still sleeping and I sat on the Swede's bed and rubbed his arm till he was awake and then gave him a kiss on the forehead. He smiled and laughed as I got up. I went to German's bed and rubbed his arm till he woke up with a big grin on his face. Pure love. So I got up higher and smooched on him all over his forehead as he giggled and squiggled like a boy. They both loved it. Weeks later I finally gave the Aussie his kiss when I felt he was ready for it. He accepted it with a smile. Good men they are.

We even had a guest walk with us for a few days. I will call him Atlanta. He was a very kind man, great smile, big heart. He was lying in his bunk snuggled in his sleeping bag so nicely. I just walked over to him and kissed his forehead as I left the room. I kissed him before any of the others. All he said was, "He is a good guy, that Drew." Don't ask me why I felt I could kiss his forehead, I just did it on instinct.

Facebook, June 25—Drew—
Having lunch and beers with my Band-of-Brothers, I love these guys, good men.
—Ken—
Adventures make lifelong friends, keep it up, u inspire me. My dad told me when we lived in Germany to remember everybody u meet, the things u see, the feelings u have, it may be the only chance u have in life to experience them. Treasure them. Glad u are, be safe, have fun. That was 1975 and I remember everything, life is good.

When you're walking as a group you figure out who is the strongest and weakest and you make adjustments according. Luckily the Swede with his bad knees kept himself medicated and was very interested in walking our slightly faster pace. The only one with a deadline to leave was the Swede who was as invested in arriving in Santiago on a timely basis as the rest of us were.

After six days of walking we had a genuine rhythm that was working really well. The four of us tended to keep up in the front while the Aussie's coworker with his blistered feet, tended to take his time a bit more and walk in the rear.

Facebook, June 25—Drew—
I used to wake up not knowing who I would meet, where I would go or who I would talk to. I don't anymore. Now I know. I love these boys and they love me. And I'm proud to say, I am the oldest. LOL.
—Ann—
Drew…You've come a long way from that scared boy who left Wilton Manors… You're now a Camino Man in Spain… Amazing Journey… I am loving every minute watching you grow…

On the Camino groups form and fall apart all because of walking rhythm. You could really love your Camino family but if their

Camino rhythm isn't jiving with yours, then you need to let them go. It's their Camino, Namaste!

However, we had been working really hard on our rhythm, pace, honoring the need for individual quiet time and the ability to talk endlessly with each other. It was a magical exchange.

On the seventh day, our rhythm was interrupted...

Posted on June 29, 2016 by Drew Eric

Chapter 22 Can I be my best self?

Facebook, June 26—Drew—
We have a new guest in our midst.

We had another amazing walk on day seven. Everything was perfect. The five of us were in sync with rhythm, conversation, quiet time and walking speed. What could happen to break this apart?

That night Boise walked into our lives causing a shift. We transitioned from what was to what it would be. Our honeymoon stage was over. A new reality started that night.

She sat with us just before dinner. She was very pretty and similar in age to the Swede and the German. She was friendly, confident and easily shot back some quick one-liners. She seemed as if she would be a good fit and meld well with our established rhythm. Her city of origin is Boise, Idaho.

She told us it was her plan to finish the Camino in ten days and make her flight connections. I, of course, understood the Camino much clearer than she did and knew her plan would never work. The Camino has its own plan for finishing. Try as you might, you cannot fight the Camino and win.

Over dinner, drinks and conversation I could see her connecting with the charming Swede. I said no less than six times, "Don't fall under his allure and charm, it's intoxicating". Clearly I must have been having an intuition of some kind.

I invited her to walk with us knowing she might not be able to keep up since most new walkers get blisters and have leg problems. We all had them in our first few days.

Sure enough the next day, her painful blisters slowed her pace. The Swede chose to walk more slowly matching her pace while the rest of us walked at our normal rhythm.

We could feel the connection separating with one of our own like a long tether about to snap. I observed, all day, a shift in the energy flow from us, towards her. At one point even the Aussie asked me, "Why am I feeling jealous?"

I explained to him that it will be fine and all will work out in the end. He loves us and he has our back. There's nothing to worry about because of the love and care we all share for each other."

That day when we arrived in town, we ventured out for lunch and electrolytes (beer).   During lunch we talked. However this time, our rather liberal views were in conflict with her conservative point of view.

She brought up her interest in attending a bullfight which surprised us all. None of us felt comfortable with the treatment of the animals in such a manner. Remember the snail loving German!

It was during this lunch I began to realize Boise might not be a good fit for our Band-of-Brothers. My Camino has been filled with loving individuals that I have chosen to walk with. Now I was faced with walking in the company of someone whose opposing views make me uncomfortable. Having different views wasn't the only problem.

We make it to the hostel later in the day and check in. Now we are a bit offended, jealous and disappointed she is walking with us and changing the flow of the group we have worked so hard to develop. We felt like our brother was slipping away from us.

We can clearly see that the Swede and Boise have a "connection." Their chemistry is palpable. What most concerns us about their connection is how the Swede's girlfriend will feel about his connecting with another woman on the Camino. My concerns about this situation run deep because I care for all my brothers.

Facebook, June 26— Ann—
Interesting situation... All I can say is if the Swede and Boise hook-up the Swede's girlfriend will start to cause drama. That is NOT what any of you need because indeed you have formed a great Band-of-Brothers... I'm afraid that you may have to walk away from the Swede if this happens... It will disrupt your harmony. This will definitely affect everyone involved... If this should happen, walk away from the drama... You have worked too hard for the Swede to disrupt these connections... Too bad Boise stepped in...

That evening, while the Swede and Boise were taking a nap, the Aussie, the German and I planned our walk into Santiago— how long it will take, how many days and miles and what our plans are when we arrive. We decide to average 20-24 Kilometers a day and not rush ourselves, arriving on a Friday. The German wants to walk onto Finisterre (The end of the earth) while the Aussie has a flight on Sunday. I am open, with a flight on Tuesday, and have no rush.

We decide to get in early on Friday and spend Saturday together. Sunday we would all go our separate ways after two days of relaxing and drinking together in Santiago. Our plan was set. All we had to do was let the Swede know to see if he is on the same page.

The next day we walk and, in general, the familiar energy connection was evident between the Swede and Boise, although today they seem to be even closer and further separated from us. This feeling leaves a break in the circle, our connectedness.

Later in the day we checked into the albergue. Once checked in they showed us the dorm. The Swede picks his bed first. The bunks all around him are open and we each take one surrounding him, leaving no room for Boise to be near him. I am sure it was just a coincidence. It would appear we were feeling a bit protective of him since we all sensed the potential impact this could have on his relationship back in Sweden.

When Boise approached us and asked me if the bunk next to the Swede was open, I said no it was mine and pointed out the bunk across from us was open. With a sad face and turndown eyes, she took the further bunk. I felt I might have been a little harsh, I wasn't really sure what to do, I was going on instinct, as we all were.

Facebook, June 26—Drew—
Practice the Pause…
Pause before judging,
Pause before assuming,
Pause before accusing,
Pause whenever you're about to react harshly, and you'll avoid doing and saying things you'll later regret.—Lori Deschene

As drinks and dinner progressed the two of them all but ignored the rest of us and were giggling and talking with each other. We were all getting very uncomfortable. I even overheard her ask him to "move bunks". My concerns grew by the moment.

On and on they giggled, touched and chatted. The sexual tension was filling the room. Remember, he was giving me/us the same flirty energy just a few days ago. It appears to be one of the tools he uses to win people over, being charismatic, flirting and sending sexual energy in all directions. Now I am witnessing his sending that energy to a woman that isn't his girlfriend.

I needed a break from this, in walks a homosexual, I assume, my Prince in bright clothing. The Brit was sitting at a table behind me. I noticed him and his friends during drinks. It peaked my interest since it had been almost three weeks since I had a conversation with another gay man. So I jumped up and entered a conversation with the Brit and his friends. It went well.

Now I am jumping back and forth between two groups, two tables and making new connections with some Brits. I like them and they seem to like me. What a joy it is to flirt with a boy. It's been so long since I have had the opportunity since everyone I have met for the last two weeks or more has been straight.

My other table of brothers and the guest from Boise weren't getting along so well, apparently Boise was over sharing her conservative views again upsetting the rest of the men.

Boise and the Swede finally left the table and went to bed earlier than the rest of us. The Brit's girlfriends went off to bed leaving us alone to get to know each other a bit better. My Band-of-Brothers joined the two of us for the tail end of the evening before leaving for bed.

I was happy to see my brothers show an interest in my new friend. I felt so loved when they both came over to join us for conversation. It was a gesture of kindness that I noticed and appreciated. I felt worthy of their friendship because they were interested in my wellbeing and my new friend.

We finished up since the Brit needed to head back to his albergue before curfew; they set a door closing time, out of respect for the sleeping pilgrims.

When he left I mentioned to my brothers what I overheard about the Swede switching bunks—to be closer to Boise. The German couldn't understand how this could be happening. The Aussie shared with me his discomfort with all Boise's oversharing. We were placing bets whether the Swede would actually have moved. I also heard him say at one point he liked to be the little-spoon while sleeping.

In this albergue, the bunk beds were side by side putting two beds up against each other. This was not a common practice in the albergue's but it was here.

When we went into the dorm, he had moved and was the little-spoon, asleep on the shared bunk. Holy crap, we were stunned, upset and concerned.

I woke the next day with an overwhelming foreboding feeling. I was uncomfortable with the changes in our group and I wanted to do something to restore what we once had. I was afraid of losing the connections we worked so hard to develop. And, I was concerned for our brother's relationship with his girlfriend, even if he didn't appear concerned.

The German couldn't understand how he could be spooning with a woman that wasn't his girlfriend and he was visibly upset. The Aussie was feeling rejected and a little jealous that she was pulling his attention away from us.

I asked the Aussie if I should talk to the Swede or her. He said to talk to him, so that's what I did. I didn't know what to say or how I was feeling really. We were all feeling conflicted and didn't know where this was headed. I could be overstepping my bounds. I could be doing the right thing looking out for the Swede's best interest. I could be screwing up everything. I really didn't know. I decided to stick with honesty.

I found the Swede and asked if we could speak and he agreed, appearing a bit confused. I didn't want to come right out and ask his intentions with Idaho or remind him of his girlfriend at home. I chose to discuss the matter in a different way since it was none of my business what his intentions were. This could be a regular thing for him, I really don't know.

I explained how we were feeling uncomfortable in her presence since she was excluding us from her conversations and focusing all her attention on him. In addition, some of her conversations when she does speak to us are her positive views on bullfights, and other conservative beliefs, all deepening our discomfort.

Our pace has been pretty steady now for several days. With her being a new walker with new blisters, she seems to be lagging, making it difficult for the rest of us to keep our pace. "Do you want to walk with her or us as she doesn't seem to be working for us as a friend or a walking companion—unless she wants to walk with us and be more inclusive with our group?"

I was not being my best self, I admit this. I was trying to save our connection, however the connection was already dwindling, I see now. Our group had changed with the new member and it was never going back to the easy flow it once had. I did what was best for me and that was to be honest about my feelings. I didn't want my Camino to be impacted negatively by their budding relationship. I gave him the choice to go and have his fun and then come back. However, he wanted to stay and walk with us.

He seemed a bit confused by the exchange, so when I saw him trying to explain it to her and struggling, I stepped up and joined in their conversation. I explained what I had told him. I reiterated that if she was interested in us and being more inclusive she is welcome to walk with us. But currently she seemed to only be focused on him. I also explained we have different personal views and if she could be more sensitive to that it would be helpful while we are sharing the Camino. After consideration, they chose to walk with us.

#LifeLesson —39 Speak your truth. How your truth is received is not important. It is your truth.
Facebook, June 28— Drew—
"Open your mouth only if what you are going to say is more beautiful than silence"—Arabic Proverb
—I recently used the wrong words and I am paying for it. I was not my best self and it hurts.

That morning I extended an olive branch and struck up a conversation with Boise. I told her all about my Camino and shared my life lessons for more than an hour. I shared about how the Camino has its own plan and about the relationships I saw on the Camino start and finish along with my own past relationships. I felt it went pretty well.

She seemed moderately interested however didn't really interject or share. Later in the day they seemed to fall back into their connectedness and slower pace.

Facebook, June 29—Drew—

157

I am on a break swimming in a river in Spain, in the freezing cold water, in my undies because I have no swimwear. The totally cool life I have.
—Drew—
"Being right can sometimes directly impact your peace. Choose well."—Drew Eric

That evening we checked into our hostel and chose our beds with them choosing bunks next to each other, lots of giggling and low talking between them. I then saw him stand and turn to face her directly, preparing to change his clothes. He pulled down his pants and popped back up with a quick jerking energy, exposing his underwear. She was seated on the bed in front of him with her head waist high. The room filled with his sexual energy that you could cut with a knife. This is the same action he did to me four days earlier.

I was stunned. He was now cut off from us completely and sending her all his charismatic, sexual energy to win her over just like he did with us. I was very uncomfortable, I wanted to leave, run out of the room right then. This was not my Camino; it was very distracting from my path.

Facebook, June 29— Drew—
The Camino has plans I am not aware of. Every day I wake up expecting the Camino to tell me something new. The Camino tells me who I will see and who I will be with and what I will say. It's not up to me. I live in the Camino flow.
—Martha—
You look well but remember this is your path… You have the right to go your own way… A traveler has no set destination… It's the journey… If you are feeling cramped go see what your soul calls for… Not everyone is on the same path… and yes, your voice does count.
—Ralph—
You are still doing it, live in the flow.

I was lying on my bunk thinking about what the hell to do about this new predicament, the uncomfortable sexual tension between one of my brothers and the female guest from Boise. The door swings open; low and behold my Prince in bright clothes is stand-

158

ing there. The Brit, looking for his room accidentally came into mine.

Facebook, June 29—Drew—
"Just because something falls apart, doesn't mean it is truly falling into a better place."—Drew Eric

This is perfect. I will spend some time with this colorful new friend and walk away from my Band-of-Brothers until this situation works itself out. I felt relieved. I realized then leaving the group was necessary for my own Camino growth. I was uncomfortable and I could leave, I could walk away. I wasn't tied to anyone and didn't need to stay. I could freely walk on my own path.

We have already hit it off pretty well and enjoyed our time together. Over dinner I let him know about the drama that was unfolding with my brothers. I also told him I would be sleeping in his dorm room in the hostel since I didn't want to sleep next to the new couple with their budding relationship.

I told the guys my plans. I let them know I would be stepping away from them. I don't know if or when I will be back but this is what I need to do and what is best for my Camino, they understood. They had to stay, but I had the freedom to walk away even though I will miss them terribly.

If anything changes let me know. We can still be together in Santiago. We can still keep our plans for the weekend.

I never told the Swede of my plans. I did what was best for me since I was uncomfortable, I walked on.

Facebook, June 29—Drew—
Been having an experience the last couple days. Sorry I haven't posted.
—K.C.—
Let me see if I got this straight (no pun intended). You go on a life-changing adventure. You are living your life and enjoying yourself. You can't take time away from the real world to post in the virtual world? I don't get it. ☺ *Keep enjoying yourself and post updates when you are able.*
—Drew—
Lol, I'm sharing the fact something is shifting for me and I wanted to let you all know, that's all. Wait for the update. K.C. you made me laugh. Thanks, I needed a laugh.

—Erik—

Understood. Perhaps you should completely disconnect for a while. This is such a great opportunity to be quiet n go within. U got this.

Posted on July 1, 2016 by Drew Eric

Chapter 23 Can I reconnect with my true self?

Facebook, June 29—Drew—
"You can never predict what the path has in store. More twist and turns than imaginable. Some paths have rocks, roots, loose gravel to trip you up. Some paths have fine grains of sand, tiny pebbles, pretty little flowers that brush your pants. Yesterday was roots, today it's flowers. Tomorrow, is unknown."—Drew Eric
—Lantz—
But you are present in the moment that you're enjoying. Goals have been met!

That day my Prince and I walked together and talked. I wouldn't say it was an easy time, but it was rewarding. We come from different worlds. He is a young doctor with science and medicine as his schooling and I am a life coach with energy and intuition as my foundation. You can easily see how we had lively discussions— that amused us both. Regardless of our differences, we were able to have stimulating conversation and challenge each other on a deep level.

Let me tell you a bit about my Prince. I call him that, because he stepped into my life and swept me away from the drama unfolding like a Prince in shining armor sweeping me off my feet, except not in the actual picking me up part. I had spent several weeks not meeting anyone with the same interest in men as I. When I first saw him I was desperate to be in his company. I needed to speak and be with another man like me. Living, walking and talking with so many men without any consensual intimate contact can only be done for so long. I needed a gay break and reconnect with my true self.

He was perfect, British, young, smart (a doctor) quick-witted and demonstrated a strong intuitive nature. And, he is good looking, which certainly adds to his allure.

We opened up to each other a bit slowly, feeling each other out. I was talking about all the energy I was feeling on the Camino from people and situations. He thought I was ridiculous, always going on about energy like some stoned hippie. He made fun of me all the time. I got under his skin with all my spirituality stuff; however he secretly really liked it. We were just different and he really enjoyed it, so did I.

I was telling him all about my life, marriage, and friends and, of course, talking about why I am on the Camino. He followed along and offered observations related to my stories. He challenged me like few people do, it was wonderful. He would make a few simple comments and I would have a huge "aha."

I loved his friends—there were a couple of gal pals and an Irishman so that's three Brits and one Irishman—and me, the lone American, walking together. They all took me in as if we were long-time friends.

Facebook, Friday, July 1—Drew checked in @ Albergue Pieros —

With my British Camino family.

We stayed at a really cool vegetarian albergue with a yoga/meditation room. Of course I was encouraged to teach a class which I was happy to do. The doors were open with a breeze coming in while the sun was setting over Spain, leaving us in the colors of dusk. At one point a bird flew in the room and landed in the nest she so lovingly constructed. I ended class with a mediation that created a yoga buzz just before dinner.

That night there was guitar playing and singing with the other inhabitants, a real loving environment. It was one of those places where you feel so comfortable that you're sad to leave. It felt like a cocoon of love. The entire place was run by volunteers including the manager, what a great life, giving back to the pilgrims walking the Camino. All the volunteers have walked the Camino themselves and came back to this special place. The Manager is a private chef and her last client was Jerry Hall before she married Rupert Murdoch. Our vegetarian dinner was out of this world! Later—after the Camino—the Irishman returned and did his own volunteering at the albergue.

The next day, while we were walking and talking, my Prince volunteered information about himself. He told me about his life growing up, school and such. I listened intently and asked questions to further dig into his life. I found out his mother is a therapist with a strong intuition, similar to his.

162

Apparently during one of our chats, I started to say things that contradicted what I mentioned earlier. The kind of stuff you don't want to admit to yourself and would rather deny than be truthful. He had no problem coming down on me, letting me know I wasn't hearing my own words and I needed to admit I had some problems. That's the kind of guy he is—one that will call you out on your shit, in a really nice way. He was just what I needed.

After a couple wonderful days getting to know the Brits, I ran across my Band-of-Brothers. I went over to see how they were all fairing. I wanted to know if I was still loved by them and what the future entailed for us all.

They seemed genuinely excited to see me. They wanted to know if I was well and asked about my new friends. I totally felt the love they had for me. I even sensed a good feeling from the Swede.

Boise then said goodbye since she needed to take a bus ahead in order to complete the Camino in ten days. She would be leaving the next night. The Camino has a plan for everyone and she was following hers.

Hmm, maybe its time for me to join my Band-of-Brothers again. With Boise leaving maybe things will be as they were—one big happy family.

I discussed it with the Brits and made my plan. The next day I would spend the morning walking with the Brits, getting in some last minute quality time, then walk back to the city I just left and wait for the Band-of-Brothers to join me. The Brits were sad for sure. We all grew to love each other in such a short time. But I really felt I had unfinished business with my brothers and needed to complete any loose ends in our relationships.

Yeah, I like this plan. Sometimes you must go backward in order to move forward.

Facebook, July 1—Drew—
"Like the pieces of a puzzle, you begin with not knowing. With laughter and presence, you realize as the picture presents itself, not knowing is worth it for the reward of the portrait that is unveiled."—Drew Eric
—Drew—
#ActOfKindess —11 To all my British friends who extended a welcoming hand when I needed one. You all took me into your nest of love and kindness and adopted me as your own little chick. You

are all so wonderful. It was an honor to give my gift of yoga to you all in thanks for the warm nest you made for me out of kind words of support, friendship and wisdom. Thank you all.

follow my… path

Posted on July 4, 2016 by Drew Eric

Chapter 24 Can I walk backwards to move forward?

Facebook, July 1—Drew—
Sometimes you must go backward in order to walk forward. Today I am walking two hours along the path in which I came, changing Camino families for an extra day on the pilgrimage. I have taken a well-needed identity break for the last four days. Checking back in with my true self, my safe place, my comfort place, my place of home. Now I am adding one more day to be with my Band-of-Brothers. This is the second time on the Camino I have walked in reverse. I can't wait to see the fun the Camino has in store for me now. Here is a picture of my shadow this morning.
—Peter—
Look at the shadow of your walking stick. It looks like a machine gun!
—James—
Peter, I thought the same thing, it does look like a machine gun.
—Drew—
There is so much subtext in the post, LOL and you're seeing the shadow?
—Michele—
Personally, I agree that it looks like a gun and your shadow looks like a soldier with combat gear and helmet. I think it's the perfect subtext for what I've seen you become on this journey. I've seen you turn into a fighter, a soldier, a warrior, a strong man.
—Drew—
"I was a survivor after some mishaps and missteps. Today I am stronger and step into my new Warrior life."—Drew Eric

When I walked back into town I found my brothers but something seemed strange. I didn't see any cohesiveness. Everyone seemed a bit separated and withdrawn—misalignment everywhere. I spent some time observing to see if I could get a sense of what was going on. I started with the Aussie and asked him. He really wasn't sure but he also felt something was different and uncomfortable in the air. He was doing his best to be normal around all the tension but even he wasn't his usually jovial self.

I continued to observe body language and moods with the rest of them. Yes, something was different. I wasn't sure if it was my presence or something else.

Aussie was still concerned and making sure everyone was taken care of, other than himself. I suggested he take a break so we could do some catching up. He was happy to oblige and was soon back to his old cheerful self without assuming the caretaker role. Our conversation was quickly comfortable and easy like we were never apart.

The others walked in and chose to sit at the bar for a drink while we were at a table, yes different energy happening over there for sure. After our beers we joined the others and went outside to walk about a bit, to see this small town.

Body language tells all. I did observe a difference between the Swede and Boise. They seemed to have calmed the closeness. I didn't see any more giggling or whispering and casual touching. Hmmm, I wonder why the change. They don't seem mad at each other but I can definitely see a shift in their energy.

I continued to observe them over dinner and I noticed something that was a bit more telling. The Swede—while sitting next to Boise— had turned in his seat leaving his shoulder out, effectively cutting her off from him. I also noticed there was little to no conversation, touching or contact of any kind. At which point I made an assumption. Something over the last few days has caused the Swede to turn his back on his new friend from Boise, Idaho.

I was now upset at how much has changed since I left. I was desperately trying to hold on to what we once had and not really sure how to handle what we have now.

Facebook, July 2—Drew—
Back with my men. 141,314 kilometers to go. I love this life.
—Mark—
I don't think you realize how much you are inspiring us all… Keep on. Keeping on! Thank you!
—Jorge—
141k KM? You sure?
—Drew—
141,314 km
—Jorge—
One of the longest routes is 610 km tho…
—Drew—

Actually I am walking 800 km. I guess I am not sure what the sign means then.
—Jorge—
Right. The sign must mean you have 140 km to go. Not 141 thousand. That's a lot! You're almost there!!!
—Drew—
Yes, almost 😊

After dinner we split up and all went to our separate beds for the evening. The next morning, after she left, the Swede said he was going to walk with another friend that he has not spent time with in a while.

He seemed different to me also. He wasn't making eye contact, not being his jubilant self and made it clear he wasn't walking with our Band-of-Brothers today. Yes, things are not the same.

I decided to be direct and honest and ask what's happening for him—rather than making assumptions.

I shared my observations about him seeming different towards me and he chose this time to explain how he was actually feeling.

He said he was upset at how I spoke with them. It reminded him of being bullied when he was a child. Just the way I was direct and told him how I felt about Boise. He told me I was a bully and that's not how I should speak to someone.

I didn't see that coming. That was a blow. I don't want to be perceived as a bully, ever. We parted ways for the day. I had a lot to think about.

This was a dramatic blow. I spent the day getting present to all that has happened. I knew this would be a big lesson with many painful benefits.

I walked with the German and the Aussie. We were terrific together. For the three of us, it flowed wonderfully and the day was just as it was before.

Facebook, July 2—Drew—
Lunchtime, Empanadas and beer, we are reliving our moment with the cross.

That night the Swede was back and we spent the evening together. He was moderately friendly after a few drinks. I was beginning to think maybe forgiveness was on the horizon.

Facebook, July 2—Drew—

So I am with a bunch of Germans watching football/soccer in a bar in Spain. Germany and Italy are playing. I am This cool. This is my life. Camino/friends/football. I love my life.

—Courtney—

I love your life.

—Drew—

It is so unreal, but it is.

—Laura—

I bet they went nuts! Going crazy here in the Alps for sure!

—Diana—

Eurocope! Yeiii

Facebook, July 3—Drew—

About 115 km left. This will be over soon. And my new life off the Camino will begin. A new adventure, new people, new sites, new feelings. I will be in the unknown.

—John—

But knowing yourself so much more!

—Drew—

Yes I am.

—Marcus—

You sound so happy.

—Drew—

I am so happy, and it is just beginning.

—Drew At Casa Barbadelo—

I am enjoying a beer at the pool. Life is hard on the Camino. But I can do this!!!

—Wes—

Doesn't look too hard

—Drew is feeling happy—

I have watched the movie "The Way" and I have to say, actually doing it is 1000 times better. Even the hard, emotional, crying is worth it. The personal growth and challenges are so worth it. I am in the right place with the right people doing the right things. My life is amazing.

—Anne—

Really happy for you, and proud of you for challenging yourself and putting yourself in some uncomfortable/unfamiliar situations for personal growth!!! Enjoy every moment!!!

—Drew—

And I have been UNCOMFORTABLE, but the growth makes it worth it.

—Martha—

I got a lot from the Reese Witherspoon movie when she walks the trail in search of herself. It seems we all need time to really look at where we have blinded ourselves in so many ways. When it comes down to the essence, we truly just need to focus on our purpose here... love and light. M

—Drew—

Yes, love and light. I am struggling right now with love and light. This to will pass...

—Drew is feeling ecstatic—

Today is six days till I reach Santiago. What an amazing journey. I feel so new and fresh. Reborn!

—Courtney—

I don't want it to end.

—Drew—

I will still be on an adventure. My flight back is September 29, however I might stay longer. We shall see.

—Jeanne—

Ross and I watched, again, the movie "The Way" just to be a little more connected with your journey.

—Drew—

That is awesome!

However the next day when he walked with us he was back and forth with niceness and shortness. I didn't come on the Camino to walk with someone who was unhappy with my presence and not willing to forgive.

The next morning I chose to apologize again. I let him know I was truly sorry for not being kinder and supportive. He reiterated his feeling of being bullied and emphasized, that's not the way a family treats one another. He said we walked too fast and we shouldn't be leaving family behind. That's not how he would handle it, indicating himself, Boise and the Canadian.

I didn't say much and left the conversation the way it was. I apologized for the second time. Now it was his turn to see what he wanted walking forward. Interesting how he called her family since I said that she wasn't including us in their conversations and walk. I began to wonder about his observation skills on human behavior.

He continued to switch moods throughout the day. I was getting less interested in continuing our walk together if he wasn't going to forgive and move forward. I was beginning to see that we were not going to regain what we once had.

Clearly he had made up his mind about my character and had chosen not to forgive. After walking with my Band-of-Brothers a few days I realized my relationship with the Swede was complete, I needed to walk on, again. I loved the time we had together, however, I wasn't comfortable in his company and decided not to walk into Santiago with him. I love my Band-of-Brothers but I needed to do what was best for me and walk ahead, for the second time. This was too distracting for my Camino.

Facebook, July 4—Drew is at Casa Cruceiro—
We are 100 km to Santiago. What a thrill! What an accomplishment! What a journey!
— Drew is celebrating—
Celebrating the 4th of July with 100 km left till Santiago. What a great day!
—Brenda—
Wait till you walk into Santiago, I found it so, so emotional. I leave Spain Wednesday. If I was to do it again, I would so do it on my own, you are lucky you are.

I text my Prince to find out where he is—only 13 kilometers ahead from where I was staying. Hmm, If I got up at 4:00 a.m. and started walking, I could potentially catch up with him at 7:00 a.m.

I told them I was coming back to walk with them. They were all excited to hear the good news. They were finishing the Camino Thursday now and catching their flight on Friday.

I wrote down the name of the hostel where the Brits were staying. Their plan for the next day's walk was 27 kilometers. I would be walking a whopping 40k that day, it would be my longest day yet.

Facebook, July 4—Drew—
Life moves pretty fast if you don't stop and look around once In a while, you could MISS IT!!!

Over dinner I let my Band-of-Brothers know my plans. The Canadian suggested I send my backpack ahead, walk with just a small bag, since I plan on doing a 40k, what a great idea. I filled out the paperwork with the address of the albergue where they are staying. In the morning I would leave my bag at the designated drop off spot and out into the world I would walk, free of 15 pounds.

After settling the bag situation I told them we will still be together on Friday and Saturday in Santiago. We would still have our time together; I just needed to move ahead. Today was Monday night and they were finishing the Camino early Friday morning.

That night, after a considerable amount of wine, the Swede and I were doing some joking. Now that I was leaving the Swede seemed a bit friendlier or maybe it was the wine. It was fun and again I thought maybe he was prepared to forgive. I asked him if we could have a few more minutes together and he agreed to another conversation—now influenced by the wine. It was going pretty well. The conversation was flowing along with more wine. Then a disagreement ended the conversation.

Facebook, July 4—Drew—
I have been struggling the last several days with emotions, attachments, fear of separation and worthiness. Today I am making another decision that is painful but is what is best for my wellbeing. What I want most I cannot have. What I most want to avoid I must face. Keep me in your thoughts.
   —Ann—
You can't always get what you want... Face the unavoidable... Remember, pull up those big boy pants... Mr. Camino Man...
   —Lori—
Things are meant to be as they are!
   —Richard—
Drew–You are a beautiful human being! Enjoy your ability to face life's innermost questions by bringing them to the forefront!-R
   —Michael—
I can't help you with some of those things, but I know that you are worthy! You matter! Love Ya! —"You is kind... You is smart... you is important..."

With a few minutes of cooling time, I saw him sitting alone and I attempted to finish our talk once and for all.

He said without mincing his words, "You are a bad person for leaving a family member behind. That's not how we do it. It's wrong to leave her behind because she is slower. You are a bad person, period!"

I got up and said, "It looks like we are done here" and I walked away. I saw now my reflection in his eyes and I didn't like it.

I did what was right for me at the moment of uncomfortableness and spoke my truth. His perception of me is right on how I appeared to them at the time. I can see this clearly now.

Facebook, June 29—Drew—
"I was a survivor after some mishaps and missteps. Today I am stronger and step into my new Warrior life."—Drew Eric
#LifeLesson —40 There are times in life when two people can both be right, regarding the same position.

Since the first day on the Camino, each time I met a new person, I wondered "Is this who I am going to walk into Santiago with?" I put a great deal of emphasis on completing the Camino and sharing the experience with people whom I enjoyed and respected. Completing a 500-mile pilgrimage is no small feat, so walking into Santiago should be treated with respect.

I woke up early the next morning and walked away. It felt great, no one angry at me for my actions and no one withholding forgiveness. I was going to walk with people who genuinely wanted me to be with them.

Facebook, July 4—Ruben—
Drew this a beautiful opportunity to stretch out of your comfort zone that you've co-created with your Band-of-Brothers. The constant lesson of letting go. The only thing that is ever constant in this life is change. Change of our thoughts, perception, beliefs and experiences. As you continue on your "Camino" be mindful and present of your thoughts and energy and allow them to flow through you. Love is love no matter what, so allow yourself to share the love 🙏 💚 🙏

172

follow my… path

Posted on July 5, 2016 by Drew Eric

Chapter 25 Can I let go and walk away?

Facebook, June 29–Drew—
"One day, you'll be just a memory for some people. Do your best to be a good one."—unknown

The next morning my alarm went off at 4:00 a.m., I brushed my teeth, left my bag and out the door I went into the early morning. This was the earliest I had been awake to walk since I started the Camino and I only have three days left to complete the pilgrimage. It was several hours before dawn, but I enjoyed the early morning darkness.

Facebook, Tuesday, July 5–Drew–
"Wake up everyday and be your best not your easiest."—Drew Eric
—Drew is feeling determined—
So today is a fantastic day. I stood my ground, faced my fears and walked away from people I love. Just for a couple days till I see them again on Friday and Saturday. But I needed to feel the freedom of the road, on my own. Well, at least for a couple hours. I got up at 4am and walked into the pitch dark. Sill in the darkness of morning I walked upon a new pilgrim I hadn't met. He is Danish, 25 and an American political expert. So we spent the dark, then dawn talking about the state of affairs in the USA. Wonderfully intelligent man and a fast walker. At 7:15 I finally arrived at my friends albergue, luckily he was starting his day late and was still in his albergue. It took me three hours to walk 13.5 kilometers. Today will be my longest walk ever at 39 kilometers. I'm having a beer now and octopus now for lunch, which is the specialty in this area. I love my friends.

I never expected to run into someone so early in the morning but after almost two hours of walking alone, I did. He was from the Netherlands. It was such a delight to make such a great new friend.

He told me he likes to walk early because he is a fast walker and generally people can't keep up with him. I laughed and said I thought he was a bit slow since I was able to catch up, we laughed.

Crazy thing happened next. I was telling him about my Camino and even told him about falling in love with a boy on the Camino. After a few minutes he said, "Wait a second, I feel like I have heard this story before. Was it a pair of cousins walking together?"

Apparently he walked with them earlier and heard all about me and my connection with the young man. That was a crazy moment to meet someone who had already heard great things about me. The Universe works in mysterious ways. It was very reaffirming and comforting to hear.

We finally reached the town where the Brits were staying and I said my goodbyes. I also needed some food and coffee. I spent a few minutes messaging the Brits to see if they were still in town. It was only 7 a.m. and there was a good chance they could be just getting ready to leave.

I headed towards their albergue to see if they were still there. And they were—crazy cool. Woo hoo! I was very pleased to see them. Now I would spend another amazing day with my friends and I couldn't be happier to walk into Santiago with these great people.

We settled right back into our routine of walking and talking except this time we were even closer than before. The time spent apart seemed to deepen our friendship.

Later in the day I talked about my childhood again and I heard myself differently this time. There is a funny thing that happens on the Camino, at least for me. I told my life story multiple times and each time I told it I learned something new about myself. I saw things slightly differently than the last time I told the story and this phenomenon continued.

Facebook, June 29—Drew—
"You never realize how strong you are until strong is all you can be."—Drew Eric

The Brit asked me "What was your earliest sexual experience?"

"Hmmm" I replied. "I was pretty young, maybe five or six, with a boy. I assume we were playing truth or dare—all I remember is the dare, now—and he dared me to kiss his thing. I do remember the smell, it was a little pungent, the beginnings of a young boy having smells down there. The whole experience was scary, confusing, exciting and gave me butterflies in my stomach. The game was under a sheet in our bedroom with a flashlight while our parents were in the living room."

I continued talking, "When I was in 4th grade, another boy showed me how to pull on my thing. He told me it feels really good when you do this as he demonstrated. I was very nervous and didn't want to do it. He encouraged me till I did. It was really early for me, I wasn't even thinking about sex at that age, I was so young. I am not even sure I was in puberty yet. This continued for many years, escalating until we were having oral sex on a regular basis".

As we were walking through the woods on a small dirt path, I said all this to the Brit with a very, matter of fact detachment. The sun was peeking through the trees and it felt like it was just the two of us in the world. So we ran off into the bushes and did the same.

Facebook, June 29—Drew—
"Don't give up now. Chances are your best kiss, your hardest laugh, and your greatest day are still yet to come"—Atticus
—Drew is feeling satisfied—
The Way has plans I am not aware of. Every day I wake up expecting The Way to tell me something new. The Way tells me about whom I will see and who I will be with and what I will say. It's not up to me. I live in the flow of The Way.

The Brit told me about his first experience although he wasn't nearly as young. He also shared his mother is a Psychotherapist. I already knew he is very intuitive. Perhaps he gets that from his mother.

We started talking about our childhood and I told him mine was pretty unconventional. My relationship with my mother wasn't filled with boundaries. For example, I told him about the first time I had sex with a girl when I was 15.

"It was the summer I moved out of my father's home—where I had been living for the past seven years—and moved to

175

Fort Lauderdale area with my mother and her long-term boyfriend. There was a girl in the apartment complex that was staying with her grandmother. We met, went on a date then back to my room. My mother and her boyfriend were sleeping in the bedroom next door."

"I was old enough to know exactly what I wanted to accomplish in my first sexual experience with a girl. I had a checklist of positions in mind and accomplished all of them over a couple of hours. I was well versed, I had been studying so to speak. I might have been a surprise for her since she had experience and I didn't." I continued.

"Then I asked her if she was willing to try a vibrator. She agreed and I crawled into my mother's room—naked—and took her vibrator out of her bottom draw in her nightstand while she slept. I brought it back in the room and plunged it in. It was a Sear's back massager with the ball head. Once it was plugged in, I aimed for my date." I said.

Continuing, "The next morning after my date was long gone; I came bopping down the hall into the kitchen with a satisfied, perky smile crossing my youthful face.

First thing my mother said was, "You got laid!" I was caught. How did she know?

She grabbed her 16-ounce tumbler of Pepsi, Egg McMuffin and her Eve lights Slim 120 cigarettes and headed for the couch for a long discussion on the details of my coming of age. I shared every detail, leaving—crawling on all fours and naked into her bedroom—for last. She got visibly angry with me, which surprised me a little.

Mom said, "You get up right now and wash my vibrator, then you return it to where you found it". I felt like her anger was more for show, I thought I saw her smirk while lighting an Eve.

Once the washing up was complete, I rejoined my mother for cigarettes and Pepsi and continued. We talked about how it felt and what I thought about sex. Somehow we got on the subject of anal sex and she told me, "Don't knock it till you try it, it's not that bad".

Even at my young age of 15, I heard that statement and instinctively knew, "file that baby away for later, you just heard a line from your mother you will never forget". Clearly, I never did,

I shared all this with my new friend on the Camino, along with a few other details about the boundary-less relationship with my mother.

"Yea, my upbringing wasn't exactly normal, but it was normal for me. Oh yea, and my baby sitter was a pedophile. I knew it and my mother knew it. He was her gay neighbor and good friend who just happened to have a thing for young boys." I said casually.

She told me, she told him, "If you ever touch my son I will cut your dick off!"

"I was probably between eight and ten years old at the time". I blurted this out with little to no reaction from me or him and we kept walking like this was as normal as talking about the first time I rode a bike.

So when I was sharing about my childhood I realized that something wasn't sounding acceptable. I was describing my young years and just slowly but surely I realized my childhood wasn't normal or OK. Some persons, places and things from my childhood weren't OK and I was just beginning to have this realization—connecting the dots of my life.

The Brit said he was waiting for me to realize it myself. He told me he was curious why I was just brushing over some delicate matters and treating them so lightly. I was just now putting some of the pieces together and seeing my childhood in a new light.

I cried for a few minutes and he held and comforted me. Eventually my crying subsided, I wiped my tears and we continued walking. I wanted to walk away from the pain like I always had. All the while I felt this heaviness, knowing, I have more work to do, this isn't over.

Facebook, June 29—Drew—
"I am learning to trust the journey even if I can't comprehend it." —
Drew Eric
Facebook, July 5—Drew—
I just finished my longest walk, 40 kilometers with four hours sleep. Basically I went in reverse a few days ago to complete unfinished business with my Band-of-Brothers. Once this was completed I followed my intuition and chose to move forward to reconnect with my British family. I know, it's complicated. Now that I am reaching the end of my pilgrimage, I am realizing my journey has

177

been about connection. I have learned to meet, attach, then sepa-rate with ease and love. I am getting really good at it. I follow my intuition and I am very happy.

This morning I sent my backpack ahead because I chose to walk 40 Kilometers. However I sent it to the wrong city. I sent it to the city where my friends were staying not where my friends were go-ing, ugh. Apparently I must learn to attach and separate from my own minimal belongings.

I love the Camino life. Another first, I challenged being uncomfort-able and wore my purple tights. There are many men just joining the Camino these last few days, wearing tights, presumably Ital-ians from their looks. I was too chicken to wear them before, but these last couple days I said yes to the tights. Funny thing is, I can't change out of them since they are the only clothes I have.

We finished walking that day and reached the albergue. I realized the bag debacle and now have no belongings, nothing to sleep in, shower with, change into or a toothbrush—only the clothes on my back and my water bottle. I felt overly needy and tried to compensate by telling the Brit I am not a needy person, I was a mess.

I thought, "This isn't going well". I am feeling needy, scared and in pain from the last couple of days. I have no belongings and my friends don't seem to be volunteering any assistance to get me through the night. The blankets have all been handed out and it's a little cool out tonight. My clothes are wet from when I washed them and put them back on after my shower.

My Prince, after drinking just a bit too much beer, seems combative. I am at a loss at why?

When the evening was over we all went to our rooms and climbed in our bunks. I was laying there alone, cold with no sleep-ing bag or sheets. Finally my Prince gave me one of his T-shirts, I layered it onto my slightly damp clothes. I desperately wanted to be warm and held and comforted. I thought, "Why don't I craw up to the Brit's bunk and cuddle for a bit, warm up and return to my bunk later". I joined him and we snuggled, I was warm.

I placed my hand on his crotch and he got hard. I scooted down under the sleeping bag while we were pretending to be asleep in the shared room. He came quickly. I crawled out of his sleeping bag and went back to my bunk without ever saying a word.

Wait, I don't feel better, I feel worse. What did I just do? I feel dirty. What just happened? Then it hit me, I just reenacted my childhood sexual behavior.

I secretively carried on an unhealthy friendship with one of the boys from my childhood, for many years. We would take turns pretending to be asleep, encouraging each other to essentially, molest the other, all in an effort to resist the truth of what we really wanted. Instead we lived this shameful, secretive lie.

I couldn't sleep. I tossed and turned and shivered most of the night, sleeping maybe a couple hours. Replaying all that happened that day, that evening and how I essentially just molested my friend, in this bunk, in a room full of sleeping pilgrims.

follow my... path

Posted on July 6, 2016 by Drew Eric

Chapter 26 Can I finish the Camino
and stop the pain that is this path?

I woke just after 5:00 a.m. and laid in my bunk turning the horrific events in my mind. I jumped out of bed and grabbed my belongings. I needed to get out of there.

I could feel a panic consume me. From experience, I knew I had some learning/personal growth to do because of what I uncovered the previous day about my childhood. I could feel the pressure building like a weight on my chest and I knew I needed to get on the path. I have my best realizations while walking these days. I decided to walk out alone.

I woke my friend and told him, "I gotta go; I will see you later in the day." And out the door I went.

I had envisioned my last few days on the Camino much differently. I dreamed about walking into Santiago with all my beautiful best friends—all the people I had gotten to know and had grown to love. From that first day, each and every person I met I wondered, "Are you the one? Will I be walking into Santiago with you?"

Facebook, July 6—Drew—
"If you want to be strong, learn to enjoy being alone."—unknown

I wasn't out the door five minutes before I started crying. Dawn was just peeking over the horizon, birds were just starting their songs and dew was on the ground, quenching the plants and animals. I wanted to run, fast and hard.

Step by step I walked. I was walking out of a village and into the between land. There are no businesses, homes or people on the road. I was all alone and able to cry openly and hard. It was an exceptionally difficult day. So many pieces fell into place for me. So much new found awareness. I kept running through everything that happened to me when I was young.

- I was sexualized too early by two boys before I was ready.
- I carried on a long, inappropriate relationship with a boy that was based on secrecy and molestation.

180

- My mother placed me in the home of a known pedophile to babysit me.
- The pedophile's home was an uncomfortable, sexually charged space that was confusing for me at a very young age.
- Said pedophile encouraged naked day.
- Said pedophile took pictures of me sleeping in my underwear.
- My mother kept child porn photographs of me.
- My mother gave my child porn photographs of me, to me when I was 25-years-old.

Facebook, July 6—Drew—
"Your willingness to look at your darkness is what empowers you to change."—Iyanla Vanzant

On and on I walked and cried. I was walking hard, slamming my feet on the ground causing new blisters to form and physical pain in my legs and feet. I couldn't stop. I kept thinking I need this pain to stop. But it didn't stop, it continued for five hours.

I felt the urge to expel my pain. I felt the urge to remove it from my chest. I felt the urge to post it on Facebook.

Facebook, July 6—Drew—
I'm feeling pretty sad today. I didn't sleep well. I didn't have my backpack so I was cold. I couldn't charge my phone or brush my teeth. Yesterday I faced some pretty hard shit. In my childhood, my mother left me in the care of someone who put me at risk. Yesterday I finally realized how bad that was for me and it was wrong. I need to forgive my mother. This is hard. I have two days left on the Camino and I'm scared and in pain.

Wow, what a relief. Once I expelled the pain and posted on Facebook, my crying started to trickle. Slowly but surely my pace slowed a bit and my heart rate began to normalize. I could breathe again. People were beginning to show up on my path. The Camino was coming back to life and I was rejoining the living, the pilgrims.

All while I was walking as fast as my disintegrating shoes would carry me. I wasn't sure I was going to make it into Santiago with them on my feet. Funny, the way I was feeling I wasn't sure I was going to make it into Santiago at all.

181

I was walking so hard and fast and feeling so much emotion that I just kept walking. When I finally stopped crying I had already reached 20 kilometers and still felt like walking on. It was then I decided to finish the Camino alone. I wasn't going to finish with the Brits or my Band-of-Brothers.

I was going to walk into Santiago with my shadow. I realized it was my shadow that earned the right to be my partner and walk with me into Santiago. My shadow has been there since the beginning, silent, loving and supportive throughout.

Facebook, July 6—Drew—
I'm realizing so much. I woke up scared and confused. I am being flooded with realizations. Clarity is coming so fast. I am walking so fast. Yesterday I walked 40 kilometers with the intention of finishing the Camino on Thursday. Today, Wednesday I have only 40 kilometers in total to finish. I have been questioning who I would walk into Santiago with. Who has earned the right to walk by my side into Santiago? That person was with me the whole time. I have posted many pictures of him. My shadow has earned the privilege to be my companion today. My shadow has always been there each and every day. I will finish this Camino today. I need to put the pain behind me. I need to put the Camino behind me.

It's midday now and I am only 20 km to Santiago. In my mind I tie my pain with the Camino. I decide if I finish the Camino I can stop the pain, the personal growth and stop the self-evaluation that is so difficult today. I decide to keep walking till I complete this shit. I need to finish, I need it to stop, I need it to be over.

Once back amongst people and after my Facebook post, realizations started flooding me. Like the string art Lucite lamps from the '70s, I began to tie the pieces of my life together. I slowly saw how my early sexualization and behaviors tied my life together with one continuous thread. How each individual act in my childhood impacted my life as I lived it. As each notch in the Lucite got closer to finishing the sculpture, that is my life, I clearly saw the finished product. I didn't like it.

- The way my mother raised me without boundaries—how we talked about everything. This showed up for me, by not having the ability to understand what appropriate conversation was and what wasn't. I turned many people off with my uncontrollable mouth.

- My having a loveless, secretive relationship as a child showed back up with casual loveless sex with strangers.
- How a childhood where I struggled with friendships and sex, continued as a struggle in my adult years with friendships and sex, many times with my confusing the two.
- How I took drugs, drank alcohol, had casual loveless sex and ate my emotions rather than face them.

Each time I walked by a Camino mile marker I counted down thinking it's almost over. Then I decided to post my realizations on Facebook. Knowing it wouldn't necessarily make sense but I needed to expel my emotions. They have been tied to me for so many years, hidden in those places we dare not look.

Facebook, July 6—Drew added a photo—
I can do this! I can finish the Camino today!
—Drew added a photo—
My babysitter was a pedophile! I can do this! I can finish the Camino today!
—Drew added a photo—
My mother gave me a three-inch stack of photos of a boy, asleep in his little boy underwear. ME! I can do this! I can finish the Camino today!
—Drew added a photo—
I just realized I am walking into Santiago with my shadow and with all my friends following my journey here on Facebook. Thank you! Thank you! Thank you! Please cheer me on today, as I am crying my way into Santiago. I can do this! I can finish the Camino today!
—Drew is feeling broken—
"We are all broken, that's how the light gets in."—Ernest Hemingway
Facebook, July 6—Drew–
Never forget 3 types of people in your life:
1. Who helped you in difficult times.
2. Who left you in difficult times.
3. Who put you in difficult times.

Later in the morning I got some messages from the Brit. He was very concerned for me since the previous day was so difficult for me. Wanting to walk alone, he felt, was out of character for me and knew intuitively something was up. I was also posting cryptic information on Facebook which he read, giving him cause for alarm.

Eventually, when I was feeling better I told him I would see him that night since I still didn't have my bag. Hopefully it would be dropped off at the hostel where he was staying that evening.

Facebook, July 6—Drew—
I finished. This was pretty difficult, physically and emotionally. I still don't have my bag. Hoping its at the last albergue which I am taking a cab to. My shadow and I finished together. I don't understand why I had to finish today I just felt pulled to get it done. Hoping the learning and growing would also be complete, we shall see. I am going backward for the third time now. I do not know why or what will come of it. I just know I must go back again because my backpack is behind me.

Exhausted, I kept walking, with new blisters and worn out shoes, until I reached Santiago. I got my certificate of completion, my Compostela, and sat down at a restaurant for some food and beer. This was not as celebratory as I would have expected. I was alone, raw, vulnerable, exhausted, in some pain from walking so hard and still had no belongings.

Facebook, July 6—Drew is feeling exhausted—
"Releasing the past is like putting down a heavy backpack you have been carrying for 500 miles. Only then can you walk into your future with lightness."—Drew Eric

184

follow my… path

Posted on July 9, 2016 by Drew Eric

Chapter 27 Can I get a redo?

I grabbed a cab and informed the Brit that I was on my way back to meet them and retrieve my bag. He was pleased and concerned for me. When I arrived he was making dinner and received me warmly. It was appreciated as I was physically and emotionally exhausted. They offered me clothing, food and toothpaste since I hadn't brushed my teeth in two days.

I shared about my day and let it go after that. They were in the mood for some wine since it was going to be a short 20k day for them. Then the celebration would begin with the completion of their Camino. So we got a bit tipsy, a welcomed feeling for me from my emotional day.

Facebook, July 7—Drew–
"Friends, laughter, sleep are the best cures for anything."—Drew Eric

The next morning my bag didn't arrive in time to walk out with the Brits. I told them I would meet them at the halfway point and walk into Santiago once again. Walking was my thing so why not continue? Besides, I would have a new memory of the experience and it would give me a second chance to complete the Camino. Who doesn't like second chances?

Facebook, July 7—Drew—
I am waiting outside Santiago for my backpack. Once it's here I will taxi up and meet the Brits, to walk the last 10k, again. This time with loving people to share the experience. Yesterday's arrival I was pretty cried out, in pain, exhausted and hungry. Today's arrival will be a celebration with good friends. That makes me happy. Sometimes in life, we actually get a redo. My shoes are really shot though, hope I make it.
—Drew is feeling determined—
Not only can I do this but I can do it twice.

We walked into Santiago, found our hostel and relaxed. I was still a bit of a mess, not quite back to normal yet but I was better. That night we went out to dinner and celebrated. The drinks came and we stayed out late. We ended the night with some crazy drinking and we might have played truth or dare, I dare not confirm nor deny. It was a great evening with friends that helped me feel normal again.

Facebook, July 8—Drew is feeling sad—
#ActOfKindness —12 My goodbyes have started. Last night I said goodbye to five amazing people, the Brits. I spent more than a week with them—which in Camino time is over seven years. They were kind, loving, supportive and there when I needed them. We grew and became better individuals because we were friends. I left them for a short time and came back. They loved me even more on my return. I love you all and look forward to the day we will be together again. Luckily they have invited me to visit them in England. So I will see you again soon.
—Drew at Plaza de Fonseca en Santiago de Compostela—
Touring! Apparently I really needed to decompress after my Camino. I finished Wednesday, today is Friday and I am finally feeling the love that finishing the Camino brings. Or maybe it's the wine.

The rest of the byroads is not planned in the slightest. The only concrete "must do" item on the agenda is a flight from Amsterdam to Ireland on July 12th—just days from now—with a return flight two weeks later. At the moment, I do have a flight back to America at the end of September but my plan is perhaps to change the flight, leaving my European road completely flow accessible.

I have been dreading this moment for the length of the Camino. I have avoided making new travel arrangements until the last moment. My fear and anguish around figuring out how to use Google and then choosing a roadway, out of many, to get from Santiago, Spain to Amsterdam.

I know this sounds like a small task but for someone who hasn't made travel arrangements for themselves, it's huge. In my 20 year marriage, my husband enjoyed the research and booking. Since I was apathetic about it, I allowed him that simple pleasure. It also allowed me to limit my google use.

186

I thought I was pretty good with the World Wide Web prior to this path. However when I actually sat down to begin my adventure, I realized my lack of experience translated into, "I really don't know how The Google really works". It's a crash course for me now.

Finally on Friday, two days before leaving Santiago, I am sitting here reviewing options and coming up with the cheapest, easiest way to get there. Looks as if I'm going to Lisbon, Portugal. Sunday is the day of the World Cup, which finds Portugal and France in competition. Apparently, no one in Portugal is flying out during the match but me.

It amazes me, I spent hours upon hours over 32 days, dreading the action of finding transportation and it only took three hours to do so, albeit painful. This is an imbalanced experience I need not repeat, I should choose to live in the flow.

#LifeLesson —40 Avoidance is always a clear sign of what I should tackle next for your own wellbeing.

#LifeLesson —41 When something takes three hours to accomplish but you spent 300 hours avoiding it, take note. This is an imbalance that need not be repeated.

Facebook, July 8—Drew at Catedral De Santiago De Compostela Espanha—

I'm feeling a real sense of accomplishment today. Feeling better about completing the Camino and transitioning back into the semi-real world of emails, bank accounts, bills, wiring money and all. Taking time out to accomplish travel plans has been a burden these past three weeks, I was avoiding. I finally sat down and worked it out, it took several hours. Along with getting on couch-surfing.com and starting the full-time job of looking for free places to stay in an effort to conserve money, to extend the experience on the road as long as possible. I have been invited to several countries through Couch Surfing and from my new friends on the Camino, it's exciting.

This road is about connection for me and I am looking forward to making more deep connections while I am on the roadways through Europe. If anyone has family and friends in Europe please connect us.

My motto on the Camino and in life is "Who shall I meet today, What shall I say, What will I learn, Where will I go, I am open to all connections, I am open to what will enrich my life today, I am open-hearted today and every day, I am open to all new possibilities.

—Drew is celebrating—
I am with my Band-of-Brothers, and we are touring the bars in Santiago. 'Cause really, that's how we roll.

On Saturday, I have located a bus that will take me to Portugal for a quick overnight then a flight to Amsterdam. Who would have thought, me, a single guy from South Florida with virtually no travel experience alone, booking buses and flights around Europe?

I also found a Couch Surfing host in Lisbon who offered a room for the night, so kind and helpful. I am so happy when it works out. I do hope this will be one of many kind people I meet on the road through Europe. If I put faith in the flow and trust that I am being shown the best path, I can be confident in knowing the Universe conspires for my benefit.

Facebook, July 8—Drew—
I have left my Band-of-Brothers three times and have come back to my boys three times. We are finishing our last night together here in Santiago. I have to say, we separated and come back together and it only takes a few minutes for us to connect deeply as if we never separated. We are completely in sync; we share our heart and love each other openly, with kindness and understanding. These are some of the best relationships I have had in my life. We even laugh about how I need to bring so much love and emotion to everything. Secretly, they love it and love me. They have my back and I have theirs. This has taught me what kind of relationships I will have in my life, going forward. I want men like them, emotional, sensitive, with an open heart. I will have this for the rest of my life. We are even making plans to meet up in Canada next year.
—Drew—
This is my life, hanging in the Santiago Plaza while the bell chimes for 7:00 p.m. Mass. Last night in Santiago. I just randomly walk up on stuff all the time here. Concert in the plaza, enjoying a little street music.

Now the Camino is over and I am saying my goodbyes to my Camino life and all the friends I have made along the path. This is hard, scary and profoundly emotional.

Facebook, July 9—Drew is feeling emotional—
Leaving these men was the hardest part of leaving the Camino. I can't remember feeling so much love in my heart. Crazy thing I felt loved by more than one man and they loved me right back, equally and openly. Until we are all together again in Canada, I love you all dearly. Tears of love feel so wonderful on my face.
    —Courtney—
Making me cry.
    —Drew—
I cry every day at least. Feeling is wonderful!
    —Ray—
Happy cries are cleansing.
    —Luis—
How are you my darling? U have been very emotional lately, you are a sweet soul!!! Love you!!!!
    —Drew is feeling anxious—
Ok, I found the bus station, found the ticket booth, got my ticket printed, have fruit in my bag but no substantial food. I'm a little concerned about being hungry. Seven minutes till the bus leaves. All this makes me anxious. I can do this!
    —Drew is feeling nostalgic—
Goodbye Camino… Now I am officially complete as I bus out of Santiago. It's a feeling of loss. I am letting go of an amazing life of living in the flow called "El Camino de Santiago." I started on June 4th and I finished on July 6th.
For 32 days I got up and walked, prayed, cried, meditated, talked, was silent, present, loved, controlled, bullied, angered, opened my heart, closed my heart, pushed people away, pulled people in, formed families, left families, felt pain, self evaluated, grew, withdrew, made friends, made enemies, forgave, let go of grudges, saw people in their space, accepted people in their space, acknowledged people who did not work for me, loved people who did work for me, was my best self, was my worst self, drank—sometimes a lot—felt like a kid, felt like an old man, I didn't sleep much, lost weight, stopped eating meat that doesn't swim, ate fruits and vegetables all the time.
This path changed me down to the bones, on a molecular level. I couldn't have predicted this prior to the path. It was beyond my comprehension. My blog has been "Can I do this?" I now know I

can do anything I put my heart and soul into. This is my official pronouncement.

I am writing my first book, "My Autobiography!" my own "Eat Pray Love," my own "Wild," my own "Camino Adventure," my own "Journey-of-Self-Discovery". I have an editor who will help me clean it up and fix some of the crappy mistakes that make me, Me. My writing is as flawed as I am and that's great for me. I love Me and now I know who I am. Now I can write about who I was. Look for new pages soon.

—Drew—

"We do not heal the past by dwelling there; We heal the past by living fully in the present."—Marianne Williamson

—Juan—

Pretty interesting Drew. We all, one way or another, have or do experience this, earlier or later. Some are not even aware of it. It seems that this journey is making you more aware of you and also others. The new you… Until it also becomes the OLD you. And then you have to look again for that NEW you, just to become old again. It is a Journey. Now you know how to walk it. Good job and get going.

—Sunny—

Flaws can sometimes be our greatest characteristics. You're an inspiration.

—John—

Drew, you gave us all seats on that bus. Thank you for an incredible journey.

—Sherry—

Drew—You have accomplished not only what you set out to do, but SO much more!!! 👏 You have discovered what most of us already know about you… You're an amazing person inside and out!!! And you can do and be anything you want!!! Know you are loved dearly and encouraged to follow your dreams—all of them –

- whatever they are! ✊ 👍 👏 Love you bunches my friend!!!

—Beverley—

Wow, just wow. I can't wait to read your book! I loved being on this adventure with you even though it was from afar, it was so wonderful to watch the transformation. Treasure this time and keep it close to your heart.

—Drew—

"Regardless of good and bad, all experiences eventually move into the past. We only remember the emotions that we once clung to so dearly."—Drew Eric

I once again find myself moving through the traveling experience that causes me much anxiety. Over the last month, there was no thinking involved when making travel arrangements. You simply walked up to an albergue and asked for a bed. I look forward to the day I can move through airports, bus stations, trains and subways with the same ease, patience and peace. Until that day, I am a mess.

My Camino has ended. Looks like I can get a redo, with loving friends.

Facebook, July 9—Drew—
"Facing the ugly truth can be difficultly rewarding."—Drew Eric

Posted on July 12, 2016 by Drew Eric

Chapter 28 Can I live in the flow of life
while on the road in Europe?

Facebook, July 9—Drew—
"When you feel the sand beneath your feet shifting and sliding, keep moving forward your feet will find the flow of stability. "—Drew Eric

This is a story about living in the flow (letting the Universe/God/ Higher Power/Destiny/Inner Guidance System, take the lead). This is also a story about being comfortable with the unknown, trusting, and not letting fear stop my flow.

I struggled with the unknown and the fear that crept up every day on the Camino. I practiced living in the flow allowing minutes to pass, being present, no expectations and observing everything the Universe put on my path. It was a tremendously rewarding experience to be fearless and present for the unknown. It didn't go well every day, but in the end, every day was for my benefit, whether it was a good or an uncomfortable experience.

Facebook, July 9—Drew—
"Books are inspired through unknown, unplanned, undiscovered adventures."—Drew Eric
—So I just got present to the fact I am on a bus riding through Portugal going to Lisbon writing my book which will be made into a movie someday, crossing fingers. This is a very surreal feeling. So much to look forward to.

Soon I will be meeting my second Couch Surfing host on this road. I decided prior to leaving America that I would Couch Surf. Living in other people's homes is an experience that leaves me vulnerable. This concept is scary, unknown and uncomfortable to say the least. I didn't have an understanding what its like to live in stranger's homes and I knew I would have to figure this out on the fly. My plan is to travel for an extended period on the road through Europe, so with this in mind, keeping expenses down is the utmost priority.

192

As a reminder, couchsurfing.com is a website where you post a profile, like a personal ad and you are invited into someone's home to share your time, adventure and your dynamic personality as your payment for a room/couch/bed. The homeowner makes the rules according to what they are comfortable with offering. Presumably you agree to their rules. This may or may not include any food, towels, laundry service and or simple coffee in the morning. All these details aren't necessarily listed in their bio and you need to just figure out when you show up—so many unknowns.

I arrived at 9 p.m. and taxied to my host. He's a nice man and a tour guide in Lisbon, which is perfect for a Couch Surfing host. We chat, while he offers me a beer and half his pizza, very kind. I guess food and beer are included with this stay. Note to self, I should better prepare in the future by having a supply of food, just in case my hosts aren't as generous with me. I should be a better Boy Scout. Be prepared!

I inquired "What's nearby? I should see something before I leave in the morning."

My host replies "Well there are no gay bars near, however, you could walk to the end of the street and see the bridge copied after the Golden Gate Bridge you have in America."

Eventually, he offers to take me on a car ride around the city and show me some sights. This is perfect because I have been celebrating (drunk) the last two nights in Santiago, I am really tired and would prefer a ride rather than walking around town.

On the ride, I learned the city hired the same bridge builders used for the "Golden Gate Bridge" and it does look the same. It was a beautiful, comforting sight to see an American landmark in this far off land.

I am marveling at my manifesting. Such a great example of flow and I wonder will this same manifesting continue as I navigate the rest of my journey.

After checking out the Lisbon sights, I went straight to bed. Set the alarm for 8 a.m., much earlier than my flight, just in case, to get a good start to my busy day.

I woke at 7 a.m., dozed a little longer while waiting to hear my host scurry around the apartment to get ready for work, and then joined him in the kitchen. He offered me coffee which I gladly accepted.

I inquired "Is there a store nearby where I can pick up some food for the road?"

He set me up with directions to the store, then at my request, called the taxi company with a pickup time for 10:45 a.m. My flight is at 1:20 leaving me two hours and 35 minutes to make my flight. I want to be prepared for any unusual, unforeseen problems. Then off to work he goes, leaving me a key to let myself in and out. Lisbon is working out very well for me.

Next, I pop down to the store for tuna, bread, avocado, hard-boiled eggs and fruit, plus a yogurt for breakfast. Eating in Europe is so different than home. As a gift for my host, I bought a six-pack of beer, his brand, and spent six Euros. It's a polite gift of thanks.

I finish packing, preparing my food and I'm ready to go. I plan on being downstairs by 10:30 a.m. for the taxi. I realize now the host is gone for the day, once I leave for the taxi I won't be able to get back into his apartment. I have to triple check for my belongings prior to leaving the key inside and locking the door. The anxiety starts up.

Facebook, July 10—Drew—
"Relax and feel confident, nothing is in control."—Drew Eric

The time has come to leave; I made the bed and cleaned all his dishes that were left about. I want to be a good surfer. I walked out the door at 10:31 a.m. perfect timing. I sent him a text, left his apartment and waited downstairs for the cab. In my mind I am reviewing all my belongings, where I put them, piecing together everything I packed.

I have everything. I finally give up due to the stress of making sure I have everything. I need to let it go and live in the flow—and trust.

Facebook, July 10—Drew—
#ActOfKindness —13 My second Couch Surfing host supplied so much on my short overnight, a warm bed in a private room with a private bath, pizza, beer and a driving tour around Lisbon. So much in so little time. I do hope someday to swing back around with more time and give a warm hello and thanks again.

The cabbie arrives on time, however, he doesn't speak English. I say, "Aeropuerto", which could be Spanish or Portuguese, I have no idea, I speak neither.

What did he say? I believe he asks "Which airport, one or two?

OH, F*CK ME! Exactly what I thought would happen—unusual, unforeseen problems. Is there more than one airport in Lisbon? I don't know which airport it is, shit, shit, shit. Eventually, I realize he means which terminal because my email say's "Terminal one". Now I am panicking about all the things that can go wrong. For instance, I have a tall walking stick that I used on the Camino. I decided to cut it in half and strap it to my backpack prior to leaving the apartment, hoping security will let me take it on the plane.

As it turns out I am ok, it is Terminal one, I find my gate and check-in. Now, at the counter, three women are deciding about my stick and eventually tell me to try going through security with what are now two sticks. Maybe making one weapon into two weapons was a bad idea. The last thing I'm told is to read the boards for my gate once I'm through security.

I'm thinking, "What the hell does that mean. Don't they know the gate where the flight will depart?" Panic, panic, panic! Not realizing until later that I am so early they haven't marked the gate yet. (I get snippy when stressed, not my best trait)

TSA security calls over the senior TSA security agent to let decide if I am using my walking stick—with my mother's ashes tied on the handle—as a weapon on the plane. I explain El Camino de Santiago, walking and my mother's ashes.

He asked, "Why did I cut the stick"?

I replied, "I didn't think I could get a 4' waking stick on the plane".

He said. "Have a nice flight."

Wow, good thing I am almost two hours early, whew. I'm through security and now waiting near the board to find out where my gate is. I'm calmer now. I would say I am getting a tiny bit better at this travel stuff, and if I keep at it, maybe, just maybe I will reach slightly better, then someday somewhat better.

Anxiety is still high but leaving plenty of time really helps my stress. I realize now, anxiety/stress are the opposite of living in the flow. Maybe I can't do this travel thing, I'm so conflicted.

Facebook, July 10—Drew—
Today, flight day, all is well, let's see how my journey to Amsterdam goes, wish me luck.

While waiting in the terminal for my flight, I decide to have some comfort food and a beer, maybe two. As the beer washes my insides, I peruse Facebook in an effort to calm my nerves. It works. Alcohol is a great way to reduce anxiety. Why didn't I do this before, maybe I could just drink alcohol all day and night, that makes so much sense now. Facebook is doing the trick also; I am smiling again and chuckling at photos of friends back in America.

Facebook, July 10—Drew—
When I feel insecure or sad or scared I read the comments on Facebook and I feel better. Thanks Facebook friends. You know who you are.
    —Kitty—
❤ *so proud of you Drew, and happy for you! This is an amazing experience! I have had a much smaller, but on its own, was a scary journey to find my perfect home. Now that it's done, the next big joy will be for us to engage in some travel. I hope to get back to Europe and other places, I will carry the choice to stay open to everything from your example. In fact, it's a way to walk through even a regular old day at home* ☺ *Thank you for sharing all this with your friends.*
    —Lin—
We love you, I think what you are doing takes courage, there are many people out there that couldn't do what you are doing right now, I'm proud of you Drew
    —Christopher—
Hang in there Drew, what an amazing experience this is for you and for everyone who is following and supporting you on your adventure.
    —Tamara—
What a beautiful journey you are on... Stay true to yourself... And better yet find a piece of yourself you didn't know about... And then love and accept it... So happy for you!
    —Cindy—
So proud of you! I wish I would have the guts to do something like you're doing. Keep on going you are growing so much, and learning so much about yourself! So happy for you! Love you!

I wonder what Amsterdam will be like? A girlfriend from college, who along with her family, offered me a place to stay prior to leaving America so that I can practice sleeping in other people's homes. She also set me up with her sister in Amsterdam as another Couch Surfing host. It seems to work out for me thus far.

Facebook, July 10—Drew—
I was just informed after I arrive on my flight, I will get on a boat and explore Amsterdam from the canals. My life is that cool and amazing things are happening for me.
—Drew is feeling wonderful—
I just landed and look at me now, someone pinch me. I am sitting on a balcony, overlooking the canals of Amsterdam, this is so cool.
—Sally—
Kelly and Alexander are fantastic hosts. Enjoy! Love you!
—Ruben—
Now you have memories that no one can take away!

It is hard to believe my eyes, a boat, canals, bridges, all while listening to my host point out all the landmarks from the water.

"Look, there is the Anne Frank Huis," she said. These are the seven bridges of Amsterdam. "Look down the center, from this point you can see through all seven bridges. It makes a great photo," she continued.

Facebook, July 11—Drew—
My boat ride yesterday in Amsterdam was breathtaking. Thanks to Kelly and her family. I really resisted crying in front of them. I was so overwhelmed with love and beauty. God, I love my life, not a bad first day in a new country.

Once the canal rides 'finiSHt (finished in Dutch) we drove back to their home to retrieve my belongings I had when I started the Camino in France. I was informed by my host that the box looked intact. This made me happy since I have my camera in there along with more clothes. I have been wearing the same five items of clothing for the past several weeks now. Oh, to have fashion choices again after so long.

Facebook, July 11—Drew—
Facebook, June 10—Drew at Albergue Villamayor de Monjardin—
I just had one of the most profound conversations in my life. I will never forget this moment. Life can get better for me!

197

—I posted this on June eleventh shortly after I started the Camino. My friend Tamara—all the way back in America—felt compelled to memorialize the event. She had no idea what happened or any details on my conversation. She only felt the energy and impact it had on my life and choose to take action and help me remember. She ordered a custom made bracelet with the coordinates of the location I was at when I checked in on Facebook.

The company that made the bracelet is the WandererBracelets.com. Then she messages me for an address to mail me a present. I couldn't imagine what she could possibly mail me that was so important I needed it on the road in Europe. What could she mail from America that was so important I had to carry it on my body while backpacking?

The day I posted that comment was the day I told the boy that I fell in love with while walking the Camino, our time together is over and I was walking out of his life the following day. Not knowing if we would be friends or ever see each other again. We were mad at each other all day. I decided it was time to walk on. This was not going to define my Camino, it would only be a chapter.

He cried for 45 minutes. Never in my life had such an experience happen to me. Someone I was not in a relationship with was crying over our pending separation. He was upset he treated me so poorly on our last day. He didn't want our last day together to be filled with anger. I promised him I would walk with him in the morning at least a half day and we would have fun. Our last day together would be a really enjoyable day. I held his hand and wiped his tears and put my head on his shoulder.

I just had my moment on the mountain and realized I needed to move onto the path, solo. I felt calm and at peace with my revolution on the mountain. That even upset him more that I wasn't crying. He pictured me crying and him not crying when our time together ended.

This moment changed my life. I opened my heart and learned I could be myself and men will still like me, even love me. This moment was profound for both of us and I realize now it touched so many others at the same time. We will all remember these moments when our lives changed. I am so touched someone so incredible was so moved to help me memorialize it. Now you all can share this moment in my life. I wasn't straightforward then with what happened. So here is my life, here is my crazy, here is my open heart for you all to see.

198

#ActOfKindess —14 My American girlfriend, who was so moved to memorialize a life-changing moment in my life, had a Wanderer's bracelet made and mailed across the pond to find me in Amsterdam. This is a loving expression of friendship. I thank you and will remember your gift always and the inspiration behind it with your love.

I only have a couple of days in the Netherlands. I started the Camino a week late while waiting for a new phone to replace the one I lost on the first day of my adventure in Barcelona. If I could have had more time in this city I would definitely have chosen to stay longer. Just to be able to drink in the culture and feel the energy of Amsterdam.

Facebook, July 11—Drew—
I made it to the train to Amsterdam. I'm getting so much better at this travel thing, maybe.
—Beverley—
You're a pro now!
—Darcy—
Practice makes perfect!

Today, my second and last day in the Netherlands, I am off to explore the city. My host lives in a city named Haarlem on the outskirts of Amsterdam just a short train ride away. The name reminds me of New York's Harlem and after a quick Google search I find out it is named after this Dutch City. My plan is to walk about town, visit the Van Gogh Museum and definitely see the Anne Frank House. I know it's a short roadworthy trip but I want to squeeze out as much of the experience as I can.

Facebook, July 11—Drew—
I think I found the red light district. Haven't seen that before. I was looking at a leaning building then looked down into the windows and saw the window display and she moved. WOW!
—Peter—
Bingo!
—Courtney—
Have you been to a coffee shop?
—Drew—

No, not enough time.
—Corey—
Yay. I wish I could meet you at a coffee shop…
—Drew checked in to Van Gogh Museum—
I love Van Gogh, he is my favorite.
—Ann—
Vinny is the bomb!
—Corey—
So weird cause my friend from L.A. was there the same day. I love Van Gogh. Hope it was an amazing day.

The first time I saw a Van Gogh painting I was moved to tears. It was in Washington, DC in the late '90s. I believe the painting was one of his series on sunflowers in a vase. That same summer is when the Van Gogh museum was being remodeled, If I remember correctly, many of his works from the museum were on an American tour. This was my second time seeing some of the collection. I am in awe.

Facebook, July 11—Drew—
#ActOfKindness —15 I met a lovely young girl in line waiting to get into the Van Gogh museum. We hit it off so well she bought me the headset tour as a thank you. Totally random happening I will always remember. So many generous people in the world extending kindness.
—Drew—
"What would life be if we had no courage to attempt anything."—Vincent Van Gogh

Incidentally, the only time I lived outside the state of Florida was the seven months my husband and I lived in DC. Our stay lasted from spring to fall, it was beautiful to see the city come alive and bloom then change colors in the fall. My only hope is this experience on the road last longer than my DC stay so I can say, "The longest I have lived outside the state of Florida is the _____ time I spent in Europe."

While finishing up at the museum I decided to go on Grindr to see if any locals were interested in entertaining a tourist. I did get a message from an American living here. I shared where I was and he offered to show me his art collection when I was done with Van Gogh. "What the hell, I am on vacation, sure, sounds good."

200

After my tour of the museum, I went in search of his apartment to make a new friend and share some wine-enhanced quality time.

Facebook, July 11—Drew—
I just met a really nice younger man in Amsterdam. We shared wine and great conversation. He is a self-described art collector. To me, it looked more like art HOARDING. Art was everywhere in his flat. So much so it was stacked on the floor. The art was out of this world. One piece was an 8' rubber newborn baby girl, with the expression of screaming on her face, a bit terrifying. He had a chandelier so big it was lifted with a crane into the backyard then brought in. That was a great connection. Maybe my new adventure won't be a lonely one. On the way to the Anne Frank House, I met a girl and we talked for a long time. I told her all about my book. I will work hard at staying in the flow of traveling and let people come into my life. I like this travel thing so far, it suits me.
—Michelle—
Omg, you look so beautiful and happy. Ty Universe. Let's do this. I'm coming to the next one w u. U should have it down by then love. Happy travels, exploring new peeps, embracing where ur at and letting go of familiarity. Love #StrongestPersonIknow
—Ron—
You look so handsome and enlightened. You really do! You are really giving us a great history lesson. Much love to you. Ron

Next up, Anne Frank. I have read the "Diary of Anne Frank" a couple of times so this is an exciting moment. While waiting in the long line I can hear the bell chime. I remember from her diary she could hear the bell from her secret hiding place. My host shared in Amsterdam they built houses behind houses. So the front house was obstructing the view of the back house. She called them Hinder Houses, which is where Anne Frank hid.

The museum was entered through a secret passageway in a bookcase making the experience real for all the tourists who were crawling through. The space was small, empty and difficult to envision their life. There was a model and photos of how it could have been arranged with furniture and belongings which was an attempt to help us see how it was. Regardless, it was deeply moving to be walking the empty halls, knowing all that transpired in those upsetting days.

Facebook, July 11—Drew is feeling amazed—
I was in the Anne Frank home today, she wrote in her diary the following: "Last night the four of us went down to the private office and listened to England on the wireless, I was so scared." June 11th, 1942. That's today, I am stunned and humbled!
—Drew is @ Anne Frank House Amsterdam— "I long to ride a bike, dance, whistle, look at the world, feel young and know that I'm free."—Anne Frank 24 December 1943 – I feel free in this place.

When I was returning to the train station after my tour of Amsterdam, I noticed just how many bikes were chained up outside the station. It was a shocking number of bikes. So many you could hardly imagine that many bike owners. I did hear some residents have several bikes depending on what they need them for at the time, casual to the more expensive and the advance bike. Even some bikes are specifically owned and used just in case they get stolen, geen probleem (no big deal).

Facebook, July 11—Drew—
They LOVE BIKES here. How do they find theirs? "kerel waar is mijn fiets"(dude, where's my bike)
—Kitty—
I know!!! I went at age 14, would love to go again and see it as an adult and most of all, do a tour on a bike!
—Jorge—
I remember being shocked at guys in suits commuting by bike.
—Peter—
They look really good flying with their ties flapping behind them.
—Drew—
And girls in dresses.

That evening while back at home in Haarlem, I searched the internet looking for lodging in Ireland. Hostels are always an option if I don't find a Couch Surfing host. Finding lodging and making travel arrangements is turning out to be a full-time job.

Facebook, July 12—Drew—
Ok, I am getting anxious again. Today I fly to Ireland and I don't have a place to stay. I have been on the Couch Surfing website and haven't gotten a confirmation. There are several hostels in the

area so I don't think I will have a problem with that as a backup. Basically, I arrive in Dublin, have to figure out how to get downtown, walk around finding hostels and move in for a few days. I feel the sand beneath my feet shifting and moving. Now I have to get to the airport, get through all that stuff and get on the plane. So many moving parts. I can get better at this. I will be in Ireland for two weeks and this will give me some time to better prepare for the rest of my journey. I am purposely not planning my time on the road so I can live in the flow and trust that all will work out. I don't even have a sweater or jacket; I will need to find an H&M straight off or a thrift store. It's colder than expected.

—Michael—

The sand is always shifting. Now you're better at balancing.

—Laurie—

Well, at the very least you Look AMAZING! And you are shaving? I expected a full-on grizzly bear beard. I have tons of jackets and sweaters. Just tell me where to send them! I Love you. Keep on Shining my Beautiful Friend.

—Richard—

I went to Dublin airport in 2001, there are regular shuttle buses into the city centre directly outside the airport building, I think it takes about a half hour into the city, I didn't see much of Dublin apart from the bus journey as I only went to Dublin to catch a train from Dublin to Galway. Regarding a jumper or sweater, there are two Penney's stores in Dublin where you will definitely get sorted out. I wish I knew someone in Dublin who I could ask to put you up but I am positive you won't have a problem.

—Drew—

Thanks for the shuttle info. Facebook is so helpful…

—Brenda—

Ok, stop worrying. First, a bus will take you into the city center from the airport. There are few hostels in the city. Second, go into Penny's on O'Connell Street very cheap get anything you want and just enjoy my hometown. You will love Ireland, get into the country on cheap rail and buses gets you around. Enjoy, I am jealous, wish I had got home to see my son's and grandkids.

—Ken—

Worry is a misuse of imagination. I see you going through all these changes with ease & joy. Meeting wonderful people all along the way. The Irish are very friendly. Enjoy.

—Marcus—

You will conquer these obstacles...
—Drew is feeling loved—
So I have figured out that leaving the warmth of a loving home and safe place is difficult for me. Leaving safety for the unknown makes my ego-mind reconsider my adventure. I am sure I will get better at this, that's why I am on this journey. But that doesn't make today any easier. Kelly and her family are the kindest people ever to welcome me into their home and give so much love and kindness to me, a stranger. I love them. Thanks Sally for setting us up.
—Scott—
To take chances of the unknown, it's challenging... Keep going just to scc what's out thcrc... Because you never know when you're in your older years you will wish you had done something about it.
—Oya—
Enjoy the Journey. I am so proud of you. You are full of love and that's what you will always receive.
—Anthony—
The biggest fear for anyone is the unknown. You have faced that fear time and time again and then conquered it. Never give up faith in yourself. You are taking the expression "Life is about the journey, not the destination" and made it true.
—Martha—
The thrill of adventure... history... every step you take someone from a long time ago stood in that exact place... Oh, when in Ireland, respect the little folk (fairies)... they are quite a force still in Ireland. Peace and may light show you the way to your next stop. Love, Martha

One of the many items I brought on the road(too many) were my art pastels and pastel paper. Since I graduated from Ringling College (art school not the clown school) I thought I would try my hand at creating art again. As a Thank You to my kind host, I created an original pastel using their garden as my subject. Before I left America I did a practice piece to work out the kinks. Now this second pastel is making me just as nervous. I haven't been on the "art" bicycle in a long time, I am not sure if I will remember how to ride it. Since the Netherlands loves their bikes, I should at least try.

Facebook, July 12—Drew checked in at Amsterdam Airport Schiphol—
Ireland here I come. I made it all the way to the gate, now, a beer *Next stop, Dublin. Find a hostel and I'm done, safe in a new country. Crossing fingers.*
—Sherry—
You are now a pro traveler Drew! 😊
—Kitty—
You got this Drew!

As I sit in the airport sipping my beer, I am reflecting on the past four days. They seem like a week. I was in Spain, Portugal and the Netherlands, now I'm off to Ireland. When I was separating from my husband 18 months ago, I never imagined this for myself. I could never have dreamed that sad day would pass. Nor could I have dreamed in less than two years I would be traveling the world, solo.

I am the same person who never made travel arrangements throughout my marriage. I resisted using Google, instead relying on my husband to do all the work. Thinking he enjoyed it, I let him do it and thus save me the trouble. I was wrong for many reasons. I realize now how codependent I was, never doing anything by myself and resisting doing basic life responsibilities in an attempt to make my life easier. As I reflect today, I needed the practice. I am sure he would have appreciated my taking on the task occasionally. Actually, I am very sure he would have. Open note to my ex-husband, "I'm sorry, I should have done more in our marriage".

Now I am taking on this task—what I now consider my new full-time job. I instinctively knew when I left America I would get the necessary training I needed to bring me up to speed on life. I am getting a crash course.

I am learning how to live in the flow of life, knowing

"Trust would settle every problem, now." — A Course in Miracles.

This powerful quote was on the phone that I lost and has been my motto on this journey. I might not always see how the Universe is conspiring on my behalf, but I do feel it.

Can I do this, can I live in the flow of life while on the road in Europe? I guess I can because, hey, I am doing it. TRUST!

Facebook July 12—Drew—
#ActOfKindness —16 My first friend host on the road. The Netherlands really know how to welcome a stranger into their home. A boat ride on the Canals of Amsterdam, really? Never had I ever, and boy was it wonderful. Along with the food, drink, conversation, rides in and out of town and much more. It is so rewarding to be in a loving warm family home while on the road. This feeling is hard to leave. I am forever grateful for your welcoming of me into you're loving home. I thank you.

Posted on December 30, 2015 by Drew Eric

Chapter 29 Can I have the life of my dreams?

"My chains are loosened. I can drop them off merely by desiring to do so. The prison door is open."—A Course In Miracles

I feel close, closer than I have ever been to living the life of my dreams. I am not talking about RICHES, I am not talking about LOVE. I am not talking about FRIENDS or FOLLOWERS, I am talking about my inner self, my true self, the self of my soul that is… HAPPY, CONTENT and at PEACE.

I am seeing glimpses of peace and happiness in my life, moments of clarity and moments of love a good percent of my day. Then, I go and do things that aren't in my best interest, focus on things that don't bring me peace or happiness, dwell on things that encourage stress, frustration or even depression.

It is moments like now when I feel connected and at one with myself, that life makes sense. Life is right, joyful and peaceful. I went for a jog today and I was talking and listening to my inner self, running over my life as it is now, my actions and who I am and who I want to be. It was in that moment I heard my inner voice, "You can have your dreams come true". What I realized that next moment was that my dreams won't come true if I keep taking actions or doing things that aren't in my best interests. Let me explain.

"The Soul always knows how to heal itself. The challenge is to silence the mind."—Caroline Myss

I have come to realize on any given day, we have a finite amount of time that we are awake, creating and thinking. This time changes every day, minute by minute, hour by hour. I do observe where my creative thinking goes and what my actions are. Where is my focus and what I am doing? Am I present to how my thinking, focus and doing affects my happiness? If my thinking time is finite, how much of it is spent making my life better or how much of it is spent resisting my divine happiness? I do have room for more divine happiness in my day!

We all have addictions and tools we use to escape: Drinking, drugs, sex, gambling, gaming, eating, complaining, television and many others. What I am observing is how much of my time is spent using any of these tools to escape. How much of my time is filled up with empty meaningless actions and treating my body and mind lovelessly when I could be doing something that would be fulfilling and rewarding?

We are taught to pray at an early age. We are taught to sit for a few moments and be grateful. We are encouraged to meditate for 3 to 30 minutes a day. All of these actions are healthy and beneficial. But the question is what are we doing the rest of the day? Where are we spending the other 14-16 hours of awake thinking time?

I get up each morning at 6 a.m. and love to be in bed at 10 p.m., leaving me 15.5 hours of awake thinking time. If I spend 30 minutes meditating, five minutes on gratitude and 25 minutes praying, reciting a mantra or reinforcing words of encouragement, that leaves me with 14.5 hours. How am I spending my time?

Here is where I spend my time that is beneficial to my wellbeing: working, teaching yoga, coaching clients, meditation, reading and listening to audiobooks, watching inspirational television (Super Soul Sunday, Sunday Morning on CBS, Super Soul Sessions on SuperSoul.TV), quality time with friends, quality time with my three pups, Center for Spiritual Living CSL, spiritual conversations, Tuesdays with A Course in Miracles study group.

Here is where I spend my time that is NOT beneficial to my wellbeing: Television that is mindless and/or somewhat entertaining, beating myself up, dwelling on sadness or difficult situations, looking outside myself for love, eating comfort food and sugar, drinking, isolating myself at home, getting upset with my three pups, feeling bad and/or depressed.

The point I am trying to make is that I want to focus on the list that is beneficial and limit my time spent doing anything else. I am awake 15.5 hours a day and I want to spend 15.5 hours a day doing things that lift me up and make me a better person, friend and leader in my community.

I no longer want to spend hours tearing down what I build up each and every day. If I spend three hours creating joy in my life, I don't want to spend six hours counterbalancing that joy. I want to be free of my old ways of being and let go of old habits that are no longer needed. I am not defined by my actions, I am defined by

208

who I can aspire to be and who I believe I am. I can create joy and happiness without counterbalancing it. I can have the life of my dreams and create Heaven on Earth here and now. This is my call to action.

Will you join me and create more joy and happiness in your life?

"The only person you are destined to become is the person you decide to be."—Ralph Waldo Emerson

#LifeLesson —42 Fill your time with experiences that bring joy and minimize the time that diminishes, take away or destroy your joy. Finding joy in your life is not counterbalanced with reduction. This is one balancing act you want to tip the scales.

Facebook, December 30—Sherry—
That was very well written and something I needed to hear today. Thank you, Drew!
—Tim—
WOW! Well said my friend! I will join you!
—Todd—
I applaud you Drew for being so open and bearing the intimacies of your soul. You're making your journey not only your own but a journey for those reading as well. We're all so different, but yet also so much the same. I think so much of these things
—Mark—
Your writing today has moved me. Please know that one person now and much more will follow to hear, listen, learn and be touch by these incredibly honest brave thoughts you are sharing. They are truly gifts from your soul and I thank you! Namaste

Posted on July , 2016 by Drew Eric

Chapter 30 Can I surrender to the will of the Universe?

Facebook, July 12—Drew—
"When the need to control takes grip, hold up your hands, open your fingers and surrender all. Peace will quickly find you."—Drew Eric
—Drew checked in @ Dublin, Ireland—
Ok, I made it safely. Once I got off the bus an overwhelming calm came over me, very surprising. I still didn't have a place to sleep, I do now. I am here for two weeks. I really need to relax, everything has been moving so fast. I haven't felt stable, grounded in a week. The last two days were amazing though—my host family in Amsterdam was incredible. I am so looking forward to not doing anything for a couple days. My hostel is a shared room with ten people—an improvement from 50 people on the Camino.
—Kitty—
Whoot! An Irish blessing for you! —
May you always have walls for the winds,
a roof for the rain, tea beside the fire,
laughter to cheer you, those you love near you,
and all your heart might desire.
—Drew is feeling full—
Comfort food then a comfort beer. Garlic cheese fries. I'm in heaven.
—Pedro—
You gonna gain some pounds. Who cares! Not regrets man! Lol
Facebook, July 14—Drew is at O'Connell Bridge—
Taking a walking tour.
—Peter—
It's about time you need some exercise.
—Drew—
Right, 500 miles wasn't enough.
—Drew is feeling optimistic—
I arrived on Tuesday and found a hostel. Wasn't crazy about it and left the hostel the next day. I spent some time looking on couchsurfing.com for a place to stay. Finally I was offered a place for the weekend, which is nice since the beds at the hostel go up in cost

over the weekend. I have someone offering me a room on Sunday also if that pans out. Finding cheap lodging is a full-time job. I like the hostel where I am now. It's clean, nice and I can use the kitchen—which cuts costs on eating out. Tomorrow I check out of this hostel with my 50 lbs backpacks and hopefully get a bus or something to the new Couch Surfing host. Wish me luck.

—Christopher—
You'll be fine for sure...always go with your gut.
—Drew—
The Sunday room did not pan out.
—Sherry posted a photo—
"Stress makes you believe everything has to happen right now. Faith reassures you that everything will happen in God's timing."— unknown

What is a BIGAM? I flew into Ireland three days ago and took a well-needed vacation from my vacation. I know, it sounds crazy but yes, I needed to ground myself and get centered after two flights and four countries, in four days. Moving so fast does that to me. Now that I have rested, I'm finding myself curious how the rest of the road will unfold. I am just off the Camino where traveling was easy. Basically there was no thinking involved. Everything was laid out for me—food, lodging, sights to see and a constant flow of people to meet. Every day I would walk with someone who could be a potential new best friend.

However I am not on the Camino anymore and I am observing that life on the road isn't as easy as it was while on the pilgrimage. I walked for 32 days figuring out how the whole thing works, how to live in the flow of the Camino. Now I have to learn how to navigate the roads in Europe and let the Universe guide me in whatever direction it sees fit. The act of surrendering has proven to work for me thus far. I learned this from "A Course In Miracles" and whether at home or here on this road, I do not know what's best for my personal growth, but the Universe/God/Holy Spirit/ Destiny/Inner Guidance does, if I let It.

About midway through my pilgrimage, I observed my own fight against the Camino. It became apparent, I must surrender to what the Camino (Inner Guidance) wanted for me versus what I wanted from the Camino. This transpired right out of the medieval gate at Saint Jean Pied de Port when I met the young man who would so significantly impact my life. My heart was closed after my divorce and meeting him opened my heart and with everyone I came in contact. I feel in love with me and by doing so this it allowed me to love others.

Living in the flow of the Camino, I observed, was a struggle for many others on the pilgrimage as well. People who were fighting the Camino had injuries, illnesses, all kinds of blocks preventing them from achieving their selected goals, i.e. finishing the Camino by a certain date, walking at a certain pace, finding peace.

Eventually, after surrendering, I learned how to live in the flow while walking my path. I recited a mantra from "A Course In Miracles" every day in an effort to open myself to all the Universe has to offer.

"Universe,
Where would you have me go?
What would you have me do?
What would you have me say and to whom?" —*A Course In Miracles*

The Universe provided for me life lessons beyond my imagination. I came on this adventure to open up, to grow and learn. I intuitively knew this time on the road was exactly what I needed to kick start my life after the divorce in early 2015. So far, just over six weeks, the personal growth and self-reflection have been deep and powerful along with unsettling and difficult, as most lessons are.

By reciting my mantra, often throughout the days of my path, I consciously chose to be open and accepting of the flow, the unknown—all while feeling confident the Universe will bring to me exactly what I need to be my best Self and have the most amazing life-altering pilgrimage. Where will I walk? Oh, the sights I saw were breathtaking from the mountains to the valleys. Who will I meet and share with? I made some beautiful friendships and ended some new acquaintances. What new experiences and growth will I have today? More then I bargained for and it was completely worth it.

Now that the Camino is in the past, I don't want to lose that new found excitement of living in the flow and surrendering to the unknown. I learned when I want or need something, all I have to do is ask the Universe and it will be provided, Flow. Every time I tested this theory it proved accurate. What I noticed, all I have to do is get still, observe where I am closed down, open myself up and ask for possibility. Sometimes I am more specific and while other times I am more vague, not limiting what the Universe wants for me since the Universe knows best.

Facebook, July 13—Drew is feeling optimistic—
"I believe, today and every day, everything will work out for my best and highest good."—Drew Eric

I have been enjoying some alone time this past week through my fast moving travels. It was greatly needed after my intense experience in Spain. It's easy to get some quiet time for self-reflection while moving around so quickly from Santiago, Spain, Lisbon, Portugal, Amsterdam, Netherlands, and finally landing in Dublin Ireland in just four days.

However, now that I feel more grounded and centered, I'm noticing I have begun to feel isolated. I am longing for my Band-of-Brothers and the amazing time we shared when our paths crossed. It felt amazing to be "One of the guys" since I never felt that way growing up. Being a sexually confused young man I tended to shy away from other boys in fear of being seen as potentially gay since I was so unsure myself. With my Band-of-Brothers, I was just another guy, not the gay guy, just a dude.

This morning I began to wonder what I was doing to limit myself and just how am I living outside the Flow. So I decided to get still, present and ask my inner guidance for help.

Facebook, July 14—Drew—
"I trust, I know it comes when I ask, I am patient, I surrender to the process."—Drew Eric

I am a social person by nature and I accept my need to meet and make some friends along the way. I read blogs about meeting travel buddies, although I couldn't envision the concept, I am open to the experience. My plan is to backpack the roads of Europe for several more months, seeing as much as I can, meeting new people, make some lifelong friends and memories. How will I do all this with my social anxieties, can you see my confusion?

Facebook, July 14—Drew—

I am getting some helpful advice how to meet people while traveling. Hang out in the common room of hostels. Go to meet-up groups, do walking tours, do bus tours. All good advice I will put into action.

Through my research I found couchsurfing.com to be very helpful. The website has a social component with a calendar where you can look up events in whatever city you find yourself. Here in Dublin, lo and behold, there is a meet-up at an Irish Pub this evening(the funny thing in Ireland, wouldn't they just be called a Pub)? On the way to the meet-up, I recited my mantra "I am open for all possibilities". I decided if anyone ask me to do anything, I am going to say, "Yes." I will not be crippled with fear and social anxiety, I will remain "Open to all possibilities" and surrender to the flow. The Universe knows best.

Once I entered the pub and located the meet-up, I ordered a beer and found myself next to a friendly English bloke. We spent some time chatting over our Guinness, I could feel my social anxiety loosening its grip on me.

Eventually our conversation waned and we joined the rest of the travelers and locals at the meet-up. A short time later, I was in the middle of conversing with a young couple when my new English friend found me and shared what he just heard.

"Hey, another traveler inquired if anyone was interested in renting a car and exploring Ireland over the weekend, what do you think?" he asked with a tentative, uneasy look on his face.

This was my chance, insert mantra here: I am open to all possibilities, don't say no.

"Yes!" I replied emphatically.

As it turns out, the Brit, I and three other guys showed interest and, like the Guinness in my glass, a plan began to bubble to the top. After a few minutes of conversation, we decided to form a Whatsapp group (a texting and calling application that uses Wi-Fi) and make some plans for the following day. I left the meet-up feeling a little excited and anxious at the same time about a possible car share over the weekend with four strangers.

The next day we gathered at a hip place called Library Bar. It had the feel and appearance of a 200-year-old, private smoking club. It's described online as "Plush embroidered armchairs, open fires and leather sofas dot the inside of this calming hotel bar."

We jumped right in with the planning and getting to know each other. After a very few minutes, we were laughing loud and enjoying each other's company. I was thinking, "This could work, still nervous, but this could work."

Facebook, July 15—
"Loving life will always create opportunities for Life to envelope you in love."—Drew Eric
—Drew with 4 others at Library Bar in Dublin, Ireland—
Ok, here I go again, my life is so cool. Last night I met four guys at a meet-up for Couch Surfers, host and travelers. One of the travelers suggested renting a car on Saturday and driving to Cork. All five of us said yes, what the hell.
—Joe—
I have driven all over Ireland, watch out for livestock!
—Laurie—
Oh Dear! Good Luck. You are making me nervous.
—Drew—
LOL, Don't take on my anxiety you have enough of your own. Isn't this crazy? I was actually feeling sad and concerned about not meeting people on the road through Europe. Now I'm on a road trip with four strangers.
—Ron—
It all sounds perfect! You guys are displaying how the world wants to be in community together. So sweet to see the progress of your journey!!!
—Jenna—
That is what traveling and being in Europe is all about. If only more people would leave this country and open their hearts and minds to people from other places and new experiences we'd have a lot more love and tolerance in the world, or here. Enjoy every second my friend. xx

I spent the last month on the Camino making friends and learning how to travel with them. I felt this prepared me for a new bunch of men. I saw the Brit, typing something on his phone, then he chuckle, and hand his phone around, everyone did some laughs, then it reached me. The Brit wrote a post on Facebook and wanted my approval. I read it.

Facebook, July 15—The Brit—
The gnarly crew, A Brit, a Mexican, a Homosexual, an American and an Italian (he's in the boot) in a VW all around Ireland. What could go WRONG!

I laughed out loud and thought how wonderful it was he could make such a joke, not knowing how I would react as the "Homosexual". Clearly, his view of me was as just another guy. I told him I loved it and thought to myself, "This weekend is going to be good, I can feel it." Maybe I can live in the Flow, off the Camino, maybe I just need to surrender and see where this car ride takes me. As the Brit's famous last words said, "What can go wrong?"

Not all of us were there at the Library Bar, the Italian from the meet-up was at work and wasn't able to make it to the planning meeting. Unfortunately, this meant he was a bit more vulnerable to our jokes. We couldn't exactly remember his name and started calling him Fellatio (Google it), his name is Feliciano, you can see the similarity. We couldn't stop laughing each time we said Fellatio and we weren't even drunk, yet. This was the closest I felt to be with a new Band-of-Brothers, and I liked it.

The Brit fancied a name to call our group. This made sense to me since I named my last group of guys the Band-of-Brothers. We started throwing around letters seeing if we could create an acronym. We had a British guy, a Mexican, two Americans, one gay guy and an Italian. We ended up choosing "British, Italian, Gay, American, Mexican or BIGAM" and the Brit coined "The Gnarly BIGAM Crew" as our official name. They were all under the age of 27 with my being the oldest at 48, so yes, I was thinking this is crazy and I surrender.

Facebook, July 15—Drew—
"I release control and go with the flow. No amount of stress will disrupt my peace. I will breathe into the unknown and surrender."—Drew Eric

It was time to head over to the rental car. "Are we really doing this"? I thought.

When we arrived it was just before closing time. There weren't many cars and getting the cheaper rate seemed to be out the window. After discussing it with the rental company and amongst "The Gnarly BIGAM Crew" we decide it was just too expensive.

216

The manager overheard our discussion and chose this time to offer us a deal just to get us in a rental so they could close.

My mind exploded with, "Whoop, whoop, we have a rental car, living in the Flow! What can go wrong, we are The Gnarly BIGAM Crew"! I had possible plans this weekend with a Couch Surfer host, but nothing committed. I am making a conscious decision to see this through, wherever the car takes us. The only solid plan I have for the next week and a half is a return flight to Amsterdam. Let's see where this goes first before I make any further commitments. Hell, I could be in an Ireland prison before the week is out. :)

Facebook, July 14—Drew—
Last night I met a young doctor from Malaysia. He is a pediatrician here and a professor. We spend hours talking about coaching, the Camino and the interaction of people with each other. It was awesome. So nice to connect with really great people. I will see him again this weekend hopefully.

Facebook, July 15—Drew with 4 others—
Today we have rented the car until Monday morning. We will get on the road tomorrow. We are planning on visiting six cities in two days. So to recap, five strangers, an Italian, Brit, Mexican, and two Americans that don't know each other will be driving through three cities on Saturday, doing an overnight somewhere and three cities on Sunday then arrive back in Dublin, completing a circle around Southern Ireland. What can go wrong!

—Drew—
#ActOfKindness —16 I met a local resident Doctor who invited me over for a home-cooked meal. We really hit it off and he offered to host me the night before my big adventure, tomorrow with The Gnarly BIGAM Crew. I saved some money and that is always an act of kindness to have a place to sleep and fed wonderfully. I thank you.

Posted on July 19, 2016 by Drew Eric

Chapter 31 Can I have a big adventure with some blokes?

Facebook, July 16—Drew—
"I breathe through uncomfortableness, I trust it will be ok, I let go of uncertainty. No other plan is needed!"—Drew Eric

We went out that night for some "getting to know each other" quality time prior to our full-on adventure the following day. I was still a little nervous with my new mates, but I didn't focus on my nervousness. After an evening of fun and jokes, I chose to head back to my hostel early as to get a good night sleep, early meaning midnight. I believe the rest of The Gnarly BIGAM Crew, stayed out late, or early in the morning, whichever way you look at it.

As morning arises, I receive a message and make it down to the car for them to pick me up. I then found out about the adventure they had to send a message to me. They had to tailgate a public bus to access the bus's Wi-Fi in order to send me the message. They recounted a hilarious story about them working hard to not hit the bus while keeping their Wi-Fi connection.

I feel that we're off to a good start. It's only been 24 hours and already jokes and memories abound. Ireland better watch out, The Gnarly BIGAM Crew is touring a town near you.

When we were at the rental car place I spoke with one of the agents inquiring where in Ireland we should do some sightseeing. She gave us some recommendations and a direction to drive, looping around Southern Ireland from Dublin, on the East, heading south, then crossing west, driving up the West coast until we circle back to Dublin in two days.

Let me remind you that Ireland drives on the wrong side of the road. The two Americans are the designated drivers, which is funny since the person used to driving on the "wrong side of the road" is the Brit and he is 24, too young to drive a rental car.

We, five strangers, worked together in an effort not to get killed while driving around Ireland—hilarious. The four of us are working in tandem as backseat drivers, with different responsibilities in order to keep us on the road and safe i.e. staying in the left lane, where to look when turning right, left and keeping an eye out for red lights and stop signs. There are so many things to see and watch out for while you're driving on the wrong side of the car and the road.

Facebook, July 16—Drew is @ Abbey HSE with 4 others— Checking out the sights.
—Ann—
Finally you look at peace... You have made an awesome change... Don't let anything bother you when you return... Remember where you've been, how you got there, and where you are now... You did this! And it worked... Be safe my friend... You look fabulous... You are a long cry from a break-up... Whether you see it or not...

We made our first stop at the ruins of a monastery. Our first group outing included a tour in a beautiful setting. We took pictures, made jokes and generally poked at each other like school kids on a field trip. "Classic," became our go-to phrase when referring to any one of us. As if we knew what "Classic Drew" really is or what "Classic Mexican" really means since we only met two days ago.

Facebook, July 16—Drew checked in to Kilkenny Castle with 4 others—
We have made it in one piece. The American drove first with the Brit giving directions. Next up, Drew the American driving with the Italian giving directions. We are eating lunch, seeing the castle, walking the town a bit till we head to Cork with me at the wheel, God help us all.
—Drew, eating fish and chips at Dinos Kinsale with 4 others—
We got the grilled fish and garlic cheese chips. Along with curry chips and battered sausage. Yummm!
—Drew, with 4 others in Kinsale—
Should I be driving on the wrong side of the road? Oh goodness. The Gnarly BIGAM Crew made it to Kinsale. I am still driving poorly, they are nervous and they are making me nervous.

Continuing on the road, we enjoyed a lunch of "Fish & Chips" at a small fishing village, strolled through a shopping town named Cork, then on to our final destination, Tralee, where we will spend the night. We choose a hostel—only one available—and it has less than desirable ratings online. We are actually excited about the adventure this poorly rated hostel would deliver.

Facebook, July 16—Drew with 4 others—
Back in the car! Hoping we make it to the hostel before it closes and we get a bed to sleep in.

Once we arrived, the host recommends we stay as a group with several other guests in a big room, leaving no empty beds. We inquired about a room of our own since there are five of us and she informed us that we don't want to share a room with the other two men in the only other room available.

She stated, "They're a bit dodgy, and for your safety, I wouldn't recommend it".

Facebook, July 16—Drew, is drinking beer at Roundy's Bar with 4 others—
The Gnarly BIGAM Crew made it to Tralee and checked into our hostel. All is well but one of the bunks looks a little dodgy, not mine though. It's the Brit's; hopefully he doesn't get crushed in the bunk bed while he sleeps.
—Shannon—
Dodgy, eh? Yep, you're definitely hanging around a Brit!

We took her advice. When we ran into them later that night her suspicions were confirmed. One had a black eye and both looked a bit, ruff, quick darting eyes and a walking pace with purpose.

With the Brit's bunkbed concerns, he chose to pull the mattress on the floor rather than lose his life in a bunk bed mishap in Tralee. He chose wisely.

It is Saturday night and "The Gnarly BIGAM Crew" decided to see what kind of nightlife is to be had in Tralee. I was a mix of nervousness and excitement since I didn't want to stay out too late and feel hung-over on our second day of the road. I also didn't want to abandon my new crew so off we went into the night in search of a happening place where they have girls (for them) and Guinness for all of us.

Wow, is all I have to say about Tralee. These Irish folks like to DRINK. I saw quite a few passed out drunk, throwing up, dressed up, partiers out on the town. I was concerned for my safety while at the same time found comfort knowing I had a crew that had my back, just in case this evening goes awry.

While out, we had some beers and the boys attempted to flirt with girls, possibly dance with them and attempted wing-man services for each other. This became our pattern, drink, be a wing-man, try to meet girls and flirt. I was the only odd man out since very few men in these pubs were interested in other men, but that was ok with me, I am here for the ride and excitement it will bring.

After midnight we called it and headed back to the hostel, laughing, recounting the girls they flirted with and making plans for the next day. We decided to get up early and visit the "Ring of Kerry". The Ring of Kerry is a scenic drive around the Iveragh Peninsula in Southwest Ireland. It's a 179km-long, circular route that takes in the rocky coastal landscapes and rural seaside villages.

Facebook, July 17—Drew—
On the way to Kerry and Skellig Ring, stopping for a quick photo op.

The Ring of Kerry included a short ferry ride on one side of the ring, giving us an opportunity to take the rental on an ocean voyage. Eventually we find our way back to town for lunch then on the road again. Next stop is "The Cliffs of Moher" which is a mountainous cliff edge jutting 214 meters (720 feet) above the Atlantic Ocean. We will experience spectacular views of the cliffs and hopefully see the ocean splashing at the shoreline many frightening feet below.

Once back in the car a magical thing happened. The other American "A" of BIGAM asked some in-depth questions that gave us a chance to get to know each other on a more personal level. We have been together a little over two days and with these new insights, a shift happened, so subtle we didn't even notice. However, it had a huge impact on the rest of our time on the road. Closeness was formed, a deeper bond, a connectedness that felt more spiritual in nature. My anxiety almost completely disappeared and I now saw these guys as true mates. We all felt the same way it seemed.

The American could have easily been the G in BIGAM because his family is from Guatemala. I got the G for Gay so he was dubbed the American. He is a kind man, super easy going. He is a little shorter, more of the Latin type, tan with dark hair and a warm

221

smile—good-looking guy. He has an interesting way of speaking that is calming, direct with little expression. He almost speaks in a monotone with little to no fluctuation. It's interesting to watch him talk since I tend to be more animated with my expressions and personality. He makes you feel relaxed in his presence he is so easy going.

His best friend is gay and he and another girlfriend are meeting up with him in France for a couple weeks. He describes himself as being extremely comfortable with his sexuality, so comfortable in fact he has no problem cuddling with his best friend. He even shares his bed at home when they have a sleepover after a night out on the town. Hearing this surprises me since I haven't met many men in my life so comfortable with themselves. It's refreshing. Clearly he is a kind, warm, friendly man and I enjoy his company immensely.

The Brit: Is dirty blond, with greenish eyes and a really charming smile. He has fair skin, probably easy to burn in the sun. He kinda has this devilish grin that draws you in. He is a super sweet guy however in typical British fashion, I would say he isn't as comfortable with the touch of a man—which, of course, encourages me to attempt to push those British buttons. He is always up for the adventure, willing to go anywhere and do anything. He is super friendly and easy to get along with. I would probably say he is the most reserved of us all, proper even, again, in typical British fashion. Still, a very likable guy.

The Italian: Is attractive with thinning hair and a very typical Roman nose, appropriate since he was born just outside of Rome. When he speaks he can't quite pronounce his R's so when he says Rome it sounds more like Woooome leaving out the R altogether. I believe he doesn't quite understand everything we are saying, especially if we are talking fast. Back in Wome, he lives with a girlfriend. He is temporarily working in Ireland at the moment and will be back in Wome when the summer is over. I find him attractive honestly. Maybe it's the Mediterranean thing he has going on and his adorable smile. He exudes a warm friendly feeling that is comforting.

The Mexican: He is the quirkiest of us all. He is thin with long limbs and loves to dance around at a bar being unusual and fun. His English is good; I even forget his first language is Spanish. He has a brother who is gay and has no issue being physical with me or any of us. That is a quality I like most in the men I am meeting on the road. He is full of expression, moving around and using his whole body to talk. He even came up with a calling card when he wanted to find us. Cocoo, Cocoo, he would call like a bird searching for his mates.

When we arrived at the Cliffs, the fog had rolled in. The rangers said the parking lot for the Cliffs is closed due to the fog. We could drive up but there is nothing to see. Earlier at lunch, the cashier recommended a private viewing spot just down the road from the parking area. She said it was private land, with a path running down the fence line to the Cliffs and is great viewing, very popular. We decided to give it a try. Amazingly, we actually found the location.

It was mid-day, gloomy with fog, not able to see but a few feet ahead. The path was wet from dew and rain with a mud trail running up the middle. We did our best to follow the path, trying not to step in the mud; the grass gave way to large puddles. I eventually stepped directly into the mud ruining my H&M tennis shoes. Fortunately they were only seven Euros.

As we moved down the damp path through the horse pasture towards what we hoped—but didn't want to fall over—were the Cliffs of Moher. We felt like trespassers walking towards our doom. Then, out of nowhere, we could hear the sounds of waves crashing on the shore and knew we were edging close to the cliffs and sea far below. I had visions of one of us dying on this very day. I could picture the breaking news article, "One member of "The Gnarly BIGAM Crew" fell to his death on a road trip to the Cliffs of Moher, due to deep fog, full story at 11:00". All I could hear in my head was the Brit saying "What could go wrong?" which is a clear indicator that the shit is about to hit the fan.

Luckily we could see the cliff's edge. It was even better than expected. We spent almost an hour playing on the cliff, taking selfies, hanging over the cliff's edge and pretending to be Superman. There we were, standing as if we are on the actual cliff edge when there was a safe distance from it—all for the photo op.

There was no other human around; we were all alone on this private scenic cliff edge. It made for a special surreal feel and was the highlight of our experience on the road. Because of the personal sharing that morning in the car, I believe the Cliffs of Moher were that much more enjoyable.

Facebook, July 17—Drew is with 4 others—

The Gnarly BIGAM Crew had an amazing time on the road. Here are the photos. I love these guys, so much fun.
—Summer—
Dang, does the sun ever shine in Ireland lol?
—Drew—
Every other day, LOL.

Once back to the car we made the long drive back to Dublin getting in that evening with plans to drop the car off the following morning. The Italian invited us over to his apartment for a final get together, farewell dinner of sorts. It would be our last time as the full Gnarly BIGAM Crew. Of course he cooked spaghetti and I brought the wine.

Facebook, July 18—Drew, with the American and 3 others—
#ActOfKindness —17 The Gnarly BIGAM Crew were invited to the Italian's residence for a home cooked Italian dinner. This is the life. The Italian is a great man. He is kind, giving of himself and deeply contributed to an amazing road trip. Thanks for all you gave me and the guys.

Over dinner, we discussed our traveling plans and as it turned out, three of us are on long-term road trips. My backpacking experience has no end in sight, I do have a flight back to Amsterdam but no plans after that. The other American has another month while the Mexican also has no plans on returning home in the immediate future. The Brit has a flight back to London in a couple days and the Italian is remaining in Dublin with work.

Hmmm, maybe this doesn't have to end in Dublin. Three of us hatched a plan to train up to Belfast, Northern Ireland and spend a day or two, ferry over to Scotland where we can catch a bus to Edinburgh. Stay in Scotland a few days then who knows, maybe head down to London from there to visit the Brit.

The Brit was even interested and said he would check flights to Edinburgh from London. Amazing, not only did I meet some great guys to drive around Ireland with, I also met some travel buddies who would go country hopping. My dreams are coming true. I now have a clear vision of how to meet travel buddies and make life-long friends. Thank God I surrendered and went with the flow regardless of anxiety and fear.

Facebook, July 19—Drew—
"Someday, everything will make perfect sense. So for now, laugh at the confusion, smile through the tears, be strong and keep reminding yourself that everything happens for a reason."—John Mayer

—Drew is with the American @ Hostelling International N.I/ Y.H.A Northern Ireland—
BIGAM has mostly disbanded. It's just GA right now. The two Americans are off to Northern Ireland, (Belfast) for an overnight then a ferry to Scotland. We shall be traveling together for the next week. However BAGM will be back together Friday in Edinburgh Scotland for the weekend, the Brit is flying up. What can go wrong?
—Beverley—
What a road trip you are having!

A little bit about Belfast—In the '80s there was the Catholic—Ireland, Protestants—Northern Ireland conflict. In Northern Ireland, they are the descendants of 500 years of Protestants from England and Scotland with fewer Catholics, while Ireland is predominately Catholic. These two conflicted religious and culturally different areas struggled with the English rule and the country has been split since 1921. Ireland wants their land back from English domination and rule, while Northern Ireland has English roots and feels more tied to England. The English suppressed the Catholics with discrimination and regulations. Many years of bombings and fighting neighbor-against-neighbor ensued and the IRA (The Irish Republican Army) is blamed for more than 1700 deaths between 1969 and 1993. I had wondered what kind of condition I would be seeing when we arrived. To my surprise, Belfast was new and shiny with new buildings and shopping districts all around.

Facebook, July 19—Drew with the American at Titanic Museum, Belfast, Northern Ireland—
Checking out the exhibit. This is how we roll in Belfast.
—Drew—
#ActOfKindess —18 A kind student in Northern Ireland for school —through Couch Surfing—put me up for a night. He cooked me a beautiful Indian dinner then joined my friend and me at a pub. Even a student can extend kindness to others. Thanks.

Facebook, July 20—Drew, Drinking beers with the American at Morrisons Lounge Bar—
Hanging on our last day in Northern Ireland. Tomorrow we ferry over to Scotland, bus and train to get to Edinburgh and meet up with the Brit. Thursday to Sunday the three of us will be together. Sunday, the American and I are renting a car in Edinburgh, dropping the Brit at the airport, then driving a stick shift to London where we will stay together till Tuesday. The American will head to France and I will stay in England for a while to burn up some time out of the EU Visa treaty. I made some friends on the Camino I plan on seeing in London and can't wait. I read a blog once about meeting people and joining with them as travel buddies. I couldn't imagine this for myself since I have struggled for so long with sustaining friendships. I have grown so much in the last two months that I was able to create this reality for myself. I have made some great friends and will have known them for 13 days and have been with the American continuously. Life is great. Bonds can be made over drinking a Guinness.
  —The Brit—
Sweeeeeet! And thanks in advance for the lift to the airport, nice surprise!
  —Joe—
Guinness !!! <3 THE Breakfast of Champions!

After a restful couple days and a visit to the Titanic Museum—Titanic was built in Belfast—we caught the ferry to Scotland where we will rejoin the Brit and the Mexican for a few fun filled days in Edinburgh, Scotland. Sure would be nice if I met a guy interested in guys :). I can only hope the joy and excitement continues once we gather back together. What can go wrong?

Facebook, July 20—Drew—
"From good days I find happiness, experience comes from difficult days, lessons from bad days but the best days bring memories that sustain you throughout your days."—Drew Eric

follow my... road

Posted on July 26, 2016 by Drew Eric

Chapter 32 Can I be a wingman?

Facebook, July 21—Drew is with the American, at Stella Line, Belfast Docks—
I am on my way to Scotland on a ferry. It's like a small cruise ship. Really upgraded and nice. Life is so cool when you live it.

Recently I found out my Father is 67% Scottish making me somewhat—insert unknown % here—Scottish. I haven't done my genealogy yet but I am very much interested. My excitement level is unusually high. I hadn't realized how much I truly wanted to visit Scotland. I really had no concrete plans for my time spent on the road and wasn't sure if or when I would visit. Now that I am on the ferry I am so looking forward to arriving. Just for this occasion, I wore my kilt that I have been lugging around in my backpack since I left America. It weighs five pounds so I better get good use out of it. What comes to mind is the movie "Highlander" released in 1986. The beautiful countryside and landscapes are breathtaking. I saw it with my mom all those years ago. I have this Moorish ancient city fantasy in my head, with no real clear image of what to expect. This is all new to me.

Facebook, July 21—Drew is with the American at Stena Line, Belfast Docks—
Ferry to Scotland-check, bus to the train station-check, first of two trains to Edinburgh-check. We are that much closer. A funny thing happened on the windy deck. I gotta be more careful with my kilt.

What beautiful countryside we saw while riding the trains into Edinburgh. The American is staying at a different hostel; the rates are cheaper at mine however they only had one bed available. I dropped him off at his hostel then walked past the Edinburgh Playhouse in the direction of mine, which took me to the North Bridge with a spectacular view of the Edinburgh Castle in the distance. It was breathtaking. I felt like I was home. Ahead of me is a building with a sign on it that says, "The Scotsman". I used it as a backdrop for a selfie and you can see the excitement of home-coming on my face.

It was still pretty early in the day which gave us enough time to do some sightseeing. The American and I visited the castle. Unbelievable views of Scotland can be seen from all around, rolling hills with the river in the distance and the city down below.

That day the Brit arrived making us a threesome again joining the American and me. We spent some time out, just us boys, looking for beers and girls for them to talk to. We ended up in a cool bar with a live band. I have to say, it felt pretty good to be with some 20-somethings out on the town drinking beers and being a regular guy. Something I didn't get to do in my 20s so much as just another guy. Here I am doing it for the second time on my journey, thanks Universe.

A funny thing happened while we were out. My mates started keeping an eye out for guys I could meet. They have been wing-manning for each other since we have been hanging out and on this night they started searching for me. I felt so honored to be included equally with the guys. I never thought young straight guys would be so comfortable around gay men. It never crossed my mind but here we were and they were treating me like anyone else, I was just looking for the same gender, not the opposite.

As the night progressed they showed me a couple guys as they were chatting up the girls. That's when it happened; a young man started talking up the Brit. It was innocent at first then he came back around working a closer angle. Just like these guys had been trying to do with the girls.

The young man said to the Brit "Hey, its cool, the whole gay thing is cool, no big deal to me".

My friend, thinking he was speaking about me, agreed with him and kept on dancing.

The young man circled back again, this time asking how long we had been a couple, referring to the Brit and myself. My friend was like "No, wait, we aren't a couple, I'm not gay".

The young man nodded and took his empty pint back to the bar for another. When he returned, he chose to get even closer. He spoke to me, asking if his talking to my friend made me jealous. He spoke to my friend again saying he wanted to make me jealous and my friend was getting nervous at this point. This was all getting weird now.

At one point I had to step between them on the dance floor to save the Brit from this drunk Scottish guy making a move. Since I have no experience in straight bars or mixed bars I was very confused thinking, "Does this happen all the time? Do straight guys go Bi and hit on other guys in bars after a few drinks? I'm intrigued. Is this what I have been missing all these years?"

After I squeezed in, the young man proceeded to get further hammered and wouldn't leave my friend alone. He got so confused about who he was and where he was, he tried reaching around me to grab my friend like a possession or a stolen toy he wanted to keep for himself. This really crossed the line and was pretty funny at the same time, at least to me.

Facebook, July 22—Drew with the American and the Brit @ The Standing Order, Edinburgh (Wetherspoon)—
Having breakfast/lunch/beer, with me mates. First full day in Scotland, out till 3 a.m. and up at 12:45 p.m. This is the life baby. I'm living it. I am one of the boys, so much fun.

In my hostel are a couple of guests, a sweet redhead from America—another American—and an Italian. The Italian was well worked out, muscled and good looking so I was more than happy to invite them both out for the evening. Being a wing-man, my work is never done. Here is a lovely Irish looking American girl, any one of my mates will gladly sweep off her feet. Also, the beds have unusual names like climax and cuddle, what kind of message are they sending I wonder?

The Brit once lived in Edinburg and worked at a local shoe store. He mentioned his friends were heading out later and meeting up at a jazz club. But first, let's visit the one bar that's open now.

229

Facebook, July 22—Drew—
Nightlife in Scotland. Funny thing, I am at a Latin bar with salsa dancing, it feels like being back in Miami, only in Scotland. We met some new friends in my hostel. An Italian and American and brought them out.

We left the Latin bar venturing out to meet his friends. My buds pull me aside and told me they want to take me to a gay bar tomorrow. It's time we are wing-men for you. I was flattered at the kindness and told them I am having a great time just watching you all.

Facebook, July 22—Drew—
"In time you will look back on these troublesome days and realize what you stressed about doesn't even matter. Keep on going."— Drew Eric
—Last year I had so much stress, I don't even remember. I wonder what I will be thinking in a year from now:)?

Our next local Scottish hotspot on the tour is a Jazz club that is rocking with a full live band, trumpets and all. They are playing Latin Jazz, whatever that means.

Encyclopedia Britannica: Latin Jazz, also called Afro-Cuban Jazz, a style of music that blends rhythms and percussion instruments of Cuba and the Spanish Caribbean with Jazz and its fusion of European and African musical elements.
Facebook, July 22—Drew checked in at The Jazz Bar in Edinburgh, Scotland—
Wow, is this really happening? Am I really doing this? Is this really my life? Why yes, yes this is your life, your life is this cool, Latin Jazz cool!

It was one of the more surreal moments of my life on the road. Have you ever been somewhere doing something and thought to yourself "Is this for real?"

Facebook, July 22—Drew is feeling amazing—
"Always believe, amazing things are on the horizon!"—Drew Eric

The energy is electrifying. The place is packed and you can feel the excitement in the air. The passion behind the instruments is strong, loud, and captivating. I just stood around looking and watching the band and the crowd with awe and excitement.

I noticed in the crowd a tall, very young, attractive man. He appears to be about 20 years old. I am not entirely sure what the drinking age is in Scotland. People are dancing and swaying, it is amazing how packed it is in here. I can't see an inch between the people but yet everyone is having a good time, dancing and bumping each other—plain old rubbing each other—such heat, such percussion.

The boy looked up and caught my eye, we locked eyes for a second and I looked away towards my friends. Joining them I shared my excitement on how this place is making me feel. I shared with the Brits friends—some girls he used to work with—how I met everyone and the crazy time we had in Ireland. My mates are off flirting or talking or doing something, I don't really know.

They asked if I found anyone interesting and I replied. "Oh, I'm gay and I couldn't imagine anyone here also being gay, I'm great just having fun with all you guys". With that, I walked back over to the dance floor observing the crowd.

I noticed the young man again and he was somewhat near the middle of the dance floor, kind of swaying, kind of not moving much. I was standing just one step up on a platform near the dancing directly in front of the band. He looked up and caught my eye again. This time I didn't look away. The dance floor opened up around him and time stood still. What happened next was very unexpected. It was like in a movie when the dance floor opens up, the crowd pulls back, the music softens and the only people that are in the spotlight are the two main characters. He looked up at me, stared deeply into my eyes and before I had a chance to do anything he stepped forward, grabbed my arms and pulled me into him and onto the dance floor quickly wrapping me into an embrace of tangled salsa dancing. WHAT THE F*CK JUST HAPPENED?

"Ok," I think, "This is happening. There is an adorable young man in my arms."

Surreal didn't begin to explain this—confusion, dismay, shock and fear come to mind. I immediately start scanning the room to get an idea how the crowded bar is handling two men salsa danc-

231

ing in such an intimate way. No one seems to be bothered. I glance up at my shocked friends and they smile with thumbs up. So I return my brain to the young man, by now he is talking deeply into my ear.

"You are so good looking. Wow, you are a really good looking guy" he says while he has me so close I can feel his breath on my ear and feel his body up against mine, tightly as we move in a small circle on the dance floor.

He is talking again, what is he saying? "You really are such a good looking man, but I'm not GAY" he yells over the music.

Ah, he isn't "GAY" but he is dirty dancing with me in a Jazz club in Scotland. Ok, Sure, I don't care, I surrender. This road experience is turning out to be far more bizarre than I ever imagined. I am living in the flow and if a 20-year-old, "Straight boy" wants to dirty dance with me, in assumedly what is a straight, Latin Jazz club in Scotland. Fine, I'm game.

He keeps whispering, "If I was gay I would totally be into you, you really are hot."

He goes to dip me and I take his guidance and throw myself back. My head probably gets pretty close to the ground and happily he doesn't drop me. I teach yoga and backbends are my specialty, so I just blew his mind.

"That was the most amazing thing I have ever seen" he screams over the music into my ear.

"Yeah, want to see it again?" I say

He throws me back again and once more my backbend is spectacular. When he pulls me up he embraces me with glee and amazement repeating again how attractive I am and how he isn't gay! He sure is protesting a lot.

This lasts for what seems like 20 minutes but probably wasn't that long. Eventually he says he is going outside for a fag (cigarette). The irony of it all makes me smile.

As he steps outside I stumble back to my friends, dizzy and confused with an "I have no idea what just happened" look on my face. The guys are like "Cool, alright, go on then." The girls are asking what was that all about.

I told them all what he said and they unanimously agreed he didn't look straight from their angle, which I agreed with "Right"!

I stayed with the group a while, trying to compute what just happened. It didn't, but who cares. Twenty, thirty minutes later I saw him again near the bar. I decide, what the hell, I am going in for round two. I will put myself in his sight of vision. Let him know I am still around and... "Single". Let's see if he takes the bait.

I step up next to him at the bar and order a Guinness. I resist the urge to say anything and he just smiles at me. Good, the lure is set, the hook is baited, let's see if he bites me.

I cross the dance floor back to the platform with the group, all the while keeping an eye out for the young man. I drink my beer and listen to the amazing band and enjoy some small talk with my mates. I finish the beer and peer out to the dance floor. I spot the young man, not too far away.

As we catch eyes again the dance floor opens up, once more he reaches and grabs me, pulling me into him except this time he isn't talking. He is no longer interested in protesting his "Straight-ness". This time his tongue is deep in my mouth caressing mine.

His hands are moving all over my body while he passionately kisses me. I glance around the dance floor to, again, see how the crowd is reacting. I almost get the sense, the patrons rather enjoy the idea of two guys getting it on. Ok, I will surrender and enjoy it too.

Mind you, I am wearing a kilt—since it is Scotland and I brought one hundred's of miles—but I rather think he didn't notice or doesn't realize because he stuck his hand down my waistband. Any normal person would go up the kilt verses down the waist-band. Wow, we are basically now having sex on the dance floor, I am astounded, but not willing to stop. Hell, when in Scotland do what the Scots want, who I am to stop him from finding what he is searching for.

He hasn't uttered a word and we go from grinding each other to kissing, fondling and back to grinding, on a continuous loop. Again, this lasts for what feels like 20 minutes or more. I am certainly enjoying the hospitality these young "straight men" offer here in Scotland. I do feel like I could certainly live here or at least visit more straight bars.

As we catch our breath he finally pulls a little away and whispers these sad words in my ear. "I gotta stop, this is done. I'm going outside for another fag but this is done, I can't anymore".

And with joyful sadness, he slips out of my arms the same way he entered them and I rejoin my mates. I felt a mixture of shock and happiness while left with the feeling of wanting more. In an effort to respect someone else's struggle, I understood his plight. I began the process of accepting what is and leaving it at that. With a time check and the realization it's 3 a.m. I choose to leave, guide my roommates home and dream about my Scottish boyfriend, back at the bar.

I will probably, forever remember this fondly with the thought, "I wonder what could have happened?" One thing I have learned on the road is "I am always in the right place, doing the right thing with the right people" in other words, going home is the right thing to do. There is always tomorrow and who knows what that will bring in the next bar.

Facebook, July 22—Drew checked in at The Jazz Bar in Edinburgh, Scotland—
I can't begin to tell you all how much fun this place is… The locals are really friendly. :) I wish I could stay out all night dancing.

In the morning my friend, the Mexican, told me the young man was still there when he left at 5 a.m., however he didn't notice him dancing with anyone after I was gone. I guess I could have stayed and maybe done some dirtier dancing, literally. We will never know.

I woke up the following day—late morning—to a message on Grindr. Not from the young man the night before but from another admirer. He is 24 years old, blond and very tall, from New Zealand, here on vacation. What is it with all these young men! Oh, and he identifies as bisexual.

The new young man inquired if I wanted to go on a date tonight.

Wow, last night I met a 20-year-old and had a deep connection and incredible kissing, tonight I have a 24-year-old wanting to go on a date. Hell yes, I am game for that. I am living in the flow. Let's see what else Scotland has to offer.

To recap the group I am traveling with: My three guys from BIGAM, the Brit, American and the Mexican, with the added two from my hostel— an American girl along with an Italian guy. The Brit and the other American are rooming with a young dating couple from Croatia. Including my date, nine of us will be hitting the gay bars tonight. Funny thing is I am the only gay person while my date is BI and the rest are straight. It will be a crazy night I am sure. What can go wrong?

As the day progresses and I figure out where the gay ghetto is, we make our plans for the evening. My date will be meeting us at one of the bars in the ghetto. I am still wearing the kilt, hell, why take it off until I leave Scotland, no better place to wear a kilt in the world.

My date is shy and concerned whether I will like him or not. I am just coming off the Camino, basically five weeks of little to no romance and last night's escapades got me going. I am ready to cut loose and be adored by a 20-something. My worthiness is high; I deserve a night like this. My guys are excited for me also since they have been wing-manning for each other these last couple weeks.

I still do not understand all that is happening here. Surrendering to the Universe is new for me. I meet a group of guys in Ireland, we travel together for almost two weeks and now we are all heading out for a night on the town in the gay ghetto. How did this happen? Is this what I will expect for the rest of the road in Europe? Or, is this my crescendo, my swan song and the rest of the road will never peak quite as high. Nothing to worry about now, I surrender today, let the Universe guide me for what is best.

Facebook, July 22—Drew checks in at CC Bloom's Gay Nightclub & Bar with 8 others—
Let's see what the gay scene in Scotland has to offer. I am out on the town touring gay bars with seven straight mates. Hard to believe this is my life. The people I am meeting are so open. I love it.

We gather everyone up, then we head out to the bar to meet my date. He is tall, over 6' while I am 5'8" not short but certainly short to him. He has a great smile, a shy demeanor, with a little bit of an embarrassed, unsure look on his face— it's pretty adorable. We talk, he buys Champagne for us all, my friends are certainly kind and willing to be bought for the price of a glass of Champagne. He easily melds into The Gnarly Crew. This bar has a dance floor and it is filling up. We dance, chat and begin the night with some heaving kissing after a few more glasses of Champagne.

Facebook, July 22—Drew checks in at Infinity Gay Nightclub with 8 others—
Bar #2, let's see how much fun this one is? Gay bar hopping in Scotland. Wow, just WOW!

Then it's time to head over to the next bar, down the street and around the corner. I don't know how this happens but next thing I know one of the guys takes off his shirt causing an avalanche of guys whipping off their shirts, pulling off mine as we enter the bar and hit the dance floor. Cameras are clicking, people are rushing to the dance floor and the crowd swells. Girls are rubbing on all my friends, not knowing, they like girls and aren't gay, I wonder if they will figure out the truth.

We didn't even get a chance to get drinks before the bouncers ask us to put our shirts back on, not that kind of a bar. We choose to leave and hit another bar instead of staying.

We walked around a bit before heading back to the first bar, just being silly all over the streets. Once back to CC Bloom's, and after a couple of bottles of wine, the dancing commenced. The Brit and the American girl are now entangled, I am a good wingman. I saw the American and the Mexican talking to some girls and I wondered how that was going since we are in a gay bar.

I am enjoying the dance floor with my date. We were making out like crazy being a little freer with our hands, feeling a bit safer this evening. The dance floor was packed but that didn't stop him from picking me off the ground and twirling me around. A woman tapped us on the shoulder to inform us after we spilled her drink and bumped her three times, she felt it was time to tell us. We got her message and danced our way to the other side of the dance floor where we could make spectacles of ourselves, maybe with taking up less space this time.

I turn and notice the boyfriend of the couple from Croatia was sitting on the ground near the dance floor and I thought, "That doesn't look right". Sure enough, they kicked him out. I thought it's 2 a.m., maybe it's time I take this date home and see where this is going. Reminds me of the quote from the movie "Top Gun" when Carol, played by Meg Ryan tells Goose played by Anthony Edwards:

Carole: "Hey, Goose, you big stud. Take me to bed or lose me forever."
Goose: "Show me the way home, honey."

Would my New Zealand boyfriend know the movie, he is from another country and the movie was made before he was born in 1986, the year before I graduated from high school?

236

We say our goodbyes and I look forward to hearing how the night went after I left all my straight friends out on the town in the "Gayborhood" What could go wrong!

Once back in his room we shed our clothes and pile onto the bed tangled in his long arms and legs, rolling around kissing and touching in a way I have not been touched in so long. It felt amazing to be caressed, adored and to have someone look so deeply into my eyes that I feel like they are seeing into me. I so needed a night like this. I so needed a man like this to worship me, if just for one evening—someone who is interested in me and wants nothing more than to give me pleasure. And that's what he did.

The following morning, late morning, we made love again. Making love isn't something I am used to since making love wasn't part of my marriage. It was a friendship more than a marriage.

Making love wasn't familiar but it did feel wonderful. I realized how long I have missed making love. I don't really recall the last time I did. It was gentle, kind, caring and warm.

I left him in his room to walk back into the real world. I rejoined my friends to make our final plans to leave Scotland for London. I guess destiny does include losing someone forever; I will always have memories of the men in Scotland.

Once back with my buds they shared their tall tale of a night. The Mexican and the other American were near the bar talking with some girls when the Mexican got the idea to pretend to "Be Gay". He asked the Croatian girlfriend to tell the girls he was talking to, "He is gay, totally gay in fact and the other guy is his boyfriend".

This sparked a night of kissing girls, allowing them to try and convert the gay couple. Then my friends shared the next bright idea.

"Let's talk about their boobs, asking if they are real and see if we can touch boobies.

Between the two of them—they kissed about 20 girls and got to touch some boobies too.

They were so brazen, they even kissed a girl in front of her boyfriend.

The boyfriend screamed over to them, "Leave my girlfriend alone!"

She yelled back "They are gay, you idiot," then she apologized for his being such a jerk.

They waved her off with their limp wrist and told her no big deal. My mates even took it so far as to kiss each other while in an embrace; essentially putting their lips on each other's necks, dry kissing. I was dying as they retold the escapades. I never imagined meeting these guys two weeks earlier, and that we would be here in Scotland recounting our big gay evening.

We were exhausted from so many nights out. I knew this evening would be an early one, at least for me. We choose to drive down to London on Monday after another day of rest.

London would be our last time together, not knowing if we will ever see each other again, whether at home or here in Europe. We were meeting the Brit back in London since he flew back Sunday morning. I never did get to find out how his evening went with the redheaded American girl. He was being a true, reserved gentleman and she had previously declared her chastity and "good girl" ways.

Facebook, July 25—Drew and 2 others at Princes Street Gardens—
We are moving again. Leaving Scotland today, renting our second car(stick shift) and I will be driving for the next seven hours. We are down to just the three of us, Mexican, American and myself, the Gay. We have been together 12 days and we have three or four more together. Love these guys. According to the "Eat Pray Love" travel idea, we are in the PARTY period instead of the Pray period. LOL. I finished my spiritual portion on the Camino. Then again, the learning never really ends. It's been a great ride hanging with the guys. Let's see what happens in London?
—Drew checked in at Enterprise Rent A Car—
Here I go again, I got the gay card upgrade to an automatic. Yay. No stick shift driving on the wrong side of the road for me.
—Drew eating dinner with the American at Cagney's Restaurant—
We made it to London. Seven and a half hour drive from Scotland to London. Never in my wildest dreams did I ever think I would, someday, drive a car into London. I did all the driving, I feel great. While the American and the Mexican slept most of the way. I played all three Adele albums and turned Siri into a British man, appropriate for driving through England. Good times.
—Drew is feeling inspired—
Yup, the Eye and Big Ben. I'm here baby!

Facebook, July 26—Drew is with the Mexican and the American—
Seeing the city on a self-walking tour. More fun...
—Drew checked in with the American and the Mexican at Tower of London—
Lunch break with me mates. The Mexican is enjoying a free left behind coffee with his meal. No joke, that's how he rolls.

Our first full day we spent sightseeing around London, really just walking everywhere. We started out from our hostel, toured downtown then over to the Tower, across Tower Bridge, along the River Thames. We then continued to the Tate Modern Museum for a quick tour. Finishing our walk to Buckingham Palace on our way through Hyde Park to see the Diana, Princess of Wales fountain and eventually making it back to our hostel. It was a full day of walking.

That evening—our last night together—we met up with the Brit as The Gnarly BIGAM Crew. We grabbed some beers and reminisced. It was bittersweet being back together. All we were missing was the Italian, but he was back in Ireland working. I do hope I see him again in Italy when I get there, eventually.

Our visit didn't last long since we had trains to catch. On that final second it was the Brit and the American heading into the Underground. I hugged them both goodbye, still trying to plant an uncomfortable kiss on the Brit because I know how much he squirms every time I tried. I kissed the American on the cheek for his goodbye then they turned and down into the underground they went.

I immediately grabbed the Mexican in an uncontrollable sobbing embrace. He held me tight and let me cry. I have such a hard time saying goodbye and the other American and I had been by each other's side the entire two weeks. We were very close. I missed them immediately. I knew the Mexican was staying in Europe longer so there was good a chance we would see each other again somewhere in Europe. Who knows, maybe we will visit the Italian together before we leave for North America.

Facebook, July 26—Drew is feeling grateful—
#ActOfKindness —19 The Brit was my travel buddy and friend. We shared food, drinks money and a rental car. He gave me a bag that said, "I love Scotland" when I said I liked it. I will always

remember our time together on the road and I look forward to following your incredible journey on Facebook and hopefully, one day, being together again. I am in England for a couple more weeks, maybe? Thanks again.

—Drew is feeling grateful—

#ActOfKindness —20 The American traveled with me for about two weeks. He shared his food, money, bought me things I needed and we spent lots of quality time together. Great man. Proud to call him a friend. He was kind enough to invite us all on this road trip and I am thrilled I accepted. I look forward to seeing you again someday on the road of life, maybe back in America, who knows.

—Drew is feeling grateful—

#ActOfKindness —21 The Mexican is funny, warm, friendly and giving of everything. What's mine is yours! We shared money, food, and hours of laughing and cutting up. I hope I will see you again somewhere in Europe since we are both continuing on this road trip. Thanks for being you and sharing in my life.

The Universe has treated me well. Looking back on that day in Ireland, I was feeling sad and longing for a new adventure on the road with some cool guys. I wanted to make some new friends. I never imagined two weeks later I would have so many amazing memories with such wonderful people. A chance encounter in a Pub in Ireland, a simple question and a simple answer, "Who wants to drive around Ireland and see the sights?" "Me, sign me up.

What could go wrong"?

Nothing, nothing did.

Can I surrender and live in the flow? Looks like I can, and believe me, it's worth it.

Facebook, July 26—Drew—

"Surrender looks like peace, it does not resemble giving up."—Drew Eric

#LifeLesson —43 Manifesting is as easy as opening yourself up and declaring what you most desire. Then, surrender and believe your inner guidance will steer you right, on the road.

—I wanted a big adventure on the road, I wanted some new mates, I wanted to find love. I created all this and some amazing memories along the road well traveled.

follow my… road

Posted on January 19, 2016 by Drew Eric

Chapter 33 Can I travel the road through Europe ALONE?

"Staying in your comfort zone doesn't bring you closer to connecting with others. You need to step outside your comfort zone and into conversation, showing others your authentic self and allowing them in your zone."—Drew Eric

2015 is coming to an end and I am alone. This past January, my husband and I chose to end a nearly 20-year marriage. We'd reached a point where the relationship was no longer working and we needed it to end. Even though I was barely making enough money to support myself, I felt an overwhelming need to be alone–just me, my yoga mat and three dogs. I spent so many years avoiding Me.

Prior to meeting my husband, I'd been adulting for nine years. I was 27 when we met and spent the next two decades in a committed partnership. Because we'd shared all decisions equally, I now found myself, at 47 years old, frightened at the prospect of making decisions alone along with many other fears.

As the year comes to a close, I'm looking back on the experience of being alone. When partners separate, losses continue with friends and family. I leaned into friendships for support, only to feel like some of the friendships were leaning away from me. I asked myself, "Where did my support system go? What happened to some of these friends I cherished so dearly? I gave so freely of my time, love and energy, where are some of these friendships when I need them most?" Now I wonder how much of a connection we really had? How much did they really know me or I know them? For that matter, did I even know myself?

I chose then to get present and remind myself "None of this is true, I do have a support system. People love me, I am not alone and I have many people I can rely on!" However, when you are in the throes of despair, it's hard to see things clearly. It is all in our perspective on how we see our life.

When I was a young boy, I attended six elementary schools prior to fifth grade. This lack of stability had a direct impact on my social development since childhood is where we learn about

241

friendships. Because of moving so often, I didn't develop beneficial social skills that allowed me to maintain friendships over a long period. I was loud, with high energy, and that often frightened my new classmates. What I did learn was when you trade a brownie in order to make a new friend, they laugh at you–while eating your brownie. Giving gifts is not an effective manner to acquire friendships.

When I was in high school, I felt isolated and alone much of the time. To further compound the situation, I was hiding sexuality confusion. I subconsciously chose to keep everyone at a distance so I wouldn't be questioned. I shifted groups and moved around in different circles often–repeating the pattern I'd developed in my younger years. In short, I hid out and put up walls.

I am including my senior quote that accompanied my senior portrait in the yearbook. I feel it clearly reflects a need for connection and love and openly displaying my aloneness. "I Like to party, I like to dance, so tell me about your party in advance."

Even in college, I used to walk into the campus cafeteria calculating who I would sit with, in an effort to be included in their weekend plans. I felt crippled without the knowledge and understanding of how to make friends and I had a profound desperation for deep meaningful friendships. I did not have the understanding of how connections work.

Having a fear of being alone hasn't exactly disappeared since my youth. I live in Wilton Manors, a place filled with activity and action and yet I feel separate from it all.

Today, many people see me as a highly social and outgoing. The reality is that I often feel uncomfortable and prefer attending parties or events with a companion to share the experience, avoiding being alone. While in my marriage I had a built-in companion.

I used to attend social gatherings and networking events and "Circle the room" meeting as many of the attendees as I could, handing out business cards along the way. Never realizing I wasn't connecting with these individuals. I wasn't able to see how saying hello doesn't bring me any closer to a connection or a business contact, it actually assists me by hiding and never really allowing anyone to get close.

Those first few months alone in my one bedroom 600sf apartment were unsettling. Turning off the television and preparing for bed, I noticed the unbearably loud silence. When I was married, my husband and I would chit chat while preparing for bed. The silence now is deafening.

Today I am choosing to face my fear. I've made a decision to backpack Europe–alone. And I'm actually excited at the prospect of taking this on, alone.

"Stop being afraid of what could go wrong and start being excited about what could go right."—Tony Robins

Now I challenge my earlier fears by attending events alone. I've learned how to just be with me. I can be at a party or event and not rely on friends or a partner. I squarely faced my social anxieties and moved past them. I've come on the other side with a new way of handling life. I live without fears.

I learned something else this year. I learned I am changing for the better. I haven't been bar-hopping which used to be a big part of my life. Bar-hopping was an easy way to make acquaintances with anyone who happened to also be bar-hopping. Now I enjoy seeing people at social gatherings, having coffee, over dinners all while connecting deeply through conversation. Something that is difficult in a bar setting.

Today I am letting others see my authentic self. I acknowledge my accomplishment of getting out of the house and being in the company of a friend and feel proud of myself for getting out of my comfort zone of isolation. I no longer want to shut myself off or hide from opportunities to connect. I want to put myself out there for all to see.

Sometime during the summer, I believe I had my "Aha moment" and my life shifted. I stopped feeling sad, lonely and depressed. I got present with a new idea–"My life is of my choosing."

I am choosing to be separated and not be married. I am choosing to be single and live alone. I am choosing to meet new people and make new friends. I am choosing to give dating a try and prepare myself for a new life. I am choosing to backpack Europe, alone. I see my new life as My choice. I can choose to connect with others and get out of my comfort zone. I no longer have to feel anything other than to be happy and love myself and others. I choose to start living again.

When I am traveling Europe, I'll be alone. I will travel from city to city alone. I will sleep and eat alone. I plan on rising early to capture artistic landscape images–creating art and using pastels

243

to record the beauty of what I see. I want to see sunsets and sun-rises. I will take my aloneness and welcome it.

Being alone this past year has been immensely valuable to me. I needed to feel the aloneness. I needed to make friends with "Alone." I needed to be OK with "Alone." I needed to sit in my aloneness–with my new friend–and chit-chat, enjoy a cup of cof-fee and share my stories. I needed my new friend, "Alone" to come into my life. I hope he stays a while so we can continue our relationship. I look forward to sharing Europe with my new friend. I like my new friend, "Alone."

I have been looking over my selfies this past year and I observe them with pride. I see myself as someone who overcame his fear of being alone and made a new friend. I hope you see him too.

#LifeLesson —44 Show your authentic self for all to see and you will connect most deeply with everyone you meet. Authenticity keeps loneliness at bay.

Facebook, January 19—Susan—
Great writing Drew :) Europe will be an awesome experience for you. I hope you will be journalling along the way, so I can "live" Europe through you. (I don't know if I'll ever have the opportunity to do what you're doing; but I would love to!) Anyway, have a safe journey & I'll be thinking of you!
—Christopher—
Sounds like an amazing ride Drew… I can certainly feel you and where you are and are going.
—Sash—
Love your positive attitude & energy my friend.
—Ronald—
Difficult to explain however reading this just helped me. Thank you
—Allan—
Oh, you are ready my friend, I'm thrilled. The places you will go! :) Loving our journey.
—Matthew—
Thank you for sharing Drew. Silence can be so powerful. I wish you luck and joy on the road. Don't pack too heavily! I bet you meet tons of people to share your journey.
—Lantz—
This could be my story, but substitute "15-year relationship/50 yrs old." Travel has always been my love, but no place has called to me like Ft. Lauderdale. I'll look forward to meeting you in

person! :) (Moving there in Summer... Finally!) GREAT read. Chin up. Alone is better than lonely WITH someone. Promise!

—Martha—

Every artist needs a walkabout... Be careful... Breathe... Walk the old churches, the little squares... Enjoy... Laugh... Live... Love... your friend from college who would always even now welcome you to my table.

—Angel—

Thank for sharing your story. Today is one month from when I became single again.

—Chris—

Thank you for sharing your beautiful and vulnerable story. I am struck how similar so many of us are, and how we struggle with the same things even though our paths may be very different... I hope your adventure is filled with all that you hoped for, plus a dash of the unexpected to keep things interesting and know that the love that the universe so deeply holds for you may find you and embrace you with your new friend!

—Berne—

When I traveled in Europe by myself over 40 years ago, I finally realized the difference between being ALONE and being LONELY. From that point on I embraced being ALONE and lived every minute in the moment on that three-month journey. I envy you. You will never forget the memories you are about to make.

—Christopher—

You are finally comfortable in your own skin. Something few people ever are. Congratulations

—Barry—

Drew, I read every last word of this and have to say you are one amazing man. You've got the guts to face and challenge your fears and for that, I take my hat off to you honey. Love you.

—Lisa—

Drew, I loved reading this and I learned so much as well. I actually spend a lot of time alone and love it. I also like to mingle and make new friends too. But there is something refreshing about being alone. I remember you from college and remember you as the outgoing fun loving guy with a huge smile. You always had such positive energy. You are doing fine with this new you and you will love being alone on your travels too.

—Donald—

Kudos!!! I've backpacked Europe solo, one of the best things I've done.

follow my… road

Posted on August 28, 2016 by Drew Eric

Chapter 34 Can I learn how to navigate
long-term traveling?

London and Paris in 18 days, this is what I learned. I arrived in London on July 25th and spent two weeks there. I drove down from Scotland in a rented car with The Gnarly BIGAM Crew. We traveled together for 13 days total, which is an amazingly long time hanging out with travel buddies you just met. Sadly, after three days in London together we all went our separate ways.

After my friends left by train, I moved in, for another week, with my Prince-in-Bright-Clothes from the Camino who lives in South London, Peckham Rye. After London, my Prince and I headed down to the beach town of Brighton for Gay Pride, the U.K.'s biggest Pride Festival.

Facebook, August 5—Drew—
I am on the move again. It's so very difficult to start moving around after staying in a home. You forget the comforts you only get in a home. Cooking and washing, not having to carry everything you need, at all times, like soap and food. Now I will be back to the nomad life after one week staying with my Camino friend.
I am off to Brighton today for Gay Pride weekend with my friend and the rest of England. However I am doing it like a 20-something without a necessarily confirmed bed to sleep on. It's a "come along, we'll sort it out when we get there, I'm sure it will be fine!" Living on the edge here. I am sure it will make a good story at least.
I left most of my belongings at my friends flat. Sunday I will be heading back to South London on two trains, picking up my backpack and catching a third train to meet the car-share that will drive me to Paris. Today is two trains to Brighton with time to spare for mishaps. I have anxiety but it seems to be getting much better the more I move around. I can do this!
Facebook, July 28—Drew is feeling grateful—
#ActOfKindness —22 My Prince-in-Bright-Clothes invited me to live with him for a week, then invited me to Brighton Gay Pride to spend an overnight and experience Pride how the English do it.

So kind to be welcomed into his home and under his roof for shelter, warmth and generosity. I was able to visit all over London while having a place to come back to and call home. Huge savings since London is so expensive. I will always remember my Week in Peckham Rye with love and kindness. Thanks my friend, you are a Prince.

Facebook, July 29—Drew is feeling grateful—
#ActOfKindness —23 My Prince-in-Bright-Clothes brought me along to a swanky BBQ at his friends flat. They welcomed a strange American into their home and treated me like we had been friends for years. I had Halloumi cheese for the first time and loved it. Later we hit a pub for more entertainment. What a great night with amazing new friends, food and drinks, thanks.

Facebook, August 6—Drew is feeling grateful—
#ActOfKindness —24 My Prince-in-Bright-Clothes brought me to Brighton Beach for a night out on the town during Gay Pride. His friends welcomed me with open arms offering a couch in a full house of partygoers without batting an eye. They gave me food, drinks, and took me out on the town for an adventure of a lifetime. Largest Gay Pride in England is what they call it. Thanks for all your generosity. I had an amazing time which will never be forgotten.

So much learning transpired. Once the travel buddies split apart I was left to find my way as a solo traveler again, although I wasn't exactly alone. I was technically living with a friend who was working and had existing plans in the works. So my time was still my own, touring days and some evenings and weekends.

I knew it was going to be difficult to make decisions and figure out, without my travel buddies to help me with what to do every day. After the Camino, I only spent about a week alone and that was traveling between four countries. I was on my own in Amsterdam and visited the Van Gogh Museum and Anne Frank house, but when I arrived in Dublin Ireland I had no plan other than a scheduled flight back to the Netherlands two weeks later, which I never made.

I floundered for a couple of days thinking about how I wanted the road to unfold. Am I a sightseer with a list of sights to check off? Do I want to walk around the city and get a feel for it? Do I want to sit in coffee shops, write and people watch? Do I want to meet people and make friends?

I heard about travel buddies from blogs but never imagined what that would be like or how I would manage that new experience. It was beyond my comprehension since I was so inexperienced in traveling and making quick friends while traveling. Making friends is something I have shied away from with the fear of there NOT being a good fit and then I am stuck with them.

I tried the dating sights and that didn't seem to attract any sustaining friendships. I looked on Facebook for some groups in Dublin but didn't have much luck. Then looked at Couch Surfing and found events section and noticed there was a Couch Surfing meet-up just a day away. I decided to give that a try.

Prior to attending my first Couch Surfing event, I was pretty confused about what I wanted for my adventure and a little down. On my way to the event, I made a decision to be open to any possibilities that might arise. My theme on the road is to remain open versus closed to possibilities. It is very easy to shut down and stay safe by doing what I have always done. But bars and dating sites don't seem to bring me satisfaction.

So when one of the guys at the event asked if anyone was interested in renting a car for the weekend and driving around Ireland for sightseeing, I jumped up and said YES. It turned out to be an exceptional time spent on the road, so completely thrilling. I learned so much about myself and acquiring travel buddies.

Having travel buddies spoiled me a bit. I thought every met-up would be like the one in Ireland. I would continue to meet amazing people and make friends and pick up new travel buddies and adventures. This hasn't always panned out but I will continue to remain open for the possibility.

I visited London and Paris once before and had several of the required sightseeing experiences. So this time, solo, I came with a new perspective. I really wasn't sure what I wanted out on the road.

I did know I wanted to experience London like a local resident. I didn't want to just run, run, run and see the sights. I wanted to drink coffee and relax a bit. After spending almost every night out in Ireland and Scotland, I was ready for some rest.

Facebook, August 4—Drew checked in @ East Dulwich Tavern—
Doing some writing in a pub, like a local would. Life is good.
—Drew is at Prince Albert Hall—

I just witnessed my first opera. I was blown away and cried through most of it. Amazing performance, I had no idea....

Facebook, August 5—Drew checked in @ London Bridge Station—
It's comforting to see a police presence and a bomb-sniffing dog, then again, why? I guess this is what it's like to be a local.

When I arrived at my friend's home I chose to have a more regular schedule. Go to bed before midnight, wake up early and start a regular routine of checking email, going on Couch Surfing looking for events and figuring out how to travel, meet people and see some sights. Most importantly, I started using public transportation, i.e., subways, buses and trains. England has a multi-use card for all three called the Oyster which made it easy.

Facebook, August 5—Drew checked in at The Mayflower Rotherhithe Pub—
This is the pub that the Mayflower sailed from to the new America in 1620. Pretty cool to see where American history came from.
—Drew is feeling curious—
So the coolest thing Londoners do is run to and from work. They strap on a backpack and run. This saves commuting time to work, public transportation, along with being able to skip the gym. I love it.

I am dyslexic and learning anything new takes twice, if not three times longer than average. One of the symptoms of dyslexia is short-term memory retention problems. I have to work really hard at keeping something in my short-term memory. For example, verbal directions, phone numbers and people's names just don't stick. I have to work hard at name association. I don't even bother with numbers. Directions I can do really well with a map/visual assistance.

Facebook, August 15—Christy—
Sounds like an amazing adventure! And from reading this I now realize I think I have dyslexia memory problems and anxiety too. You are doing great!!!
—Kitty—
OMG you sound just like me, say someone's name and I smile and shake their hand and by the end of the shake, I've forgotten it.

I check and recheck things like stops/directions over and over and over!

Happily, there is an app for getting around Europe called "Citymapper," what a great tool. You put in an address, whether it's a home, business or park and it tells you how many options you have between walking, buses, subways, trains and always the combinations of those you will need to take. Meaning, walk 12 minutes to bus stop blah-blah, ride the bus to subway stop blah-blah, take the subway to this station then exit the station and walk another 12 minutes to your destination. Huge help for someone like me. Love it!

Spending eight days in South London and being forced to use public transportation really helped me get comfortable. I have anxiety when learning anything new. Clearly, I have fears about getting lost, making the wrong choices and, in general, screwing up. Being forced to use public transpiration has now eased the anxiety.

Let me give you an example of a subway experience so you can clearly understand what it is that happens in my mind and why I am so anxious. I put in the address, check it three times by cross-referencing it with another map application(occasionally it takes you to the wrong place). I follow the walking directions to the station. I check continuously I am moving in the right direction (I have had to U-turn). I arrive at the station and have to figure out which line to get on to go the direction I need to go. Yes, I have gotten on the wrong train now several times, but with much less stress.

Once on the train, I count the stops and look at the app to confirm the first stop. I do this no less than four times because I have forgotten all the information due to short-term memory loss. I feel like Guy Pearce in the movie "Memento" from 2000. He has complete memory loss and has tattoos all over his body to help him figure out the mystery unfolding in his life. Really well-done movie but it has not inspired me to start tattooing myself to help me remember people, places and things.

So I sit on the train, I can't remember how many stops I have left so I constantly look at the map, read the stop names outside on the train platform and quadruple check all the details over and over and over again. Eventually I arrive at my destination. I'm not

251

kidding, this is for real, it's crazy obsessive but the only way I function.

Facebook, August 15—Karen—
Traveling is such a great adventure. When I was in Germany I would opt for the bus over the subway. That way my travel app would work & I could see landmarks. Underground I would lose count of the stops. I totally agree you need to count the stops, but that can be tough to do especially at the end of the day when you are tired. Travel safe & have fun.
Facebook, August 1—Drew—
Taking all these trains busses and Overrails make me anxious. I guess that's why I am staying in London for so long. Just to get used to doing it. Today, one of my rails got canceled and I had to reroute my position and it took twice as long. Getting around London is work. But I'm here, so that's not to bad.

The good news is I have been doing it for so long now the stress has subsided and it's become more routine. If I make a mistake I just go get on the opposite train and do it again. Even when I somehow was on my way home for a short half-hour train ride in London, I somehow managed to get on the wrong train and it cost me an extra hour. It happens, c'est la vie.

Facebook, August 3—Drew—
So this is my life now. I am spending today trying to decide where I should go next. It's really that open. My friend in Kiel Germany is out of town and I have to fill some time until she gets back. She lives in NW Germany so it wouldn't make sense to go east to Berlin until after I see her since once I go east I will start heading south to Hungary and other countries around there, Vienna even. So let's see, I can visit Paris, Brussels or Netherlands again, hmmm?
Facebook, August 4—Drew—
They have this really cool thing over here called blablacar.com. It's a car-share. I am paying 27 pounds for a car ride from London to Paris with three other strangers in a strangers car. How cool is that? Real savings from the train or plane.

I took my first car-share leaving London for Paris through the Chunnel. I was terrified I would miss my ride, not find the driver or any other unforeseen possibilities. It was super high stressful. I showed up 20 minutes early looking for the restaurant, "Nandoos," where I would meet the driver. I looked and looked without finding it. I called him three times to clarify but he speaks little English and we got disconnected. I text him and sent him a picture of what I look like with my backpacks on, I'm telling you, high anxiety.

Facebook, August 7—Drew is feeling stressed—
"Worrying is like praying for something that you don't want to happen."—Robert Downey Jr

When he arrived a few minutes early he walked up to me and called my name. Whew, I'm safe with my driver, but I still was getting in a car with three strangers. He went to point out the Restaurant "Nandoos" and realized it was gone, that would make sense why I couldn't find it. By the way, did I mention I had one hours sleep that morning leaving the party that was Brighton Pride?

Facebook, August 6—Drew checked in @ Brighton Beach Gay Pride—
The parade is about to start. The funny thing about London Pride is they wear the most unmatched weird combinations of clothing, on purpose, like opposing plaids.

A little about the night before: I was in Brighton Beach Gay Pride. We enjoyed the Festival all day Saturday. As the evening went into the later hours, I had to choose—take a short nap or just stay up. I choose the short nap, of the one-hour variety, figuring I could sleep in the car to Paris. My train back to London was early that next morning where I would grab the rest of my belongings. Then find my way to the car share. In other words, I left the house in Brighton at 9 a.m. and arrived in Paris at my hostel at midnight. Luckily the car ride was silent and I slept most of the way or tried to at least.

I arrived just outside of Paris and was dropped off at a rail station to train into Paris and find my hostel. With the app, I knew I would be ok. However my phone only had 10% battery life when I left London.

Facebook, August 10—Drew is feeling grateful—

#ActOfKindness —25 A kind Couch Surfing host took me in for my last night in Paris. He is a Psychologist and a kind man. We went out to dinner and he even paid. We had a wonderful conversation about therapy and coaching comparison. Such a thrill to connect with a Parisian while here. Thanks.

A little bit about what I have learned with using phones. You have to conserve your battery as much as possible while traveling. So, endless checks on Facebook have to end. No more checking in on the dating sites, Couch Surfing sights or any other interesting diversion. You can only use your phone for necessity and you must always carry your cord charger and European plug adapter for emergency charging.

Recently I thought my European plug adapter was faulty because my phone continually wasn't getting charged to 100%. I have now switched cords and it works fine--faulty cord. That was frustrating. I also bought a battery charger in London for 15 Euros that stopped working, equally frustrating. All this causes chaos while navigating the road. Now when I see 10% battery life I think, perfect, that will get me home without a problem. All I have to do is stop endlessly looking at the phone, turn it to airplane mode, and close the apps along with lowering the light. Done!

In Paris I saw someone sitting next to a bus stop with his phone plugged into the bus-stop bench. Woohoo, I found a place to charge my phone if I run out of battery. It's the little things that make me happy.

As you can see, I rely on my phone for a lot. Without my Citymapp app, I would never be able to get around town. I can't even remember the addresses or names of the places I am staying. I learned to take pictures to help my short-term memory. I do have a keen sense of direction though. But still, no phone, no bed and I don't want to sleep outside.

I learned with my travel buddies, seeing the sights with companions increases the joy in the experience. This is something I accept about myself and I am consciously working on making friendly connections to share experiences. I know it will make for a much better experience and memory when I do.

Every city I land in I go on the Couch Surfing events page looking for meet-ups. I did so well at my first event in Ireland I wanted to continue looking for meet-ups in order to be around other sightseeing travelers looking for connections. Apparently there is a tribe of backpackers traveling around the roads of Europe all doing the same things. Looking for connections is my new part-time job.

My first Couch Surfing meeting in London proved to be worth it. I was interested in doing something outside London and wanted to find a buddy for the ride. I met a man my age from New Zealand and asked him if he was interested. We settled on Stonehenge. In just a few moments, while at the restaurant, I Googled "transportation," found a cheap tour, and booked a ticket for both of us for the next morning. He was a bit surprised and uneasy but after a beer, he was all in.

The next day we met and all went off without a hitch. He even reimburses me for the road trip. Stonehenge was amazingly beautiful and I made a friend on the two-hour ride over and back. We had some great conversations and the whole day was fantastic. We are still keeping in touch on Facebook and WhatsApp, another communication app that travelers use.

Facebook, August 2—Drew checked in at Victoria Station—
I made it on a bus to Victoria station to catch my bus to Stonehenge. Looks like I will be an hour early for the unexpected. Giving me enough time to grab some food and coffee. All is well, so far.
—Drew—
Safely on the bus with me mate from New Zealand. Had plenty of time to eat, drink and use the loo prior to boarding the bus for Stonehenge 2:15 bus ride.
Facebook, August 15—Ray—
You have learned this—trust yourself—in doing so you take chances, but isn't everything about life chances? The mere fact that we as humans being here on this rocky planet, that has an average star as a companion is a chance, a big chance. Appreciate chances. It's all we have.

Not every Couch Surfing event is as fruitful. Not all people I meet turn out to be fantastic. We have different views, politics, personalities and opinions. I am learning this is ok. I used to be really fearful of getting mixed up with someone I didn't want to spend time with. Now I just talk to anyone and I am completely open to them letting the conversation unfold and present new opportunities or new learning. Sometimes it works great, sometimes

I get stuck with a political opponent. It doesn't last long and I just roll with it. One thing I have learned is NOT to engage in any negative conversation or try to sway someone's opinion. That is not why I am talking to them. I am here to make friends and travel buddies. Not convince someone that my opinion is the correct one.

Facebook, August 15—Drew—
"Would you rather be right or happy"—A Course In Miracles

I did realize finally how this traveling thing and making friends thing works. I am completely open to meeting these people for one minute, five minutes, one hour or longer. I am also realizing someone can be a fit for an hour, then, the next hour it takes a turn. This is perfectly fine. At least for the first hour it was fun. That is better than being alone wishing I had someone to talk to.

I also realized and accept that I am not a perfect fit for everyone. I work hard at accepting that. I work hard at not making assumptions about why I might not work for someone. Who cares, in a few minutes I will never see them again. I follow the principles of Miguel Ruiz book "The Four Agreements" religiously, at least I try hard.

- Be impeccable with your word.
- Don't take anything personal.
- Don't make assumptions.
- Always do your best.

I learned when you are making new friends and you think you might like them and want to see them again you go ahead and exchange all the necessary contact information. Whatsapp is first, then Facebook. Once you establish future contact points you start working on what you might want to do in the future.

This could work out or you might not ever see them again. There really is no telling and that's ok. Sometimes they don't respond and sometimes you don't feel like meeting up with anyone and that's ok. At least you made the effort and for a few bright moments, you had something potentially wonderful to look forward to.

Once I was talking to a girl and realized I was being negative. I couldn't stop. I knew I was tired and I wasn't at my best for conversation. She eventually struck up a conversation with someone else and so did I. I never saw her again but it was a good learning for me. Sometimes I am not at my best and that's ok. Sometime later she Whatsapp messaged me asking where in Europe I was. I was happy to hear from her. Apparently, I wasn't as harsh as I thought I was.

My biggest learning at all these events is to keep talking, keep being vulnerable and keep opening up to all the people around me. It is so much more enjoyable then isolating myself with fear of meeting the wrong people or fear of being the wrong person for someone else. I am letting all that go and just opening up on a continuous basis all in an effort to connect with others.

Facebook, August 15—Ralph—
Everything that happens is happening for you to evolve. Bring those wounds of feeling alone and unsure of where and what to do next, bring them up and sit with them, let them release. Begin to go with the flow—the Universe is for you, not against you.
—Drew—
I practice that every day
—Ralph—
Good—I am learning to let go and embrace the powerful person I am—there are no limits. For me, it is a long slow process. I am a slow cooker for God, but when it is done and all have marinated together—WOW.
—Drew—
Yay, for me it was fast, fast, fast on the Camino. Now even faster.
—Ralph—
I'm a crockpot for God. No microwave for me. I'm a slow cooker. Sounds like I have a hit song brewing in me today. "Jesus crank up the crockpot."
Yea—you are kind of a fast food guy. But we can't always be in the drive-thru. Sometimes we have the need to be in the slow lane. I am in New York City next week. Will experience first-hand trying to navigate unknown territory. It all happens outside our comfort zone, right? That is where we really are alive. This is my first baby step in preparation for my next summer in Europe.

One of my favorite moments is when a conversation really hits home with someone. I can tell because I start telling my story, about my book, my life, the Camino and/or all the above. I see a shift in their attention with me. They slightly adjust their posture towards me and I notice a subtle deeper interest in me and my story. Several more minutes in and I get the question, I want your Facebook information so I can follow you.

WOW! This has happened several times now. I love it when it does. It usually follows with them having to leave or my having to leave and never seeing each other again. In just a few minutes, I managed to deeply connect with someone to the point where they want to follow my life even knowing we might never meet again. I am open to this. I want more of this. It's way cool.

I met a young man recently at a Couch Surfing host home. I was a little uncomfortable in the home and wasn't really sure how to feel or what to do. The young man said loud and clear something I will always remember on the road through Europe, "It's all a part of the adventure." He is right.

I won't let the stress of forgetting everything while moving from place to place ruin my road trip. I just left Paris and I feel like a public transportation master now. I am on my way to Brussels in a car-share for a couple of days to learn a new transportation system. Then off to Germany to learn theirs, and so on and so on.

I still have no solid plans on the road through Europe. I do know one thing; each meter forward on the road, avenue and byways, leads me to a future that will create a roadmap directing me for the rest of my life.

Looks like I can navigate long-term traveling on the road well traveled.

Facebook, August 3—Drew is feeling happy—
On the highway of life, I found my way."—Louise Hay
Facebook, August 4—Drew—
I have requested to stay with someone in Brussels. He sounds like a really interesting character. It will be unusual I assume. He has hosted over 800 Couch Surfers. He likes to treat his Couch Surfers like a king. What can go wrong? Oh, right, it is naked Couch Surfing. You are required to be naked when indoors. Hmmmm… Living outside of my comfort zone.

Facebook, August 11—Drew is feeling nervous @ Brussels Belgium—
#ActOfKindness —26 I have been taken in by yet another Couch Surfing Host in Brussels. He is a chauffeur for a businessman and has taken in more than 800 Couch Surfers. This is the list of offerings you receive once you arrive. Free breakfast and home

cooked Belgium dinner almost every night. He will wash your clothes if you need. Beer is included in the meal if you so choose. Please, don't clear the table or offer to help clean up, that he prefers to do it himself. Lodging is of course free. You have a choice of sleeping on the Murphy bed in the dining room or sharing his king size bed(which is actually two separate beds pushed tougher). He prefers not to accept gifts unless it's good Belgium beer, that he will accept.

I thought what the hell, sounds like an adventure, sign me up. What do I have to lose? Oh, one thing I lost was my clothes, he is a nudist and everyone in the house must be nude at all times. Yup, I stayed in a naked Couch Surfing home. When I arrived I was greeted by a charming 23-year-old Mexican. We found a deep spiritual connection I would never have expected in one day. Overall the experience was stupendous. One I will never forget, along with the Mexican.

—Drew is feeling curious—

"Live outside your comfort zone! That's where the magic happens!!!"—Drew Eric

Facebook, August 12—Drew checked in @ Grand Place Brussels.

Made it safely. Apparently once every two years Brussels makes a rug out of flowers. I was in Brussels two days. The day they set it up and the day they made it. What luck!!!

—Drew—

I am still getting used to this moving around thing. I don't ever remember taking a late bus like this. What am I, 20 years old? God help me through the night. Anxiety is going up. I am leaving Brussels tonight at 2:30 in the morning because my car-share fell through, twice. The bus gets in tomorrow at 5:30 p.m. I have a three-hour layover in the morning in Germany before I catch my second bus. Then a third before I reach Kiel. All this so I can spend Sunday with my girlfriend from America on her day off. I'm a bit nervous so keep me in your thoughts. I will be walking to grab the bus at 1:45 a.m., who does this?

—Drew checked in at Gare Bruxelles Nord/Station Brussel-Noord—

#ActOfKindness— 27 Good news, a nice man gave me a car ride to the bus station. So I didn't have to walk, Yay!! Now I'm waiting with all the other bus people, in the middle of the night.

Facebook, August 16—Drew is @ Freilichtmuseum Molfsee - Landesmuseum für Volkskunde—
I made it to Kiel safely. I am with my girlfriend touring an amazing outdoor museum showing how rural homes were built over the last 400 years, really nice. All these homes were moved here from all over northern Germany and Denmark.

Facebook, August 18—Drew is feeling comforted @ Kiel Germany—
#ActOfKindness —28 Five days in Kiel, Germany went by so fast. I spent them living with a girlfriend from America who just moved back to her hometown. We walked around sightseeing. Toured gardens and museums, we ate our favorite food—Sushi—something we used to do in the States, it was our thing. We watched movies. I rode a bike and toured parks. Oh and we walked her dogs, they are adorable. Thank you, my friend, for an amazing stay. I love you and miss you already. So happy I was your first visitor from the States. Who would have thought all those months ago when this was just our dream we shared over sushi, you moving back to your birthplace and I hitting the road in Europe, it would come true. It did for us both and I love you. What I most wanted to do is feel like a local and do regular things and I did just that. I also got lots of sleep, relaxed and meditated. It was just what I needed most. I was able to get centered and clear my head. Thanks so much xoxo

Facebook, August 18—Drew @ Kiel Hafen—
I needed some time in a warm, loving home in Kiel. This gave me the peace to figure out the rest of the road trip. Where am I going, how many days? Who am I staying with? The big question on my mind is... am I going to stay and change my flight back to America from September 29th to another unknown date of my choosing. I am in a car-share on the autobahn currently driving to Hamburg. Today's travels have been with less stress. I am getting more confident all will work out. I have a Couch Surfing host for two days in Hamburg then it's off to Berlin for a few days. Life is good.

Facebook, August 19—Drew—
My new travel plans will include a travel buddy. The guy from New Zealand I met in London and went to Stonehenge with, invited me to meet him in Poland. So the new itinerary is Hamburg today, Berlin, Poland, Leipzig Germany. Still in the cities and countries to explore in the East are Czech Republic, Vienna Austria and Budapest Hungary. Sounds like a plan right? If you look at the map I

am zigzagging south, I find that very amusing.   Facebook, August 20—Drew is feeling optimistic @ Hamburg Germany—
#ActOfKindness —29 Another Couch Surfing host in Hamburg. I received a two-night stay, coffee, food and a warm bed during the cold stay in Hamburg. Kind people are everywhere in the world. Thanks for the stay and the company along with the history lesson of Hamburg. The poor city was destroyed during the Second World War. But it is rebuilt now.

Facebook, August 19—Drew @ U-Boot Museum U-434—
German U boat—never did I imagine during my youth watching black and white war movies—I would ever step foot in one. Weird seeing something like this. It makes that time in history that much more real for me since I can touch it with my own hands and see this city with my own eyes.

Facebook, August 20—Drew—
On the move again, leaving Hamburg for Berlin. It's a three-hour car-share. I have had several days now with no sleeping pills and I am feeling better. My stress is down, which is unusual on a travel day. I feel good. Through the Couch Surfing app and chat rooms, I am able to make travel plans with people. I will be in Berlin a few days. I am meeting another traveler tonight, he leaves tomorrow. In a couple days another group of three travelers from America arrives and I will spend two days with them. Then I meet up with my New Zealand friend in Poland for a couple days. Travel buddies are the best. Wish me luck. I will write all about it.

—Drew @ Gesundbrunnen-Center Berlin—
I made it safely to Berlin. Let's go see the wall.

Facebook, August 21—Drew checked in at Mauerpark—
I like to go where the locals are. Went to a market in the park. I love hanging with the locals. Met an Australian on Couch Surfing and made a cool friend. We had a great day in the park. It's a funny thing meeting people and spending the day with them. Then saying goodbye and realizing you will never see them again, It twinges your stomach but you get used to it.

Facebook, August 23—Drew is @ Memorial to the Murdered Jews of Europe.
Memorial to the murdered Jews of Europe, Pretty intense name and monument. There is no getting around the meaning. Beautifully breathtaking.

—Drew is @ Badehaus Berlin.

Ok, I am at a German Reggae bar, they are singing Rap and Reggie on a Tuesday night. This is how cool I am. Wow, life is great!!!

Facebook, August 24—Drew—

We are on the move to Poland. I am with my Mexican friend from The Gnarly BIGAM Crew, one of my travel buddies from Ireland. We spent two weeks together a while back. He caught up with me in Berlin and we are going to spend another week together, Poland today, Prague, then maybe Austria, not sure what else.

I will be doing a breakaway overnight to Leipzig, Germany to visit a friend from the Camino between Poland and Prague.

No issues whatsoever with the travel plans today. Arrived at the train station 25 minutes early, got directions to the bus and was on it ten minutes early. All is well, virtually no stress.

Facebook, August 27—Drew is at Wrocławski Rynek—

I'm traveling today from Wroclaw, Poland to Leipzig, Germany by car-share. My two travel buddies went south to Prague while I am heading west to visit my friend I met while walking the Camino. I will meet back up with my travel buddies tomorrow in Prague. It's a quick stop back to Germany to fit in a visit. It is so interesting, I am on this cool circuit of travelers in this area going from one major country/city to each other. Apparently its a thing here and we get to see and run into each other on the road.

My friend left such an impression on me during the Camino that I wanted to squeeze in some time for him while on the road across Europe. Tomorrow night I have been invited to Couch Surf at someone's home in Prague. That will be nice to be in a home again.

I am leaving an amazing hostel in Poland. They cooked us a free dinner last night and each night they took a group out for a pub crawl. We met lots of great visitors at the hostel. Sometimes hostels have a big heart while others are just a bed. I experienced both this week. So much more fun when they have a heart. You make some great memories and add lots of friends on Facebook you can follow. Maybe someday I will be able to visit some of my new Facebook friends in their country. I hadn't been going out too much since I split up with The Gnarly BIGAM Crew a while back. So it's been nice to have the Mexican back in my life. We made up for some lost time with some great fun. My stress level is around a 1 out of 10. Traveling is really getting easier and more familiar. Time has been my teacher.

Facebook, August 28—Drew is feeling grateful @ Leipzig, Germany—
#ActOfKindness —30 I spent almost 24 hours with my Camino buddy. He is an amazing fellow from England. Deeply spiritual and connected to his life and friends. He has big plans for his future. He casually asked how good I am on a bike. I said great not realizing we were going on a 40-kilometer bike ride around the city. Boy did we do it all and see it all. Biking, swimming, coffee in some high rise overlooking the city, ice cream, climbed a watchtower, saw several monuments and churches. Finished with some food and back to the apartment. I love living like a local. A 40k bike ride is certainly that. I was fine by the way, he said I was a strong rider. He put me up for one night. Such generosity, I am forever grateful for his kindness.

Facebook, August 28—Drew—
On the road to Prague to catch up with my travel buddies. We will spend a couple days in Prague before we head south to Vienna, Austria. I was stressed for about 15 minutes when I couldn't find the bus stop. I was hot, sweaty and carrying almost 50 pounds of backpack. I still made it to the bus station with 15 minutes to spare, thank goodness. On the bus now and I will be staying at another Couch Surfing home. Someone who invited me from a post I did in a Couch Surfing group a long time ago. Every time I Couch Surf it's a new and exciting adventure, also a little nervousness. You never know what you're going to get yourself into. My next home in Vienna will also be Couch Surfing. I have been taking cheap busses and car-shares over short distances. Hopping from city to city making my way south, it's worked really well. I only had one problem on the way to Poland, there was an accident that added six hours to our bus ride getting us in at 2 a.m. instead of 8 p.m. Oops. Hopefully my new host and Prague are amazing.

Facebook, August 31—Drew is feeling thankful @ Prague, Czech Republic—
#ActOfKindness —31 I am blessed to have been welcomed into the home of a great guy. He took me on a tour of Prague and showed me the city along with the John Lennon Wall and the Vltava River with the amazing scenic views of the castle and bridges. We went to dinner a couple times. I had three blissful nights in this beautiful city. I am grateful for meeting him and receiving his kindness that is his home. Thanks.

Posted on September 2 , 2016 by Drew Eric

Chapter 35 Can I find the answers I need
on the road well traveled?

Facebook, August 30—Drew is feeling confused—
"No one said you have to have it all figured out, it's ok, let it go."—
Drew Eric

A little about my crazy head—a peek into my travel mind.

My mind is all over the place. So many questions arise while I am on the road well traveled in Europe— not the common questions you might think: Should I visit the Eiffel Tower or the Louvre Museum today? But difficult questions: Will I like my Couch Surfing host, or can I overcome my fear of missing a plane/bus/train or, how do I make friends on the road?

Facebook, August 31—Drew is feeling energized—
"You are emerging from the cocoon of your former self. There are no limits to the extent of transformation that's possible for you"—
Marianne Williamson

I arrived in May and it's now early September. I have moved through 13 countries and countless cities so far. I walked "El Camino de Santiago" through Northern Spain, flown a couple of times, went underground through the Chunnel from England to France and have ridden in cars, buses and trains. Still, I don't have all the answers on how to navigate the road.

I love mystery novels. I am always looking for insights and clues that will help me see the truth through the words of the story and lead me to solve the puzzle that's unfolding. In other words, I am approaching this journey as if I am Sherlock Holmes or Hercule Poirot, looking for clues to uncover the secrets on the roads of Europe.

When I learn something new I try to submerge myself, really throw myself into the ocean's deep end, of whatever it is I want to learn. I take notes, try new things and swim in the sea of the unknown until I arrive on the shoreline with answers. Here are a few of the questions I have found in a bottle on the shoreline of my mind.

Can I:
- Rely on my Spiritual practice and find peace on my journey?
- Face my fears/challenges and overcome?
- Make friends while traveling?
- Understand the nuances of Couch Surfing?
- Navigate new cities and countries with ease?
- Figure out when to go home?

Let's start at the top and I will give you a clue on what happens in my travel mind.

Can I use my spiritual practice and find peace on my journey?
I follow the teachings of "A Course in Miracles-ACIM" which basically tells you not to believe what your crazy ego and insane mind tells you to believe. My ego mind wants me to be on high alert, DEFCON 2-Red: Next step to nuclear war.

Wikipedia— DEFCON—The DEFense readiness CONdition— Prescribes five graduated levels of readiness (or states of alert) for the U.S. Military and the United States. It increases in severity from DEFCON 5 (least severe) to DEFCON 1 (most severe) to match varying military situations.
DEFCON:
- 1 White: Cocked Pistol—Nuclear war imminent—Maximum Readiness
- 2 Red: Fast Pace—Next step to nuclear war—Armed Forces ready to deploy and engage in less than 6 hours
- 3 Yellow: Round House—Increase in force readiness above that required for normal readiness—Air Force ready to mobilize in 15 minutes
- 4 Green: Double Take—Above normal readiness—Increased intelligence watch and strengthened security measures
- 5 Blue: Fade Out—Normal readiness—Lowest state of readiness

ACIM teaches you to avoid making up and believing in illusions. My DEFCON rating is an illusion since I am always safe and prepared. The foundation of ACIM is you're always in the right place at the right time, doing exactly what is best for you.

Knowing all this and having a spiritual practice still doesn't lower my DEFCON rating to 5-Blue: Lowest state of readiness. For me, only time and repetition seem to reduce the anxiety of trying something new. What my spiritual practice does do is to remind me I am safe, everything will work out and all will be exactly how it should be. I just might not like the result.

Can I face my fears/challenges and overcome?

I made a decision in preparation for my adventure; I want to put myself in as many uncomfortable situations as I can in order to grow spiritually.

When I was planning my adventure I couldn't comprehend traveling without an itinerary, direction or schedule of any kind. How do I backpack Europe with no plans? My first thought was to visit a girlfriend who recently moved back to her hometown of Kiel, Germany. The idea of starting my adventure visiting the home of a good friend was perfect and safe. I was considering at the time, possibly staying in Germany for an extended period—all to be safe and close to a friend who speaks German and could assist me in navigating my adventure.

As my plans progressed and I started to envision my adventure with a little more confidence, I was reminded of "El Camino De Santiago." Immediately my excitement grew because there was one thing I knew. "I can walk 500 miles."

From that moment on, my adventure began to take form. The Camino is well supported with albergues so you really have no worries about housing and food with restaurants and supplies all along The Way. I no longer had to worry about my first month in Europe. All I would have to do is walk, walk, walk.

Once I finished the Camino and got on the roads in Europe, the stress and anxiety of doing something for the first time was overwhelming. I meditate, do yoga and consider myself a pretty chill guy. So this level of fear and stress was new for me. I had no idea I was capable of such a high level of anxiety. I was on DEFCON 2-Red, teetering on DEFCON 1-White: Nuclear war is imminent. At least it felt that way to me.

Doing so many things for the first time contributed to my stress. I just began Couch Surfing, navigated travel arrangements and learning how to Google, tried Airbnb, car-sharing, started using my new MacBook Air leaving my Windows computer in America.

As with flying, my crazy ego mind attempted to convince me of all the possible things that could go wrong when changing countries, i.e. taxies, purchasing the wrong tickets, transportation to and from the airports, arriving on time, luggage, customs, the list goes on. I have only taken three flights on the road so far, regardless of worrying; I made all the flights without a hitch.

Every time I change cities it's as if fear and challenges knew I was coming as they both are waiting for me at the station ready to escort me into town. As a first-time solo traveler, all the potential pitfalls could stop me in my tracks if I listen to my crazy ego mind and let my fears and challenges lead the way.

Can I make friends while traveling?

Friendships have been a lifelong challenge for me and the Camino was no different. I knew going on the Camino I would have to face and overcome my attachment and separation issues. When I meet someone and instantly fall into friendship, I want to stay in the comfort of their company and never leave. When the friendship is complete I have a difficult time walking away. I pine over a relationship once it has ended, way past an appropriate amount of time. I miss people from my past and I miss the connectedness we once shared.

I also attach easily to people and want to be their "best friend". This I have done since I was in grade school. Moving around to six elementary schools prior to fourth grade, taught me to "2 Red-Fast Pace" connect quickly because next semester I could be in another school.

In addition, I have a big personality. Sometimes I come on too strong while making new, best friends "DEFCON 1 White-Maximum Readiness". While walking the Camino I knew friendships, attachment, separation and toning down my big personality to a manageable level was my work "DEFCON 5 Blue-Normal Readiness". It was hard in the beginning but it got easier as I made new friends and let them go. Each time I walked away I learned and got stronger.

The Camino really helped heal this part of my past. However when I left the comfort of the Camino and got on the road through Europe on my own, I felt like I was starting over again at DEFCON 1 White-Maximum Readiness.

There were built-in people to meet and befriend, walking in the same direction while on my pilgrimage. Crazy people just like me that thought walking 500 miles was a good idea. I knew I needed to figure out how I was going to manage this new speed of the road and make friends when they weren't so readily supplied. Where and how do I walk upon someone and make a new friend?

I tried everything I could think of. I asked other travelers how they meet people on the road and where are some good places to meet other travelers? I learned hostels are a great place and the Couch Surfing app has events on their website for meet-ups and activities. So I went to as many meet-ups as I could and talked to many travelers in hostels about what was happening, where to go and what to see.

Facebook, August 8—Drew—
I have a bottle of wine from a Paris tenth-century vineyard and I'm off to a Couch Surfing meet-up on the canals in Paris. This life suits me.

Facebook, August 9—Drew checked in @ Paris Quai De Seine
—
My second Couch Surfing meet-up by the River Seine, this is the way to live like a local. This river is very popular on a Tuesday night. So many people here and it's so cool.

In Paris, I attended two meet-ups on the River Seine. I put my new found people skills to work and made some real progress. I settled into a comfortable space of acceptance with everyone I met.

I learned you can talk to someone for a minute, an hour or several days. You never know how long a friendship will last or if you will ever see them again. You can think your friendship is going well, you're looking forward to what you will do together then; the next thing you know they disappeared into the crowd and you never saw them again. How did I lose them?

I have trained myself to enjoy a conversation as a complete package each and every time. Like a "Moment Capsule" (a moment in time that is contained and complete). If you're lucky you get to repeat the experience. If not, then it was complete at that moment and all is well.

When I make new friends I wonder how we can enjoy our capsule of time. Are we:

- Drinking mates?
- Deep conversationalists?
- Sightseeing pals?
- Travel buddies?

I seem to want them to be all four, but I settle for one or two of my choices. Sometimes the Gods are kind and I get all four and it's Heaven on Earth. But when I want them to be deep conversationalists, I might only enjoy a drink with them. Or, if I think they'd be travel buddies, I share only a great conversation in a park. My Spiritual work is to accept and let what is, be all that it is.

Facebook, August 4—Drew—
I have been posting in Couch Surfing groups letting people know I am backpacking Europe. I have been getting invitations to come and visit them once they read my CS profile. The Italians apparently love me... I have 14 invitations in Italy and I am only giving myself seven days. Maybe I should extend Italy, Hmmm.

Can I understand the nuances of Couch Surfing?

This is an unusual one to figure out since most people aren't invited into stranger's homes. Picture it; you're staying in someone's home for free, in exchange for conversation and companionship. You aren't there to be too needy, require too much assistance or be a nuisance to the host. You are just supposed to know exactly what each host's requirements are and the level of help they are willing to offer.

Every time I enter a host home, I am on "DEFCON 3 Yellow-Increase in force readiness above that required for normal readiness" in an attempt to figure out what the host needs and wants and how they fit my needs and wants. Sometimes this can be disappointing. However my spiritual work tells me not to have expectations and send everyone I meet love regardless of how I am being treated or mistreated. When I leave a host home, sometimes I have mixed feelings and questions; did they like me, did I contribute to their life in a positive way, or vice versa.

One of my strongest fears prior to my adventure was being stuck with a person I don't find rewarding or doesn't positively contribute to my life. With Couch Surfing this is a legitimate fear. The length of time I am staying with them is approximately three full days and two nights. If we aren't compatible and the purpose of my stay is to be a friend and companion to them, this can be a really uncomfortable situation.

This is a cross-section of Couch Surfing I have observed:

- Sometimes you get a key and can come and go freely, other times you rely on them being home to let you in.
- They offer you food, drink, coffee in the morning and even laundry. The opposite is also possible.
- You can have the freedom to come home when you like or you must be indoors when they go to bed.
- They want you to make your own plans or they want to show you the town themselves and/or both.
- The space can be as large as a full apartment or as small as a single bedroom with no real room to hang out in.
- They could want you around to chat and hang out or be too busy to talk while you are in their home.

All this has to be "figured out" each time I enter into someone's home. Clearly, my observations skills have to be on a higher DEFCON alert and intuition comes into play. I joined Couch Surfing just before I left America and happily was invited to a host home in Barcelona. It was my first time living in a stranger's home and I was just plain old scared, of everything really. Overall it went well, although I was somewhat of a burden especially after I lost my phone. He saw the fear in my eyes and wondered how I was going to survive on the road in Europe.

Facebook, August 31—Drew—
On the move again, I am reaching Vienna, Austria now. Meeting a new Couch Surfing host today. I hope we are a good connection.
Facebook, September 2—Drew—
"Trust your intuition more because it will always steer you in the right direction."—Drew Eric
—Drew is feeling blessed @ Vienna, Austria—
#ActOfKindness —32 Such an amazingly beautiful city. Right after arriving my host took me on a walking tour, then we grabbed a pizza and chilled at home. The following day we spent touring the Schönbrunn Palace grounds with more than 300 years of history. Today it is a popular tourist attraction with breathtaking views throughout the gardens. He was so knowledgeable of the history and the city it was a great honor to hear him share. Tours, a couch to sleep on in a warm home. I am sometimes a little nervous

about Couch Surfing, you never know what you will receive when you're there. I was thrilled and relieved with the experience, all was beautiful. What more could I ask for? Thanks.

Can I navigate new cities and countries with ease?

After the Camino I had to figure out what I wanted out of my European road trip. In the past, I had a husband and didn't really put too much thought into my needs or what I wanted. Now I had to figure out as a solo traveler in a foreign country what I wanted.

Do I want to:
- See the sights?
- Meet people, hang out and connect?
- Drink too much or not at all?
- Create art, take pictures and do pastels?
- Keep up my yoga practice?
- Experience a city like a local and do what locals do?

Facebook, August 27—Drew—
"We paralyze ourselves when we worry about making the right choice. Pick a path. Give it your all. Learn. Grow. Reassess. Make a change if it feels right. And know that no matter what happens, you can still enjoy your life and be happy."—Lori Deschene

What I am figuring out is that I want all of it, delicately balanced. Fear Of Missing Out(FOMO), is rearing its ugly head again. This has plagued me over the years and now it's a daily challenge. If I stay out too late drinking with friends I feel guilty I didn't sightsee the next day. If I go to bed early and leave my friends out on the town, I feel I missed something fun. If I see the sights solo, I wish I had friends to share with. If I see the sights with a friend, I might not have time to take all the photographs I want. If I do something like the locals I wonder what landmarks I'm not visiting.

My Spiritual teaching tells me to accept what is. This is my constant battle with my ego mind. I am trying to get to know myself and figure out what I want and what would I like to do and see. So I constantly evaluate/judge what I have done and think, could I have done it better and squeezed just a few more sights in, met more people, hung out longer, did more local stuff. This judging negatively impacts my memories of the experience. I am learning not to judge in an effort to have more joyful memories. You are al-

271

ways in the right place at the right time, with the right people doing what you should be doing.

"We, tend to overthink, control and stress about everything. Let it go!"—Drew Eric

Can I figure out when to go home?
I have a return flight on September 29th to America. I have less than a month left. I am on a bus traveling to Venice to spend a few days. After Venice I will spend some time in Croatia then Budapest, Hungary to visit a girlfriend whom I met on the Camino.

Facebook, September 2—Drew @ Port of Trieste—
I just left Vienna, crossed through Slovenia and entered Italy. Wow, Italy. I'm here. Can't wait. Just a short rest off the bus before Venice. My first espresso in Italy, Bongiorno Italy. The bus takes us around the coast of Italy on my way to Venice with the ocean just to our left for miles and miles, it is beautiful scenery. Not a bad way to travel.
—Drew—
I thought my hostel was moments away, lol. But the place I am staying is 30 minutes outside of Venice on the mainland. I might have to reconsider where I am staying and spend more money for a closer hostel. Now I have to use a new transport app to get in and out of Venice. Luckily Google has a good one, trying new things. My stress is almost not existent, time and experience pays off.
—Drew checked in @ Venezia, Italia—
The Venice of Venice.
Facebook, September 3—Drew—
I made a new friend today. He is my roommate in my hostel. It's a two-person room. We talked last night. We talked this morning. Rode the bus into Venice together. Walked and talk some more. Next thing we knew we spent the whole day together. We will hang again tonight. I love making new friends.
—Drew @Piazza de San Marco - Venezia—
I have always dreamed of just sitting In a square having a drink and enjoying the moment. And here I am.
Facebook, September 5—Drew—

I had the pleasure to meet a model in Venice. He had just come from the Venice Film festival and he received a compliment from Tom Ford and a picture with Amy Adams. Whose life is this, wait, it's mine... Crazy cool adventures.

　—Drew—

I am on the move again, leaving Venice heading for Zagreb, Croatia. Stress is at an all-time low which is amazing since I started the stress was at DEFCON 1 Maximum Readiness, Nuclear war imminent. I will spend three relaxing days out of the EU in Croatia before visiting a friend from the Camino in Budapest Hungary for several amazing days. I have dreamed of Budapest and my dreams are coming true.

　—Drew—

Ok, I am waiting for my bus and panicked a little bit thinking I'm not in the correct place. No one seems to be waiting for a bus here. I called the bus line and she is calling the bus. She will hopefully call me back. Crossing fingers. Nervous face, lol. Anxiety is back up to DEFCON 2 next step nuclear war, is how it feels.

　—Drew—

I see my bus... Disaster averted, on the bus safely. DEFCON 5 normal readiness.

　Facebook, September 4—Drew is feeling entertained @ Venice, Italy—

#ActOfKindness —33 Wow, what an incredible experience in Venice I met with the kindest man from Couch Surfing. He wasn't able to host me however he was able to take me on a walking tour of Venice Friday night then he invited me to watch the Regata Storica along the Grand Canal on the first Sunday in September, how lucky am I? The Regata is 1600 century gondola race down the canal where the participants are dressed in period costumes of the highest ranking Venetian officials, such as the Doge and the Doge's wife. The race is colorful and exciting. My new friend is American and works at Jesolo college. Our viewing spot was on the campus, floating dock. As a participant on the campus dock, I received a costume of a wig, feathered boa and a t-shirt. Guess who won the gondola race between the colleges, yes, you guessed it, JESOLO. The stands where I was viewing erupted with cheers, what an amazing day living like a local in Venice. Life is remarkable when the Universe conspires in your favor.

　Facebook, September 2—Drew—

"The Happiest people are those who live in the moment, day by day. No need to complain, enjoying the little things that life offers."—Drew Eric

When I arrived in Europe I received a 90 day Visa over a 180 day period, allowing me to stay in countries that joined the Schengen Treaty.

Wikipedia: The Schengen Agreement is a treaty which led to the creation of Europe's Schengen Area, in which internal border checks have largely been abolished.

Having 90 days means I can pop in/out of the European Schengen area as many times as I wish as long as I don't surpass 90 days over 180 day period. I am running out of Schengen time and I am now facing a tough decision whether I am ready to return to America or postpone and extend my flight. Venice, Italy is in the Treaty along with Hungary, however Croatia is out of the Treaty. As you can see I am using the popping in/out of the treaty literally.

The question still remains, do I want to spend an extra couple months out of the Treaty here in Europe and automatically receive another 90 days in the Treaty or return to America?

After Hungary I will head back to Croatia (out of the Treaty) and figure out the next step on the road. I will consider looking for work, work exchange, coaching, teach yoga, helping at a hostel or anything else I can find. I will consider traveling outside the Treaty waiting for another 90 days, at which time I will go back into the Treaty area.(The Balkans, Old Yugoslavia, is out of the Treaty) Or I could go home to America, stay a couple months, attend a friend's wedding then come back to Europe. I am open to all possibilities...

Facebook, August 4—Drew—
I can potentially visit any of the following countries, it is amazing to have such freedom to travel the road. Quick question for my Facebook folks? Which of the following countries do I want to visit, are safe, speak English well and are inexpensive??? These are all out of the Schengen treaty and do not count against my three months in Europe: Romania, Bulgaria, Croatia, Albania, Macedonia, Serbia, Bosnia and Herzegovina, Montenegro, Kosovo. So many possibilities... Can I do this???

I often find myself scratching my crazy ego head while traveling; I have no idea what I am doing. Some days I am thrilled, while some days I am sad and lonely. Some days I have both feelings several times going back and forth from sad to happy to sad to thrilled. There is no predicting.

I feel guilty if I have feelings of sadness or unhappiness. As if I am supposed to feel thrilled and joyful every day, all the time since I am in Europe on the road trip of a lifetime. Why aren't I happy all the time? Why can't I just instinctively know what I want to do? I certainly can't tell my friends at home, "All my days aren't joy filled days," some days yes, some days, sometimes. Being happy all day every day is an unattainable goal. My spiritual work tells me to move past these feelings of guilt and shame because they are unnecessary emotions that don't help my overall wellbeing, as I remind myself often.

Facebook, September 2—Drew—
"Being at ease with not knowing is crucial for answers to come to you."—Eckhart Tolle

What I know for sure is it's a mixed bag. I am uncomfortable every day. I am scared at least once a day. I am happy every day. I am sad every day. I am emotional and vulnerable every day. I don't know if I will ever figure out what I want because what I want seems to keep changing. I do know I will get better at this. Traveling wonderfully sucks! Traveling is terribly terrific. Traveling is fantastically horrible, every day.

Facebook, September 2—Drew—
"If you suffer, it is because of you. If you feel blissful, it is because of you. Nobody else is responsible, only you and you alone. You are your hell and your heaven too."—Osho

My spiritual work tells me not to judge. I have recently learned my judgments are getting in the way of my happiness. If I spend so much time judging everything, It has a negative impact on my experience during my travels. If I just accept and enjoy life as it comes and treats everything as the adventure it is, I am much happier. That takes a great deal of work and concentration.

275

So now I am coming clean about how hard my travels have been. It's a roller coaster in the dark, thrilling and disappointing when it's over because you want to do it all over again with your eyes open. I haven't practiced yoga but a few times on the Camino. I meditate, sometimes. I read "A Course In Miracles." I have done one pastel and I struggle learning how to use my Rebel Cannon camera. My art supplies and camera add at least 10 lbs. to my backpack; it's my burden to carry.

I work at being positive. I have been judgmental far too much. I have been angry, disappointed and hurt many times. I have been lonely and sad. I have also loved, been kind and thrilled to be alive. I am feeling emotions I haven't felt in years.

I also know I will continue to do my Spiritual work and overcome all my trepidations and obstacles and maintain a positive attitude. I will continue to meditate, read "A Course in Miracles" and remind myself, all will work out. A quote from "A Course in Miracles" says: "Trust and all problems are solved, now." I remind myself to trust every day because God and the Universe know what is best for me better than I do, Universe, take the wheel!

I believe the answers I need will come as I continue searching for them throughout Europe. All I need is a little silence and I can hear the soft voices of direction. I can do this, I can learn from the road well traveled.

Facebook, September 3—Drew—
"Sometimes the best thing you can do is not think, not wonder, not imagine, not obsess. Just breathe and have faith that everything will work out for the best."—unknown
—Shannon—
Drew, I am so intrigued and inspired by your experiences and how you press on, even though your comfort zones are few. I just got back from a week in France with dear friends and the traveling days were the hardest part! I was so relieved to be back in the U.S. where I didn't have to worry about language barriers and getting to airports/gates/etc. You are of very strong character to keep this journey up for so long! Keep experiencing everywhere and anything you can! And thank you for sharing all of it with us!
—Drew—
Thank you my love. Yeah it's pretty hard sometimes. Then days like yesterday are amazing. It's a roller coaster of terrible fun,

LOL. Trying to make money over here scares me but I am willing to consider it as an option to extend my trip.

—Drew—

"Live outside your comfort zone! That's where the magic happens!!!"—Drew Eric

—Shannon—

Go for it! When will you get the chance again? If it doesn't work out, you know you tried! Best of luck!

—Drew—

Funny thing when you're taking out unfamiliar money in a foreign country, you should Google it prior to withdrawing. I took out $10,000 koruna equaling $412 dollars. Little to much for three days. It cost me $6.50 to exchange the money for Euros. I learn every day.

Facebook, September 8—Drew is feeling grateful—

#ActOfKindness —34 I met a great new friend. He found me on Couch Surfing from one of my posts. We discovered we were going to both be in Croatia on the same day. He found a hostel for us and made me a reservation. He gave me directions and everything. I had to do nothing but show up at around 10 p.m. from Venice. He even found a place for us to have our laundry done, then picked it up and brought it back, very kind. We spent the next two days hanging out till he moved on to another city. I might see him again after I get back from Budapest. Travel buddies are the best. Thanks.

Posted on September 14, 2016 by Drew Eric

Chapter 36 Can I keep my thinking positive and
  attract wonderful experiences on the road?

Facebook, September 8—Drew—
"My Self is ruler of the Universe. It is impossible that anything should come to me unbidden by myself. Even in this world, it is I who rule my destiny. What happens is what I desire. What does not occur is what I do not want to happen. This must I accept."—A Course in Miracles

—Drew—
I made it to Budapest safely. Only two people on the bus and it took 4:20 minutes. About to get picked up by my Camino friend. Yay. I get to spend several relaxing days here. I need to regroup and figure out my next move. I will keep you posted

Facebook, September 11—Drew checked in @ Budapest, Hungary—
I was walking down the street and a guy asks me if my name is James. I said no and we spoke for a few minutes. I learned he was on a tinder date. He was also visiting Budapest from Scotland. I offered to hang out if he was so inclined.
He said he was leaving the next couple days and didn't think he had time to hang out prior to leaving. I walked on and had lunch.
After lunch I walked towards the river and ran into the guy again and his friend James. The guy said he was heading to the River while his friend James said he was walking to the Synagogue. Their date was now complete. I offered to also go to the river. This was Friday afternoon.
We have been hanging out all weekend and have become good friends and travel buddies.
Never underestimate a chance meeting on the street. It could turn into a lifelong friendship.

My friend arrived in Budapest, in the late evening. This is the travel buddy I met in Ireland, along with my other Ireland travel buddies, the Gnarly BIGAM Crew, we spent two weeks together (BIGAM is an acronym for Brit, Italian, Gay, American, Mexican).

278

However it's just G (Gay) and M (Mexican) now. After he arrived we enjoyed some wine and caught up.

We split from The Gnarly BIGAM Crew around the beginning of August and went in separate directions. When I was in Berlin, the Mexican decided to reach out and see where in Europe I was. He wasn't that far and he met me in Berlin.

When our time in Germany was winding down, I shared with him that my next stop was Wroclaw, Poland to meet another travel buddy I met in England. He and I visited Stonehenge, which was a one-day travel excursion. He liked the idea and a new travel plan formed for the three of us. We stayed together in Wroclaw and Prague. Travel buddies can make a vacation go from good to totally amazing.

The Mexican went off to paint a mural at a hostel in Slovakia, in return for free room and food while I went to Venice and Croatia. After Croatia I chose Budapest to visit a girlfriend I met while walking the Camino. I invited the Mexican who was happy to join me; he couldn't pass up an opportunity for free boarding.

After catching up over a bottle of wine, we walked down to the Danube River, city center of Budapest. If you haven't traveled in Europe yet, all medieval cities were built on a river for trade and transportation. The river separates what was once dual cities that didn't get along, Buda and Pest. The rivalry still remains between the now joined cities. As the residents of Buda say, "The best thing Pest has, is the view of Buda." Buda has an amazing mountainside called "Castle Hill" with a Palace and church that looks like an ancient castle while the Parliament building is on the Pest side.

At the end of WWII, Budapest was one of the last German strongholds. As I was told during a walking tour, Russia was on the Pest side and Germany was on the Buda hill. They spent the last few months bombing each other, destroying the city and all its interesting buildings and character. When the war was over and communists occupied Budapest, they rebuilt.

During the construction they choose the design of the new city to have the appearance of it's past. That's why today, Europe calls Budapest "The most beautiful fake city," since its less than 100 years old but looks to be centuries old. Not a very fair description for Budapest since it truly is a breathtaking city with the rebuilt bridges, new Parliament building, Fisherman's wall on Castle Hill, Buda Castle and the picturesque Liberty Statue.

279

Fisherman's wall is a long wall directly in front of the Church on Castle Hill giving the church and the wall the appearance of an ancient castle. The wall contains seven turrets to represent the seven tribes of Hungary who founded the country in 895. This is the place where tourist and locals alike come to bask in the views of the Parliament Building and Pest and is a UNESCO World Heritage site.

The river area was quite busy, even on a Monday night. We had a couple beers and I told my friend all about Budapest from the information I learned on the walking tour. I love walking tours, you really get into the heart of a city with cool information you wouldn't know otherwise.

Facebook, September 9—Drew—
"Karma is not just good thoughts and good deeds, Karma resides in your thinking, so think good thoughts."—Drew Eric

After taking many pictures and sharing stories we moved on towards this cool hipster space called Ruin Bar—an old dilapidated communist building somewhat stabilized, giving it a cool condemned feeling—to drink and listen to music. On our way, we were stopped by two girls asking us a question in Hungarian.

I asked if they spoke English and one of the girls immediately switched over. They were asking directions to a bar that their hotel recommended. They are visiting from Transylvania, Romania. It just sounded so cool hearing these girls—in their Romanian accents—say they were from Transylvania since never in my life have I heard someone say, "We are visiting from Transylvania, Romania, you know where Dracula is from." They asked if we were interested in joining them for a drink. We agreed, happy to meet and get to know some other travelers. With their accents and intrigue, I wanted to follow them anywhere. I love meeting interesting travelers.

Romanian 1 wasn't exactly sure where the bar was but we found it pretty easily. It was small with white walls and only a few tables, with a small group of four at another table. Romanian 2 mentioned something about it being a local's bar. We sat in a booth where the waitress joined us for our drink order. Romanian 1 said let's have the Hungarian shot that is only served in Hungary and placed our order. I have pretty much given up hard liquor at this point of the road, choosing to enjoy my journey to the fullest versus occasionally being hung-over from vodka. I no longer spend long hours in a bar. But hey, when in Hungary you do what the Hungarians do or what the Romanian's say we should do.

After Romanian 1 placed our order, I told the Mexican the shot is 35 proof. I learned about it on the walking tour. The shots came along with what appeared to be small bottles of champagne. I thought that was weird as I don't remember ordering champagne, but I left it alone.

We settled into our drinks and conversation on how the Mexican and I met and where we have visited. The girls invited us to visit them in Romania and we were intrigued and happy with our luck to meet such amazing, friendly girls. This was a real possibility for us since he and I had open travel plans and we could visit any country we wanted. It was a hoot dreaming about visiting Romania and being spontaneous during our time on the road.

The Romanians said Hungary is famous for another shot and promptly placed an order for a second round. Again it came with more champagne and I thought, "Hmmm, that's strange."

Romanian 1 said, "Fenékig" which is Hungarian for "Until the bottom of the glass", while Romanian 2 said, "mai multe băuturi" which is "more drinks" in Romanian. The Mexican said, "Salud" and I said, "Cheers."

It was shortly before midnight when our waitress asked us to settle up the bill since they were closing soon. I pulled out my card and she said, "We don't take cards, but I can walk you to the money machine." I agreed since I had no more Forint (Hungarian money). The waitress, Romanian 1 and I head out into the street on our way to the money machine. I thought it was weird for all of us to head out but didn't think much more than that.

I put my card in the machine, changed the language to English and begin my transaction. Romanian 1 steps up and says, "Let me help you since it's in another language" and starts pushing all the buttons. I thought, "That's weird for her to step up and take control of my transaction."

Money comes out and I retrieve it along with my card. The waitress steps and says, "I will take that to settle the bill" and proceeds taking bills out of my hand. I thought, again, "That's weird for the waitress to settle the bill right here on the street, not back in the bar." Then I thought, "I need to come up with another expression than "That's weird, I keep saying everything is weird.""

We work our way back to the bar to meet my friend and Romanian 2. My friend seems to be having a good time with Romanian 2 since they are in deep, animated conversation. The waitress comes over with the bill and mentions we have a remainder to pay. At which time Romanian 1 tells me they didn't bring any Hungarian money and don't have any cards with them, but we can pay you back tomorrow.

"HOLD UP! WAIT, WHAT?" I thought. I am a little disoriented from all the activities, conversations and bill paying. I am not sure how much money I took out of the machine or how much I have paid the waitress on the street. I don't understand why the waitress is asking me to settle the bill saying we still owe more money.

I don't care how much I have had to drink or what language you say it in but I know bullshit when I hear it. I don't have cards or money is clearly bullshit and alarming. I now realize something is up.

The waitress puts down a bill/receipt on the table and speaks with the Mexican. I'm distracted by Romanian 1 while I am trying to look at the bill. I barely notice the Mexican leave with Romanian 2 and the waitress. I vaguely think, in my confusion with all that is happening, he is on his way to the money machine and I need to figure out what this bill says.

Before the waitress left with the bill, I glance down at it and notice how many "Zeros" it has. "Wait a second, if I remember correctly that is too many zeros on the bill to make this exchange typical for my budget." I thought. If I remember my conversion correctly HUF (Hungarian Forint) 1000 divided by 300 is somewhere close to $4. If my eyes are seeing correctly, there is an extra zero on this bill that I am not paying. If my blurry eyes are correct, that bill says HUF 300,000 something. I am not entirely sure but I am pretty confident that's too much money and I am not paying it. It is somewhere around $1,200 possibly.

I am beginning to realize this bar is ripping us off and the girls are acting like they want some free drinks from us. I am thinking this was screw top champagne and this bar is trying to charge us for Dom Perignon. I am not letting this bar charge me for Dom when I got screw top. I am not paying for the girls' drinks especially since I am not into girls. I am way too, let's say, Frugal.

Romanian 1 is running at the mouth and I realize she is attempting to distract me. I pull out my phone to "Google translate the currency." The bill has now disappeared so I am only guessing it actually said HUF 300,000 something. If it did, then I am able to see in Google translate it is entirely too much money and we are getting robbed by this bar. I keep my cool while Romanian 1 is still talking nonstop attempting to distract.

My friend arrives back from his adventure to the money machine with Romanian 2 and the waitress. Romanian 1 joins them outside while I am left alone with Romanian 2's purse. I wonder, "Does she have any bargaining chips in her purse just in case this goes completely out the window, which it pretty much already has." I grab her purse and check it out. Wallet is empty; purse is basically empty other than a cell phone that slipped out of her purse and magically into my pocket.

The Mexican comes in and looks me straight in the eye and says, "I think we are getting taken advantage of." I reply back with a very loud "We are totally getting taken advantage of." Mayhem ensues.

Romanian 1 again says she will pay us tomorrow. I am thinking this waitress isn't getting any more of my money tonight and the Romanians are going to have to find a way to pay for the remainder of the bill. It doesn't actually occur to me at the time that I don't know how much I paid on the street or even how much I took out of the money machine. I do know my wallet is still pretty full of HUF. I am getting louder by this point. They encourage me to "Calm down". I inform them about the weather outside and it being summer and all and snow and freezing something.

The Mexican is talking and saying something I am not entirely sure what about, all I want to do is get out of this thieving bar and leave the girls to pay the remainder of the bill. By this point they are saying we could leave since we are being so loud and I inform my friend, "We are leaving now!" I was thinking, "Let's go before they try to get more of my money."

Once outside the bar away from the girls we start comparing notes. He informed me of his adventure, trying to take money out of the money machine. After several attempts and several different amounts—with Romanian 2 taking over his transaction—he wasn't able to get any money. They informed him the "Money exchange office" is also nearby and if he has a credit card they will take money off it.

So off they went to the money exchange office. It was there he realized the rate exchange and he was taking out WAY too much money and he started to push back with the waitress on the bill. She then tried to explain "You should have looked at the menu closer before you ordered."

"Crazy since we didn't order champagne or receive a menu," I thought while he was relaying the story.

He continued saying he did pay the waitress on the street, same as I did. Once he was back in the bar he was then trying to look at the bill to figure out the prices and what we were getting charged. Romanian 2 was helping/taking control of the addition of the bill. She took the menu and the bill, gave it back to him, then took it away again, not really giving him time to figure it out for himself. Since he just arrived in Budapest, he hadn't had a chance to determine the Mexican Pesos to HUF conversion and both have a lot of zeros.

I did not know he also paid while he was out at the money machine or he was trying to figure out the bill. I would have stayed longer if I knew he paid cash on the street. I asked him if he thought the girls were in on it. We just didn't know. It was very upsetting. He also wasn't aware how much he paid or took out of the money machine.

The next day over breakfast, feeling awful with a hangover from the drinks we paid for, we started piecing together what actually happened.

I went online to my bank and saw my withdrawal and was surprised it was $544. He had withdrawn $135 off a credit card. Fortunately, I am not exactly sure how they got only $217 of my money. I had a nice amount of HUF still on me. In total, the bar made off with $352. Again I asked him if he thought the girls were in on it. It was highly unlikely at this point that they weren't. We vacillated all day whether they were or were not in on the robbery.

Later that evening we met another traveler. We relayed our story to her and she, sadly, told us she was told to watch out for nice girls that want to take you to a bar, as they will try and rip you off. It was now confirmed. The Romanians (if they were actually Romanian travelers) were part of the scam with the bar and we were robbed, no question.

We were pretty angry the night before. I remembered how angry I was. Then I remembered picking the Romanian's phone up off the ground when we were outside on the street. I noticed it was smashed into a million little pieces and I figured she wouldn't want a broken phone back. So we just left her phone on the street with the trash. The good news is, her phone cost more than the amount they robbed from us.

"Your journey is of your choosing. Think IT and see IT unfold for you along the road well traveled."—Drew Eric

"A Course in Miracles," tells me "What happens is my desire." So I thought long and hard about that. I remembered at the time I was concerned about spending, overspending and losing money on the road. I am a student of "ACIM" and I believe I attracted this mishap to me, for me. This was a learning lesson on how my thinking impacts my journey.

It's my belief I attracted someone to take my money because that's the energy I was karmically putting into the world. All the Universe heard was "I am losing money" and so it happened, prophecy delivered. I must be more mindful of my thinking.

I still LOVE Budapest. This is now just an amazing tale about my adventures/miss adventures on the road well traveled. Wouldn't you agree?

Going forward I will be mindful of my thinking. I can attract positivity to my life, on my journey, I can and I shall. Prophecy delivered.

Facebook, September 15—Drew is feeling joyful @ Budapest, Hungary—
#ActOfKindness —35 I spent an amazing nine days in Budapest. I love that city. I walked, saw and made friends. The most wonderful person in the world, my Hungarian friend from the Camino invited me to visit and gave me her bed while she slept on the couch the entire time. Who does that, she is so incredibly sweet. I was thrilled to see and visit with her. Thanks.
—Jason—
This is quite a common scam in lots of cities/country's across the world... But I'm so glad that this has not dampened your spirits buddy!!! It's just another 'experience' to have had...
—Celia—
On the bright side...you're fortunate they only scammed you out of money.
—Carleen—

285

Taken down by a couple skirts!
—Frank—
A bar did a similar thing to us in Budapest. The bartenders would charge us a different price every time we would order the same drinks and would get aggressive when we confronted them about it.
—Christopher—
Wow, guess that's why they call it an adventure right?
—Anne—
Don't trust anyone… Trust yourself and only your gut… Even with your travel buddies… When some people from other countries see friendly Americans they automatically assume you are good prey… As you have now learned… It could have been worse… So change your password and if you don't understand how to use the ATM or what you are being charged for in a bar, call a cop… Not everyone is looking for friends… Some people are just looking for prey… Keep aware… Don't trust anyone… Remember you are in a foreign land… and out of your comfort zone...
—Gregory—
Unfortunately, a common occurrence in Budapest (and elsewhere). Know others this has happened to. Stay vigilant.
—Goffredo—
Glad ur safe. That's what matters! Have a blast!!!
— Frieze—
The same kind of thing happened to us in Beijing—two well-spoken Chinese guys saw us looking at our tourist map and offered to show us around one afternoon then mentioned one of their favorite bars nearby—they ordered 4 beers, then 4 glasses of crappy wine and a pot of tea. We were grateful for the mini-tour so I offered to pay thinking it couldn't be more than $40 or $50 dollars. As I was just about to give my card to the person at the register I did a double take and found it to be $432—the pot of tea alone was $70. That's when "scam" became obvious and foolishly I said to the two guys "you ordered this, you pay" and walked out on them. When we got out on the street I had second thoughts about what I'd just done—I was waiting for the Chinese Police to pop out and arrest us but we made it away without any problem. I found out later it's a very common scam; they share in the proceeds from this with the merchant. It's a shame that you have to be so suspicious of people in your travels but seems to be the ways of the world these days. As the Brits say, "Keep calm and carry on".

—Morie—

That's exactly happened to a friend of mine in Budapest, but he was robbed $1,000

—Charleen—

Wow! Glad you are okay. That is a good lesson for all of us.

—Chris—

The old Romanian champagne in a Budapest bar trick...

—John—

They are called B girls, we have them in Miami too.

—Robin—

But it makes a great story

—KC—

I have to make this comment. I read your story about being scammed by the "Romanians." I am sorry you got scammed, glad to see you got her phone as payback. I do have to admit I found it amusingly ironic a gay man(men) got scammed by cute babes. Anyway, keep posting, I don't get to read all your posts, but I am enjoying the travel log, as I am sure many others are. Glad to see you are enjoying this adventure and that you are learning so much about yourself.

Facebook, September 16—Drew checked in at Ljubljana, Slovenija—

We have changed cities again. My friend/travel buddy spent some of the time with me in Budapest. Today we took a car to Slovenia. Sadly it is raining and I hear it's going to rain in Europe all week. Meaning everywhere we go. I am in the kitchen at the hostel after making dinner and we are all talking about our travel plans. We are changing them according to the weather that is before us. This is the life. The nomad life.

Facebook, September 19—Drew checked in @ Zadar, Croatia—

I am on the road again. I have been to Slovenia, Ljubljana, Zagreb, Croatia and Zadar, Croatia. Now I am heading to Sibenik, Croatia to visit waterfalls. Then I am taking a ferry to Italy to visit a friend in Rome for a few days. I will have to make it back to Croatia/Balkans since I am almost out of time in the EU. I have been lucky enough to spend the last week or so with my friend from Mexico. We split apart today but he will be in Rome with me.

Facebook, September 21—Drew—

I am booked on a bus to Split, Croatia to catch my ferry for an overnight to Ancona, Italy arriving at 7 a,m, just in time to catch

287

my bus to Rome, Italy at noon. That's an overnight ferry with a travel time of 16 hours. What can go wrong? Oh wait, I already booked the bus to the wrong city to catch the ferry, or you can say I booked the wrong ferry to Ancona, whichever. I will see my friends in Rome.

Facebook, September 23—Drew is feeling excited—
BIG NEWS!!! I just changed my flight from September 29th... My new flight home is... January 10th!!! I will spend the holidays and winter in EUROPE!!! OMG... I can't believe it... I am so excited... This is so far out of my comfort zone I can't tell you. I'm scared, nervous, excited and so many other emotions. I am pushing past all my fears and anxieties and accepting. The longest I have ever lived outside of Florida was in 1998 when I lived seven months in Washington DC. Now the longest I will have lived out of Florida will be the eight months I lived in Europe. A little boy from Clearwater, Florida living in Europe, who would have guessed.

Facebook, September 26—Drew is feeling missing @ Rome, Italy—
#ActOfKindness —36 My Italian friend from Ireland returned to his home in Rome and invited myself and the Mexican into his home that he shares with his loving girlfriend. We slept on the pullout couch in the living room for five days, while visiting Rome. We went on bike rides, tours, visited parks, ate Gorgonzola/Honey/ Walnut gelato, dinners, breakfast, lunches all at the generosity of my loving friends. I even visited Shakespeare's Globe theater and watched Romeo and Julieto in Italian. It was beautiful. I also was able to ride their bike to the Vatican and see it for the first time. The Vatican was powerful, both positively and negatively. How I love to do things like a local. I even got hit by a car like a local after I cut across traffic and the driver didn't appreciate it and sped up to RUB my tire for crossing him. I ended my stay with a brunch and got to meet a multitude of their friends. They welcomed me with kindness. I am forever grateful to my friends for taking me into their home and showing me their Rome. I love you both and am forever grateful. xoxo Thanks.

Facebook, October 4—Drew is feeling blessed in Mostar, Bosnia—
#ActOfKindness —37 I met another kind American man when I returned from Italy and landed in Split Croatia. We met in a hostel and started traveling together. He has made all the arrangements, planning how we travel and where we stay, great guy. We met in

288

Split, took a ferry to Hvar, then a bus to Mostar, Bosnia. Making travel buddies is such a joy, especially when they do all the hard lifting. Thanks my friend.

Posted on October 14, 2016 by Drew Eric

Chapter 37 Can I overcome fear and
  continue on my trek through the Balkans?

Facebook, October 3—Drew—
"We have 2 choices at any given moment. We can attempt to control an uncontrollable moment or we can control our response to the same moment."—Drew Eric

I entered Bosnia with a vague memory of its history. I remember there was a war however I couldn't recall any details. I remembered the Olympics in Sarajevo but not when it was. My knowledge of Bosnia today was completely unknown. I quickly learned.

I arrived with a friend, a new traveling buddy that I met two hostels/cities prior in Croatia. We were greeted by the owner's brother who checked us in.

Facebook, October 4—Drew is feeling thankful—
#ActOfKindness —38 Free upgrade to a two bed shared room from an eight-bed dorm, for my new travel buddy and I. Free coffee and morning breakfast. Love this place, Mostar is great so far. Thanks.

The original Facebook post included the name of the hostel. However, after the death threats, my feelings have changed towards the hostel and their act of kindness.

Once checked in I spent some time in our private room and unpacked. I went on some apps and the dating sites to see if there were any locals who would be interested in showing me around town. I have learned while traveling, several apps work well for meeting locals and other travelers. When you're traveling solo, having local guides makes the city that much more enjoyable. Couch Surfing, Tinder, and other gay apps are great sources for meeting people while traveling. Both Couch Surfing and Tender have "hangout" options and meet-ups for people to gather.

I was surprised how quickly I received messages from men offering to show me around town. Three locals specifically offered to show me the sites. On my tour that evening, I learned all about gay life in Mostar. To my surprise, it sounded like a difficult life for the gay community.

Facebook, October 4—Drew feeling grateful—
#ActOfKindness —39 I met a local here in Bosnia and he took me on a tour of Mostar. What a great kind man taking time out of his life to show a tourist his city and share in the history of this tumultuous town. I thank you.

Before I jump into the gay life in Mostar, let me give you a little history of Bosnia. I learned all this from my tour guides and I used Google to fill in more details.

After the death of the very popular dictator Josip Broz Tito in 1980, Yugoslavia floundered for several years. Eventually it failed without a strong president/dictator that could keep Yugoslavia together. Slovenia and Croatia were the first two cities to separate and form their own countries in 1991. Then Yugoslavia fell in 1992. It was 1991 when the war started in Bosnia after they also wanted to separate from Yugoslavia. Serbia, the capital of Yugoslavia, let Slovenia go. I was told, because of its location adjacent to Italy and Austria. However Serbia was reluctant to let Bosnia go.

In 1999 Kosovo separated from Serbia. However the Serbs do not recognize it as a separate country either and chose to go to war "again" to keep it, as they did with Bosnia. As you can imagine, there is much unrest in this area remaining from the Serbian/Yugoslavian days.

Bosnia was not allowed independence from Serbia/Yugoslavia. Sarajevo, who held the Winter Olympic Games in 1984, the first communist country to hold the Olympics, was eventually surrounded and blocked from all supplies for three years. Mostar is ranked the sixth largest city in Bosnia currently and was also a front line for the war. The BBC did a graphic depiction "BBC - War In Mostar Bosnia" you can watch it on youtube:

https://www.youtube.com/watch?v=Ipua2Mh_F_c

In 1995, under the eyes of the United Nations (UN), the Serbian military committed genocide against Muslims during the years 1992-1995. In 1995 the Serbian military killed more than 8,000 Bosniak ("Bosnian Muslim") men and boys in and around the town of Srebrenica in Bosnia and Herzegovina, as well as the mass expulsion of another 25,000–30,000 Bosniak civilians. This was a very bad time in history for Bosnia and Herzegovina.

The Croatians and the Serbians both had their part in the war on Bosnia and Herzegovina. In 1993 the alliance between Bosnia and Croatia fell apart and they went to war against each other. Today in Bosnia there are Croats, Bosnians and Bosniaks. From what I gather, the three religions are Catholic, Orthodox and Islam.

With Bosnia wedged between Serbia and Croatia, there are great tensions lasting today with the older generations holding grudges along with long memories of the atrocities of war. The younger generations that didn't live through the wars however have a more accepting attitude of each other. Still, some hold animosity and extreme views. During the time I spent in Bosnia I learned a great deal about how hurt and angry the Bosnians remain today towards so many people and religions.

From the multiple offers of tour guides, I chose two. Both guides are gay men and my first tour was that evening while the second one I set up for the following afternoon. Both guides confirmed the same sad tale about how gay life is in Mostar, Bosnia. I also learned about the economy, political corruption and high unemployment.

With the war memories, unemployment, corruption, separate group identities i.e. Croats, Bosnians and Bosniaks, along with religious differences; you can imagine the anger and separation each person feels in Mostar. Now add in homosexuality and they are just another group to hate amongst all the other groups to point their finger and say, you are different from me and should be removed, killed and/or imprisoned.

After unpacking and before my first walking tour, I watched the BBC special on Mostar during the war, basically setting the tone for all I was about to see. I had no idea then what I would eventually learn and see for myself.

While touring the city I saw the charming medieval bridge that was completely restored after it was destroyed during the war. (UNESCO, the World Bank along with Croatia, France, Italy, the Netherlands and Turkey, paid for the restoration of the old bridge) Leading up to the bridge are adorable small river rock roads with tourist shops on both sides, along with restaurants bustling with business, even after summer has ended. I was genuinely surprised how many tourists are still walking, shopping and eating in this small town.

When I joined my first local tour guide we walked towards the Sniper Tower. I was informed during the war, snipers were atop the building taking aim at the residence of Mostar and they still call it the Sniper Tower today. Originally it was a bank building in the '80s and it will "soon"(or probably not knowing how Mostar operates) be restored to a working building again.

There were many, many war-torn buildings crumbling along the side of the road with shrapnel marks, bullet holes and missing walls and roofs. Clearly you can see the destruction living among today's inhabitants as an uncomfortable reminder. Whether you lived through the war or were born after the war, you can see and feel it all around you, there is no escape.

On my tour, I was taken up to the "Partisan Memorial" which is an old Yugoslavian/communist memorial built in 1965. It's been neglected, abandoned and vandalized since the end of the war in 1996. It once had a cascading fountain and was a relaxing area for the community to gather but today it's enjoyed by tourists and vandals.

My eyes tired of the destruction and my ears worked at not listening to the sadness that was coming from my guides. It was then I started to learn about how life is for gay men in Mostar—even how they treat each other which compounds the difficulties they all face. Needless to say, they do not have gay pride in Mostar.

On the dating sites, most men don't post their faces in fear of being outed. They rarely meet up with each other and even more rarely date since the gay life is so secretive. If they do show someone their face, it is usually received with silence or criticism I was told. They have a constant fear of being gossiped about among one another, supporting their secret lives.

Gossip has remained a concern, drawing from the communist lifestyle when your neighbors turned you in for not following the rules put upon you. I learned this is why so many locals seek out the companionship of visitors. Out-of-towners are safe, enjoyable and don't talk about the people they meet to other locals since they leave town in a day or two.

When I entered the Balkans I noticed gay men generally don't hold eye contact with each other. I noticed this in Croatia and then

293

again in Bosnia. Something as simple as looking someone in the eyes is too intimate for them. I am not entirely sure why.

I inquired if they are "out" with their families or friends and I was told no. Their life is very secretive among everyone in their lives. Secrecy perpetuates the lack of community and acceptance. The more they keep themselves hidden, the longer it will take to live the life of their dreams. For now, their life is small, quiet, limited and hidden from sight. Clearly they have no gay bars or any outlet whatsoever for the gay community to come together and feel safe while living their lives.

This was difficult for me to hear since I spent the last 20 years in an openly gay relationship. One of the many lessons I learned after leaving America is becoming comfortable with heterosexual men. I realized I lived in a gay bubble and had very little dealings with men. I had to learn how to be myself among men while in Europe. I was afraid men wouldn't like me. I was wrong; I have found many men who like me for who I am. I wrote this in a blog, The Camino is teaching me how to be a MAN:

https://dreweric.wordpress.com/2017/10/11/the-Camino-is-teaching-me-how-to-be-a-man/

Now I am in a city that appears to live in secrecy. I still didn't put two-and-two together for my own safety, never thinking the very person who is most responsible for my wellbeing, by keeping me safe with a roof over my head, will be the person to threaten my life. With all the secrecy in Mostar, location between two rival countries, atrocities of war and living in a community that is still separated by religions and groups, it is clear this is a powder keg of separation, maintaining a life of hate, anger and placing blame on others. So I completely understand where this community comes from when they hate others. It's understandable in this city.

In addition, Bosnian politics appear to be very corrupt. One of the guests in the hostel was there to observe the elections and found several disturbing situations—everything from buying votes to a convicted war criminal being elected into office after 15 years in jail. One politician even received 100% of the vote. After the 1996 wars, America sent over a billion dollars to help Bosnia recover. I was told most of the money went into offshore accounts owned by the politicians in charge of restoring Bosnia's infrastructure. They didn't even have enough money to rebuild the Mostar Bridge.

Unemployment is exceptionally high. Reportedly you need to be a member of a party, have a friend recommend you for a job and pay the employer for the job once it is offered to you. Both of my tour guides are unemployed, living at home with family for more than 15 months combined. They do not appear to have job opportunities on the horizon.

Meeting visitors is one of the relief points in their life, distracting them from their four walls that act like a prison in their own homes. We discussed leisure activities, working out and I was told it's hard to leave home for activities like that when they don't have a job or money so they end up staying in most days. Home life means they have nothing to do but continue to think and dwell on their circumstances.

Most hostels are run by volunteers and/or employees that tend to be younger, liberal thinking and open to all races, religions and sexuality—because that's how the 20-somethings see the world. They don't see separation as much; they are more open to new ideas and people. In my travels I haven't come across a family-run hostel, so this was my first.

I met the brother who checked me in. He was very helpful, gave me coffee, a simple breakfast and told me about the BBC movie on Mostar during the war. He also upgraded my friend and me to a 2-bed private room. Later that evening, I met the owner for a brief moment. I believe he is about my age if not a bit younger, but over 40 most likely, putting him in the war during the '90s.

My second day started with the second tour of Mostar, leaving me tired, drained and relieved to get back to my hostel. I felt such sadness after my tour, learning about the area and life in Mostar.

Facebook, October 5—Drew is feeling heartbroken @ Mostar Bosnia—
#ActOfKindness —40 I was offered a second tour of Mostar by another kind man. He took me to see an old communist memorial no longer admired. He shared many of the difficult stories I heard in the tour from the day before. Hearing how difficult life is here in Mostar is heartbreaking. My heart hurts for the people of Mostar, my heart hurts for the gay community here since it is so behind

the times. I am blessed to have met two wonderful guys with the generosity and courage to share their stories. Thanks.

The previous day I made plans to meet my first tour guide again back to my hostel to hang out. Since I had a private room and my friend was out, I didn't think it would be a problem. It was mid-afternoon when my new friend arrived. The hostel has an open courtyard which divides the main living area and kitchen from the dorm room and our private room.

Shortly after my friend arrived I heard what sounded like the brother screaming outside, "NO, NO!" We thought that was weird and wondered what the screaming was about. Shortly after he screamed my friend knocked on the door telling me our host wants my friend to leave the premises. Concerned for his safety I agreed this was best.

I chose to let the whole incident go since I was feeling uncomfortable with the yelling and what seemed to be anger on the part of the owner's brother. I went back to my room for a bit then headed out to make a video on "Overcoming fears of the Unknown". I had no idea how much my own words of wisdom would be so beneficial and timely.

I went down to the bridge and shot my video. I felt great, accomplished and headed back to the hostel afterward. On the way back I had a hint of intuition, "I could very well be asked to leave the hostel." I noticed that just a couple doors down was another hostel and thought, "I could easily walk the few feet and check in there if something does, in fact, go amiss."

I passed through the courtyard on the way to my room. Within minutes we got a knock at the door and it was the owner asking to speak with me in the hall as to not disturb my roommate. He stated "You have broken my rules and you need to leave. You have two minutes to pack up your things and leave the premises." I did not argue with the man since he was the owner and I chose to leave a place where I was not welcome. I would rather be safe than right.

I shared what just happened in the hall with my friend and he was shocked, confused and scared since he had booked a van ride with them the following day to another city. I packed and headed out the door to leave. The owner called out for me to pay for the one night I slept in his hostel. I agreed to pay and walked towards them. They got behind me as to block me from escape and told me to head into the kitchen to settle the bill.

As I turned towards the kitchen I got pushed from behind. I am wearing two backpacks, one on my back and one in front, weighing around 45 lbs. After I got pushed I stopped in my tracks, looked them in the eyes and let them both know they do not have permission to touch me. I was getting louder at this time and people were coming outside to see what the commotion was. They told me to walk into the kitchen to pay for my room, equally as loud.

Once in the kitchen I reached into my pocket and told him "All I have is Croatian money" which infuriated the owner. He replied, "I am not taking that communist money; you will need to pay me with something else." When he spit those words out of his mouth I realized something. This isn't about me, I am just another person for him to point his finger at and say, "You're the reason my life is so bad." It was a surreal moment.

I told him "I don't have any other money" leaving us in silence looking at each other. I again told him a little louder "Seriously, I have no other money."

One of multiple guests in and around the kitchen softly spoke up and offered to exchange my money for Euros, allowing me to pay the 10 Euro bill. Quietly we took a minute to exchange money; all the while several guests and my friend were observing the commotion.

As I paid and moved to leave, he stepped in front of me and told me "Your friend is in the mafia. You invited someone from the mafia into my hostel. Do you know he is in the mafia?"

I said, "I don't know anyone in this town." (I later found out the brother took 50 Euros from the man as bribery for silence and threatened him with harm. This didn't seem to be a reasonable behavior for someone suspected to be in the Mafia).

Then he said, in front of his other guest, "I want to kill you right now". I got out of there quickly. His anger was at a boiling point and I wasn't feeling safe. Children were playing outside when I was leaving the building and his brother told the kids "move out of his way, he is GAY!"

When I reached the road I quickly went to the other hostel hiding at the entrance so he couldn't see where I was going. During my check in I told my new host that I had just arrived on the bus today since I was afraid she might be friends with her neighboring hostel. I never told her the truth.

My roommate and friend, afraid for his own safety, decided to stay at the hostel and remain hidden away in his room. Once the owner was away, he joined the remaining guest in the common room. They were all a bit shaken and kept talking about how crazy and homophobic the hostel owner was.

After I checked in to the new hostel and got situated, I went out to meet back up with my friend for coffee. He wanted to give me a coat and hat for my travels now that Fall has arrived in the region.

Facebook, October 5—Drew is feeling inspired @ Mostar, Bosnia—
#ActOfKindness —41 I told my local friend I didn't have a winter coat. Last week I was swimming in the ocean in Split, Croatia. This morning it was 35 degrees. Winter comes fast here. He gave me a hat and coat and said he hasn't worn them for a while. He has been unemployed for more than a year and lives at home with his family. Generosity is free and is tremendously rewarding for everyone.

As I exited the hostel to meet for coffee, I came across another friend from the hostel in Hvar, Croatia. We chatted for a few minutes. I was so shaken, I could only talk about my troubles. As I was sharing the story, the angry hostel owner came walking my way. He passed by without saying anything. I felt safe with the guys I was with. I was still very nervous seeing him again. I hurried away shortly after to meet my friend.

Later in the evening the angry owner attempted to apologize to my friend for the troubles earlier. My friend said it was upsetting to him and he was concerned for me. It was then the angry owner got distracted with his thoughts and told my friend, "He was probably dealing drugs in the room. I should call the cops and tell them to arrest him before he crosses the border!" He walked over to the phone and started dialing. My friend ran to his room to message me "Get out of Bosnia as soon as you can, this guy is crazy!"

Facebook, October 4—Drew—
"Try to believe, however briefly, that nothing can harm you in any way."—A Course in Miracles

During coffee with my friend is when I got the message. I jumped up, thanked my friend for everything, grabbed my new coat and started back to the hostel to hide out for the rest of the night.

Back in the safety of the hostel, I shared my story with one of the other guests. I wanted to talk about it just in case the police stormed in, taking me to jail for dealing drugs. My thoughts were crazy for sure. The living room was full of people eating and talking. I felt warm and safe with all the friendly travelers.

When I got ready for bed, I checked my messages one last time. My friend messaged again saying the volunteer at the hostel knocked on his bedroom door. She told him the owner was drafting an email to send out to the "Balkan Hostel Group" saying I was a "drug dealing homosexual" in an effort to get me blacklisted for the time period I remained in the Balkans. She also told him she was ending her volunteer service at this hostel tomorrow because of the owner's homophobia.

My plan is to leave on the 7 a.m. bus, figuring the angry hostel owner won't be up that early. I am truly concerned for my safety at this point. So many fears are creeping into my mind. Having to explain to the police that I am not a drug dealer, fearing I will be blacklisted in future hostels and possibly physically hurt. I took two Xanax and read my book for a bit as a distraction until I fell asleep.

Facebook, October 4—Drew—
"Life happens For Us to grow whether we have vision to see it or not. As we look back, we can clearly see the trek that got us here."—Drew Eric

In the morning I left my hostel and was able to reach my bus safely. Two police officers stepped onto the bus and I silently panicked. I thought for sure they were here for me—they weren't, they were just passengers.

My next stop was Sarajevo, Bosnia. I worked hard over the next few days to let go of the fears that came up for me. It was strange having so much anxiety again. I was feeling so comfortable with my travels after the third month. I really felt calm, relaxed and at peace with living the nomad life. Mostar seemed to interrupt my peace, I was so enjoying. But I didn't let it win. I have again found my peace.

I chose not to leave the Balkans. I chose to continue my travels through what used to be communist countries and are now democratically based. I am still observing a different world in this eastern bloc. I still feel uncomfortable but I am not letting fear stop me from experiencing this part of the world.

Facebook, October 4—Drew—
"Fears are not Stop Signs. The purpose of fear is to give us warning and proceed with caution while remaining alert and observe our surroundings. Do not confuse warning signs with stop signs."—Drew Eric

Fears are warning signs not stop signs. I wrote about this as a coaching tip. Now I am following my own words. I got present with my trek, found courage and controlled my thinking, not allowing negativity and fears to metastasize in my mind.

Facebook, October 5—Drew—
"Bravery is acknowledging your fear and doing it anyway."— Cheryl Strayed

I will continue to grow from this experience. I came to Europe to be uncomfortable. I also wanted to see how others live their lives in another land. I am happy to have learned and seen so much. It hasn't always been easy but even this experience has changed me for the better.

On this trek, I have visited 20 countries thus far. Before the Balkans I took for granted how many cities had gay bars and businesses. Now I see none and it's unsettling.

Facebook, October 4—Drew—
"How to overcome fears of the unknown:
Fears are warning signs
Have courage
Be present
Control your thinking"—Drew Eric

In the Balkans I have traveled through Croatia, Bosnia, Serbia and I am currently in Romania. I am planning on visiting Bulgaria, Macedonia, Kosovo, Montenegro and Albania, then off to Greece. There doesn't seem to be gay pride or gathering areas for men to meet and mingle in the Balkans. When I lived at home over the past 20 years, I lived in a gay bubble of safety and security with many bars and gay businesses. Now I am experiencing a life without such privileges and safety.

The hostel owner is working hard at making a living in a city with such corruption and lack of employment. He has carved out a real business for himself. Besides the hostel, he runs a shuttle business to neighboring cities and countries, helping his guest navigate transportation while visiting this end of the world. Another creative source of income is a day tour his family provides bringing his guests to neighboring sights and shares history about the war. One business supplies three sources of income which shows resourcefulness and ingenuity. I admire this about him and the effort his family makes to provide in a difficult economy. I don't blame him for his lack of awareness and limited acceptance for others, who are different from himself. I see the environment in which he has been raised.

Elizabeth Lesser presented at TED Women 2010 a talk with the topic: Take "The other" to lunch.

From the TED website: There's an angry divisive tension in the air that threatens to make modern politics impossible. She shares a simple way to begin a real dialogue—by going to lunch with someone who doesn't agree with you and asking them three questions to find out what's really in their hearts.

http://www.ted.com/talks/elizabeth_lesser_take_the_other_-to_lunch?language=en#t-521050

I was moved by the TED talk and shared it on my Facebook because of the division we are seeing in today's politics during this 2016 presidential election. If we continue to see each other as wrong, separate, different or even as the enemy, we will perpetuate hatred and wars. In order for us to survive we must start seeing each other as one and the same. See our enemies as brothers with a slightly different view on life.

I have friends on Facebook who support different views. I love and respect them as human beings and I won't unfriend them or block them from my life. I accept them for who they are, as my brother or sister.

I hope someday gay pride will make its way through the Balkans. I also recognize they have other issues to deal with. There is so much hurt anger and separation.

"Imagine all the people living life in peace.
You may say I'm a dreamer
But I'm not the only one
I hope someday you'll join us
And the world will be as one"—John Lennon

I am not paralyzed by the strong grip of fear. I can move through my fear and emerge on the safe side, where love and unity lives.

Facebook, October 4—Anthony—
Good read Drew..terrible intolerance and the use of fear as powerful weapon is disturbing..no country is immune to its reach

follow my… trek

Posted on November 15, 2016 by Drew Eric

Chapter 38 Can I live in this world and
   remember we belong to each other?

   Facebook, November 8—Drew—
"I live in a world where I see everyone as family, friends and colleagues, not as Others to fear."—Drew Eric

Trekking the Balkans while Gay… This is my story…
   I spent the past seven weeks trekking the Balkans, across the Adriatic Sea from Italy and above Greece, from Albania in the South, to Romania in the North. Part of this area is formally known as Yugoslavia which collapsed in 1991 after the fall of communism.
   While traveling the Balkans I learned about wars, genocide, political corruption, anger, finger pointing, gossip, rebellions, dictators, ruling empires and the realities of being gay in Eastern, formerly communist countryside. In Bosnia I was told "I want to kill you right now" and I feared for my safety. All this was happening in my life while the presidential election was happening at home, this seemed like a far-off world to me now, but today I found the two worlds colliding in the present.
   The countries in and around the Balkans are Croatia, Bosnia, Serbia, Kosovo, Romania, Bulgaria, Macedonia, Montenegro and Albania. Traveling the Balkans while gay has been eye-opening. I have learned so much more than I was comfortable with.
   While on the road around Europe I have met men (interested in the opposite sex mostly) who became travel buddies and great friends. When we were together I didn't always have time to seek out the gay life. Occasionally I was able to break away for a date but for the most part, I did what my friends did. I mention this because I always thought there would be a gay life available if and when I wanted it, just like it was throughout Northern and Western Europe. I did expect that when I arrived in the Balkans, but all that would change.
   When Yugoslavia was a country the main capital was in what is now Belgrade, Serbia. Other larger cities around the country

eventually became Capitals of the new emerging countries, meaning, not all capitals have a thriving city life and are still growing.

In Germany, Poland, Czech Republic and Austria, all the wars and unrest dated back to WWII in the mid-'40s. Today in the Balkans everything is more recent and raw. I even remember it from my childhood dating back to the '80s and '90s.

My Balkan experience started in Croatia. While seeing what Zagreb, the capital of Croatia, had to offer, I took a walking tour. I love history and I was interested and willing to dive into this region and learn about their lives and cultures the same way I experienced it in the rest of Europe. In Croatia I was informed about the 1991-96 war with Bosnia and Serbia along with political corruption and life in Croatia. I didn't know what I was getting myself into. Croatia was my first country in this region and I felt as though I was just an observer. Later, much later it became real for me.

I did have some time in Zagreb to visit some gay businesses since my travel companion was also gay. My impression of these businesses was a bit disappointing, especially for the capital of a country. I still maintained it would get better as I traveled through the area.

I visited several Croatian cities Googling gay life and finding none but the occasional gay-friendly bar. This was my first indication I might not be able to rely on having a gay life available when I wanted or needed it. However, there are always the dating apps where I can meet some locals or fellow travelers for some sightseeing and quality time.

I came to Europe to see as many of the sights I could see. I had no plan, no itinerary and no real time limit other than my three-month Visa in the Schengen Treaty.

(Entering the Schengen Treaty you automatically receive 90 days over a 180 day period. The United Kingdom along with the Balkans are two areas not in the Schengen Treaty where most long-term travelers spend their time if they want to extend their trek through Europe)

I dreamed of visiting places like Berlin, Prague and Budapest. These are big cities with established names and long, rich histories. I had no idea what I would see while visiting these cities but I knew their names and was thrilled to visit them. I am a regular American with limited geography memory and knowledge. I know the big sights to see like "Big Ben," "Eiffel Tower" and the "Berlin Wall" but that was about it.

However, when it came to the Balkans I knew nothing. I didn't even know if it was safe to travel. I remember it being communist and I vaguely remember wars but couldn't recollect anything.

My 90 days were pretty much finished in the Schengen Treaty when I entered Croatia. I never thought about the Balkans and knew nothing about this side of the world. After visiting several Croatian cities I decided to keep moving through the Balkans and visit as many cities/countries as I could, meeting vacationers and travelers along the way.

While in Split, Croatia I met an American who is a long-term traveler. He had lived outside the country for several years, just traveling around, living the nomad life. My new travel buddy identifies himself as more fluid with his sexuality so it was a refreshing change from men just interested in the opposite sex.

While visiting Croatia I continued to Google gay life finding none other than that in the capital. Still it hadn't occurred to me the rest of the Balkans could be the same. The next city my new travel buddy and I chose was Bosnia. It all changed in Bosnia.

When I enter a city I usually open the Couch Surfing app that has a great meet-up and hang-out features. You can also post in groups on the website telling other travelers and hosts your travel plans, in case they want to host you or meet up. This is a great resource for solo travelers.

A new dating app for me is Tender. My travel buddies in Ireland had me join so we could form "going out" groups to attract other folks, mainly girls for them. The gay apps work as well for meeting people, making lifelong friends and snagging a tour guide to show you around.

In Mostar, Bosnia I opened the gay apps and to my surprise several people offered to show me their city. I was optimistic about my Mostar experience as I met up with my first tour guide.

We began our tour with the war-torn buildings in the area. He informed us about the destruction of the city from both Croats and Serbs along with the genocide in 1995 at the hand of the Serbs. He told me all about the political corruption with the politicians embezzling money. He also shared the corrupt hiring policies. "You need to be recommended for a job interview then once offered the job; you need to PAY them to receive the job". My first tour guide has been unemployed for a year, living at home with his family.

He then shared how the gays are not a cohesive group. They are terrified of gossip. This is a communist throw-back about your neighbor turning you in for anything and outing you in public. So my friend said he doesn't really date and meet guys in Mostar. One of the last things he told me was "If it wasn't for you and our tour, I would just be at home looking at my four walls contemplating my life." He spoke about his dream of leaving Bosnia for a job in Germany since he has dual citizenship in Croatia/EU and Bosnia/not EU.

I found it very difficult to focus on what he was telling me, I couldn't put my finger on why but it was difficult to hear such unsettling words. I felt sad and struggled during our conversation. He was so nice and open.

When he found out I was heading to Sarajevo next and I didn't have a winter coat, he offered me one of his old coats, even though he has been unemployed for a year. We made plans to meet.

On the second day I met my second tour guide for another tour. All the same information was relayed—even confirming the fear of gossip amongst the gays. He also shared he was unemployed for three months. He is 37 years old and living at home with his family. He doesn't have dual citizenship and isn't interested in leaving Bosnia for a better life. He wants to stay and make a go of it. I struggled again hearing his words. My ears wanted to shut it all out and not listen. Later I realized my reaction to such sadness was to run away and not listen to them describe their lives. It just hurt too much. So much finger pointing, hate and fear of each other, in this region.

I didn't know it then but my life was changing. My observation of this new land was shifting.

When I finished my second walking tour I went back to the hostel and invited my first tour guide over for some quality time. I had a private room with my travel buddy and the room was on the outside with a separate entrance. I didn't think it would be a problem bringing someone back to my hostel in the middle of the afternoon. I was very wrong. I was kicked out and threatened to be killed by the hostel owner.

This was a very disturbing experience. I have since learned so much about the hostel owner and his practices from other travelers who stayed with him. It would appear the experience was about homophobia rather than rule breaking and I make this conclusion from his continued actions against my friend and me.

As an example, I found out the hostel owners brother extorted 50 Euros as hush money, something I Googled and saw as common in Bosnia. That evening the hostel owner told my friend he was going to call the police and tell them I was a drug dealer and get me arrested before I left the country. He said, "People like him need to be in jail." My friend immediately messaged me to get out of Bosnia as soon as I could. That same night I received another message that the owner was sending out an email to get me blacklisted from the Balkan Hostel Group, so I won't have any accommodations in the Balkan area.

My friend posted a video blog about what happened to us in Bosnia, at the hands of the person who was providing us shelter. Several weeks later he got a comment on his blog from the hostel owner saying we were both kicked out of the hostel. In addition, he stated when he contacted the police, they already knew about us because we were wanted in Split, Croatia for prostitution, all lies.

Until today I have been silent about naming the hostel owner and his business. I see now how my silence isn't helping my fellow travelers. Today is the first time I am publishing his name and business. I have been frightened by his backlash because he does comment on every post he can find. I would rather receive his backlash now, then to allow someone to stay in his hostel since he is so volatile.

I met a woman much later who stayed with him and she shared how he was pinching her cheek. She had to tell him he wasn't allowed to touch her. She felt very uncomfortable in his presence. I heard others had similar feelings when they stayed in his hostel as well. In his defense he has plenty of positive reviews.

His name is Miran at Hostel Miran Mostar. #hostelmiran

I do not recommend anyone staying at his hostel due to his volatility and uncontrollable anger along with inappropriate touching and homophobia. I am still slightly nervous about his backlash even now.

I left the next morning early to catch the 7 a.m. bus to Sarajevo, Bosnia. I wasn't going to leave Bosnia out of fear, I stood my ground. When I arrived in Sarajevo I found Hostel Miran posters on display. I kept my mouth shut about my experience out of fear.

It wasn't until a couple days later I shared my experience with the two young individuals working at the hostel. They were horrified and apologized for my experience in Bosnia. Later, they warmly let me know they took down his posters and will no longer be promoting his business.

I met some wonderful friends in Sarajevo and recuperated from my traumatic experience. I shared my story and everyone was supportive and kind.

Next up was a walking tour with some of my new friends. The reports of hate continued as we learned all about the horrific siege surrounding Sarajevo during the Serbian/Bosnian war. As if this wasn't difficult enough we also went to a museum describing the atrocities put on the Sarajevo, Bosnians during the war in front of the United Nations.

Some of the atrocities were the constant sniper shooting of residents including women and children. We learned all about the Bosnian genocide of 8000 Muslim men, boys and male babies while the world watched on television. The museum described three buildings housing Muslim women and young girls, who were used as imprisoned sex slaves. This shit got real for us.

For three years the Serbs did not allow food, water, electricity or any medical supplies into Sarajevo. It took the residents of Sarajevo 21 months to dig a secret tunnel for supplies. The UN and Serbians never found the secret tunnel.

On an upside, we heard about the Sarajevo people embodied a rather unusual sense of humor in an effort to cope with the atrocities of war. They still have this sense of humor today. I was not coping well with all I was hearing especially with my time spent in Mostar so fresh. It was hard to see and hear but I couldn't turn away or close my eyes or plug my ears any longer.

I was so frightened by my experience in Mostar I didn't pursue meeting anyone in Sarajevo other than hostel travelers. I have no idea how the gays live in Sarajevo or how they treat each other.

The highlight of Sarajevo, and a pleasant relief from the atrocities was visiting the site of the 1984 Winter Olympics, mainly the bobsled track in the mountains. We got up early in the cold, took a taxi to the top of the mountain and walked the downhill track.

There were about five of us sharing in the experience. We took so many beautiful pictures of the graffiti bobsled track while the morning dew rose off the landscape. It was an amazing sight to behold. Less than a decade later, what was once a celebrated location around the world would be the site of atrocities while the world watched on television and remained silent.

I would like to point out how we are all still watching the atrocities of war, such as Syria and doing little about it. History keeps repeating and silence kills.

On our way down the mountain we came across two bombed out homes that were on the front line of the war. A shepherd, with his flock in toe, told us about them. He was an older shepherd who lived through the war and knew about these buildings. He said he was here fighting the Serbs in this very spot where he lets his sheep graze. It was a breathtaking view of the valley with Sarajevo in the background and the sheep grazing on the hillside. In contrast, war and destruction obstructed the view of the rest of the mountains.

As we made it down the mountain into the city we passed a huge graveyard with newer white crosses just below the old Fort. I was curious to see when the residents were buried in this location, 1996, another reminder of hate and death in our view.

Two of my hostel buddies were planning on traveling to Serbia next and visit the capital city, Belgrade. I decided to join them; the three of us got a shuttle and headed for Serbia, the main culprit of all the wars in this region. We openly discussed our feelings about visiting Serbia since we were all a bit overwhelmed with our learning about the atrocities in Bosnia at the hands of the Serbians. All three of us felt a bit guilty giving Serbia our money, supporting their economy; however we wanted to move past our ill feelings and give Serbia a chance.

We took a walking tour first thing. Have I mentioned how much I love walking tours? Our tour guide, we learned, was probably a bit more of a nationalist then we had wanted. He mentioned the war against Bosnia and stated: "Bad things happen during wars and both sides did some bad things." Then he moved on. We were surprised how he gave such a small amount of information on something so horrifying.

Later he discussed a few bombed out buildings in Belgrade and how the residents wanted to keep them as reminders of the atrocities of war. I inquired which war and he explained they were from the 1999 war when Bill Clinton bombed Belgrade.

The Serbia war against Bosnia ended in 1996. Then when Kosovo wanted to secede from Serbia, because they feel more Albanian then Serbian, Serbia went to war with them. Apparently the only atrocities of war this nationalist wants to remember is when they were the victims of bombing.

During the tour, our guide told us the measures they took to join the European Union (EU) by giving up "War criminals" and other measures. Then the EU came back and said to let Kosovo go. The guide told us, "90% of Serbs would go to war tomorrow to keep Kosovo, we feel it belongs to us." Later he said he didn't understand why they aren't accepted into the EU. I am not sure why he couldn't see their warring attitude as a deterrent for acceptance in the EU, it seemed obvious to my friends and me. Again, more hate, finger pointing and placing blame.

While in Belgrade I Googled gay bars and found one that was open on a daily basis. I took my two travel buddies, a German guy and an American girl, to get a look at the place. It was small and pretty cute but not a lot of patrons on a Monday night. Still I was happy to be in a place of comfort and safety while traveling the Balkans.

Serbia isn't all bad though; my German friend told me that after Berlin, Belgrade is the hip place to be for bars, nightclubs and techno music. Many people from around the Balkans and Europe come here to party, who knew?

I finally went on the dating apps the last day in Belgrade and met a young man for coffee. He confirmed all the same information about gossip and gay life in Serbia. He is "out" at work however not "out" at home with his family. He wasn't dating and rarely meets up with other gays for dates out of fear of gossip. Again, I was confronted with the fears the gays feel in their own lives and country. He also said he doesn't visit the bars much for the same reason.

My travel buddy from Croatia told me just before I went to Sarajevo, about his experience in Belgrade. When he arrived and came out of his hostel the streets were blocked and full of police with guns. He inquired what was happening with fear of terrorism and they replied it was a gay pride parade that day and they were out to protect the citizens from harm during the parade.

He made a video blog about the experience and posted it online. This video blog turned out to be his most popular blog post to date with views and comments, most with hate and anger towards the gay community. It terrified him so much he left immediately and vowed never to return to such a homophobic country.

Time had come for the three travel buddies to part ways. I enjoyed them and appreciated their support during my difficult time in Bosnia.

Facebook, October 11—Drew is feeling super @ Belgrade, Serbia—
#ActOfKindness —42 After more then a week traveling with two new travel buddies we are splitting apart. They have been so kind and supportive during my troubled time. They made the travel arrangements for us to Serbia. We cooked food together, I received chocolate and love. We played cards, took walking tours, laughed and visited a gay bar in Belgrade where they treated me to a beer. I love these two, a German kerl(guy) and a spitfire American girl. Thanks for being there for me in so many ways, helping me heal from Mostar. Thanks.

Next up, crossing the border from Serbia to Romania. I had a difficult time getting across the border.

Facebook, October 11—Drew checked in @ Centar Vrsac—
Always an adventure... I am traveling from Serbia to Romania. I take a bus to a small city near the border. Where I catch another bus for a short ride to the border, where I walk across, LOL, really I walk across! Then on the other side, I will find another bus to the city I am going to, Timisoara. I didn't have enough money so I had to walk to two petrol stations to get Serbian money. Not too much because I am leaving Serbia. I assume I will have to take out Romanian money once I walk across the border. What a hilarious trek I am on. The transport bus teamed me up with a few other kids going to Timisoara, I think. We will all have to figure it out. At least they might speak Romania, maybe, hopefully!
—Drew—
I have taken two buses, dropped at the border walked into Romania only to discover there is no transport on the other end to take me to my city. Oops. I thought the kids I was teamed up with on the bus were crossing however they got off earlier. I thought this was a bit more organized when I started this morning. Online it seemed like it would be. I have now hitched a ride to what appears to be an old train station. A man walked up when I did and said the train to Timisoara is this way. I boarded, sitting on the train now. I don't have a ticket. I only have Serbian money and

311

there doesn't seem like an ATM is going to be handy. Wish me luck.

—Drew is feeling relieved @ the Romanian/Serbian Border—
#ActOfKindness —43 After I walked across the border from Serbia to Romania on my way to Timisoara I realized there was no city, no buses or transport to move me along. So I stuck out my thumb. Two guys picked me up after 15 minutes, drove me a few miles to a train station where I was able to take a train directly into Timisoara. All is well in Romania.

—Drew is feeling optimistic @ Romanian train station—
#ActOfKindness —44 When I didn't have Romanian money, the train conductor gave me a free train ride to Timisoara.

#LifeLesson —45 Trust and all problems are solved now. A quote from "A Course in Miracles" Yesterday was very adventurous walking over the border and hitchhiking. I was walking between Serbia and Romania thinking, "Oh this isn't looking right" then my next thought was to trust and take this as part of the adventure. I laughed and shrugged off any negativity. I was afraid of hitchhiking while on this trek. A couple friends were doing it and it was beyond my comprehension. However, once I was in Romania and seeing I was several miles from a town hitchhiking was a great idea. Even when I got in their car I totally didn't care where they dropped me off I figured it would be better than walking in the middle of nowhere.

In Timisoara, I didn't have a chance to meet any locals and learn about gay life since I was there such a short time. However, I did Google gay life in Timisoara and learned there were no gay bars anywhere. I did visit a Romanian Revolution Museum with a couple of guys from the hostel. Did I mention I love history? The revolution against their dictator started in Timisoara and spread throughout the country within a week in 1989. At the end of the week, Nicolai Ceausescu and his wife, Elena were captured. They were tried and killed on Christmas Day for the atrocities they committed against their people, more hate, blame and finger-pointing, it just doesn't let up.

Facebook, October 12—Drew is feeling lucky @ Timisoara Romania—

#ActOfKindness —45 A nice traveler from my hostel loaned me money for a museum and lunch after we just met, as we toured together in Romania.

Between history lessons, I was able to hang with people in the hostel and play cards with other travelers. So it wasn't all doom and gloom. However, It rained the entire time I was in Romania, sad but true. It probably contributed nicely to the spooky ambiance and my history lessons.

Facebook, October 12—Drew is feeling delighted—
#ActOfKindness —46 To all the travelers that entertained me with hours of cards. I thank you for your kindness. Cards came with wine, popcorn, beer and chocolate, who could ask for more. Thanks.

I remember hearing about the Victorian age and Victorian architecture as it relates to haunted houses. From what I learned on National Public Radio(NPR), around the time television was creating "The Munsters" and "The Adam's Family" and directors were filming Frankenstein and Vampire movies, Victorian homes fell out of popularity and into disrepair. Victorian homes reached their popularity from 1830-1910 and are very ornate with elaborate trim and bright colors. So when the film industry was creating spooky homes, Victorian's where the ones that fit the bill since the colors had long faded and the ornate decorations had only partially remained. I am assuming Timisoara was built up during the Victorian age because that's exactly how it looked, Victorian, dark, old and spooky. This architecture only added to the allure of Romania, coincidently the birthplace of Dracula. Did I mention it never stopped raining while I was in Romania?

Facebook, October 13—Drew checked in @ Romania—
I'm on a bus riding through Romania with a violent war movie playing on two TVs. I have been learning all about the wars, rebellions and the fall of communism in this region of the world. Outside it's grey rainy and cold. The bus is silent but warm. I just finished a crime drama written by #davidbaldacci. The landscape is barren and the buildings are in need of repairs. This feels surreal and haunted from the deaths gone by.
—Drew is Feeling amazing—

Next city was Sibiu and I stayed in playing cards with the new travelers at the hostel. I went on the apps but didn't meet anyone right off. I was feeling a bit lonely and still recovering from Mostar. The next day, my first full day in Sibiu, I decided was the day I needed to finish my short story on Mostar. I spent five hours writing, proofing then posting the story. It was difficult to relive. It left me depressed in this strange new city with rain and darkness beating me down.

I decided to give Sibiu another day so I could see a little of what the town had to offer. Most all the other travelers were leaving the next day. I did get to do some morning sightseeing with them before they left. There wasn't a walking tour available, just a descriptive map of the city and what to see. I didn't get any history or learn anything about gay life in Sibiu. Overall my emotions during Sibiu were raw and I struggled with my mood. So a break from history was fine with me.

When I reached Bucharest it was still raining, of course, and I had to make my way to the hostel on foot. It was dark, wet and cold on this autumn night but I was optimistic, barely.

I Googled gay bars and found out the only gay dance club was open on Friday and Saturday nights. Today was Sunday so I missed out. The only place available was a gay-friendly bar.

So what do I do on my first full day in the Capital of Romania? I join a walking tour for some history, of course. I met a lovely young gay couple from Israel. We spent the entire day together. We did the walking tour then we visited the Capital building for yet another walking tour, WOW, two tours in one day, I am in heaven. I learned so much. At the capital we met a couple of Americans from my hometown. The world is small.

Facebook, October 19—Drew is feeling hungry @ Berarie Gambrinus—
I had tripe (cow stomach) and pork brains for dinner. I am living on the edge in Romania.

Now a little about the history of the Romanian dictator: Apparently he got mad at the World Bank in the '70s and decided to pay off all their debt. At the same time he created a massive building project in the Capital, and I mean massive. He tore down 34,000 homes and displaced families so he could build his own Empire/Palace/Germania.

(Hitler had plans drawn up to remodel Berlin in the style of a Roman empire that would last for 1000 years and solidify his place in history. He wanted to call it Germania. Something I learned while on a walking tour in Germany of course. The people living in this region during the Roman times were called Germanic People and the Romans also referred to this region as Germania.)

While Nicolai and his wife were building their empire and paying back the World Bank through the 1980s, he was starving his country. This eventually led to a one week revolt and the end of his life. Touring his Palace/Parliament building I was able to see his vision. It was the most beautiful interior imaginable. Today, it stands as the second largest government building in the world. The Pentagon is the largest.

During this period he was also exporting goods, such as new tractors the Romanian citizens were building in factories. However he was selling them at a loss to other countries just to show Romanians were able to produce goods and export into the world economy. The tractors he sold, and melted down for their metal since the metal was worth more than the tractors. This would be called self-destructive economics. Further examples of how power is destructive to the people you are governing.

I went on the dating apps for some friendly conversation. Unfortunately a consistent theme throughout the Balkans is to chat for a bit then never meet up. I hear and saw it over and over again.

With so much fear and closeted gay men you don't always get to know people.

I did reach out to a person when I was out with my friends at the gay-friendly bar. He was at the same bar, however he was with someone and couldn't let them know he was gay. Sad, but true.

The next night I made a date with another traveler on business by using the dating app. I got ready and took a 30-minute bus to where he was staying. When I arrived it became apparent I was lured to a hotel room with no guest. I was cat-fished and my cat-fisher was somewhere else bearing witness to my foolishness in believing he was a real person. This didn't help my already fragile mood from Mostar. I left Romania feeling down.

Off to Sofia, Bulgaria.

Facebook, October 19—Drew is feeling crazy @ Romania-Bulgaria Bridge—
Crossing the border from Romania to Bulgaria… Never in a million years did I expect to experience this moment. But here I am, on a bus, crossing the border. Can't wait to see what happens in Bulgaria. So excited.

Now is a good time to share the tourist sites of the Balkans. It was about this time I started to realize there isn't that much to see as compared to the "Eiffel Tower" or "The Berlin Wall" and "Tower Bridge" (thought to be London Bridge). The Balkans can be a beautiful place to visit however it's a lower level excitement as compared to France, Germany and England.

I am not sure who said it first but we quickly created and played the "Balkan Bingo". Which consist of:

"B" the old stone bridge,
"I" river,
"N" fort/castle,
"G" clock tower and
"O" the mosque.

Most all cities in the Balkans has them on their "Top 10 list of sights to see" along with a few statues and monuments.

I am not saying the Balkans isn't a great place to visit, but these countries are a lower level excitement. Each city had the Bingo/ five things to see. Combine that with wars, dictators, political corruption, famine, genocide and hate along with the 1950s gay lifestyle of secrecy and fear of gossip, it's no wonder I got homesick around this time.

It was probably halfway through my seven weeks in the Balkans, I started to realize the impact it was having on my wellbeing and happiness. Sadness was slowly creeping up on me, each day, little by little.

Home was a war zone of finger pointing and hate for the "others." The 2016 election was full-blown shit-throwing. It was all over the news media wherever I was traveling at the time. On my journey I regularly used Facebook to lift my spirits for those moments of sadness I occasionally experienced. However now, hate was in my feed and I didn't have a safe place to retreat to.

I thought at the time I would rise above the petty fighting and not chime in with my opinion on politics. I was wrong. From all I learned here in the Balkans I can't keep quiet. I must speak up and point out where I see attitudes and opinions that could use some new insights.

Back to Sofia, Bulgaria…

I arrived in Sofia still a bit down. I'm feeling homesick, sad from being cat-fished in Bucharest and not meeting anybody in my last hostel to travel or hang out with. I decided to make some changes and shake things up in Sofia to break this feeling of despair.

I log into the apps and let my presence be known. I haven't been on Couchsurfing.com for a while and I tried a new tactic for meeting locals. I sent out messages to all the men on Couch Surfing that had similar interests as I, letting them know I am in town and looking to meet some locals for drinks and hang out. This turned out to be a great way to get the ball rolling because two people responded and we scheduled a time to meet. I was meeting one that same evening for a drink at a local bar.

He gave me some insights about the gay scene in town. They have a big club with great music open on Friday and Saturday nights. I planned on being here in the Capital with the idea of going out Saturday night. My new friend told me he was happy with the gay life in Sofia. He has friends, he dates, he even travels to Serbia to go out (the party town of the Balkans). I mention gossip and people remaining in the closet and all the other issues I heard about and he agreed. That is all still present here, but overall he was happy with his life. This was refreshing to hear.

Later that day, I planned to meet another Couch Surfer host for a drink and conversation. Months earlier he invited me to stay with him "if and when" I arrived in Sofia. However I hadn't couch-surfed in a while and completely forgot about the invitation. Once I messaged him, I read over our previous conversations. He seemed nice and I looked forward to meeting him.

Also that evening was a Couch Surfing meet-up that I was interested in attending. Meet-ups are great places to hang out with other travelers. You never know who you will meet and there is always a chance you can be traveling in the same direction.

I mentioned to my new Couch Surfing friend about the meet-up and we agreed to check it out. It was a small group of three attendees. A Columbian who organized it was about my age. Another Latino (I didn't get his country) and a 19-year-old from Finland. Guess who ended up being my new travel buddy for the next couple weeks, yup, the Fin, more about him later.

Over beers, I connected the Fin and my Couch Surfing host friend so he'd have a place to stay. The Fin mentioned he was heading to Macedonia after Sofia, which was my plan. I decided to stay an extra day in Sofia with them, Couch Surf one night, then leave Monday morning on a bus for Skopje, Macedonia with the Fin.

Saturday we made plans for a walking tour of Sofia, with our host as our guide. We walked for several hours as we saw all Sofia had to offer. He shared so many interesting tidbits we wouldn't have gotten if we toured on our own.

Facebook, October 23—Drew is feeling excited @ Sofia Synagogue—
#ActOfKindness —49 My new Bulgarian friend took three of us around Sofia on a private walking tour for several hours. He is a kind man to give so much of his time to strangers! Thanks.

Coincidently we ran into our other meet-up Couch Surfing friend, the Latin who was around my age, then we were four touring Sofia. This type of thing happens all the time when you run into people over and over again, as you are all touring the same areas. It is always a welcome experience while traveling solo. You never really feel completely alone.

Saturday evening I had plans to hit the town and see what Sofia's gay bar had to offer. I was still down and homesick and was hoping to meet and make some friends.

Once the bar filled up I was able to meet a Bulgarian who drove into town for a night out. He was from a city an hour and a half outside Sofia and came in to share in the city's gay life. We talked for a bit as we watched the locals dancing and mingling with their friends. It was refreshing to be out among other gay men in a regular environment. It felt like home again and I forgot all about this being the Balkans.

As the night progressed, I reached my quota of fun for the evening. I saw, I talked and I was ready for bed after a long day and an enjoyable night out in Sofia.

It's a funny thing how your attitude impacts your vision. Here I was struggling with my attitude about the cities, the Balkans, meeting people and I wasn't really giving Sofia a chance. I was doing everything to my best ability and I was getting everything I was hoping for. Yet I couldn't see it as easily as that.

Once I realized I wasn't giving Sofia a chance my mood shifted and improved. Then I was able to see all my efforts were working well. I was able to make friends, get a place to stay and even found a travel buddy. It was a struggle to pull myself out of the funk I created in Romania.

Sunday night my Bulgarian Couch Surfing friend offered shelter to me and the Fin. This gave the Fin and me time to plan a visit to Skopje. Macedonia would make my sixth country and twelfth city in the Balkans. We were not prepared for what we were about to see in Macedonia.

Facebook, October 24—Drew is feeling loved—
#ActOfKindness —50 My Bulgarian tour guide invited me and a friend into his home for shelter and warmth my last night in Sofia, great hospitality. Loved his big old lab and his adorable kitten running around the house leaving a wake of fur and mayhem. Thanks.

We called Skopje the "Las Vegas" of the Balkans, not the cool hip Vegas but rather the over the top, ridiculous Vegas.

Skopje, Macedonia (The Former Yugoslav Republic of Macedonia, pronounced Skopy) has the fifth largest cross in the world and the largest cross in the Balkans. It also has an "Arc De Triumph" or rather an "Ark De Accomplishment" since they have never triumphed over anything. They have a fountain with the world's largest "Warrior on a Horse" also referred as "Alexander the Great." Greece has a patent on Alexander so they can't use the name. Greece also has a patent on the name Macedonia so they can't use that name either. The UN has accepted the name "Macedonia FYROM-The Former Yugoslav Republic of Macedonia." This city is bizarre. I am talking really BIZARRE. Nothing is real or authentic, not even the names.

They have multiple fountains and more than 1600 statues in the city center. The main fountain "Warrior on a horse," (not to be confused with Alexander the Great) was built for a modest eight million plus Euros, while the beggar and shoe shine bronze statues were cast for a modest 80k, which is more money than both the shoe shiner and beggar will make in a lifetime. It's been reported they have spent between 200 and 500 million on what is now infamously called the "Skopje 2014" construction project which includes a complete redesign of the city center.

In a region recently torn from wars and communism, in an effort to attract tourists, Macedonia is ordering bronze statues from Italy to create a city with the most bizarre appearance. One fountain has lions that don't really fit on the marble base. Buildings have more than 20 statues adorning their exterior, similar to old Roman monuments and the original Coliseum. Bridges have statues running along the railings like the bridge in Rome.

It's not just bizarre statues; in addition they are building three pirate ships to hold restaurant/retail space. During the walking tour (I love walking tours) we were told the mayor visits other famous cities and sees things that intrigue him. He comes home and has them built or shipped over, hence the pirate ships and "Arc de Accomplishment."

Once he saw three islands in France in the middle of the River Seine, with three willow trees growing. He was so inspired he spent thousands having the same three willows shipped to Skopje. However, without three islands he had three stainless steel planter boxes placed next to one of the pirate ships where he planted his willows. Sadly it would appear two aren't doing so well. We were told during the walking tour that he even has plans for the London Eye and Spanish steps from Rome.

The old stone bridge and the old stone fort along with the Byzantine heritage area and Ottoman district are easily overshadowed. New construction is everywhere—museums, government buildings and a National theater. Advertising is not small either. Huge signs adorn building tops and one giant video screen that shows advertising directly on the square near the multimillion Euro fountain of the "Warrior on a horse" (not Alexander).

One positive note, the city holds the honor of baptizing Mother Teresa. There is a modest museum and church on the grounds of the original church(destroyed in an earthquake) where she was baptized. Several of the Balkans countries have special ties to Mother Teresa—or as she is now known, Saint Teresa—and are proud of her. She was sainted just a couple months prior to my visit to the Balkans.

Facebook, October 25—Drew—
"What can you do to promote world peace? Go home and love your family"—Mother Teresa

Overall Skopje was uncomfortable. I couldn't help but be over-whelmed and concerned for the citizens of Macedonia. They have started to protest the "Skopje 2014" project. It is the second year of protest and this year they chose to call it the "Color Revolution" by using paint balloons and throwing them at sculptures and build-ings. This along with painting the statues in conspicuous places, i.e., lions balls are painted red. The paint adds to the allure of the unusualness. All this reminds me of the dictator in Romania build-ing his Germania.

Our walking tour guide told us that calling the demonstration the "Color Revolution" has had a negative impact on tourism. In-evitably the word "Color" gets left off the "Revolution" and tourists assume the worst and choose a different country for their vaca-tion. I would be interested to go back in ten years to see the final results. I am sure it will be powerfully entertaining and grotesque.

Since I was with the Fin, I had little time to socialize outside our time together and didn't meet any local gays. I did a quick search and found no gay establishments for a drink or conversation. Our next stop is Prishtina, the capital of Kosovo.

Facebook, October 28—Drew is at Prishtina City—
"We are all a piece of the bigger puzzle, together we fit."—Drew Eric

Bill Clinton is a huge deal in Kosovo. Now we are traveling back in time to the 1999 war with Serbia (again with Serbia) and Koso-vo. Just a reminder, Serbia doesn't want to let any of the Yugoslavian cities go, including Kosovo. So when Serbia goes on the attack shortly after the war with Bosnia, Bill Clinton and the UN respond. Bill Clinton sees an opportunity for a well placed, strategic military base and tells the United Nations, America is bombing Serbia and defending Kosovo. They love Bill Clinton for this. More war and devastation in the Balkans.

When the Fin and I arrived in Prishtina, we chose a hostel right on the main walking street in city center. I pull up Trip Adviser for the top ten sites in Kosovo. This time the sites were so limited they only listed several statues. After coming from Macedonia, the statue capital of the world, seeing Bill Clinton, Mother Teresa and another warrior on a horse in statue style, made it amusing. There was no old stone bridge or fort. We didn't see a river but they did have a couple of mosques, no Balkan Bingo here.

I opened the gay apps and immediately met a nice guy who joined us for lunch. He was Indian and has lived in Kosovo for many years and just moved back to town. He was our tour guide in this city. He told me all about Bill Clinton and what Kosovo is like. He also said the UN threw tons of money at Kosovo to no avail. He called it the UN's biggest mistake in history.

All these years later, Kosovo is still struggling to make ends meet. Soon the UN will be pulling out of Kosovo and leaving them to govern. Like the rest of the Balkans, politics are a bit of a mess, including corruption. It just never lets up here.

Prior to lunch, I noticed several men and even teen boys holding hands, kissing each other's checks and walking arm-in-arm down the street. I saw so many coupled men; it was the first thing I questioned my lunch companion about. He confirmed my observation stating the men here are extremely affectionate with each other, however, not gay. It's a strange twist here in the Balkans—being affectionate with each other while still maintaining homophobia.

The rest of our Prishtina consisted of an American movie "Snowden," and a jazz club with a Gypsy jazz live band, great fun. So it wasn't all doom and gloom from wars and lack of gay life.

Prizren, Kosovo was our next stop. Once we arrived in Prizren we were back on the Balkan Bingo: bridge, fort, river, mosque and the clock tower were all present. Once we finished Bingo in five minutes, I took a Fin break and met a couple locals who told me about gay life here in Prizren.

322

Apparently gay marriage is legal however gays don't marry each other because of fear of being killed or ostracized from their family and friends. He has a wife which allows him to maintain his cover. I met him and his best friend/workout partner. He told me they workout every day in an effort to see each other. Occasionally they meet travelers allowing them the opportunity to have intimacy since they can't date in this small town.

There is a local business/hostel that rents for a few hours. It is a large apartment with a bathroom and a garage to pull your car into and close the door for added privacy. It costs ten Euros which is a lot of money for Kosovo. One of the men is 37, has a job but only makes 300 Euros a month while the younger 29-year-old recently graduated from college and has been unemployed for a few months. Meaning travelers have to pay for the private hostel if there meeting goes in that direction. He expressed his discomfort with asking tourists to pay for the room but explained: "Ten Euros is just out of my budget living in Kosovo." I felt his sincerity and sadness simultaneously.

My travel buddy and I were splitting up the following day heading in different directions. The Fin was going to South Albania while I was going north to Southern Montenegro. We planned to reunite in Shkoder, Albania, the week after for a hike up the Albanian Alps, also affectionately called the Accursed Mountains.

Facebook, October 29—Drew is feeling sad—
#ActOfKindness —51 After more then a week my little buddy, the Fin and I are spitting up till we meet back up in Albania. We shared money, meals, drinks and laughs. He was always there to lend a hand and help out any way he could with ideas and making travel arrangements. Travel buddies are the best. He is one of my youngest travel buddies at 19, however, more traveled than I. He has visited 40 countries in his young life as compared to my 22. He is an inspiration to all with his courage to solo travel the world. I thank you for your kindness and friendship. Thanks.

I did a quick two nights in Podgorica, Montenegro, the capital. Saw most of the bingo then moved on. It was my first time in a hostel solo, felt weird.

Kotor, Montenegro did not disappoint. There was Bingo along with an amazing view of the sea from the mountains. What a beautiful little town, no wonder it's a port-of-call for cruise ships.

There was no walking tour, no gay bars and the nightlife ends at 11:00 p.m. Something else I noticed, once you reach the coastline and the Mediterranean Sea, you leave behind the Balkan wars and politics. It's all beauty and relaxation and touristy as if it was always this way. The coastal areas of the Balkans are the gems of the Mediterranean Sea for new tourism. I met some really nice people in this hostel, another American along with a trio of Australian girls in a comedy group.

Budva, another beautiful coastal city in Montenegro is next. I met more travelers in the hostel and we shared wine along with stories of our adventures and the wars of the Balkans and homophobia. All this was fading into the distance with each kilometer that I separated myself from inland Balkans. Here on the coastline it felt like touristy Europe again.

Next stop, a bus to Shkoder, Albania to meet up with my Fin friend one more time and then hike the Accursed Mountains. On the bus is a mash-up of hostel friends—some from the hostel I am leaving in Budva and some from the hostel in Kotor. My Kotor buddies are heading to Shkoder, while others are moving on to the capital of Albania, Tirana.

The Fin and I arrived around the same time in Shkoder. Just before dark so we have a little time to hike up to the fort/castle on the hill for breathtaking sunset views. We could also see the river from the fort. My Kotor buddies join us for the walk. As we climb to the fort one of the many wild dogs throughout the Balkans follows us as our leader and protector. He stayed with us all the way up to the castle, toured the top then came down with us midway until he got distracted and we lost him. It was the first time a wild dog attached to my group and was so friendly.

The next morning the Fin, I and an English bloke caught the bus to Theth, the mountain base camp, before the hike. On the bus was none other than the American from Kotor. Crazy how that happens. The American was hiking that same day, we were planning to hike the next day and the Brit was just going to visit the town. After a long bus ride and a couple of shots of Albanian Rookie (Albanian moonshine), the four of us decided to hike the same day. This meant we needed to get over to the other side of the mountain rather fast to reach town before nightfall so we weren't lost in the dark and unable to find the trail.

All went well during the hike and an amazing group of new friends was formed. Next stop is a ferry down the river back to

Shkoder then onto Tirana, the capital of Albania. The four of us decide to visit Tirana together rather than split up—more travel buddies.

The first thing we did—of course—was to join the walking tour and learn all about Albania. Albania was not a part of Yugoslavia; it had its own dictator named Hoxha who was at one time friends with Yugoslavia, Russia and China. However, later he unfriended them for not being more Stalin-like. He died in 1985, pretty much freeing the country just before Yugoslavia fell after their dictator Tito died in 1980.

What a terrible dictator, in the sense he had no friends and cut his country off from the entire world. This left his country with no trade, no products and no friends, they had to produce everything. Citizens of Albania never saw a banana and were afraid to eat it once it was introduced. They weren't allowed to have cars or watch outside television or movies. The only thing they saw for a while was old Chinese movies and the Chinese coincidently were watching old Albanian movies at the same time.

I had heard about Albanians being friendly. I mean like super friendly. They are so happy you are in their country and happy to help you with any of your needs while you are here. They were like that neighbor on the block with no friends who eventually be-friended one of the popular kids and was catapulted into the popu-lar crowd while still remaining kinda awkward. What a pleasure to be in Albania, they were so hospitable.

In Croatia, Romania, Bulgaria and such, I observed men in their workplace; they tended to be gruff, short or even just harsh/mean. I was told not to take offense, it's just the nature of men in the Balkans. These Balkan men are smiling, friendly and kind. What a change,(workplace i.e. money exchange, shopkeepers, salesman)

These people were poor and their Capital showed it. But man, were they happy. One startling change was everyone drove a Mercedes. I was told it was possibly nouveau riche but hell, I don't blame them since they weren't allowed to own cars under Hoxha.

After Tirana we all split up. It was the last time I would see my Fin friend. The Brit and he both moved on while the American and I went south for our last Albanian City before Greece. I was finally leaving the Balkans after almost seven weeks. It was difficult be-ing in the Balkans. So much war, so much destruction, so much distrust among the Balkan people and gay men. So much finger pointing, blaming dictators, other countries and other gays for everything wrong in their life.

Adding to the difficult experience of being gay in the Balkans was the lack of rewarding monuments and tourist attractions. Of course I saw some great things and had some amazing times, but I never dreamed of visiting the Balkans as a child, so spending seven long weeks was wearing on my soul. Not like visiting Venice, Paris or London where your soul can be born again.

When I left America, Bernie Sanders was still running and Trump was just bullying everyone including his opponents on the Republican side. My last day in the Balkans ending seven long weeks coincided with November eighth, election day in America.

Facebook, November 8—Drew—
"I pledge allegiance to the Flag of the United States of America, and to the Republic for which it stands, one Nation, indivisible, with liberty and justice for all."

I just spent the last seven weeks seeing the impact "remaining quiet" and staying in the closet does to a gay community. The Balkans was 1950's gay life in America all over again.

Because the Balkan residents remain quiet, people don't know who is gay and it perpetuates homophobia. In order for their life to improve they need someone to stand up and take the lead. They need to throw the door open on homosexuality and scream from the streets like Americans did in NYC at Stonewall when the drag queens rioted for three days burning cars and beating cops.

They need unity not fear. They fear each other and their happiness diminishes from lack of dates and relationships. They need to come together, get organized and come out, causing homophobia to be pushed out of Balkan society.

While on my trek, and during the entire election period, I said nothing. I chose to rise above what I saw as petty fighting and let the "Others" fight it out on Facebook and in the news. I chose to keep my political views silent as to not offend anyone.

So when I went to bed election night it was way early for votes to be counted and when I woke to my alarm at 6:00 a.m. it was 9:00 p.m. in Los Angeles, perfect timing for some serious poll numbers. I was shocked to see the preliminary results, Trump is in the lead. As the morning progressed the election was called and it was done. I, among many, was in a state of Shock and Dismay.

Facebook, November 9—Drew—
I am joined in the kitchen of my Albania hostel by one Canadian and three Americans. We woke up early to share in the American experience.

Now let me tie it all together for you. While traveling gay, through the Balkans I saw a consistent theme, silence and hate. When I went to Facebook for some relief I was silent and all I saw was hate for "The Others" with different beliefs and political views. I saw Deplorable and Nasty Americans, blaming, hating and not listening to each other regardless of their political views.

Facebook, November 9—Drew—
I choose peace, Peace for all Americans. I send you all love, De-mocrats and Republicans alike. I send love to all religions, all na-tionalities, all races, and all sexualities. We are all the same and we all want peace. Let's start a new campaign of peace now that the election is over. Let's!!!

The following week, while I joined my fellow liberal Americans in a state of shock, I saw America and the Balkans, with new eyes seeing for the first time, similarities. Americans aren't any better than Balkan citizens willing to start a war because of different reli-gious views. Americans don't rise above blaming others for their problems. Americans don't welcome other immigrants. I am not better than gay Balkan citizens because I remained silent during such an important election.

Facebook, November 9—Drew—
I REFUSE TO HATE…
Religious People
Atheists
Black, White, Asian, Hispanic People
Trump Voters
Clinton Voters
Gay People
Men & Women
I REFUSE TO HATE…—anonymous billboard

Wars and genocide start because conversation ends. When two parties can no longer listen or communicate, forts with protective walls are put up and concentration camps are created. I saw so many of my Facebook friends stating they are blocking anyone who has a different opinion than them. Those same people shared and posted hate statements and negative memes, to people that only believe the same as they do, in other words, preaching to the choir. I saw Americans degrading each other, calling others lazy Liberals and uneducated Conservatives. And those are the polite terms.

What I realized, if we come from a place of hate and blame we will never get anything accomplished. We need to listen to each other. Hear why the other team feels this way. How can we help them while protecting our own rights and beliefs? That's all we want, is to live the American dream as free-thinking individuals.

Like we tell our children, use your words. Unkind memes and name calling only perpetuate anger and hate. We need to speak intelligently and state what we want. We also need to listen to "The Others".

Facebook, November 9—Drew—
"If we have no peace, it's because we have forgotten that we belong to each other"—Mother Teresa

Honestly, I don't know the needs of middle America. I don't know why they want the swamp of Washington drained. I don't know why they feel a man with no political experience is better than a Senator/Secretary of State with experience. I don't know anything about them.

I have traveled the world now and I have learned so much. Soon I am going home to my land of the free and I want to learn about it. I need to learn about it. I want to be the change in the world I want to see. My country needs me and my opinion. I want to make a difference by learning, listening and speaking up for my needs and rights in an intelligent way.

Facebook, November 7—Drew—
"When you have seen one thing differently, you will see all things differently." —A Course In Miracles

So I would like to challenge you all. Stop posting hateful comments. Use your words. Learn what their needs are and why aren't their needs being met? Then share why your needs are important. Figure out how you can make a difference in our country, in a constructive way. Try a new approach because what we have been doing apparently didn't work out so well.

I can live in a world where we all belong to ourselves and to each other. I plan on co-creating that world. Will you join me, as my co-creator?

Facebook, November 9—Drew—
"I can see others in my own likeness, searching for connection and love amongst others, searching for love and connection."—
Drew Eric
—Drew is feeling concerned—
This is my open letter to Donald John Trump. I am using my words and speaking my truth. I am taking a stand and declaring, I will be watching and speaking up.

Dear Donald John Trump,
I would like to start with congratulations on your being our new President-elect. I have been out of the country since mid-May and really have little knowledge of your policies or expected direction. I have watched your acceptance speech and I am very happy how supportive your speech was.

I was happy to hear you say, "We need to bind the wounds of division".

What great words and so true at this time. You also stated, "It's time for us to come together as one united people, it's time". I couldn't agree more.

We have so many political parties, races, sexualities, ethnicities and religions. You are exactly correct, we need to come together to work as one for the great land we call America.

What I most appreciated and was happiest to hear was your pledge to me and all Americans. "I pledge to every citizen of our land that I will be President for all Americans and this is so important to me". Those words are so valuable for me to hear and believe.

As an American man, I can practice any religion I choose because America was founded on freedom of religion. I can marry any person I choose because the Supreme Court has deemed it

329

legal. I have free speech as my right as an American and can speak out honestly and openly about my government at any time because we are not a dictatorship or a Communist country. I will choose to do this going forward.

I have seen and learned so much while traveling in Europe. I have seen oppression from wars, dictatorships and bigotry. I have been threatened with my life because I am a gay man. I am pleased you consider me an American and want to be my President—not because I am straight or gay or belong to a certain religion. I am an American and that's good enough for you. You said so in your acceptance speech and I will hold you to those words.

This past election I chose not to voice my beliefs or opinions on any candidates. I allowed others to battle it out on Facebook, television and in the papers. Now you, as our new President-elect has put out a request to us.

"I am reaching out to you for your guidance and your help, so we can work together and unify our great country."

I pledge to you, Donald John Trump, here and now, I will no longer keep quiet. I will work to inform you of my views and beliefs, on how I see what needs to be done in this country. I will do this with respect and kindness and consideration for all Americans. I will continue to stand for our rights in this country and the fundamentals it was founded on.

As our new President, you will have the House, Senate and potentially a seat on the Supreme Court. I look forward to the new opportunities you will bring to our great land while keeping the foundations we have always believed in—human rights, health, religious freedom and liberty. If I feel you are pivoting away from our American foundations, I will let you know. I will not use profanity or divisive words because I am well aware that I will not be heard. My intention is to be heard, clearly and respectfully and with heavy concern.

I attempted to vote from Europe and wasn't able to. I am at fault for that. I am at fault for not expressing my opinions and values for all to know. I will not make that mistake again. I am on your team, Donald John Trump, as my new President-Elect and I will use my right to free speech to let you know how I want you to govern our great land.

Respectfully,

This is to you, the reader:

I encourage you to use your words and speak your truths. Inform our new President-Elect in your words, as a concerned citizen with your voice, letting go of divisive words in an effort to be heard, and let him know how you want him to govern. Let's release our anger and move forward together, believing in us, American Citizens. Together, we can make a difference.

Facebook, November 15—Drew—
"I believe something good arises out of all experiences whether they are good experiences of not so good. We just need to see it that way."—Drew Eric
—My Balkan trek wasn't all breathtaking mountainous views and sunsets, however I have been deeply moved. This portion of my journey has given me new eyes to see the world. I will never see it the same again. I hope you see these words and the world differently too.
"Never doubt that a small group of thoughtful committed citizens can change the world; indeed, it's the only thing that ever has"—Margaret Mead

follow my… journey

Chapter 39 Can I simply enjoy the journey
  through Greece, Turkey, Italy, Spain?

"When travel is in your heart and you are the only one who wishes this wish, then go solo. You will never regret granting yourself this wish."—Drew Eric

Facebook, November 10—Drew is feeling positive @ Kalaja E Gjirokastres—
#ActOfKindness —52 I am on the move with my American friend/ travel buddy! We are heading to Greece. This will be the first time leaving the Balkans in many, many weeks. I have been to all the Balkan countries located in and around ex-Yugoslavia. What a TREK! My buddy and I met a few hostels ago, we took a hike over a mountain together and are now spending a few more days in Greece. He has shared with the travel arrangements and all decisions I needed to make getting out of the Balkans. When I accidentally took out too much money, one extra zero, he helped me exchange it for Euros so I wouldn't get hit with another exchange fee. We also shared meals and laughs. Undecided whether we will visit Turkey or not. For now... Greece :) Life is good.
Facebook, November 14—Drew is feeling inspired in Thessaloniki, Greece—
#ActOfKindness —53 People from all over the world are staying in my hostel. They are volunteering at the refugee camps here in Greece. They said 40% of the refugees are children in the 20 camps. They offered me free breakfast and to eat with them before they went to the camps. I wanted to cry from their kindness.
Facebook, November 15—Drew is feeling blessed—
#ActOfKindness —54 So many volunteers cooking for the homeless refugees here in "The Soul Food Kitchen." I got invited to cook for refugees. I will spend the next eight hours cooking and handing out food to the homeless refugees. I am not a registered volunteer so I won't be entering the refugee camps. I am blessed to be around so much love.
—Drew is feeling honored—

#ActOfKindness—55 I met a man from Austria while volunteering. Every day he picks up refugee children and takes them to the playground here In Thessaloniki. This is his contribution to help the children have a little joy in their day. I am deeply moved and honored to witness such love and kindness.

—Drew is feeling proud—

#ActOfKindness —56 There is a mom and son team that came to Greece to volunteer and cook for homeless refugee families. In addition to them, there is a father and son team also doing the same. I am proud to be among so many people giving up their busy lives to come to Greece and give love to the refugees. No words can express my joy here.

—Drew is feeling honored—

#ActOfKindness —57 I met an Iranian refugee that is working on his asylum and he is a translator/volunteer for other refugees. He had decided to give back to other refugees while he remains a refugee himself.

—Drew is feeling proud—

#ActOfKindness —58 The chef is stirring the giant pot of food—with love in her heart—for the homeless refugees. She left her home in August to volunteer in Greece while on her one week vacation. She is still here in November cooking every day with no days off. She gave up her own life in order to give nourishment to others.

—Drew is feeling honored—

#ActOfKindness —59 A group of the volunteers are sorting clothes for refugees in the 20 camps here in Greece and handing out some items to the homeless refugees on the streets. So many volunteers here helping out. Beautiful acts of love.

Facebook, November 17—Drew is feeling excited @ Athens, Greece—

Wow, just wow! Rich with history.

Facebook, November 21—Drew is feeling excited—

I am booked on a flight from Athens to Istanbul in just a few days. Then I have a flight from Istanbul to Milan. I will spend December in Italy, Christmas and New Years in Rome. Then I have to make it back to Barcelona in January for my flight home. My journey is winding down. I fly back to America on January tenth, almost eight months here on my journey. Where did the time go?

Facebook, November 22—Drew is feeling ready @ Mykonos, Greece—

I have dreamed of Greece since I was in my 20's and I saw my first movie on location in Greece, "Summer Lovers" with Daryl Hannah. I will be here for Thanksgiving. Thrilled to see the island.

—Drew is feeling thankful @ Mykonos—

#ActOfKindness —60 I met a local and he took me all over Mykonos on his motorbike so I could see the island. I got to see the "Shirley Valentine" beach(from the movie in the '80s that also inspired my journey to Mykonos) which was on my list of must sees. Thanks for taking time out of your day for a tourist.

—Drew is feeling thankful @ Mykonos—

#ActOfKindness —61 I met an Irishman living in Mykonos and he invited me out for wine and conversation. People on this Island are so kind to tourists. Thanks

Facebook, November 23—Drew is feeling thankful @ Mykonos—

I made a new friend today, a wild dog. His name is PITA(pain in the ass) his favorite game is fetch with his pet rock. I had to take his rock away because he wouldn't let up playing fetch while I was eating lunch, in a restaurant, which he had to sit at the table and watch me eat. I took a picture of him sitting at the table looking at me and the rock. I assume he is a wild street puppy. He spent all day with me. I finally had to separate from him. I was very sad. That evening I was telling my new American friends about him and I kept saying he would turn up. Sure enough, WOOF, there he was and so excited to see me. He stayed again for several more hours. Following me into the restaurant, market, home, every-where.

—Drew is feeling thankful @ Mykonos—

I have had such great luck meeting people here in Mykonos. I met two locals and a dog. During the day I saw a guy wearing a grey hat four times walking around town. Later in the day he walked up and we had dinner and a beer together. We bumped into this bunch of tourist and spent the rest of the evening with them. One is Brazilian and three girls are American. While one of the girls leaves tomorrow the sisters will remain and we will celebrate Thanksgiving together. It will be my first Thanksgiving without fam-ily. I don't think I have ever been without family on Thanksgiving, I might be feeling homesick today.

—Drew is feeling thankful @ Mykonos—

#ActOfKindness —62 The Americans had four-wheelers. They took me for a ride and sure enough, PITA jumps on. We rode him

around Mykonos for a good hour and a half. He got really good at jumping on and off. I wonder if he will find me tomorrow? Thanks to the Americans and the ride on their four-wheelers, it made my journey that much more enjoyable. PITA thanks you too.

Facebook, November 24—Drew is feeling thankful @ Mykonos —

My little friend Pita, how I miss you. He was pretty well groomed and neutered so I assume he had a home. He spent two wonderful days with me and now he must be off with his real family. After our four-wheel adventure with our American friends, we hung out and played fetch with his rocks till eventually, he walked me home. That next morning was Thanksgiving. This was my first Thanksgiving without family and I was terribly homesick. I woke up early feeling pretty sad. Opened the shutters and window and there was PITA. He waited all night outside my window, waiting for the morning to see me again. I got ready and out I went to get PITA some Thanksgiving breakfast. We spent all morning together. We sat on a bench, played fetch, ate and simply enjoyed the time we had. Eventually, we were walking in the early afternoon and as young dogs do, he got distracted or simply decided it was time for him to go home. He got me through a difficult morning here in Mykonos feeling homesick for my family and extended families. I am leaving in two hours. I give thanks to PITA. My little friend. Goodbye, my friend. I will always remember you and I will always love you.

—Drew is feeling thankful @ Mykonos—
I'm reading #TheMartian in Mykonos on Thanksgiving day and I read this line. "In other news, today is Thanksgiving. My family will be gathering in Chicago for the usual feast at my parent's house." I love it when this happens. When I was in the Anne Frank house, there was a passage from her diary written on the wall with the very same date I was in the museum. I love it when that stuff happens.

—Drew is feeling thankful @ Mykonos—
#ActOfKindness —63 My American friend and her sister spent Thanksgiving day with me, what a treat. We even got to watch my favorite movie, also filmed in Mykonos, "Shirley Valentine". Thanksgiving turned out to be amazing, not lonely at all. I am forever thankful to my American Sisters for the gift of quality time.

Facebook, November 25—Drew is feeling thankful @ Mykonos —

Goodby Mykonos, you will forever be in my heart. I give you thanks for a beautiful and warm Thanksgiving.

Facebook, November 26—Drew is traveling to Istanbul, Turkey from Athens, Greece—
On the road... Athens to Istanbul, Turkey... This is my first plane flight in several months. I have been taking buses, cars and trains mostly. I have learned I am not the only one who has anxiety traveling. I have seen many of my fellow travelers show signs of stress while on their journey. That has been reassuring. I am pretty good at it now. I get thoughts of anxiety and fear, I accept them as not real then let the thoughts go. It's a much quicker process. My body even feels better, not showing signs of stress. I'm sleeping better and waking up at a decent time instead of too early because of stress. I feel so much better. After Istanbul... Milan! I fly from Istanbul to Milan because I am that cool. Wow. Life is great. I am living on the edge.

—Drew is feeling inspired @ Istanbul Turkey—
I made it to Istanbul... Found a bus to take me into the old town and it's an hour bus ride, which was a surprise. I never expected to visit Turkey, but here I am. I just finished reading "Inferno" by Dan Brown. Can't wait to see all the places he talked about in the book. This will be way cool.

—Drew is feeling thankful @ Istanbul Turkey—
#ActOfKindness —64 I land in Istanbul & get on a bus to city center, the nice man that sits next to me pays for my bus ticket. Random act of kindness.

Facebook, November 30—Drew is feeling grateful—
#ActOfKindness —65 A nice fellow tourist bought me coffee, and some food while we are touring Istanbul. He is from Columbia.Thanks.

—Drew is traveling to Milan, Italy from Istanbul Turkey @ İstanbul Sabiha Gökçen International Airport.—
My business is complete in Istanbul and I will be flying into Milan for a little fashionable people watching today.
—How cool is that sentence? Istanbul you did not disappoint. The smell of the spices and the jewel tones of the city and the rich history. I loved you Istanbul. Thanks

Facebook, November 30—Drew is feeling excited @ Milan, Italy—
Let's see what this city has in store for me!?

Facebook, December 1—Drew is feeling optimistic—

#ActOfKindness —66 An Italian helped me plan/map my journey through Italy for the month of December. Grazie Grazie

Facebook, December 2—Drew is @ Leonardo DaVinci's Last Supper Museum—
This just happened! I had my last supper!!!

Facebook, December 3—Drew is feeling great @ Torino Citta—
I hear good things Torino, let's do this. I am staying in a hostel that was originally built for the 2006 Winter Olympics to house the Olympiads.

Facebook, December 4—Drew is traveling to Genova, Italy from Torino, Italy—
On a train to Genova, Italy where I will be Couch Surfing. It's been a while since I have Couch Surfed. This will be a refreshing change. In Torino my hostel was way out of town. So I didn't meet anyone in the hostel which is one of the best reasons to stay in a hostel. Along with meeting potential travel buddies. Hostels, I am finding, are much more expensive in Italy so I will need the break from spending. It's not the Balkans anymore.

—Drew is feeling positive—
#ActOfKindness —67 Couch Surfing host invited me to stay in his mansion in city center Genova, Italy for three nights. He fed me many meals, he sets the table every night & gave me wine with a home-cooked meal. Kind man I will always remember. Thanks.

Facebook, December 6—Drew is feeling disappointed—
Change of plans... Looks like there are no cheap hostels in Cinque Terra Italy. I will have to do a drive-by, meaning I will get off the train and walk around a bit take photos and get back on the train. I have found a Couch Surfing host in Pisa though so all is well. Pisa is the next stop after Cinque Terra before Lucca, Italy. There are so many amazing cities to see in Italy.

—Drew is feeling frustrated—
"Patience is being at peace with the process of life."—Louise Hay
—Drew is feeling perplexed—
This leg of my journey is different than the rest of my journey. I am seeing more cities with less time. I am traveling a bit faster also. This causes me to change my daily routine which has been moving pretty slow. Also, I am Couch Surfing a bit more. Couch Surfing is a great way to meet locals and save on expenses. However hostels are a great way to meet travel buddies and people to sightsee with. I have been a bit more solo on this leg of my journey. I won't get a chance to meet travel buddies until I reach big

337

cities where I will stay in one location longer and can work my network, Couch Surfing meet-ups and hangouts along with dating apps to meet locals interested in showing tourists around town. I am doing more research now to figure out what there is to see in the upcoming cities. When I stayed in Genova I was more scattered without a plan on what I wanted to see. This lead me to figure out a new way of traveling that includes planning. Today I left Genova to visit Cinque Terra. I have all my stuff with me. I will sightsee for an hour or two then visit the second city in Cinque Terra before heading to my final destination in Pisa where I have a Couch Surfing host. Tomorrow I head to Lucca for the day or possibly spend the night before I move onto Florence for several days. I will be enjoying some day trips using Florence as my home base. I should have one or two more trains before this day is over. I purchased a ticket yesterday for my train today not realizing I put the wrong day in. I had to buy another ticket this morning. My stress is a little higher with all the shifting of my routine.

—Drew—

"I have endured, I have been broken, I have known hardship, I have lost myself, but here I stand, still moving forward, growing stronger each day. I will never forget the harsh lessons in my life. They made me stronger."—unknown

Facebook, December 7—Drew is pleased @ Mura di Lucca—
I am "Under the Tuscan Sun," charming city.

—Drew is feeling amazed @ Pisa, Italy—
Apparently, it is just a bell tower for the church, who knew.

Facebook, December 8—Drew is feeling thankful @ Pisa, Italy—

#ActOfKindness —68 My Pisa Couch Surfing host gives me a place to sleep for two nights. We are now friends for life. Feels like we have been friends forever. We fell into conversation with ease and truly hit it off. I hope to see him again someday. Thanks.

—Drew is feeling optimistic @ Bologna, Italy—
Arrived today in Bologna. Haven't seen much but I am excited. Every night in Bologna it is foggy, no kidding, all the time. It is a really cool look.

Facebook, December 10—Drew is feeling grateful @ Bologna, Italy—

#ActOfKindness —69 Couch Surfing host offers me a night in his home. Sadly we didn't get to spend much time together but I appreciated saving a little money. Thanks.

—Drew is feeling frustrated—
Trains in Italy: I did everything right... I even paid to download the app. Then I purchased a ticket. The app doesn't read that well or work that well. It seems I can't scroll up or down. I arrive at the station 30 minutes before my train and attempt to print the ticket. The machine isn't really clear on how to print the ticket. I use the confirmation number from the app. Somehow I hit the back button and lost the confirmation number, it's gone. I didn't screen-save it either. To no avail, I cannot log back in and get the number. I purchase another ticket and run to my train just in time. Yay, why pay once when you can pay twice the price for one ride. Good thing I remembered to validate it before I got on the train.

Facebook, December 12—Drew is feeling perplexed—
Update: yesterday I got a train ticket to Siena. When I got to the second station the train was canceled. I took another train to another station and the train to Siena was canceled again. I then found out about the train strike. When I asked about a ticket back he gave me one free but forgot to give me a refund for my purchased ticket. Hmf, couple hours travel that ended where I started. ONLY IN ITALY! Well, and Paris, lol. Today I am on a nonstop bus to Siena. Cheaper ticket and not on strike.

Facebook, December 13—Drew is feeling surprised—
I have 28 days left in Europe. OMG time is running out. NOOOO more time left.

Facebook, December 15—Drew is feeling happy @ La Botteguccia di Valeria, Tuscany region—
I am on a photo exposition in Tuscany. I think I found THE AREA! Wow, I am driving around Tuscany this is truly amazing.

Facebook, December 16—Drew is feeling accomplished—
After several months backpacking Europe, I finally figured out how to visit a city and maximize my experience. 1. Create a Google account/log into the account on your phone. 2. Google "Top things to see in blablabla" 3. Select all things regardless of what it is. 4. Hit the star icon leaving a star on the map. 5. Include where you are staying and star it. Then, while you are walking around the city you will walk past a location and hit the star to see what it is, read about it/decide to visit the stared location. Google also gives walking directions and times and in most cities it will tell you public transportation. HUGE BENEFIT! There are other apps that work well for public transportation like Citymapper in London and Paris.

This works great if you handle the research before you arrive. You're welcome 🤓 my fellow travelers.

—After several months backpacking Europe, I finally figured out how to pack my backpack. The packing cubes I brought are the bomb. I switched bath items to the medium packing cube and reduced my underwear and socks to the smaller cube. My electric toothbrush didn't fit well in the small cube. This allowed me to keep all my bath stuff together instead of several bags I was using. Hard to believe it took so long to figure out, LOL.

—Drew is feeling beautiful @ Ponte Vecchio, Firenze - Italy
#florencelightfestival projecting art onto the Ponte Vecchio Bridge
—

This is beautiful beyond words. Google it and see for yourself. They are projecting famous pieces of art onto the Ponte Vecchio Bridge. Amazing!

—Drew is feeling amazed @ David (Michelangelo)—
The three Davids of Florence: The one in front of the building in the Palazzo della Signoria is a copy. The original David stood there for many centuries until they made a replacement and moved the original inside the museum. The bronze is located in the Piazzale Michelangelo dedicated to the artist. This sculpture overlooks the city and all its glory. Why make one when you can make three. David was originally planned to be placed along the roofline of the Florence Cathedral "Duomo" with other statues depicting bible prophets. That's why the head and hands are larger/ out of proportion, to be viewed from the ground up. Things you learn on a walking tour.

—Drew is feeling thankful @ Florence, Italy—
#ActOfKindness —70 Another amazing Couch Surfing host. He invited me to stay three nights, I received dinners, wine and a warm private room. He was a great guy and we truly enjoyed each others company. He also rode a bike on the Camino so we had that in common.

—Drew is feeling content @ Florence Italy—
#ActOfKindness —71 I was invited to stay one night in a Couch Surfing host home. He had another surfer their at the time and the three of us went out to dinner. The night stay was short, only a few hours but I am grateful. Thanks.

—Drew is feeling accomplished—
Today is a vacation day from my vacation. If you have never had one before: basically you don't sightsee. I slept till 8 a.m., had cof-

fee and breakfast while doing administration things consisting of travel arrangement planning and such. This lasted till 10:30 when I packed up, checked out of my hostel and I am waiting for my thirteen Euro bus ride from Florence to Naples. I enjoy a long bus ride(six hours). Buses give me a chance to write, read, relax and nap. It is so much easier than a plane. I also get to upload photos to Instagram and Facebook. Can't do that on a plane. I also get to look at the Tuscany countryside one more time. Yay!

Facebook, December 17—Drew is feeling amused @ Napoli, Italy—
This is my impression of Naples: Vespas and cars literally trying to barely avoid you on the street. The sounds are beep, beep from autos and men singing Italian songs. Many people milling about with an energy that is palatable. The color is dirt and grime. Small streets with shop's selling cheap goods. Three bottles of wine for five €. The smell is laundry soap and pizza. I love the vibe, I love Napoli.

Facebook, December 18—Drew is feeling curious @ Porto Sorrento, Italy—
Wow, nice place, another amazing Italian city. I traveled here with some great new hostel friends.

Facebook, December 19—Drew is feeling excited—
I'm safely on an overnight ferry from Naples to Sicily. Having a quick bite to eat before bed and I wake up in Sicily, yay!

Facebook, December 21—Drew is feeling ecstatic @ Mount Etna—
Wow, I climbed the highest active volcano in the world: Etna... The weather was amazing until the last 45 minutes, then it was snowing. We had to trudge through thick, slippery, deep snow to reach the lift area and warm shelter. At times I felt like we would never make it, with the heavy snowfall and disappearing road, thinking we would be two lost hikers frozen in place on the volcano. Eventually we did. We stayed up there in the shelter for a couple hours talking and waiting for the storm to do something while we tried to dry and warm. Nothing changed. My hiking mate gave me his extra shoes and socks since mine were very wet summer running shoes. We took the walk back instead of taking the lift. Snow turned to rain, then snow again and back to rain. As we reach the base we were dripping wet and quite cold. Including my new shoes and socks. The landscape was barren due to the volcanic rock. Black volcanic rock against white snow was a beautiful con-

trast, a remarkable contrast. I am on the bus now, wet and cold wondering if I will ever warm again. I loved it.

Facebook, December 22—Drew is feeling in love @ Taormina, Sicily—
One day journey to Taormina, Sicily. Show me what you got baby. Sicily, oh how nice you are.

—Drew is feeling full—
#ActOfKindness —72 A woman hears me say I am looking for a pizza place and can't find one open. Apparently I am an American who likes to eat before 7 p.m. but can't find a restaurant open before 8 p.m. in Sicily. She gives me half a pizza and it was amazing. Best Pizza I have had in Italy. I thank you from the bottom of my stomach.

Facebook, December 23—Drew is feeling full @ Sicily, Italy—
Another first, red meat straight from the horse's backside, in a gyro, I will try most things at least once. When in Sicily…

Facebook, December 24—Drew is feeling excited @ Naples, Itlay—
I am back on the ferry to Naples. I am sleeping on the couch in the common area. Goodbye Sicily, thanks for the amazing pizza. Whoa! I am heading back to the hostel in Naples where I stayed before Sicily. There are two Americans and a Netherland lad managing the hostel and preparing a Christmas feast, party and gift exchange. I am so excited. Merry Christmas to you all.

Facebook, December 25—Drew is feeling happy @ Naples, Italy—
I want to wish you a Merry Christmas from Napoli, Italy. Buon Natale... To all the people I Amore. Merry Christmas to you all. Before the party tonight I am exploring the Catacomb of Napoli. There is no better place on earth to explore then an ancient catacomb with deceased Catholics on Christmas Eve.

Facebook, December 26—Drew is feeling amazed @ Pompeii, Italy—
Pompeii is totally amazing, the coolest old city ever. There was one house they claimed two bachelor brothers lived in. There was a wall fresco in the foyer when you entered the home off the street, which depicted Priapus, the God of sex and fertility, with his oversized erection. I am not buying they were brothers, they must have been a gay couple. It was the first impression of their home. It is a big impression, so to speak.

—Drew is feeling wonderful @ Pompeii, Italy—

#ActOfKindness —73 I met a nice American girl getting off the train in Pompeii and she joined my hostel friend and me. She has a guidebook and takes us on an informative guided tour of Pompeii. So very cool and grateful to have had her company.

Facebook, December 27—Drew is feeling peaceful @ The Path of the Gods, Almafi Coast—
Today I hiked with two great people across the Almafi Coast. It was breathtaking and a thrill to have done it. It was some of the most picturesque views I have seen of the Italian coastline.

Facebook, December 28—Drew is feeling delighted @ the Colosseum Rome, Italy—
I made it back to Rome, for my Roman Holiday.

Facebook, December 29—Drew is feeling loved @ Rome, Italy
—

#ActOfKindness —74 I am back with my loving friends staying with them a second time. They have invited me back and we will be driving to Florence for a New Year's Eve house party. We have taken a walking tour of the area looking at the street art. Such a beautiful city, I love you Rome. Thank you guys for taking me in again. xoxo

Facebook, December 30—Drew is feeling festive—
I am making my first apple pie. I am attending a house party on New Year's Eve in Florence and I have been asked to bring something from America to share. It's a funny thing to make my first apple pie in Rome. There is no mixing bowl, no measure cups or measure spoons in the home I just throw it all in and see how it comes out. I made the crust from scratch. What can go wrong?

Facebook, December 31—Drew is feeling sad @ Rome, Italy—
Arrivederci Rome, until next time. One last visit to Florence then it's goodbye Italy, I leave you tomorrow. Goodbye 2016, you changed my life forever. I spent a total of 43 days under your Italian sun. I enjoyed 21 of your cities, more than many Italians. Thank you for your beauty, warmth and history. Amore ITALY!

—Drew is feeling interested @ Orvieto Cathedral—
Another beautiful Italian city. Happy New Year to you all. We stopped here on the way to Florence for some wine. I was told it's the best in Tuscany.

—Drew is feeling festive @ Firenze, Le Cure—
#ActOfKindness —75 I am having a traditional Italian New Year's Eve dinner with some wonderful people. I am living the Italian life one last night. The same lovely people who I met at brunch way

back when in Rome. They invited me into their home for this NYE festive night. I am forever grateful for their kindness. I am so looking forward to all the interesting food we will be sharing. Felice Anno Nuovo, Happy New Year everyone!

Facebook, January 1—Drew is feeling optimistic at Firenze, Piazza Del Duomo—

Good news everyone... 2017 is so much better than 2016 🔥 *Felice Anno Nuovo - Happy New Year everyone it's 2017 here in Italy...*

—Drew is feeling tired—
Thanks everyone for the well wishes. I am home safely from an amazing night out in Florence at 3 a.m. I have an 8 a.m. flight to Madrid. Wish me luck. Happy New Year to you all. I love you.

—Drew is feeling thankful @ Florence, Italy—
#ActOfKindness —76 Strangers I never met, offered their home for six of us to sleep New Year's Eve off, or at least the rest of them slept since I have had an early flight. I have been so blessed throughout my journey with so many kind acts. Thank you all.

—Drew is feeling excited @ Madrid, Spain—
Madrid you madman, show me what you got...

Facebook, January 4—Drew is feeling nostalgic—
"To know yourself as the being underneath the thinker, the stillness underneath the mental noise, the love and joy underneath the pain, is freedom, salvation, enlightenment."—Eckhart Tolle
—I am feeling this Journey-of-Self-Discovery has brought me to Freedom, Salvation, Enlightenment! I am forever grateful.

Facebook, January 5—Drew is feeling thankful @ Madrid, Spain—
#ActOfKindness —77 My last Couch Surfing host on my journey. I truly enjoyed his company. He offered me food, coffee and a warm bed, along with all the comforts of a home. We instantly hit it off and had a fun time. He is a nurse and had a couple days off while I was with him which was a pleasure to share some quality time. We visited the Modern Art Museum and had a dinner out. Thank you so much for the time we shared, you are a good man and I look forward to seeing you again someday. Hopefully my home if you come to America.

Facebook, January 5—Drew—
My last train as I prepare for my last visit to Barcelona. Sad but true.

Facebook, January 8—Drew is feeling amazed @ Basílica de la Sagrada Família—

Facebook, January 10—Drew is feeling nervous—

I am on the bus to the airport, it's 9 a.m. I'm staring out the window and my eyes are so wide I don't feel like I can blink. As fearful as it was for me to travel to Europe solo, I feel going home is equally as frightful. My first stop is Indiana to visit family for a week. I am slowly easing back into America and real life with the support of family and friends.

—Drew is feeling heartbroken—

I am in line for the plane tearing up. This reminds me of that moment in the movie "Shirley Valentine" where she sends her bags home and doesn't get on the plane. Choosing to remain in Mykonos forever. Hmmmmmm?

follow my… journey

Posted on January 10, 2017 by Drew Eric

Chapter 40 Can I go home and create life anew?

Facebook, January 2—Drew—
"You know that voice in your head telling you to travel? Listen to it.
Because 10 years from now you'll wish you had!"—unknown
— I heard this voice in 2015. It started out as a whisper then got
louder. Everyone I knew supported me and I had to listen to the
voice. I was afraid of the voice. What if the voice is wrong? What if
I can't do it? What if??? I listened to that voice and it saved my
life. I am a new man because of it.

I can do it! I did it! I completed my Journey-of-Self-Discovery. I
just boarded the plane in Barcelona jetting back to America. This
is really strange, everyone on the plane speaks English, and it's
been so long since I've heard my native tongue. I feel so many
emotions—sad, excited, nervous and confused—these emotions
are shifting as fast as the jetliner. Now my question is "Can I go
home and start a new life as a new man?"

"There is nothing like returning home"—Nelson Mandela

For the very first time, I am happy to be where I am. For the 48
years prior to this journey, I dreamed about living in a foreign land,
visiting strange ancient cities and experiencing cultures far different than my own, now I have. I am flying home to begin a new life,
see old friends and inevitably make new friends. I am ready to be
in America.

#LifeLesson —46 A journey's beginning, day one, happens with
a single step forward into the unknown. Standing, rooting, inac-
tion, barricades a journey's path.

Something I didn't expect was to feel like I am needed back in
America. My friends and followers need a shining light among so
much hate and darkness. The country feels so divided with hurts,
anger and blame after the 2016 election. Then there are the ter-
rorist acts in Turkey, a country I just saw with my own eyes and in

my hometown at the Fort Lauderdale-Hollywood International Airport.

Facebook, January 3—Drew—
My heart goes out to Turkey. I just visited Istanbul a month ago, shortly before the attack and now there is another. Such a beautiful city, rich with culture, music and beautiful people. My heart aches for the victims of terrorism everywhere.
Facebook, January 6—Drew Miller marked himself safe during The Violent Incident in Fort Lauderdale, Florida—
I am marking myself safe after several people inquired where I was and if I was at the airport. I am still in Europe for anyone who is concerned. Prayers to my friends at home in Fort Lauderdale.
I just finished my last blog in Europe. While here, I was impacted by what I was learning and what I was hearing from back home, a call for love in so many ways.
Facebook, January 9—Drew—
My last blog post in Europe. See the entire story on my fan page: Traveling the Balkans while Gay... This is my story...
I spent the last seven weeks traveling the Balkans, across the Adriatic Sea from Italy and above Greece. This area is formally known as Yugoslavia which collapsed in 1991 after the fall of communism. While traveling the Balkans I learned about wars, genocide, political corruption, anger, finger pointing, gossip rebellions, dictators, ruling empires and the realities of being gay in Eastern Europe, formerly communist countryside. In Bosnia I was told "I want to kill you right now" because he found me out as a gay man, I feared for my safety. All this was happening in my life while the presidential election was exploding at home. I found the two experiences colliding in my life. Both reflecting hurt, pain, anger and separateness.

America needs leaders who can bring darkness to the light. Leaders who will uplift Americans and take them out of fear. There is so much fear with my community believing all our rights will be stripped away. I do hope these are unfounded fears. I have seen what gay life is like here in Eastern Europe and it isn't a life I would choose for my country.

I want to return and help our country heal. I want to be a leader spreading positivity and light. I want others to be inspired by my growth and journey and hopefully find that drive for themselves. If

347

I can I will, I won't give up regardless. With more positive leaders in the world, we can change it. I believe this to be true.

"Be the change you want to see in the world"—Gandhi

Throughout my journey, I shared inspirational quotes that came up in my Facebook feeds. Quotes that seemed to be exactly the words I needed to hear at the moment they materialized. There is no coincidence. As part of my shining light, I hope others get inspired by the words of wisdom from the leaders in our world. I believe these words heal and I, for one, believe it is important to keep them alive and share them. We all need these words of enlightenment when we are desperately in search of our own voice in the world. I even choose to use my own voice and write my own. Light begets light.

"If your actions inspire others to dream more, learn more, do more and become more, you are a leader."—John Quincy Adams

We need to be reminded to be kind to one another. That's why I felt it was important to document and share #ActsOfKindness I received while on my journey. So much love and kindness is in the world, we just need to look and observe. Kindness can go unseen during the mundane of our existence. We need to train ourselves to be vigilant and observe when, where and how we are kind to each other. Kindness is not just of the same race, religion or nationality, kindness is an extension of oneness in the world. Kindness translates into all languages. Kindness is free, you don't have to leave home to discover and see kindness.

"Be kind whenever possible. It is always possible." —Dalai Lama

#LifeLessons are abundant. I want to live in a world full of personal development and growth for myself and others. I want nothing more than to discover, talk about and share my #LifeLessons, clearly as I have written a book about them. If we aren't present to our own Adventure, Path, Road, Trek and Journey and what we learn, we will lose the growth and remain stuck in that tiny town, never leaving to see something new. When we acknowledge and document our #LifeLessons we create a toolbox to be used when

348

life breaks down. If we forget our toolbox filled with useful personal development, we won't look for answers. We will move into the breakdown and make it a fortress with high walls never to escape. I choose to move out and see the world, I will no longer live in a prison I created, a prison without #LifeLessons.

"Life lessons are the tools we use to demolish the fortress we created as our prison. The tools are growth, strength, power, enlightenment. These tools will build a passageway to an inspired future."—Drew Eric

I have grown far beyond my wildest dreams. I knew when I left America that it would change me. I even felt as though this journey would save my life. My intuition said this journey would be exactly what I needed to find myself, know myself and love myself. Way back when in 2015 I set into motion, manifesting, a Journey-of-Self-Discovery. I have accomplished this and much, much more. My manifestation skills are now fine-tuned and I will use this new tool the rest of my life. I can create a future of my dreams.

Facebook, January 9—Drew—
Almost eight months ago I landed in Barcelona. I was scared, alone and didn't know what to do or how to travel. I lost my phone in less than 24 hours. Now I have seen most of Europe—more of Europe than most Europeans. I'm no longer afraid to travel. I now know what I like when I travel. I like big cities. I like to take my time moving through a city. I like history and architecture. I like to feel the energy, smell the food and hear the sounds of a city. I like my alone time and I like to meet and make new friends. I like traveling. It suits me.

The last few days I have been reading over the short stories that I published on Facebook. I have been reading the comments from old friends and new friends. I even went as far as documenting my life lessons. While reading through the stories I pulled out the lessons and numbered them as a research tool for my book. I have counted more than 70 life lessons I have discovered and grown with, an astounding volume of #LifeLessons.

Before I start sharing some of my learning and lessons, I do want to tell you about my last few days in Barcelona.

Facebook, January 7—Drew—
My hostel just got robbed! The thieves climbed through an open window and stole three pieces of luggage, two suitcases and my big backpack, while I was sleeping in the room!!! I lost most of my clothes, some gifts, a camera lens, odds and ends, nothing of real value. Funny thing is I had my Canon Rebel camera, passport, a credit card and $100 in the backpack. Just before I went to sleep my intuition told me to put everything in the locker. I didn't listen specifically; I decided to remove the valuables and move them into the locker. I should have just listened and put both backpacks in, one on top of the other.
Now I get to go home with one light backpack. Sadly, the other guy lost two suitcases with everything from a toothbrush to a computer, watches to his passport. I followed my intuition, mostly.

I brought a ridiculous amount of stuff to Europe, weighing approximately 50 lbs. So when my backpack got stolen, believe it or not, I was relieved to see it go. My belongings had become a burden. I was carrying, literally on my back, items I wasn't even using. I used the camera lens maybe once. I bought a pair of espadrille shoes at H&M for five Euro's before it got cold, wore them twice and didn't leave them behind at a hostel. I carried those summer sandals for three months. It amazed me how, with so few items, I was still able to hoard, on the road. It was a real-life lesson once the backpack was gone. The Universe did what I couldn't do, which was lighten my load and allow me to leave Europe without the burdens of hoarding. I should have sent a package home with some of the important items I wanted to keep as mementos, and then leave the rest in some hostel.

#LifeLesson —47 Hoarding comes in many forms; possessions are things we carry on our back preventing us from moving forward with lightness, peace and grace.
Facebook, January 7—Drew—
Each day this week I have felt tired and run down. Prior to getting robbed, I realized finally, I'M SICK. I got a cold my last week in Europe. I am here in Barcelona lying in bed watching "Star Wars" in honor of Carrie Fisher's passing away. RIP. So far I watched the last one she was in and the first one from 1977. I have two more to go. The force/internet is strong with this hostel. I will be better

tomorrow and I will get out of bed and enjoy Barcelona in the last days before I leave for America. May the force be with me.

Facebook, January 9—Drew—
Even my shoes are telling me it's over, they are breaking apart slowly. I have posted my last blog, taken my last walking tour, visiting my last city in Spain. I am saying goodbye to my first Couch Surfing host, seeing my last church, eating my last meal. I will come home a new, lighter man, changed forever.

—Drew—
#ActOfKindness —78 The gift of kind words, love and support. I thank all of you who helped me grow on this journey. I thank all of my followers, you, too, have helped me grow. Thank you Europe, thank you America, thank you.

Facebook became the lighted path to my past. I felt such love through the posts on Facebook. As I continued to journal my stories and post them, my friends followed me with cheers and warm wishes. I connected and reconnected with people from my past on a deep level. I never expected to gain followers of my journey. I never believed by being vulnerable and putting my crazy on Facebook, my friends would connect more with my authentic self. If I had known putting my crazy out for all to read would create closer friendships and connections, I would have done it years ago.

Facebook became another character in my story. This is why I choose to include my friend's comments and words of encouragement along with my own post. I was so moved I realizing Facebook helped me heal old wounds and greatly contributed to my new self.

I am on the plane reviewing my post, stories, photos and personal growth, which has been off the charts, well beyond my wildest imagination. Some #LifeLessons were easier to learn while others were groundbreaking "ah-ha" moments.

I remember the scared boy who arrived on this very plane to Barcelona from America. Once landed, my eyes were wide open with exuberance, fear and amazement. Growing up in Florida where everything is less than 100 years old, and the historic buildings are just tall modern condo high-rises, seeing these multi-century-old buildings was strange and unfamiliar. I touched them to see their realness. I stood on the ground—like a first timer in New

351

York City—looking up with a feeling of bewilderment thinking, "Am I really here?"

Once off the plane I was filled with insecurity. I felt I had no travel legs and couldn't get grounded. I left everyone behind and I was unsure if I could actually be a solo traveler in Europe. I set a colossal adventure before me, traveling Europe for an undetermined amount of time. No pulls home, no apartment I left behind, no bills or responsibilities. My journey was wide open. Some thought I wouldn't come home; unlimited possibilities were at my creating.

Within hours of arrival I chose to overindulge at a bar and got lost, then I left my phone in the taxi. My insecurities caused me to use alcohol in an effort to overshadow my stress and fear. A walloping lesson I did not want to repeat over the next several months.

I prepared for the journey by setting up my phone with every possible need I could image. Right off the plane I lose my one safety net. It was the best thing for me. Once I reached France I was forced to chill out for a week waiting for my new phone to arrive from America. I was moving so fast from Barcelona, Pamplona, then on to Saint-Jean in just a few days. A week in France gave me the peace I needed to move onto the path of the Camino.

#LifeLesson —48 Take time, move slowly, don't rush, be present.

During those days in Barcelona I had so many firsts. First Couch Surfing host of many. First solo travel. First time making decisions on my own, choosing what I wanted to do versus allowing someone else to decide. I realized I didn't know what I wanted to do. I let my past dictate what I chose after just arriving which was gay bars for socializing. I was very limited. I never had to fend for myself in the world and had no clue how to experience travel.

I immediately realized I didn't want to rely just on my old behaviors, the old way of doing things. I intuitively knew I had to forge a new path, a new way of doing things and find what works for me today, on this adventure, in Europe.

In Pamplona I began to notice and realize I was in a straight world and I didn't know how to be myself. With almost no knowledge of Self, I didn't know how to be with straight men. I saw men being intimate with each other in a non-sexual way. I was astounded and couldn't comprehend this in my own life. I couldn't see how I could be myself, whoever that is, in a world of straight men. They would never like me. My eyes were open but it would take me a long time for my sight to translate into a vision of how to be Me. Much learning needed to happen first.

"Belonging" is the word that most resonates with my journey. Looking back I see how belonging to myself and with others is the main common path through my journey. I needed to learn what authentic belonging looked like. I started to love myself and belong in my own skin when I wrote my Manifesto. I declared to the world what my needs are and what I am looking for from friends. With this new clarity I felt the chains holding my past, loosen and drop away, I was finally free. I discovered my voice; I screamed it from the mountaintop.

#LifeLesson —49 Belonging to my authentic self entrusts a feeling of belonging to others.

I was no longer willing to compromise with others. I did not want to fit into someone else's expectations. I wanted them to see me for who I am and choose to be with me because they like what I have to offer. I fell in love with Me that day in Spain on The Way to Santiago.

#LifeLesson —50 loving oneself is the key that opens the door to happiness.

As my path continued, I discovered how to be authentic. I am an emotional, sensitive, caring, warm and physical person. With each new connection I was able to test the waters and express each one of my perfect characteristics. I was able to show my authentic self and see if, for the first time, people would like my authentic self. Up until this journey, I was always shifting and readjusting to fit what I thought others wanted me to be. Never realizing I could be my authentic self and that is the person they most want to see and know.

#LifeLesson —51 Showing up authentically builds the bridges needed to connect with others. Without authenticity you can only

gaze upon, but never reach the other side where you meet con-nectedness.

I definitely met some people that didn't warm up to my authentic self. My authentic self has some drawbacks. I am needy at times, a take-charge leader and tend to be loud when excited. My authentic self can be abrasive to some. While meeting people who did like authenticity, at the same time I was meeting people that didn't care for what I had to offer. I discovered with each person who didn't care for me, there were four others that did like what I had to offer. I noticed it was never a one for one, it was much more. This realization informed me the payoff for being authentic is much greater than the loss of being inauthentic. Losing one whom I rub the wrong way isn't worth not meeting the four or more great souls who will reward my life immensely.

#LifeLesson —52 Letting go of the fear of one, not liking your authentic self, yields a payoff that quadruples in size, attracting four who require your company, authentically.

Facebook, January 9—Drew—
"People enter our lives for a reason, a season or a lifetime."—unknown

These words rang in my ear as a truth I was able to accept on my journey. Some pilgrims walked with me, side by side, while some chose to walk away. I did the same. I believed people would be there forever only to discover they came in for a reason.
I fell in love with a boy on the Camino. My first short story on the El Camino de Santiago. I did not see that coming. My heart was so closed down after my divorce. I needed to crack it open and let the love in and allow my heart to beat once more. I was desperate to feel the rhythm of love deep in my chest and didn't even know it. I met the young man and his cousin on that first day. Over the first week on the Camino I began to surrender. I let go of expectations, belief systems, stereotypes and much more. I allowed the young man into my heart and he helped heal.

#LifeLesson —53 Allowing your heart to open for others yields the love you long for when you are feeling alone, isolated and closed.

354

When I left America I had little to no experience with straight men. I only have less than a handful of them in my life. I needed to learn how to be amongst men. How to be my authentic, emotional, loving, physical, kind self, with other men? The young man helped me on that path. He was the first among many on my journey, young, attractive men who were interested in me. I began to learn how to interpret their interest and see it as a friendship versus believing they were sexually interested in me. Living in the gay bubble of Fort Lauderdale, I was used to men sexualizing each other as a common practice, like shaking hands. I was used to men coming on to me with less than admirable intentions. However here on the Camino and in Europe I began to meet men who liked my authentic self and are interested in being in my company. They warmed to my energy and relished what I contributed to their life. It is a beautiful exchange and I am blessed to have met so many wonderful men on my journey. I look forward to bringing this new fondness for the company of straight men home with me. Having buddies, guy pals, travel mates is a blessing I will cultivate in my future.

#LifeLesson —54 Having bonded with brothers, comrades, mates, travel buddies, men, looks like caring, sharing, intimacy, loving, kindness, and blessings.

There clearly was a reason that young man walked into my life that first week on the Camino. The keyword is reason. After eight days together I needed to walk away. My intuition was telling me our time together was complete. I had more to learn on the Camino and needed to do it on my own. We saw each other a couple more times over the next few days then I never saw him again. I continued to write about my path on the Camino and post it on Facebook. I reached out to him through text messages and private messaging on Facebook a few times. We stayed in touch for a while then the connection eventually receded into the past. He was an intricate part of my personal growth and helped facilitate my open heart.

#LifeLesson —55 We form attachments with people and loved ones only to experience the joy of releasing them with love, ease, grace and finally, peace.

355

I will always have love in my heart for him and I will always be thankful he walked into my life. He was my first love, of many, on my journey. My heart remains open to this day and will for the infinite future.

I discovered myself during my friendship with the young man. I saw his requirements/needs and in turn, I looked inward and uncovered my own. No longer do I need to fit-in for others. If someone isn't interested in meeting my requirements, I can accept that and release them from my life. I no longer have to allow my requirements to go unmet in order to be in someone's company. My needs are important and require attention.

#LifeLesson —56 Knowing one's self and one's needs are essential to being your true, authentic self. Without knowing, you are clay, being molded into someone else's image of who they want you to be.

Now that I am leaving Europe I have a chance to reflect back on all the people's lives I touch. I made some real connections and I look forward to keeping these connections alive, hopefully, some will last a lifetime. Even if they only last a season I will always cherish our time together in Europe.

I made some travel buddies. I learned to connect with my whole heart. I learned to accept people for who they are and what they bring to my life. I learned to accept each person and enjoy the qualities that did work well for me at the time we were together.

#LifeLesson —57 Acceptance of others is seeing and enjoying the qualities one brings to your life versus dreaming about the qualities you don't see and focusing on the qualities you don't enjoy.

I found, just because they work today, doesn't mean they will work for me tomorrow. As with the young Swede who fit well over the first week, but then his appeal shifted. With him, I cultivated a truth for myself—walk away from situations that make me uncomfortable. I no longer have to stay in an uncomfortable environment because that's what the others require.

#LifeLesson —58 When that soft voice you hear and the tingle in your gut says this isn't right, walk away, move on, let it go.

In my life prior to my journey, I compromised many, many times in an effort to fit-in with my husband and friends. On my rebirthing journey, I studiously learned I no longer have to fit-in, I can just walk away. What a joy a few steps in a new direction can bring. In my marriage, it took many years to build up the courage, strength and worthiness to put my codependent marriage a few steps behind me. I no longer need to let time elapse, I can walk away right when the going gets uncomfortable, and I hear that soft voice and my gut tells me to listen.

#LifeLesson —59 Remaining in uncomfortable environments for the benefit of others is reductive to your life's journey. Sometimes you just need to walk away.

Throughout my journey I continued to be authentic, making some lasting friendships along the way. Such a new feeling, belonging to the people I was meeting. I felt like one of the guys, they liked me and I liked them. I wasn't different because I was gay, no one cared. Each time I met a new friend and shared my interests with men they didn't turn away. My sexuality was one of my qualities not one of my defining qualities. This comfortableness made me feel closer to belonging than I have felt in my life. I also realized this came from a feeling of belonging to me. I learned to be comfortable in my own skin, with who I am and what I have to offer. I belong to me, I belong to others.

Somewhere in the middle of Spain, while on the Camino, I realized my worthiness and stopped chasing the popular kids. My old self felt a lack of worthiness, closely tied to a lack of belonging. I now let go of my childhood hurts knowing I do belong, I am worthy. All I have to do is remain open and the right people will walk into my life. People who are interested in what I have to offer and want to see me being me, will join me on this journey through life.

What was so beautiful, once I found worthiness and self-love and let my flags fly, I discovered the layers of interesting tidbits I call me. I feel more in touch with who I am on the inside: weird, different, unusual, colorful. Now I am most interested in letting my outer self—the way I dress and appear—show through allowing others to see my weird, colorful embodiment. On the Camino I tied

Tibetan prayer flags to my walking stick and let them flap in the breeze for all to see. Such a simple act of vulnerability created a sense of freedom, to be me.

Connection, belonging, loving myself and others along with letting my flags fly and being me, set the foundation for what became my journey. I could have gone home with just these lessons they were so rewarding, but I didn't. I stuck it out and kept moving on the journey of a lifetime with boundless more discoveries behind each old stone fort and church.

#LifeLesson —60 Worthiness, belonging, loving oneself and others is the granite we walk upon on this journey we call life.

Vulnerability played a big part in my growth as a gay man. While on the path of the Camino, undoubtedly, multiple times a day, I came out to other men as a gay man. I had no awareness how uncomfortable it was to out myself so often, how unsafe I felt. It was just days after the shooting massacre at Pulse Nightclub in Orlando when I had my breakdown/breakthrough. Standing in a wheat field in Spain, I realized the only way for me to move forward on my journey was to let go of the fear of my own safety and tell everyone I meet who I really am. No matter how many times, no matter how many people, I require honesty.

#LifeLesson —61 Vulnerability and showing one's authentic self is essential when you want to be seen, heard and counted.

#LifeLesson —62 The power of vulnerability is recognizing, standing and showing your true self in the face of fear and adversary.

I am now skilled in overcoming personal hardship. My last day on the Camino was unexpected with an emotional response to my childhood. Realizing my childhood wasn't ok and I needed to forgive my mother. She did the best she could with what she had in her life, in the way of knowledge and resources. So I do forgive. I cried it out for five hours that last day of walking, releasing it onto the dirt and gravel that covered Spain. I left the pain and hardship on the path. No longer will it darken my journey.

#LifeLesson —63 Turning away from painful situations compresses the pain close to your chest with the weight of an ele-

phant. Only walking through the pain will you arrive on the other side where the pain releases with the lightness of a bird, replaced with love and peace.

#LifeLesson —64 Forgiveness clears space in your heart for love and peace. Anger, pain and hatred create a blockage in your heart that reduces the flow, to your demise.

Living in the flow and surrendering are a welcome part of my life. Knowing the Universe has my back and will always put me in the right place at the right time with the right people is my foundation. I proved it works over, over and over again. I no longer have to plan or worry about the next move or if I made the right move. I learned over time my anxiety would and did subside. No amount of control or preparation would reduce my anxiety, only surrender does. Flow, allows me to let go of stress and see where the road takes me, allowing new adventures to pop up on the road. Surrender offers people who will enrich my life versus closing down and not allowing anyone to come close in an effort to protect and remain small. Nothing comes from smallness and resistance. Let go, be free, and enjoy the road.

#LifeLesson —65 Only surrender of control and living in the flow of life magnetizes infinite rewarding possibilities from all directions to you, for you.

Judging played a big part in my unhappiness. I was so concerned with having the best European experience I was judging every minuscule experience. How long I stayed in a city? How much I did? Should I have done more, or less? Did I enjoy Paris more than London or did I enjoy Brussels more, which was my favorite city?

I was in Germany when I finally had my #LifeLesson and let go of judging. I saw it like two gears, grinding together for years and years until finally, the gears had no teeth. I compressed all the joy out of both cities I was comparing. Once I let go of judging all my experiences, I was able to see my journey in a whole new light, free of bad, with only good remaining. Even the struggles that were more uncomfortable became rewarding.

I would inevitably get asked on the road, "What is your favorite city so far?" That left me to answer in judgment. With my new found freedom I would answer their question with an indirect response. "Well, I spent five weeks in Spain, It was so beautiful walking the Camino" or "I spent over a month in the UK visiting Ireland, Northern Ireland, I took a ferry to Scotland, then drove a car down to London." By this time, they have forgotten the original question and are captivated by my journey.

I remember talking with other travelers about their adventures and hearing them say, "I liked Florence and Rome, but I didn't like Venice" then giving me reasons why they didn't like Venice. I wanted to tell them "NO, stop judging your experiences, you will exponentially enjoy the adventure.

#LifeLesson —66 By judging one experience, trip, adventure with another we squeeze the juice of joy out until we are left with the bitter rind. Enjoy the juice of non-judgment.

My joy increased exponentially. I am not talking a little or a lot; I am talking buckets of juicy deliciousness enjoyment. It was as if I surrendered to the journey again. I truly started to believe, "I am in the right place at the right time doing the right thing with the right people." Meaning, I no longer had to reconsider anything because everything is exactly as it should be. It was like an explosion going off in my head, of joy and happiness. BOOM!!! I can't express enough how rewarding this is. Try it for yourself.

"You cannot but be in the right place at the right time."— A Course In Miracles

I cultivated taking care of myself, to get the job done. I schooled myself on Google, making travel arrangements and moving from city to city and country to country with ease and grace. For people who find Google easy, enjoyable and a rewarding task, that was not my experience. It was beyond foreign and uncomfortable. I have dyslexia and memory retention problems is a symptom. I would purchase flights and reserve a bed in a hostel, then forget how to find the said reservation. I lost one hostel booking and spent hours of searching trying to locate the reservation to no avail.

#LifeLesson —67 Learning something new takes tenacity and grit. We must release the fear of failure and discomfort in order to firmly grasp the reward of knowledge and experience.

Today, I feel accomplished. I walk into airports, train stations or catch a bus with little to no stress. I give myself time for what I cannot control and let the rest go. No longer letting fear and anxiety grip me like it did in the beginning.

#LifeLesson —68 No amount of preparation and planning loosens the grip of anxiety and fear. Only surrender of control and the elapse of time allows anxiety and fear to slip through your fingers.

Midway through on the road, I had to make the decision to keep going or go home. I had a flight scheduled for the end of September and that day was fast approaching. I felt like I was just acquiring my travel legs and a feeling of groundedness. I was able to move around easily, my stress was down and found a rhythm that suited me. I wanted to keep going so I considered extending my flight.

While in Rome I got out my calculator to figure out when I should fly home. I decided on a financial amount I was willing to spend then counted the days it would take me to spend that amount. This put me in January so I began the task of looking for flights. I settled on January 10th giving me almost eight months in Europe. I booked the flight finally and made that choice to extend my time on the road.

I was looking into work-exchange in one of the European countries outside of the Schengen Treaty but wasn't sure because I felt the pull of the road and wanted to continue. Around then I met another long-term nomad traveler in Croatia. We moved to a couple different cities together then he shared his interested in busing to Bosnia. I got out my phone and Google Eastern Europe and saw there were several countries in this region I could visit. I counted the countries I had visited and added the potential countries in the Balkans and realized, "Hey, if I visit all the countries in the Balkans that would only leave 12 major countries in Europe remaining for me to visit." I abandoned my idea of working and continued my trek joining my new friend on his way to Bosnia.

During my trek through the Balkans, I was shown the world. I was shown how anger, pain and hurt in the world can impact our lives. My personal/internal evaluation slowed during this period as my eyes began to see the world at large. I now envision my place.

361

I need to be a beacon of light for others. I need to remain positive, not complaining and negative. I need to offer love to others, not withhold, be fearful or run away from conflict. I need to share with others how to find oneness with all races, religions and nationalities—something the Balkans lacks but so desperately needs. I was deeply moved by my trek through the Balkans. I see the world anew.

#LifeLesson —69 Baring witness to discomfort shows you a new way, a new path, through the discomfort to peace and oneness.

The final months of my journey were wonderful. I did most of my personal development during the beginning of my adventure and path. Leaving me to simply be present and enjoy the road through Europe. Being in a peaceful state of mind is new to me. Throughout my life I longed to be somewhere else. Before my relationship I was desperate to be in a relationship. Years I pined to be on an adventure seeing the world. Very few times was I ever somewhere and fully present. Hawaii comes to mind as one of the few places I was completely present and happy to be exactly where I was at the moment. I wouldn't feel that again until this journey. I did take other vacations and had different experiences, however I never felt complete, comfortable or at peace. Looking back I realize now I didn't feel whole. I didn't belong in my own skin, to me, my life or in my marriage. Now that I am airborne on my way back to America, I am eager to be home, in America, in Fort Lauderdale, the place that has been my home for close to three decades. This is a new feeling. I have seen so much of the world and I feel whole, complete with my new self and at peace being back in a city that didn't hold peace for me prior. I know it will now. Home is exactly where I want to be. There is no other place in the world that I would rather be than home, now.

"There's no place like home, There's no place like home! There's no place like home!"—Dorothy in The Wizard of Oz

When my feet began to walk Barcelona I saw my future as an Adventure. What will I see? What will I do? What will happen for me? Everything was new, different, unimaginable, confusing. I settled into the newness and became friends with the discomfort I so longed for and needed in my life. My Adventure trained from

- Barcelona to
- Pamplona eventually leading me on a bus to
- Saint Jean Pied de Port.

Then my Adventure transformed into a Path, my Camino Path, walking, sharing, connecting, and belonging. After so many closed years, I had my heart cracked open early on. That single moment my heart opened, my path to growing was tamped out before me. Centuries ago the path was walked and all I needed was to show up, open my heart and put one foot in front of the other, just as Dorothy did. My heart rate quickened, my pace sped up, my soul awakened. I didn't think I could travel across the sea to a new land and new discoveries, as other pilgrims have been doing for centuries. The passage led me over the Pyrenees Mountains through northern Spain. From

- Roncesvalles to
- Estella where the pathway meets the beaten path to
- Burgos. Then the footpath leads us to
- Leon which eventually concludes in
- Santiago. I walked through 33 quaint Spanish cities brimming with families and children and love and, of course, churches.

Then my Path became the Road with twists and turns of epic proportions as I navigated through Europe. Over the mountains with highs and lows containing equal greatness. I didn't think I could be a solo traveler and find peace or happiness. I couldn't fathom creating such deep connections with so many kind souls. And yet, I did all this and more, much more. I bussed to

- Lisbon, Portugal to see the Golden Gate Bridge then I took to the highway in the sky to
- Amsterdam where I conversed with Van Gogh and Anne. Then back on the highway in the sky to
- Ireland. My BIGAM crew and I drove the avenues around southern Ireland visiting a Cork and a Moher, eventually guiding us to
- Belfast for a Titanic of a good time occurred. On the ferry way to
- Edinburgh, Scotland I found my sea legs. In Edinburgh I discovered the wonders of straight bars then BIGAM drove down to

- London where we got a London Eye-ful of Palaces. What road trip in England would be complete with only a Stone's throw away from the henge. After we crossed the London Bridge I took a short train ride to
- Brighton, for the largest Gay Pride in England which was a Rainbow Flag of excitement. I caught a Bla Bla Car(car share) to
- Paris through the Chunnel. I spent a loving five affectionate days in the city of Amour. This is a city that loves its Tower and has an infatuation with Pyramids. I Bla Bla Car to
- Brussels where the Manneken Pis(little pee man) endlessly flows. I only stayed a short overnight to catch a late night bus across the border to
- Klel, Germany to enjoy the company of a friend from home and chill. Then
- Hamburg, jumping the Wall to
- Berlin and
- Leipzig. When my Stein ran empty I got on the expressway bus with
- Wroclaw, Poland on the horizon. Seeing the Dwarfs of Poland was a small chuckle but not as stupendous as the Clock in
- Prague, Czech Republic. Since
- Vienna, Austria is so close I gave the Palaces a tour. Look, a cheap bus to
- Venice, Italy sign me up for a walking tour over the Bridges and Canals. I have to get out of the Schengen Treaty since I am out of time, I will head to
- Zagreb, Croatia, the capital, for a few days. I am so looking forward to visiting my good friend from the Camino who invited me into her home in
- Budapest, Hungary where I spent nine blissful days in My hidden treasure chest. This is where the river separates the old cities of Buda and Pest. I will always love my time in My house in Budapest. Let's see how many countries I can visit, next up
- Ljubljana, Slovenia for an overnight to see the Dragons. Then back to
- Zagreb, Croatia only to catch a bus to
- Zadar, Croatia to hear the sounds of the Sea Organ before I saunter down to
- Sibenik to explore the fortress on the hills. I hear
- Krk has a beautiful waterfall and swimming hole.

- Split has a beautiful beach and look, naked people. My friends are meeting in
- Rome, Italy so let's catch a ferry across the Adriatic Sea. Rome wasn't visited in a day, more like six days. Then back across the Adriatic to
- Split where I stripped down and enjoyed the sun. I met a new travel buddy and we chose the Island of
- Hvar but this party town is closed for winter.

Then the Road became an arduous Trek through the Balkans, a land of chaos, separatism, fear, wars and anger. Hearing and seeing such hardship awoke a drive to be better. I see my place in the world now, a shining light on the darkness that remains in our illusionary world. My travel buddy and I trek into
- Mostar, Bosnia where my hostel owner said, "I really want to kill you right now!" I'm not entirely sure this is a proper hello, so I hastily Bobsledded to
- Sarajevo to meet some new travel buddies and join a walking tour. What visit to Sarajevo would be complete without an in-depth examination of the atrocities of war at the museums before we shuttled over to
- Belgrade, Serbia, the hands that caused said atrocities. I am dying to cross the border into
- Timisoara, Romania on foot, walking, across the border, with wild dogs nipping at my heels.
- Sibiu is the city I trudged to next before I risked the rain and cut across to
- Bucharest, the capital of Romania. This is where the dictator built the second largest Government Building in the world, second to the Pentagon. It's a shame he was tried and killed before its completion; it is a beautiful home/government building. Never in my wildest dreams did I ever think I would be busing across the border and the River Danube separating the two countries or Romania and
- Sofia, Bulgaria. Sofia actually has a pretty decent gay life and a metropolitan city worth seeing. I met a new travel buddy, my Fin friend and we planned our trek to
- Skopje, Macedonia which is called the Las Vegas of the Balkans. Not the cool hip Vegas but the over the top ridiculous Vegas with its 1600 Statues and several Pirate Ships. With our Macedonia gamble out of the way it was off to

365

- Pristina, Kosovo where Bill Clinton is a demigod since he defended them against the Serbs, again with the warring Serbs. We saw the statue of Bill and moved on to
- Prizren to catch the Balkan Bingo. Here we saw the Old Fort, Old Stone Bridge, Mosque, Clock Tower and the River. I am trying to see as many Bingo's and capitals as I can so
- Podgorica, Montenegro was next. Not much to see after looking for the Bingo but in
- Kotor, the gorgeous port of call where the mountain meets the sea and the charm is abundant. I can see why tourists are flocking to the coastal areas of this region, it is warmly inviting. Kotor is only matched by
- Budva which is an old Fortress surrounded by a Great Wall. I heard
- Shkoder, Albania has an exceptional hike up the
- Theth Mountains sometimes referred to as The Accursed Mountains. My new friends and I drank in the views and the Raki (Albanian moonshine) over the passage to
- Val Bona where we spent a cold night in the sleepy town before we moved to
- Tirana, the capital of Albania. Here we took another climb, however, this was up The Pyramid of Tirana, an abandoned museum the tourists enjoy to climb. It's November 7th and I choose
- Gjrokaster, Albania to wait out the results of the Presidential election of 2016. The world was shocked and amazed when DJT won. Really, I was there, in the world, I saw it, shock and amazement, everywhere. With the Balkans behind me and the election over, I left Albania. I was finally able to end my bearing witness to such hate, anger and finger-pointing. I am referring to both, the Balkans and America. I am forever changed; we need more love and oneness.

Once the Balkans was behind me, my Trek metamorphoses in my Journey through the final months. Winding down the learning. Letting all that happened on my Adventure, Path, Road and Trek swirl together like the great sea that joins Europe with America. The sea with its vigorous tides and depths, with its darkened shadows rising to the surface where it meets the light and warmth. With the strength of the oceans pouring into my soul I feel the flow of my life anew. I have now seen my darkest hours and have risen to the surface to let my light and warmth shine.

- Penteli, Greece is where I spent my first sunny day, then
- Loannina before I reached
- Meteora. Magical is a limiting description of this mystical town with its breathtaking vertical cliffs and serene setting. It's where the Monasteries perch on the edges overlooking the crevasse below. Nature here looks like another planet, an ethereal look at the spirituality of a far-off place.
- Thessaloniki is adjacent to another God-like Mount Olympus. I met some charitable visitors and joined them to feed the refugees fleeing the atrocities from their own home. Next up
- Athens where the city is ancient, ancient. Who knew ancient Greece had an ancient Greece? I didn't. The Parthenon had an Old Parthenon destroyed in 500 to 400BC period. Thanksgiving is just days away and I choose
- Mykonos to share with my new American friends and the wild pup I named PITA (Pain in the Ass) who adopted me. My American gal pal gave PITA and me a ride on a four-wheeler. After the Thanksgiving Gyros were eaten it was time to head back to
- Athens to take off and visit
- Istanbul, Asia my second continent.
- Istanbul Turkey smells like spices and looks like jewel tones. With the Minarets peaking above the sky you can hear the Calls to Prayer throughout the city as music played with love. I am forever grateful I got to experience such a rich culture before I jettisoned off to
- Milan, Italy. On the roof of the Duomo Di Milano, you can see all of Italy and the Alps along with hearing the music of the city down below as if the angels were singing. With my Last Supper in Milano complete, I roamed to
- Torino then
- Genova before I saw one of the five
- Cinque Terra's. I leaned into
- Pisa before I climbed the walls at
- Lucca. I heard David lives in
- Florence so I paid him a visit. There are so many David's in Florence.
- Bologna also is famous for their leaning Bell Tower and fog, every night, fog.
- Siena is a beautiful quiet town which inspired me to rent a car and drive around
- Tuscany for a day of pictures before I fled Florence for

- Naples where the energy is palatable and the dirt is everywhere. I loved the grime of Naples, it had a character all its own. What journey to Italy would be complete without a ferry to
- Catania, Sicily for the most amazing pizza I ever had. A quick day journey to
- Syracuse and
- Taormina before myself and another hostel resident climbed
- Mount Etna to sink into the snow as we worried for our life, being lost forever in the white backdrop and black volcanic ground. With Sicily finito, it was another ferry to
- Naples for Christmas. There is nothing like Christmas in Naples. The streets are abuzz with vendors and shoppers scurrying for last minute i regali (gifts) for loved ones. With
- Pompeii so close I have to see that. I saw some Big frescos in that lost city that looked to be a couple handfuls I'm sure. Dying for another hike I visited the
- Amalfi Coast to walk the Path of The Gods that starts near
- Positano then taking a bus to
- Sorento. With New Years Eve just days away I Autobus to
- Rome where I visited
- Vatican City with my friends. Then it was off to
- Florence again for NYE but first we grabbed some wine in
- Orvieto. I rang in the New Year with friends and food listening to the bells from the Duomo. I barely slept before catching my bus in the sky to
- Madrid, Spain, my last country on this journey. With just days left on my journey, I movido back to
- Barcelona where it all began. I caught a cold and had my backpack stolen. I loved that ending to my journey.

I visited 28 countries, 111 cities, took six planes, a multitude of cars, a plethora of buses and uncountable numbers of trains, four ferries, a bike, a moped, oh and one four-wheeler. Let's not forget, I placed a foot on two continents. I rested my head on innumerable pillows in so many hostels and homes. I crossed so many borders, rivers, bridges and a Chunnel. I saw a multitudinous quantity of churches, mosques and Orthodox chapels. I made a populous amount of friends and drank copious amounts of wine. I loved this journey. I wouldn't change a thing I saw and did. I only wish I had more time and money, I would have just kept on going.

Facebook, January 10—Drew is feeling ready—
"There is nothing like returning to a place that remains unchanged to find the ways in which you yourself have altered."—Nelson Mandela

#LifeLesson —70 Anything is possible. The life of your dreams is available to you, for you, anytime you choose to manifest that dream into your reality, simple, easy, no problem. All you have to do is take that first step into your dreams.

I am crossing that sea again, hopefully not for the last time. I am no longer afraid of the future. I will embrace it with all its glorious difficulties, with love, grace and ease. I accomplished what I came to do on my Journey-of-Self-Discovery, I came to be uncomfortable and grow, accomplished, I did it. I am leaving Europe having saved my life, I am anew. My shadow was there for me throughout my journey, carrying my pains, hardships and lessons, making them known when I was ready, allowing me to overcome. My shadow will remain with me forever. I will never be alone, I never was. There were times in my life I couldn't see my shadow or didn't want to see. Now, when I can't see my shadow, I know he's there, my companion. We are connected, my shadow and me, forever linked as one. My shadow will always be there to put forward what I am ready for, to learn and grow. We are one my shadow and me.

I continuously questioned, "Can I do this?" I found my answers while navigating Europe, I CAN do it, I can do anything. I fell in love on my Journey-of-Self-Discovery, deeply and passionately, like the Europeans do everything.

I fell in love, with ME.

The end
or
the new beginning.